Writing Music

A BEDFORD SPOTLIGHT READER

Writing Music

A BEDFORD SPOTLIGHT READER

Jeff Ousborne
Suffolk University

bedford/st.martin's
Macmillan Learning

Boston | New York

For Bedford/St. Martin's

Vice President, Editorial, Macmillan Learning Humanities: Edwin Hill
Senior Program Director for English: Leasa Burton
Program Manager: John E. Sullivan III
Executive Marketing Manager: Joy Fisher Williams
Director of Content Development: Jane Knetzger
Developmental Editor: Cara Kaufman
Content Project Manager: Louis C. Bruno Jr.
Senior Workflow Manager: Jennifer Wetzel
Production Assistant: Brianna Lester
Media Project Manager: Rand Thomas
Manager of Publishing Services: Andrea Cava
Project Management: Lumina Datamatics, Inc.
Composition: Lumina Datamatics, Inc.
Photo Editor: Hilary Newman
Photo Researcher: Sheri Blaney
Permissions Editor: Kalina Ingham
Permissions Researcher: Arthur Johnson
Senior Art Director: Anna Palchik
Text Design: Castle Design; Janis Owens, Books By Design, Inc.; Claire
    Seng-Niemoeller
Cover Design: John Callahan
Cover Photo: Flashpop/Getty Images
Printing and Binding: LSC Communications, Harrisonburg

Manufactured in the United States of America.

2 1 0 9 8 7

f   e   d   c   b   a

For information, write: Bedford/St. Martin's, 75 Arlington Street, Boston, MA 02116

ISBN 978-1-319-02015-6

Acknowledgments

*Text acknowledgments and copyrights appear at the back of the book on pages 330–32,
which constitute an extension of the copyright page. Art acknowledgments and copyrights
appear on the same page as the art selections they cover.*

About The Bedford Spotlight Reader Series

The Bedford Spotlight Reader Series is a line of single-theme readers, each featuring Bedford's trademark care and quality. The readers in the series collect thoughtfully chosen readings sufficient for an entire writing course — about thirty-five selections — to allow instructors to provide carefully developed, high-quality instruction at an affordable price. Bedford Spotlight Readers are designed to help students make inquiries from multiple perspectives, opening up topics such as money, food, sustainability, gender, happiness, borders, monsters, American subcultures, language diversity and academic writing, and humor to critical analysis. An editorial board of a dozen compositionists whose programs focus on specific themes has assisted in the development of the series.

Spotlight Readers offer plenty of material for a composition course while keeping the price low. Each volume in the series includes multiple perspectives on the topic and its effects on individuals and society. Chapters are built around central questions such as "How Do We Make and Consume Music?" and "What Rituals Shape Our Gender?" and so offer numerous entry points for inquiry and discussion. High-interest readings, chosen for their suitability in the classroom, represent a mix of genres and disciplines as well as a choice of accessible and challenging selections to allow instructors to tailor their approach. Each chapter thus brings to light related — even surprising — questions and ideas.

A rich editorial apparatus provides a sound pedagogical foundation. A general introduction, chapter introductions, and headnotes supply context. Following each selection, writing prompts provide avenues of inquiry tuned to different levels of engagement, from reading comprehension ("Understanding the Text"), to critical analysis ("Reflection and Response"), to the kind of integrative analysis appropriate to the research paper ("Making Connections"). A website for the series offers support for teaching, with sample syllabi, additional assignments, web links, and more; visit **macmillanlearning.com/spotlight.**

Why a book about music in a college writing class? If *Writing Music* had one revealing moment of conception, it occurred after I included a popular culture unit in a first-year composition course. During the semester, we read, discussed, and wrote about pop-culture topics including video games, movies, music, television, and the internet. Then I let my students choose their own topics for a longer, formal writing assignment. Almost every student chose to write about music. One—a cerebral, self-identified feminist who struggled with her visceral attraction to hyper sexualized hip-hop and R&B songs—provided a fine-grained, close reading of John Hart's 2012 hit "Who Booty" worthy of William Empson or Robert Penn Warren. Another student researched and composed a brief, dense, quirky narrative history of American jazz, while another wrote an informative, pragmatic process essay about the techniques and business practices of professional club DJs. And the results cut across national and cultural boundaries. A shy Saudi student wrote a compare-and-contrast essay tying the Saudi hip-hop artist Qusai to 1990s rap culture in the United States, while a Chinese student composed a spirited defense of *We Will Rock You*, a critically panned stage musical which, she argued, gave her a key to understanding the culture of the West.

These examples are representative, not exceptional. In nearly every case, the writing was self-directed, passionate, inquiring, engaged, wonderfully argumentative, and genuinely informed: a revelation. But that knowingness and engagement should not have been a surprise. Music—and its various cultures, discourses, and contexts—are a realm of relative mastery for many young adults and college students. In fact, music is probably the pop-culture form most closely tied to the formation of their identities, both personally and socially. Several selections in the book, such as Laina Dawes's "Hardcore Persona" (p. 90) and Rob Sheffield's "Left of the Dial" (p. 70), illustrate this phenomenon explicitly. But essays in *Writing Music*—and the discussion and writing they generate—will use that student mastery and intimacy to move readers beyond purely personal responses and fandom. That is because it is impossible to write thoughtfully about music without also exploring, analyzing, questioning, and confronting themes like identity, race, gender, business, commerce, consumerism, celebrity, technology, and aesthetics, as all the writers in this anthology demonstrate.

With all that in mind, *Writing Music* is organized around five thematic contexts, which the writers here address through a range of analytical approaches and rhetorical strategies. Each chapter is grounded in a question that organizes and centers the readings, while encouraging a broad range of inquiry.

The first chapter focuses on music in the thematic context of *itself*—the nature of music, along with its significance and its appeal. From physicist Barry Parker's classification-and-division essay on sound waves as the building blocks of music ("Making Music," p. 10) and psychologist Stephen A. Diamond's inquiry into "Why We Love Music—and Freud Despised It" (p. 26), to composer Jan Swafford's attempt to define and explain the essence of melody ("The Most Beautiful Melody in the World," p. 54), all selections engage questions about the meaning of music.

The second chapter explores music in the thematic context of the individual listener: how it mirrors, expresses, and influences the formation of personal identity. The selections include Aristotle's discussion of music's role in development and education ("from *Politics*," p. 75) and Frederick Douglass's useful corrective on the meaning of slave songs as a form of expression ("from *My Bondage and My Freedom*," p. 80), along with hip hop artist Zach Moldof's critique of contemporary hip hop and proposal for a reimagining of the genre to articulate contemporary class and economic realities in "Humble Trappings: Blue-Collar Hip-Hop and Recasting the Drug Dealer's Myth" (p. 114).

The third chapter considers music in the thematic context of its creation, mediation, and consumption, as well as the different ways we experience it. The essays range from writer Meghan Daum's witty, sharply observed personal narrative about playing the oboe in the subculture of youth orchestras and music-obsessed families, to the economist Robert Oxoby's tongue-in-cheek, mock-scholarly, compare-and-contrast article about the band AC/DC's effects on listeners and musician Damon Krukowski's sober take on the financial realities of those trying to earn money from music in an age of streaming.

The fourth chapter investigates music in the thematic context of race and ethnicity, with music as a powerful lens that illustrates and informs collective identities in the United States—and around the world. For example, in "Black Rhythm, White Power" (p. 193), student writer Samantha Ainsley provides a potent and historically minded argument about the white appropriation of African American musical forms in the twentieth century; Chris Kjorness, in "Latin Music Is American Music" (p. 239), links the openness of American music with the historical openness of America to immigration, as a country and a culture; and Kat Chow offers a deft, informative inquiry-based exploration of a familiar nine-note musical riff that has come to signify "Asian" in American culture.

Finally, the fifth chapter engages music in the thematic context of sexuality and gender. Those themes may develop in the context of performance, as Amy Clements-Cortes's "The Role of Pop Music and Pop Singers in the Construction of a Singer's Identity in Three Early Adolescent Females" (p. 286) reveals by looking at how young female singers construct their performing personas by using cues from popular stars. These issues also emerge when we try to understand popular music through an explicitly feminist viewpoint as Tamara Winfrey Harris does in her spirited defense of Beyoncé ("All Hail the Queen?," p. 263), or even in the intense personal affiliation with a single artist of a different gender, as Madison Moore does in "Tina Theory: Notes on Fierceness" (p. 302), an essay that is both scholarly rigorous and profoundly personal. But these thematic contexts are not absolute: many of the selections cut across interrelated issues, problems, and questions, allowing instructors and readers to make their own connections and find resonances between themes and readings.

The essays are preceded by headnotes with biographical information about the writer, along with context for the reading. At the end of each selection, you will find three sets of questions. "Understanding the Text" questions will help focus on and clarify basic comprehension of the readings; this level of understanding is necessary for thoughtful interpretation, discussion, and writing. While the "Reflection and Response" questions that follow presume accurate comprehension, they move away from the authors' perspectives to encourage readers to form their own interpretations. The "Making Connections" questions show parallels and contrasts between essays, provoke inquiry into larger themes, and prompt writing assignments. An appendix, "Sentence Guides for Academic Writers," helps students with the most basic academic scenario: having to understand and respond to the ideas of others. This is a practical module that helps students develop an academic writing voice by giving them sentence guides, or templates, to follow in a variety of rhetorical situations and types of research conversations. While you may assign and teach *Writing Music* in a variety of ways, I encourage you to follow the spirit of the book: feel free to sample, remix, or create mash-ups if doing so takes students deeper into a topic and allows them to develop their writing skills.

Of course, good music writing provides a great opportunity to discuss and model good writing, more generally: how to make an argument and support it with evidence; how to move from the autobiographical and anecdotal to the empirical and the broadly relevant; how to view a topic through different lenses, discourses, and intellectual frameworks; how to entertain and address competing points of view and counterarguments without dismissing them or adopting them; how to gather and synthesize sources; how to key an essay or research paper to a particular audience; how to move from the concrete to the abstract, and back again. And music writing — particularly, writing about contemporary popular music — provides a space for rigorous thinking and analysis. Indeed, music can be an alluring gateway to deeper intellectual engagement. I have found this true of myself as a writer and teacher of writing — and I hope that *Writing Music* makes that experience available to you and your students, as well.

Acknowledgments

I am grateful for the insights and suggestions from reviewers who provided feedback during the development of this project: Lee Alan Bleyer, American University; Cheryl Cardoza, Truckee Meadows Community College; Anthony Edgington, University of Toledo; Benjamin Gray, English Language Center; Steve Oakey, Virginia Tech; Ryan Sharp, Huston-Tillotson University; Jay Udall, Nicholls State University; Jay Varner, James Madison University. I would also like to thank several reviewers who chose to remain anonymous.

I thank the people at Bedford/St. Martin's who made this book possible, particularly Edwin Hill, Leasa Burton, and John Sullivan, who have always been so encouraging over the years. I thank my editor, Cara Kaufman, for her smart, thoughtful, and invaluable guidance, as well as her ability to keep this project on track with such grace and ease. I am grateful for the help of Lou Bruno, who guided this book through production; William Rigby for his careful copyediting; John Callahan for the cover design; and Sheri Blaney and Arthur Johnson, for obtaining permissions.

I am deeply appreciative of all of the writers included in this book for their provocative and engaging work. I would like to thank my colleagues and students at Suffolk University, who teach me about teaching, writing, and many other things on a daily basis. Finally, I am especially grateful to my friends, my family, and, most of all, Kate, Sam, and Max, to whom this project is dedicated.

Jeff Ousborne

Bedford/St. Martin's is as passionately committed to the discipline of English as ever, working hard to provide support and services that make it easier for you to teach your course your way.

Find **community support** at the Bedford/St. Martin's English Community (**community.macmillan.com**), where you can follow our *Bits* blog for new teaching ideas, download titles from our professional resource series, and review projects in the pipeline.

Choose **curriculum solutions** that offer flexible custom options, combining our carefully developed print and digital resources, acclaimed works from Macmillan's trade imprints, and your own course or program materials to provide the exact resources your students need.

Rely on **outstanding service** from your Bedford/St. Martin's sales representative and editorial team. Contact us or visit **macmillanlearning. com** to learn more about any of the options below.

Choose from Alternative Formats of *Writing Music*

Bedford/St. Martin's offers a range of formats. Choose what works best for you and your students.

- *Popular e-book formats* For details of our e-book partners, visit **macmillanlearning.com/ebooks**.

Select Value Packages

Add value to your text by packaging one of the following resources with *Writing Music*.

LaunchPad Solo for Readers and Writers allows students to work on what they need help with the most. At home or in class, students learn at their own pace, with instruction tailored to each student's unique needs. *LaunchPad Solo for Readers and Writers* features:

- **Pre-built units that support a learning arc.** Each easy-to-assign unit comprises a pre-test check, multimedia instruction and assessment, and a post-test that assesses what students have learned about critical reading, writing process, using sources, grammar, style, and mechanics. Dedicated units also offer help for multilingual writers.

- **Diagnostics that help establish a baseline for instruction.** Assign diagnostics to identify areas of strength and for improvement and to help students plan a course of study. Use visual reports to track performance by topic, class, and student as well as improvement over time.

- **A video introduction to many topics.** Introductions offer an overview of the unit's topic, and many include a brief, accessible video to illustrate the concepts at hand.

- **Twenty-five reading selections with comprehension quizzes.** Assign a range of classic and contemporary essays each of which includes a label indicating Lexile level to help you scaffold instruction in critical reading.

- **Adaptive quizzing for targeted learning.** Most units include LearningCurve, game-like adaptive quizzing that focuses on the areas in which each student needs the most help.

Order ISBN 978-1-319-13588-1 to package *LaunchPad Solo for Readers and Writers* with *Writing Music* at a significant discount. Students who rent or buy a used book can purchase access and instructors may request free access at **macmillanlearning.com/readwrite**.

Instructor Resources

You have a lot to do in your course. We want to make it easy for you to find the support you need—and to get it quickly. Instructor resources can be downloaded from **macmillanlearning.com**. Visit the instructor resources tab for *Writing Music*. In addition to sample syllabi, the instructor's resources include a list of additional readings and music videos to assign with the book.

Contents

Introduction for Students   1

Chapter 1   What Is Music — and Why Do We Love It?   7

Barry Parker, *Making Music: How Sound is Made*   10
"Sound is a wave that is created by a vibrating object; this object can take many forms, such as a tuning fork, the human voice, a siren, or a musical instrument."

Brad Mehldau, *Blank Expressions: Brad Mehldau and the Essence of Music*   21
"A composer does not 'feel sad' and then write 'sad' music; that is a childishly reductive view of how music is created. It is the listener, after all, who assigns meaning, ideas, and emotions to music once he or she hears it."

Stephen A. Diamond, *Why We Love Music—and Freud Despised It*   26
"Music can stimulate emotions, evoke long forgotten feelings or recollections, much as psychotherapy ideally does. It can trigger childhood memories, both pleasant and traumatic. Unlike rational conversation, music penetrates our intellectual defenses and speaks directly to the heart and soul of who we are."

Leonid Perlovsky, *Music and Consciousness*   35
"Consciousness, especially as it is reflected in language, strives to split the world into pieces. Music makes it whole again, in all its manifold emotionality."

Chapter 2   How Does Music Express and Shape the Self?   67

Chapter 3 How Do We Make and Consume Music? 123

"In fact, not only does this debate have zero bearing on artists (not to mention consumers), but by its very nature it serves as a distraction with respect to what artists should really be focusing on."

Chapter 4 How Does Music Negotiate Race and Ethnicity? 183

"I would often hide Bill Evans albums when talking about jazz musicians with fellow black jazz fans for fear of being 'outed' as a sellout, given a look of disapproval, or asked, 'Why are you listening to that white boy?'"

"Beginning with jazz and leading up to hip-hop, white America has appropriated black music as its own. When whites cannot stake claims to black music—as in the case of hip-hop—the nature of the relationship between mainstream society and African-American culture is simply exploitative."

"The concept of vanity is so rooted in the idea of a singular narcissist that it can be hard to catch that Kanye speaks almost from a populist perspective—a populist narcissism, if you will."

"I've spent the past decade wondering why rock and roll, the most miscegenated popular music ever to have existed, underwent a racial re-sorting in the nineteen-nineties."

"As an expanding body of scholarship has made clear, the most important influences on Mexican American rock 'n' roll musicians were their African American neighbors, with whom they shared the experience of racial and economic oppression and segregated, marginalized urban spaces."

Chapter 5   What Does Music Reveal about Sexuality and Gender?   261

"As I now arrive at my own theorizations of black glamour and the political thrust of spectacular sartorial style, I've come to realize that it was through my performances as Tina Turner that I learned what queerness meant for me—it meant a spectacular presence."

Contents by Discipline

African-American Studies

Business and Economics

Creative Nonfiction and Literature

Ethnic Studies

History

Musicology

Neuroscience, and Psychology

Philosophy and Religion

Politics and Sociology

Women's Studies

Contents by Theme

Family

Labor, Money, and Class

Science and Technology

Spirituality and Metaphysics

Contents by Rhetorical Purpose

Definition

Exemplification

Comparison and Contrast

Classification and Division

Argument

Introduction for Students

Why Music?

Music is everywhere, from the noisy public sphere of media, advertising, and commercial spaces, to the gated private sphere within our carefully curated playlists and our noise-canceling earbuds. Indeed, music exists outside of us, of course, but it also lives in our internal soundtracks—whether in the songs that still haunt us long after we have listened to them or in the annoying jingles that we cannot shake off, no matter how hard we try. Music surrounds us, sustains us, and even annoys us. What is all that listening doing to us? What does it mean? And how would we begin to answer such questions? We might start by considering our specific encounters and engagements with music: the records or CDs our parents played; our first favorite song; our attempts—whether fruitless or successful—to learn an instrument or play in a band; the musical artists we admire; the ways in which a song or band marks milestones in our lives and reflects our moods; or the way an enthusiasm for a style or genre of music connects us with friends or a subculture of fellow fans.

Writing Music explores these experiences, passions, and connections. The book is designed to draw on your curiosity, your knowledge, and your musical literacies—which, in many cases, will be deeper and broader than your instructor's. But your initial interest in—or even mastery of—a particular band, genre, or topic is not an end in and of itself. As the authors here demonstrate, your thinking and writing about music should be directed toward reflection and inquiry. To encourage that frame of mind, each of the five chapters in this book places its subject in a different thematic context: What Is Music—and Why Do We Love It? How Does Music Express and Shape the Self? How Do We Make and Consume Music? How Does Music Negotiate Race and Ethnicity? What Does Music Reveal About Sexuality and Gender? Notice that each chapter also focuses on a question: the range of those questions shows the value of music as subject for academic analysis. That is because music cuts across physics, melody, aesthetics, and fashion. It encompasses teen idols, Auto-Tuned-vocals, and—yes—that new song with the catchy chorus that plays endlessly in your mind. In its intellectual, emotional, and visceral appeal, music sheds inward light on the deep springs of psychology, selfhood, and identity. Music constitutes and reveals social, cultural, political, and maybe even evolutionary history. It provides a space and an occasion to discuss technology, commerce, and consumption; it illuminates, informs, and problematizes questions of race, ethnicity, nationality, and globalism; it is a medium for exploring sexuality and gender.

Asking the Right Questions

So how does a writer move from the music of Taylor Swift to, say, an exploration of adolescent gender identity formation? How can a clichéd, vaguely "Asian"-sounding nine-note melody lead to a discussion of orientalist stereotypes? What do infectious and catchy songs reveal about neurology and the mechanics of our brains? Why is contemporary country music a battlefield in America's culture war? In a way, the answers lie in a preliminary act of inquiry. As you move from your own immediate interests and responses, use the following questions to interrogate your topic.

What do I already know about this topic? What don't I know? You may be familiar with an artist, a genre, song, or other musical subject, but in most cases, you will find other aspects or implications of it that require further thought and research. So begin with what you know and then use that knowledge as a scaffold to explore *what you do not know.* What is your topic's history and origins? What hidden components comprise your topic? What cause-and-effect relationships have shaped your topic? To see how this process can lead to informative writing and analysis, consider the example of Kat Chow's "How the 'Kung Fu Fighting' Melody Came to Represent Asia" (p. 245), which begins with the sentence: "There's a tune that you've probably heard throughout your life." But from this familiar melody—and shared knowledge—the writer moves to what she does not know: the history of the tune, its melodic elements in the pentatonic scale, the cultural processes that led it to become trite musical shorthand for "Asian."

In "Country Music, Openness to Experience, and the Psychology of the Culture War" (p. 105), Will Wilkinson shares his experiences with country music and the genre's well-known clichés, but this provokes "conjecture about conservative psychology and the stakes of the 'culture wars.'" That conjecture leads him to further research in political and social psychology, as well as to a deeper understanding of the formal aspects of country music and the worldview of its fans.

What bothers me about this topic? While you may want to write about a topic you like, pay attention to things that bother you or trouble you, as well. That means more than composing a purely subjective rant about a musical style you dislike or an artist who does not appeal to you. Instead, look for an angle on the topic that allows you to support your point of view with evidence. And try to make sure you have something at stake in your analysis or argument, a substantive issue or problem — one that answers a question that readers often silently ask: *So what?* In fact, you will find that several selections in *Writing Music* originate in a writer's complaint. For example, Mark Oppenheimer's "Stop Forcing Your Kids to Learn a Musical Instrument" (p. 126) begins in his frustration with the conventional wisdom that learning a musical instrument is inherently beneficial — and with his claim that in the case of his own daughter, violin lessons are "pretty well pointless." But he moves from this personal irritation to broader issues of parenting, and over-scheduled children, as well as to the twinned social history of music and American immigration. Similarly, in "Why Artists Should Stop Chasing Spotify's Pennies and Focus on Top Fans" (p. 177), George Howard turns his exasperation with stories about musicians struggling to earn money from music streaming into an essay that proposes a more productive approach to a new business model.

How has this topic — or attitudes about it — changed over time? Like a good piece of fiction, a good piece of analytical or argumentative non-fiction writing requires a "plot": a change, shift, or problem that the text explores and seeks to resolve. The evolution of a topic over time can often help provide you with that alluring storyline, so to speak. How and why has the topic changed? How does its current manifestation compare and contrast with earlier iterations or its original form? What has caused changes over time—and what are their effects and implications? How have people responded to these changes? In "Music and Consciousness" (p. 35), Leonid Perlovsky asks, "Why is music so important to us? What role does it play in our minds? What evolutionary purpose does it serve?" To answer these questions, he composes and analyzes a dense, concise evolutionary history of music and its relationship to human consciousness: a story of change that stretches from the Old Testament and Ancient Greece to contemporary hip hop. Focusing on a much narrower time period, Damon Krukowski, in "Making Cents" (p. 172), traces the profound transformations of the music industry and the significance of those changes for working recording artists, who struggle to deal with "morphing formats" and "dissolving business models." This conflict provides the tension and "plot" of his essay.

What do people misunderstand about this topic? As you work toward discovering the focus of your writing or composing a provisional thesis, you might reflect on common misunderstandings about your topic. What have others missed or failed to see? In what ways has your topic been misinterpreted, incorrectly identified, or otherwise mischaracterized? How can you correct or clarify misperceptions? Is the conventional wisdom about your topic mistaken? Several writers here address this problem as the primary focus of their essays. Heben Nigatu, for example, begins her essay with "predictable" media responses to Kanye West ("In Defense of Kanye's Vanity: The Politics of Black Self-Love," p. 203), but then argues that conventional interpretations of the hip-hop star—rooted in mistaken assumptions about his "vanity" and "narcissism"—are not only wrong, but that they obscure his significance as an avatar of African American male self-expression. Other writers make correcting perceptions a key element of their texts, if not the main focus. In the excerpt from Frederick Douglass's *My Bondage and My Freedom* (p. 80), for example, Douglass corrects a common misconception about the sound and meaning of slave songs.

What is a source of disagreement over this topic? Instead of seeking sources of consensus and agreement about your topic, look for gaps, differences of opinion, and even controversy. This approach will help you enter an ongoing discussion—and allow you to add your own point of view to the conversation. For example, in "All Hail the Queen?" (p. 263), Tamara Winfrey Harris addresses contemporary arguments about Beyoncé's status as a feminist in the context of race, femininity, and celebrity: "The dogged criticism of the way Beyoncé chooses to live out her feminism must add to the pressure of being a famous woman of color." In "My Bill Evans Problem: Jaded Visions of Jazz and Race" (p. 186), Eugene Holley begins with his personal admiration for— and ambivalence about—the legendary white jazz pianist Bill Evans. Ultimately, however, Holley negotiates larger disagreements about the status of white musicians working in an African American art form. And these disagreements *matter:* "To like a 'white sound,' or worse, a white musician who 'sounded black,' was cultural treason."

What are the paradoxes, contradictions, or ironies associated with my topic? Provocative, engaging texts focus on tensions and address problems, so look for paradoxes, contradictions, ironies, and other curious or surprising aspects of your topic. They may suggest provocative and rewarding material for writing. Consider Stephen A. Diamond's "Why We Love Music—and Freud Despised It" (p. 26), for example. Here, the writer investigates music's power and appeal, in part, from the perspective of Sigmund Freud: a profoundly important and perceptive thinker who appreciated a variety of art forms, but disliked music intensely. For Diamond, this quirk in Freud's temperament ultimately provides insight into the "enigmatic magic and majesty of music." In "I Listen to Everything, Except Rap and Country Music" (p. 117), Jeremy Gordon discovers surprising parallels between—and ironies within—two polarizing and seemingly disparate genres, particularly in the context of collaborations between country and hip-hop artists over the last several years. As Gordon notes, "It's not as weird as you might think."

These questions are only a beginning, of course—you can ask many others. Moreover, most writers explore multiple questions and problems in their essays: they correct misunderstandings while following the changing trajectory of their topics over time; they resolve contradictions as they share new knowledge from their research and reading; they move from correcting misunderstandings to clarifying and resolving disagreements over their topics.

Finding Models

Regardless of the question, angle, or topic, all the readings here model good writing. The writers push back against conventional wisdom; they pursue lines of logic and argument; they support claims with evidence and address counterarguments; they work with sources and synthesize them to further their own arguments; they pivot from personal experience to broader, more rigorous empirical assertions; they identify analogies and parallels; they make important distinctions, consider cause-and-effect relationships, and provide definitions. Similarly, these writers can provide practical guidance about constructing an essay, sentence by sentence and paragraph by paragraph: how to create effective introductions; how to craft a thesis; how to move from generalizations to specific examples, and back again; how to summarize other writers effectively; how to entertain or play with an idea without accepting it as true or rejecting it outright; how to shape and focus paragraphs; how to conclude an essay without merely restating your thesis or main point. These skills and techniques are applicable, whether your topic is the work of Aristotle or the work of Kanye West. So do not hesitate to try a rhetorical approach or writing maneuver you find in these essays. You should read with an eye for how good writers solve writing problems and build their essays, in the same way you might study an expert athlete or musician to better understand how the trick is done. At the same time, look for ways to place these texts in conversation with each other—and with your own point of view, as your perspectives evolve. In other words, the writers here provide a basic track with melodies, harmonies, and rhythms. Ultimately, however, you should take the opportunity to write about music as a chance to develop a distinctive song and voice of your own.

1

What Is Music — and Why Do We Love It?

Physicist Leonid Perlovsky begins his essay "Music and Consciousness" with a simple, unqualified claim: "Music is an enigma." The word "enigma" or "enigmatic" appears in other selections here as well, including Stephen A. Diamond's "Why We Love Music — and Freud Despised It" and Jan Swafford's "The Most Beautiful Melody in the World." Even when the term is not explicit, all the writers in this chapter confront — and illuminate — the mystery of music, as well as its power and appeal. Not surprisingly, for several of them, the questions seem as important as the answers: What is music? Where does it come from? Why is it so important to us? Is music a form of personal expression, or does it only express itself? How does music's meaning change over time? What is happening in our minds when a tune gets lodged there?

While these and other questions underlie all the essays, each writer views them through a different lens. Physicist Barry Parker ("Making Music") focuses on the physics and mathematics behind "organized noise," bringing clarity to music's building blocks such as pure tones and longitudinal waves. In "Blank Expressions: Brad Mehldau and the Essence of Music," composer and jazz pianist Brad Mehldau reflects not only on the wellsprings of musical expression and meaning, but also on the unsatisfying language we use to address the elusive mystery of music: for Mehldau, this rhetoric of the transcendent or ineffable "is simply [language] feasting on itself, on its own poverty — it has revealed nothing about music." In "Why We Love Music — and Freud Despised It," psychologist Stephen A. Diamond investigates music's appeal, in part, through the prism of Sigmund Freud's fear and loathing of the medium. While Leonid Perlovsky is a trained physicist, his inquiry in "Music and Consciousness" explores the evolutionary purposes of music and its relationship to the human mind; his essay traces the reflexive relationship between the development of Western human consciousness and the development of Western music. Writing in the context of his religious faith and revealed truth, fourth-century Catholic Church Father St. Basil considers the musical, devotional, and instructional pleasures of the Psalms as an emanation of the divine Holy Spirit in this excerpt from "The Homily on the First Psalm." But centuries after their composition, his insights about music's power may have value for both secular and religious readers. In "Brainworms, Sticky Music, and Catchy Tunes," physician and neurologist Oliver Sacks pursues the psychological, neurological, and cognitive mechanisms of "brainworms": tunes or jingles that take possession of our inner ears and play incessantly in our brains. In "The Most Beautiful Melody in the World," composer and writer Jan Swafford tries to tease out — and pin down — the essential structures and qualities of Western melodies: those instantly memorable tunes "you might whistle in the shower or sing around a campfire." Finally, in "Beethoven's Kapow," critic Justin Davidson writes about the fate of Beethoven's Third Symphony (the "Eroica") through the centuries as it transforms from an explosive and radical provocation to "settled wisdom."

Making Music: How Sound Is Made

Barry Parker

In this excerpt from his book *Good Vibrations: The Physics of Music*, physicist Barry Parker explains some of the basic principles underlying music, or as he defines it, "sound that is organized." He traces the properties and motion of transverse and longitudinal waves; the causes of loudness and intensity; the effects of a medium on sound. While his analysis may seem highly technical, it is not an academic exercise. Rather, he sees the physics of sound as one way to explore a question about music: "Why does it have such a powerful force on people?"

Barry Parker obtained his PhD in physics from Utah State University and taught at Weber State University and Idaho State University for thirty years. His other books include *Einstein's Dream: The Search for a Unified Theory of the Universe* (2008) and *The Physics of War: From Arrows to Atoms* (2014).

Music is sound, but it's a very special kind of sound. I think everyone would agree with that. In this chapter we'll be talking about how sound is produced and what properties it has to have to be music. Let's begin by defining sound. Sound is a wave that is created by a vibrating object; this object can take many forms, such as a tuning fork, the human voice, a siren, or a musical instrument. Once created, the sound propagates through a medium, usually air, from its source to another location where it is picked up by a receiver. The most common receiver is, of course, our ears.

Given that we're mainly interested in the form of sound that we call music, we have to distinguish it from the other sound we hear. What is it that makes music different? There are many ways we can define it; a simple one is, Music is sound that is organized. We can also say that music differs from ordinary noise in that the vibrations associated with it are more uniform; in short, there are no sudden changes. Finally, musical sounds are, for the most part, pleasant and pleasing to the ear.

According to the first of our definitions, music is sound that is organized, so let's look at how it is organized. We see that it consists of notes, rhythms, phrases, and measures and has an overall form. All of these things help to organize it. Another important aspect of music is melody, in other words, the tune we whistle or hum after we've heard the music a few times. This melody is usually repeated several times throughout a musical piece and is something else that helps keep it organized.

The simplest form of music is the pure tone; it is the type of tone you get from a tuning fork. Pure tones are basic to music, but as we will see, they are not heard very often. Music composed only of pure tones would not be interesting.

So music is organized noise that has a melody and consists of structured rhythms and various types of pure tones. This is, of course, a very mechanical definition and doesn't convey what music really is and what it really does. As everyone knows, its most important role is to convey emotion, and it does this well. There's no doubt that it affects us all; it can convey joy, it can give us goose bumps, and it can even make us cry. Why does it have such a powerful force on people? This is one of the questions we will look at in this book.

> "The simplest form of music is the pure tone; it is the type of tone you get from a tuning fork. Pure tones are basic to music, but as we will see, they are not heard very often. Music composed only of pure tones would not be interesting."
>
> 5

The Motion of Waves

One of the first things we learn about sound is that it is a wave. This means that our study of sound will center on the study of waves. What exactly is a wave? Waves are, of course, all around us; we encounter waves of many different types every day. Besides sound waves, we have radio and TV waves, water waves, waves in our microwave ovens, and earthquake waves. In each case they are caused by some sort of vibratory motion.

One of the most familiar waves is a water wave, so let's begin by looking briefly at one. Assume you are sitting on the bank of a pond and throw a stone into the water. What do you see? When the stone hits the water, you will see a series of concentric rings that appear to move outward from the point where the stone hit. Looking at these rings closely, you see that they consist of crests and depressions, or troughs. The tops of the crests are higher than the level of the water when there were no crests, and the bottoms of the troughs are lower. The waves move out with a certain speed from where the stone struck the water, and it appears as if the water is actually moving. There is, indeed, some motion in the neighborhood of a particular crest or trough, but this consists only of a small amount of circular motion. The water as a whole does not move. The wave passes *through* the water.

If you could take a cross section of the wave—in other words, cut it in a direction outward from the source—you would get a wiggly line that consisted of a series of crests and troughs. The curve of this line is known as a sine curve, since it is identical to the curve we get when we plot the trigonometrical function sine.

To understand this type of wave a little better, let's generate one and look closely at its properties. The best way to do this is to attach a rope to a doorknob or other projection and pull it tight, then give it a sudden upward jerk. A pulse that is similar to single wave (a crest and a trough) will travel down it from our hands to the knob. What we really want, though, is a series of these pulses. For this we have to keep jerking our hands up and down, and if we want the pulses to be equally spaced, we have to do it uniformly, or regularly. This will create an array of equally spaced pulses moving down the rope that will look exactly like the cross section we took of the water wave.

The obvious conclusion from this is that vibratory motion is needed 10 to create waves. As it turns out, though, a particular type of motion is critical in the case of music: *simple harmonic motion* (SHM). Simple harmonic motion is motion where the force on the object undergoing the motion is proportional to the displacement from its equilibrium position. It is said to obey Hooke's law.

A good example of something that undergoes simple harmonic motion is a taut string, like the string of a guitar, that is pulled to the side and released. It's easy to see that the farther we pull the string back, the greater the force pulling it back to its equilibrium position will be. So it obviously obeys Hooke's law. If we pull the string to the right and release it, the restoring force will accelerate it back toward its equilibrium position, so that it moves faster and faster in this direction. You're no doubt familiar with acceleration in relation to your car. You have to accelerate to get up to speed; in other words, you have to increase, or change, your speed, so acceleration is *change in speed.*

As the string approaches its equilibrium position (straight up and down.) its displacement from equilibrium decreases, and as a result, the restoring force also decreases. But it is the restoring force that is causing the acceleration; this is, in fact, known as Newton's second law of motion (acceleration is proportional to force). So the string moves faster and faster as it approaches the equilibrium position, but at the same time the acceleration itself is decreasing because the force is decreasing. Finally, at the equilibrium position, the restoring force is zero, and since the acceleration is proportional to the force, it is also zero. With no force acting on the string, it might seem that the string would stop moving, but it doesn't; in fact, it has its maximum velocity as it passes through the equilibrium position. Why doesn't it stop? Because of *inertia.* Inertia is something you experience every time you're in a car and it accelerates. Simply put, it is resistance to change in motion; an object will stay at rest or in motion until it is forced to do otherwise. A force will cause an object to move and accelerate, but to do this the force must overcome the object's inertia. Similarly, an object in uniform motion will not change its motion unless it is forced to do so. And in the case of our string, as it passes the equilibrium position there is no force on it. As it moves past equilibrium, however, the restoring force comes back into play, but now it's acting in the opposite direction. Since this force is proportional to the displacement of the string from equilibrium, it grows as the string continues to move. And, of course, associated with this force is an acceleration, but it is now in the opposite direction, so it's now a deceleration.

As the string continues to move to the left, the restoring force continues to increase, and because of the resulting deceleration, its velocity continues to decrease until finally it is zero. The string is now the same distance to the left of the equilibrium position as it was to the right when it started. At this point the restoring force again changes direction and is directed back to the equilibrium position. The string therefore begins accelerating in this direction, and as before, it passes through the equilibrium position with its maximum velocity and moves back to the position on the right from where it began. This process would continue indefinitely if there were no air resistance or friction at the ends of the string. But in practice there is always some friction, and as a result, the vibrations are damped and eventually die out.

It's obvious that simple harmonic motion is relatively complicated. The reason is that the velocity of the object undergoing the motion is continually changing, and so is its acceleration. The changes are always smooth, though, so there are no abrupt motions.

Stretched strings are not the only things that undergo simple harmonic motion when they are pulled aside. Pendulums also have this property. Galileo was sitting in a cathedral one day in 1583 when he noticed the chandeliers swinging back and forth. They were all of the same length, but they were not all swaying the same distance from their equilibrium positions (straight up and down). We refer to the distance from the equilibrium position as the *amplitude*. Galileo noticed that, regardless of their amplitude, the chandeliers appeared to move back and forth in the same length of time (we refer to this as their *period*). He used his pulse to time them, and sure enough, their period was the same.

The observation fascinated Galileo, and when he returned to his home he decided to look into the motion of pendulums further. He attached a bob to the end of a string and began experimenting with it. The first thing he noticed was that the period of the swing did not depend on the weight of the bob, but it did depend on the length of the pendulum. In fact, it varied as the square root of the length. This meant that if a pendulum was one foot long and had a period of one second, a pendulum two feet long would have a period of $\sqrt{2}$ seconds, and a pendulum four feet long would have a period of $\sqrt{4} = 2$ seconds.

Now, let's look at the motion as we did in the case of the stretched string. In this case when the bob is pulled to the side, a restoring force also acts on it, but this case is different because the bob moves in an arc of a circle when it returns to equilibrium. At its extreme it is raised to a higher level as compared with its equilibrium position. Because of this, when it is released, gravity acts on it, pulling it downward in an arcing curve. But it is obvious that gravity is not the only force involved. There is a force on the string — an upward pull. The gravitational pull that causes the restoring force is therefore only the part that is not balanced by the upward pull of the string.

Because the gravitational force is largest when the bob is first released, the acceleration is also the greatest at this point. As the bob drops, however, the gravitational force decreases and so does the acceleration. But because of the acceleration, the velocity of the bob increases and is at a maximum when the string is vertical. At this position, there is no unbalanced force, but because of inertia, the bob swings through this position and past it. On the other side of this position the force acts back toward it, and the bob therefore slows down. Eventually it stops at roughly the same distance on the opposite side of the vertical. At this position the gravitational force has built up again, and the bob starts back down toward the equilibrium position (the vertical). It performs this motion over and over again, and if it were not for friction it would continue to do so indefinitely.

It's easy to see that this motion is very similar to the plucking of a string. Both, in fact, are simple harmonic motion.

Types of Waves

Simple harmonic motion is basic to wave motion. One way to see this is 20 to go back to our rope tied to a doorknob. We saw that we could create a series of equally spaced pulses that moved down the rope and that they were similar to the cross section of the waves we saw on water. Looking at this wave closely, we see that it consists of equally spaced *crests* and *troughs*. The crests are the places where the rope is displaced above its usual equilibrium position (when it is pulled tight), and the troughs are the valleys created below the equilibrium position. There are, of course, places along the rope where it is not displaced from its equilibrium position; they are referred to as *nodes*. This type of wave is called a *transverse wave*. It is the type of wave that is set up on a violin string, or a string in a piano. The motion of the rope is perpendicular to the motion of the wave in this type of wave; it is, in fact, a basic property of a transverse wave.

There is another type of wave that is also important in nature. To see how this type of wave is generated it is helpful to use a Slinky.

I'm sure you are familiar with this toy; you probably played with one when you were young. It is a continuous metal coil that can easily be stretched out. If you attach a Slinky to a doorknob, pull it out straight (or at least as close to straight as you can), and then hit or pound the end of the Slinky, you will, as in the case of our rope example, see a pulse move along it to the doorknob. But this pulse is different from the one with the rope (Fig. 1.1). It's a disturbance caused by the back-and-forth movement of the coils in the Slinky. The first coil is disturbed by the blow you gave it; it pushes the second coil and displaces it from its equilibrium position. This causes a push or pull on the third coil, which is displaced from its equilibrium position, and so on. The result is a disturbance that moves down the Slinky. The disturbance in this case is in the direction the wave is traveling, so in this respect it is different from a transverse wave. In several respects, however, this wave is similar to the transverse wave we talked about above. It is referred to as a *longitudinal wave,* and as we will see, it is also of importance in music.

Let's look at both of these waves in more detail, beginning with the transverse wave. We saw that it has crests and troughs and has a regular repetitive shape down its length. And since it has the same shape as the trigonometrical sine function we call it a sine wave. In the sine wave a small section of it is repeated over and over. The distance of repetition (from one point to a similar point farther on) is known as the *wavelength* of the wave, which is usually designated by a lowercase Greek lambda, λ. The wavelength can be measured from the maximum of one crest to the next, or from a minimum of a trough to the next, or any other two equivalent points. Similarly, the distance from the equilibrium position to the maximum of a crest is called the *amplitude* of the wave. Another important property of the transverse, or sine, wave

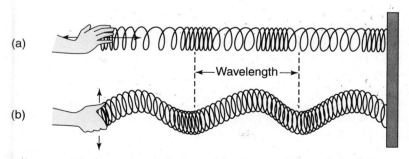

Figure 1.1   A Slinky toy can be used to illustrate both longitudinal sound waves (above) and transverse sound waves (below).

is the number of crests (or troughs) that pass a given point per second; this number is referred to as the *frequency* of the wave and is usually designated by *f*.

If we have two waves traveling down two ropes that are side by side and the crests and troughs from one line up with the other, we say that the two waves are *in phase*. If the crests and troughs do not line up the two waves are *out of phase*. Furthermore, we can specify how far they are out of phase; if, for example, a crest lines up with a trough on the other wave, we say they are out of phase by half a wavelength.

Let's turn now to the longitudinal waves we saw on the Slinky. As we look down the wave we see regions where the coils of the Slinky are closer together than usual; they are referred to as *compressions*. We also see regions where the coils are farther apart than usual; these regions are referred to as *rarefactions*. Compressions and rarefactions are analogous to crests and troughs in transverse waves. In the same way, therefore, we have a wavelength for a longitudinal wave; it is the distance between two rarefactions or two compressions (or other equivalent points). In addition, the points that remain at equilibrium correspond to nodes, and the number of compressions (or rarefactions) that pass a given point per second is the frequency of the wave.

Sound

As we saw earlier, sound is a wave created by a vibrating object that propagates through a medium from one location to another. The medium that transmits it is usually air, but many other media such as water and steel also transmit sound waves. But we now know there are two types of waves: transverse or longitudinal. Which type is sound? If you think about a sound wave moving through air, it's easy to see that it has to be a longitudinal wave. A sound wave moves through air as a result of the motion of the air molecules. When you talk or sing, your vocal cords exert a force on the air molecules next to them. As a result, these molecules are displaced from their equilibrium position. They, in turn, exert a push or a pull on their neighbors, causing them to be displaced from their equilibrium position. These push and pull motions, continuing all the way to the receiver, are like the waves that traveled down the Slinky.

Sound waves need a medium such as air to propagate them, and as a result they are referred to as mechanical waves. There are also non-mechanical waves that do not need a medium to transport them. They are called electromagnetic waves, and as we will see, they also play an important role in music. A radio wave is an example.

Properties of Sound Waves

A tuning fork is a familiar device that creates a sound wave of a single frequency. As the tines, or prongs, of the tuning fork vibrate back and forth they push on the air molecules around them. The forward motion of the tine pushes molecules together creating a compression; then, as the tine moves back it creates a rarefaction. If we place an open tube next to the tuning fork, compressions and rarefactions will be set up in it. This wave has the same properties as the longitudinal wave we talked about earlier. The distance between successive compressions (or rarefactions) in the tube is the wavelength of the sound wave. Tuning forks are made to vibrate at a particular frequency. Thus, if a tuning fork is designed to sound middle C, it will vibrate at 256 vibrations/sec. The frequency of the longitudinal waves passing down the tube would therefore also be 256 vibrations/sec.

Another way to look at this tube is to measure the air pressure at each point along it. At a compression, this pressure would be higher than normal (equilibrium pressure), and at each rarefaction it would be less than normal. We could, in fact, make a plot of pressure versus time for the tube. It looks like a transverse wave — in other words, it's a sine wave. This shows the close relationship between transverse and longitudinal waves. This is not to say, of course, that they are the same. They are distinctly different.

We've seen that a sound wave has a particular frequency, which is the number of compressions that pass a given point per second. And for years we referred to the units of frequency as so many vibrations/sec, but we now use a unit called the Hertz (Hz), where 1 Hz = 1 vibration/sec. The sound emitted from the tuning fork mentioned above is therefore 256 Hz.

Another important characteristic of sound is its *period*. Its period 30 is the time for a compression (or rarefaction) to move between two successive equivalent points. The relationship between period and frequency is frequency = 1/period — that is, the frequency is the reciprocal of the period.

Audible sound covers a relatively large range of frequencies. The human ear is capable of detecting frequencies from about 20 Hz up to 20,000 Hz. Sounds below this range are usually referred to as *infrasound,* and sounds above it are called *ultrasound.* The upper range of audible sound actually varies considerably for humans. As you get older, for example, your upper range decreases, and you can't hear sounds anywhere near 20,000 Hz. Animals generally can hear a wider range of frequencies than humans. Dogs, for example, can hear frequencies of 50 Hz up to 45,000 Hz. Bats can detect frequencies up to 120,000 Hz, and dolphins, up to 200,000 Hz.

When most people hear a high frequency, they say it has a high *pitch*. And pitch is, indeed, generally considered to be synonymous with frequency, but as we will see later, it is not exactly the same.

Intensity of Sound

Another property of sound is loudness. When a wave passes through a medium such as air, it transports energy as it moves, where energy is defined as the ability to do work (in units of joules). This energy is transmitted to the medium by the vibrations that create the wave. It depends on the amplitude of the vibration: the greater the amplitude, the greater the energy, and the louder the sound. In the case of a guitar string, for example, the farther it is pulled to the side, the greater is its amplitude, and the louder is the sound it produces.

Loudness is associated with a quantity called *intensity,* where intensity is defined as the amount of energy that is transported past a given area of a medium per unit time. But energy per unit time is power, so intensity is power per unit area, and since the units of power are watts, the units of intensity are watts/meter^2 (W/m^2).

As a sound wave spreads out in a medium, its intensity decreases. As the wave moves outward, the same amount of energy is spread over the area at 1 m, 2 m, 3 m, and so on. Since the area is bigger in each case, and the energy is the same, the energy per unit area is less. The relationship in this case is called an inverse square law, which means that the intensity of the wave drops off as the square of the distance from the source. Therefore, if the distance is doubled, the intensity will decrease by a factor of 4; if the distance is tripled, it will decrease by a factor of 9; and so on. 35

The range of sounds that impinge on the human ear each day varies considerably. It is so large, in fact, that physicists use a scale for intensities that is based on multiples of 10. This logarithmic scale is referred to as the *decibel scale*. A sound that is 10 times as intense as our threshold of hearing (the threshold being something we can barely hear) is said to have a sound level of 10 decibels (dB). In mks units (measured as meters, kilograms, and seconds) this is 10^{-12} W/m^2. A sound that is $10 \times 10 = 100$ times as intense has an intensity of 20 dB (or 10^{-11} W/m^2), and so on. So a sound of 10 dB is 10^1 times threshold, a sound of 20 dB is 10^2 times threshold, a sound of 30 dB is 10^3 times threshold, and so on.

The intensity of sound is something that can be measured exactly, and it is obviously associated with loudness, but it is not exactly the same. The loudness of a sound actually depends on several factors. All people do not hear a given intensity as equally loud. Older people, for example, do not hear a particular intensity to be as loud as a younger person. Also, the frequency of the sound has an effect. Different frequencies of the same intensity are perceived to have a different loudness.

The Speed of Sound

When a sound wave passes through a medium such as air, particles are disturbed, which in turn, disturb adjacent particles so that energy is transported through the medium. The individual molecules do not move very far, and the overall medium does not move at all, but the wave passes through it with a certain speed that depends on several factors. It's well-known that speed is defined as distance divided by time, so it has units of m/sec in mks units (or ft/sec in British engineering units).

Two properties determine the speed of a wave through a medium: the medium's *inertial properties* and its *elastic properties*. When we talk about inertia in relation to sound, we are referring to the inertia of the particles that make up the medium. Particles with greater mass have greater inertia and are therefore less responsive to a wave passing through them. This means that, in general, the greater the density of the material, the slower the wave will travel. Therefore, it will travel faster in light gases than it will in a heavy or dense gas (assuming other factors are the same).

Elastic properties are those related to how well a material retains its 40 shape when subjected to a force. Steel is a good example of a material that is very rigid and inelastic; rubber is a material that is not. High rigidity and inelasticity are related to the strength of the atomic or molecular forces within the material, and since metals generally have stronger molecular forces within them than fluids, and fluids have stronger molecular forces than gases, the speed of sound is therefore highest in solids, next highest in liquids, and lowest in gases.

Temperature and pressure also have an effect on the speed of sound; it increases with increasing temperature or pressure because both elasticity and inertia are affected. At normal pressure and a temperature of 0°C, sound travels at 331.5 m/sec (1,087 ft/sec), and at 20°C (32°F) it travels at 343 m/sec (1,130 ft/sec).

The velocity of all waves, including sound waves, is related to their wavelength and frequency by

$$\text{velocity} = \text{wavelength} \times \text{frequency},$$

or in formula form,

$$v = \lambda f.$$

This formula does not imply that different wavelengths or frequencies of sound travel at different velocities. The speed of sound does not depend on either of these quantities. A change in wavelength does not change the velocity: it changes the frequency, and vice versa. The speed of sound depends only on the properties of the medium it is moving through.

Understanding the Text

1. What kind of vibratory motion is "critical" to music? How is it defined?

2. What are the two types of waves described in the essay? Which type of wave is sound?

3. What does the speed of sound depend upon?

Reflection and Response

4. The writer offers one definition of music: "Music is sound that is organized" (2). How do you respond to that definition? What are its strengths and weaknesses as an explanation?

5. Parker is a physicist and his essay — excerpted from the book, *Good Vibrations: The Physics of Music* — incorporates principles from mathematics and physics. Does he explain these concepts clearly? What does he assume about his readers? Does he seem to be writing for a general audience or an audience already familiar with the basics of physics? Point to specific examples to support your answers.

Making Connections

6. Parker asks, "Why does [music] have such a powerful force on people?" (5). In some ways, all the writers in this chapter wrestle with that question. Do you think exploring the physics of sound helps us answer it? Does this analytical framework broaden the mystery of music's appeal, or reduce it? Is Parker's approach compatible with other ways of investigating music — for example, Stephen A. Diamond's "Why We Love Music — and Freud Despised It" (p. 26) or Oliver Sacks's "Brainworms, Sticky Music, and Catchy Tunes" (p. 46)? Why or why not?

7. In "Beethoven's Kapow" (p. 61), Justin Davidson writes about a "thrilling" version of the "Eroica" by conductor John Eliot Gardiner and the Orchèstre Révolutionnaire et Romantique. Does Parker's discussion of the physics of music suggest any insight into why this performance might have been so startling and memorable?

Blank Expressions: Brad Mehldau and the Essence of Music

Brad Mehldau

In this piece, jazz pianist and composer Brad Mehldau seeks to clarify not so much what music means, but how it means. Along the way, he addresses common accounts of music — particularly ones that seem smug, misleading, or even empty. For Mehldau, the primary agent of musical meaning is neither the composer nor the musicians. He reflects on "musical wisdom," and interrogates the supposed representational and expressive qualities of the medium.

Brad Mehldau's albums include *Introducing Brad Mehldau* (1995), *Largo* (2002), and *Live in Marciac* (2006). He has collaborated with many musicians and composers, including Pat Metheny, Joshua Redman, Willie Nelson, and Daniel Lanois.

Music often seems to suggest an emotion or a state of being — we reach a consensus, for example, that one piece of music expresses carefree youth, while another expresses world-weary wisdom. But is music properly expressing anything? Here's Stravinsky on the subject in 1936, from his autobiography: "For I consider that music is, by its very nature, essentially powerless to express anything at all, whether a feeling, an attitude of mind, a psychological mood, a phenomenon of nature, etc. . . . Expression has never been an inherent property of music . . . It is simply an additional attribute which, by tacit and inveterate agreement, we have lent it, thrust upon it, as a label, a convention — in short, an aspect unconsciously or by force of habit, we have come to confuse with its essential being."

Alas, Stravinsky does not tell us what music's "essential being" is, only that we have mistaken the property of expression with it. He seems to be repeating the gambit of thinkers from Plato onward — he tells us that what we observe is false, posits another realm that is more real, but gives us no concrete information about it. There is no information to give, after all — what is essential lies beyond our reach; we're stuck in our empirical shallowness. Essentialist tropes are everywhere in discussions about music, smugly short circuiting further inquiry, maintaining: "We cannot put in words what is essential about music."

It is probably more reasonable to say we cannot put in words what is essential about anything. Essence is a cipher, a phantom, and a perilous one at that — by the time Stravinsky was writing those words, essentialist ideas were being stapled on to notions of race and nation with horrific results. These kinds of tropes about music always persist, though, because music acts like language in its ability to represent things, yet its mode of expression, if Stravinsky will pardon us, is free of language. So we see it as the ideal form of communication—one that supersedes language. The irony and ultimately the weakness of this viewpoint is that our ability to posit this idealised communication is dependent on the very language that we wish to transcend. Language is simply feasting on itself, on its own poverty—it has revealed nothing about music.

Was Stravinsky merely perpetuating a kind of sophistry? For years, his statement confounded and bothered people who took it at face value, assuming that he meant music is not expressive, period. In 1962, he clarified what he meant—a little grumpily: "The over-publicised bit about expression (or non-expression) was simply a way of saying that music is supra-personal and super-real, and as such, beyond verbal meanings and verbal descriptions. It was aimed against the notion that a piece of music is in reality a transcendental idea 'expressed in terms of' music, with the reductio ad absurdum implication that exact sets of correlatives must exist between a composer's feelings and his notation. It was offhand and annoyingly incomplete, but even the stupider critics could have seen that it did not deny musical expressivity, but only the validity of a type of verbal statement about musical expressivity. I stand by the remark, incidentally, though today I would put it the other way around: music expresses itself." So Stravinsky wanted to do away with a subtle but pervasive notion: that of a pre-existing idea or emotion that a composer will then set to music. A composer does not "feel sad" and then write "sad" music; that is a childishly reductive view of how music is created. It is the listener, after all, who assigns meaning, ideas and emotions to music once he or she hears it. We commit a blunder when we imagine a transcendental idea that existed before music, like one of Plato's ideal forms.

When Stravinsky says "music expresses itself," he is speaking of the 5 process by which it comes into being—for himself at least. It does not borrow from language to generate itself; the composer does not have to have a particular feeling as he composes. Music's abstract quality—the way in which it does not refer to something other than itself—gives it autonomy in this reasoning.

This is not cut and dried, of course. Someone could point to any number of works that seem to be driven by a specific idea, or music that we retrospectively know was inspired by specific feelings—happy, sad, what have you—that came about from an event in the composer or performer's life. Many of Stravinsky's works seem to be related to a concrete idea—an imagined primitive ceremony, famously, in *The Rite of Spring*. And I'm excluding music with words, which is a whole other matter.

Stravinsky's statement was probably born out of frustration, as he repeatedly encountered reductive, mistaken characterisations of the composer's creative process. To the extent that he is correcting that reduction, I agree with him. It is easy to demonstrate the validity of his view by considering perceived youth in one work, and wisdom in another.

Consider two examples among many: Schubert's perfect song, "Gretchen am Spinnrade". This song changed the expressive possibility of song, upping the ante forever. He wrote it when he was 17. Or there is Jimi Hendrix's album, *Are You Experienced*, recorded when he was 24. The guitar was never the same again; rock music was never the same again; music was never the same again.

How was Schubert able to think up music like that—music that telegraphed the emotions of desire, fear, passion and unrest so uncannily? Doesn't it take wisdom to portray emotions like that? From where did young Schubert's psychological insight into female desire come? From what deep, sad place did a song like Hendrix's "The Wind Cries Mary" emerge; what informed the ecstasy of his "Third Stone from the Sun"—memories of high school?

It was not wisdom that comes with age, strictly speaking, in any of those cases. In day-to-day life, wisdom means we have grown older, we have learned much through numerous experiences, some painful and some pleasurable, we have reflected on them, and we base our observations, judgments and actions on them. Music is different. A musician does not necessarily need a wealth of experiences to express something that others will find profound. He or she obviously needs some—you can't live in a cave and pop out and start waxing profound—but not as many as one would expect. A musician can demand our attention without having necessarily lived many years.

That suggests musical wisdom has different rules than the wisdom that tells someone, for instance, not to argue a point, because he's argued it so many times before and it's an argument he can't win; or the wisdom that helps an older guy win the affection of a beautiful younger woman for a night because he understands her—he knows what she wants to hear more than the twentysomething guy vying for

> "A musician does not necessarily need a wealth of experiences to express something that others will find profound. He or she obviously needs some — you can't live in a cave and pop out and start waxing profound — but not as many as one would expect."

10

her attention. The twentysomething guy, on the other hand, might be arguing shrilly about politics, full of youthful stridency, sounding self-important to everyone except himself; he might be saying all the wrong stuff to the girl at the bar while the silver fox steals her away. But that night he might go home and write some music of profundity, music that has no stridency, music that bewitches us and soothes us.

Should we say, then, that musical wisdom arrives somehow faster than normal wisdom? That hypothesis won't do, though, because, in essentialist fashion, it brackets out the experience of composing and playing music from other experiences. There must be some way to account for the ability of musical expression to arrive before the depth of experience it seems to convey. The key word there is "seems" — it takes us back to Stravinsky, who would say, simply, that music only "seems" to convey wisdom; there is not a shred of actual wisdom in it at all. Music is only representing wisdom for a group of listeners; it is not properly exuding it. So let us not assign this agency to music; let us more accurately say that the group of listeners is attaching a quality to the music — it comes from them.

That works the other way around as well: Older musicians and composers create "youthful" music — music that sounds quirky, full of anxious energy, untamed — awkward, jagged, rhapsodic, or even foolish — at a station in their lives where they are not particularly anxious, foolish or awkward in their bearing at all. (Brahms' *Double Concerto* is a beloved example for me.)

This should be good news for the listener. I propose that we never grow out of good music — the whole idea is nonsense. Anything that is strong stays with us our whole lives. We forget about music sometimes, but then we come back to it, and it yields fresh pleasure and insight, along with a beautiful, bittersweet cadence of our past merging with the present moment. Thank goodness it is this way; thank goodness great music isn't "age sensitive" — what a sad world that would be!

Rock'n'roll is often by definition a young man's game — Led Zeppelin, the Who, the Beatles, Jimi Hendrix or the Rolling Stones released some of their most enduring music before they were 30. We don't stop listening to their music past the age of 30, though. Any music that is strong will speak to us in different ways at different points in our lives, and will never truly grow irrelevant.

Understanding the Text

1. According to Mehldau, "Essentialist tropes are everywhere in discussions about music" (2). What is he referring to? What is the problem with "essentialist tropes"?

2. In paragraph 4, Mehldau asks, "Was Stravinsky merely perpetuating a kind of sophistry?" What does "sophistry" mean? Does Mehldau think Stravinsky's argument is sophistic? Explain your answer with quotations from the text.

Reflection and Response

3. According to the writer, what is the relationship between music and wisdom? How are the two different? What is "musical wisdom"? Do you agree with these distinctions and claims? Why or why not?

4. Mehldau writes: "We forget about music sometimes, but then we come back to it, and it yields fresh pleasure and insight, along with a beautiful, bittersweet cadence of our past merging with the present moment. Thank goodness it is this way; thank goodness great music isn't 'age sensitive' — what a sad world that would be!" (14). Do you agree? Can you think of specific musical examples of this process or experience in your own life? What do you think he means by "age sensitive" in this context?

Making Connections

5. In "Beethoven's Kapow" (p. 61), Justin Davidson writes about Beethoven's "Eroica" symphony — and about how perceptions of music change over time: "Beethoven toyed with expectations we do not have and dismantled conventions that no longer guide us. As a result, the 'Eroica,' which emerged with such blinding energy that some of its first listeners thought its composer must be insane, sounds like settled wisdom to us" (4). Would Mehldau agree with Davidson's argument, particularly with regard to the meaning of music and the role of the listener? Why or why not?

6. According to Leonid Perlovsky in "Music and Consciousness" (p. 35), the "key to music's mysterious power lies in its unique relationship to the basic mechanisms of the mind" (3). Do you think Perlovsky's account of music's power and effects on listeners is compatible with Mehldau's? Explain your answer with specific quotations from the essays.

Why We Love Music — and Freud Despised It

Stephen A. Diamond

Clinical and forensic psychologist Stephen A. Diamond begins his reflections on music's power — and the powerful responses it evokes in listeners — with inquiry: "What is it about music that makes it such a popular art form? Why do we humans love it so? And why did Freud despise it?" In exploring the answers, he incorporates his experience as a therapist, as well as discussions of art, spirituality, the unconscious, and Swiss psychiatrist Carl Jung. He also argues that music stands at the core of our humanity, "an archetypal, primal means of human communication and self-expression" that emerges from deep within our DNA.

A regular contributor to *Psychology Today*, Stephen A. Diamond is the author of *Anger, Madness and the Daimonic: The Paradoxical Power of Rage in Violence, Evil and Creativity* (1996).

D id the father of psychoanalysis suffer from music phobia? I've been a musician and lover of music most of my life. Not all music. I never developed a taste for opera, for example. Nor do I care much for country music. I can enjoy classical music, especially that of Beethoven, Bach, Mozart and Vivaldi. I also like jazz and jazz-fusion, having an appreciation for its complexity and free-form improvisation, but, frankly, don't listen to either much. Unlike my parents, who came of age in the 1940s with the brassy music of big bands led by legendary musicians like Glenn Miller and Tommy Dorsey, and romantic crooners like Frank Sinatra and Dean Martin, I grew up hearing, loving, and playing pop and rock music, Chuck Berry, Motown, Beach Boys, Beatles, Rolling Stones, Kinks, the Who, and the amazing musical revolution known affectionately as the "British invasion." I was twelve and already taking drum lessons in 1963 when the Beatles arrived in America and made their debut television appearance on the *Ed Sullivan Show*. Like most impressionable American adolescents, I was hooked. And I'm still hooked. Today, as both an amateur musician (drums and rhythm guitar) and professional psychologist, I pose the following questions: What is it about music that makes it such a popular art form? Why do we humans love it so? And why did Freud despise it?

Fascinatingly, Sigmund Freud, the father of psychoanalysis and modern psychotherapy in general, apparently disliked most music with a passion. With the exception of certain bland operas, he had practically no appreciation of music as an art form. Indeed, he avoided almost all music like the plague. One might even speculate that Freud suffered from a significant fear of music, a "music phobia." Here is how Herr Doktor Freud (1914) himself explained his strong resistance to music:

> . . . *I am no connoisseur in art, but simply a layman. . . . Nevertheless, works of art do exercise a powerful effect on me, especially those of literature and sculpture, less often of painting. . . . I spend a long time before them trying to apprehend them in my own way, i.e. to explain to myself what their effect is due to. Wherever I cannot do this, as for instance with music, I am almost incapable of obtaining any pleasure. Some rationalistic, or perhaps analytic, turn of mind in me rebels against being moved by a thing without knowing why I am thus affected and what it is that affects me.*

Quite a confession! Why would someone with such a penetrating appreciation and comprehension of painting, architecture, sculpture, literature, poetry and other traditional art forms reject music so totally? One possible reason is that Freud, who is known to have suffered from various neurotic symptoms including obsessions, compulsivity, death anxiety, migraines and psychogenic fainting spells, may have also manifested *melophobia*. Fear of music. (Some even speculate that Freud suffered from an extremely rare form of seizure disorder known as *musicogenic*

Figure 1.2   "Music speaks the language of the irrational, and it cannot, as Freud frustratingly found, be broken down, analyzed, intellectualized, or rationally explained." RDA/Contributor/Getty Images

epilepsy. In such cases, music, either while played or heard, triggers an underlying neurological dysfunction, resulting in mild to severe seizures, and hence, an understandably powerful fear and avoidance of certain types of music.) As with other specific phobias (e.g., fear of snakes, spiders, flying, heights, storms, elevators, etc.), *melophobia* involves anxiety reactions to some specific stimulus. In Freud's case, this auditory triggering stimulus seems to have been music of almost any sort. When exposed to music while out on the town in Vienna or Munich, his automatic response was reportedly to immediately place his hands over his ears in order to block out the sound. What could have caused such a reaction? Was Freud's hearing, so finely tuned by decades of psychoanalytic listening, acutely hypersensitive? Or could his problem have been more deeply rooted?

One possible explanation for *melophobia* is that at some time   5 music — either all music or some specific piece or genre of music — was psychologically linked and negatively associated with a traumatic event or period in the person's past. A classical Freudian interpretation almost certainly would conclude that the music stimulates some repressed or repudiated unconscious complex, memory or emotional content, typically sexual (or aggressive) in nature, which the person feels compelled to avoid becoming conscious of at all costs. But let's take that one step further: What if someone's dislike and avoidance or even hatred of music is rooted in a fundamental fear of the "unconscious" itself? Of the "irrational"? A primal dread of what neo-Freudian existential psychoanalyst Rollo May (1969) called the "daimonic"? Or of what Jung dubbed the "shadow"?

For example, I once treated a very angry yet chronically repressed and, therefore, depressed patient who, despite his strong interests in literature, theater and film, could not read, attend or view works of any emotional depth and intensity (Diamond, 1996). He would consciously avoid placing himself in such situations. And, when he could not avoid them, he would dissociate from his feelings, numbing and preventing him from relating to the material more than merely superficially. My patient felt paralyzed with anxiety by the very activities and artistic endeavors that most stimulated him intellectually and emotionally, calling forth his fiercest passions and providing some sense of meaning and purpose. He feared that if he were to permit his self-imposed defensive walls to be breached by the sublime beauty and power of art, film, music and literature, he might lose all control of himself, go berserk, psychotic, become mad, be overwhelmed or destructively possessed by the *daimonic*. So he carefully steered clear of such circumstances, concealing his artistic sensibilities behind a crude *persona*, impoverishing his quality of life and starving his soul. When we chronically deny the *daimonic* in ourselves, our deepest passion and, as in this case, especially our rage, we must preclude activities, relationships or experiences that threaten to waken it from its unconscious slumber. (For more on the concept of the "daimonic" and its connection to creativity, see my book *Anger, Madness, and the Daimonic.*)

Fear of the feminine is yet another way of conceptualizing Freud's hatred of music. Music is all about feeling, emotion, passion, the irrational, the heart, the soul, and is closely associated with what Jung described as the "feminine" mode of being and, in men, what Jung called the *anima*. Despite his profound genius, Freud's denigrating antipathy toward the feminine and its physical embodiment, women, is well known, as seen, for instance, in his controversial concepts of "hysteria" (wandering uterus) and "penis envy." Freud devalued the feminine in his psychology as in himself, and overvalued the more "masculine" qualities of thinking, reasoning, logic, analysis, intellectualism and scientific reductionism. Did Freud fear his own "feminine" side? His sensitive, hysterical "inner woman"? Did he avoid dealing with his *anima* in part by excluding music from his world? (Freud allegedly did not permit music to be played at home, including by his children.) Or, to put it another way, was Freud unconsciously fearful of his own feelings? Powerful feelings that could involuntarily and irrationally be stirred up in him by music? Feelings he could not dissect, analyze or rationally comprehend? Feelings he therefore compulsively tried to keep under control at all costs? And did the chronic repression of his *anima*, his psychically divorced inner woman, his dissociated irrational impulses and emotions, engender Freud's own neurotic symptoms?

According to Freud biographer Peter Gay (1988), "Freud's life . . . was a struggle for self-discipline, for control over his speculative impulses *and his rage*—rage at his enemies and, even harder to manage, at those among his adherents he found wanting or disloyal [emphasis mine]." It is precisely this obsessive-compulsive defensiveness against the *daimonic* that may have produced Freud's seemingly pathological dread of music. Sigmund Freud possessed a towering intellect and profound insight into the human mind. But, like all of us, he struggled with his own personal demons. His *complexes*. Music is a two-edged sword: it has the power not only to ameliorate and sedate but to summon up and set free our "demons," our disturbing, long-suppressed emotions, memories and associations.

"Music, like a movie or good book, temporarily takes us far away from our ordinary troubles and tribulations, transporting us to a different time or another world. It can provide the solace of companionship for the lonely, lessen our sense of existential isolation, and convey compassion to the suffering soul."

It has been said (by playwright William Congreve) that "music has charms to soothe a savage breast." There is much truth to this. Music, like a movie or good book, temporarily takes us far away from our ordinary troubles and tribulations, transporting us to a different time or another world. It can provide the solace of companionship for the lonely, lessen our sense of existential isolation, and convey compassion to the suffering soul. That great American art form known as the *blues* is but one example of how listening to music created out of someone else's suffering — unrequited love, loss, trouble, bad luck — helps make us feel less alienated and alone in our problems. Misery, as the saying goes, loves company. When we hear such tragic tales and the sorrow they engender, whether in folk, country, R&B, standards, rap or rock music, we relate to the performer and feel ourselves to be part of the herd, tribe, the collective, the archetypal, the universal, the human family. For who among us has not felt the angst and confusion of adolescence, the sting of love lost or unreciprocated at some time? So listening to such sounds soothes our souls. When we're feeling sad or down, discouraged and disheartened, music can raise our spirits, be uplifting, inspirational and energizing. Music makes us want to move and dance, in a joyous, spontaneous expression of the primal life force. It can gently lull us to sleep (*lullaby*). Or it can make us want to cry or laugh. And, sometimes, music makes us feel angry. When, for example, Bob Dylan wrote, played and sang protest songs like "Masters of War" and "A Hard Rain's A-Gonna Fall," we felt his personal anger, and that he was expressing or channeling our own collective outrage. This is what differentiates *true* art from self-indulgent pretension; *real* music from mere cacophony or commercialism. The best music comes from and most purely expresses personal experiences, but arises and speaks also to what Jung called the "collective unconscious." It taps directly into our psyche at the deepest possible level and addresses archetypal and existential concerns about the human condition, ultimate concerns and universal experiences we all share. And it connects us intimately to each other.

Melody alone can be deeply moving. Consider Beethoven's *Eroica* symphony or his late string quartets composed just prior to his death. But when combined with meaningful lyrics, music takes on the additional   10 power of poetry. It becomes synergistic, speaking to us both verbally and non-verbally simultaneously. Of course, this all depends on the quality of the music and/or lyrics, and how well they complement each other. But when the combination is just right, nothing compares to the experience, whether of composing, playing and vocalizing, or passively listening to such sublime creations. Dylan did this. The transcendent yet soul-wrenchingly personal music of Joni Mitchell comes to mind as epitomizing this synergistic marriage of music and poetry. Jackson Browne is another artist whose music, vocals and lyrics work exceedingly well together. The Rolling Stones give evil and the diabolical dark side its due in their edgy and hypnotically chilling "Sympathy for the Devil." And then, of course, there is the timeless music of Lennon and McCartney. And many, many others.

But music can do so much more. Music can stimulate emotions, evoke long forgotten feelings or recollections, much as psychotherapy ideally does. It can trigger childhood memories, both pleasant and traumatic. Unlike rational conversation, music penetrates our intellectual defenses and speaks directly to the heart and soul of who we are. Music speaks the language of the soul, the irrational, and it refuses, as Freud frustratingly found, to be facilely broken down, analyzed, intellectualized or rationally explained. Perhaps this is why Freud, the consummate rationalist of the irrational, i.e., the *unconscious*, found music so deeply disturbing: He (his ego) evidently could not tolerate being affected by something without identifying the precise nature and cause of his strong emotional reactions. Being unable to place music under the reductionistic, mechanistic psychoanalytic microscope, and thus, to gain mastery and control over it, Freud may have found music's mysterious power profoundly threatening. It moved him in ways with which he was psychologically unprepared and unwilling to contend. Paradoxically, music is often associated with love, eros, romance and sexuality, another basic component of the *daimonic*. Music is commonly made use of in erotic relationships to "set the mood" for love, serving as aphrodisiacal "mood music." Music can stimulate sexual feelings. In this sense, it seems especially strange that Freud, who did more than anyone of his era to bring eros and human sexuality into the bright light of day and out of the dark Victorian shadows, showed so little enthusiasm for or interest in music. Quite the contrary. Curiously, though perhaps not surprisingly in light of the present discussion, in the prodigious fifteen-volume *Standard Edition of the Complete Psychological Works of Sigmund Freud*, the subject of music is seldom mentioned.

Freud, who considered himself inherently "unmusical" or perhaps as having a "tin ear," was not alone in his disparagement of music. Not everyone is a music lover. Some philosophers and intellectuals, including Plato, have argued that music is mere entertainment and distraction for those who cannot amuse, converse or think for themselves. A poor substitute for authentic social intercourse. For intellectual debate. For real intimacy. There is some truth to this. As there is to the fact that music can sometimes become a compulsive defense against introspection, silence and existential aloneness. Yet, in Freud's case, we still don't know why. Was the highly cultured, refined Freud simply unable to appreciate the emotional language of music? Was Sigmund Freud "tone-deaf"? Maybe, like 4% of the general population, he did in fact suffer from congenital *amusia, dysmelodia,* or *dysmusia*: an inability to expressively and/or receptively detect tonal pitch or rhythm. To follow or carry a tune. Tune deafness. This might be why Freud, a trained neurologist, sought to avoid being constantly and painfully reminded of this partly neurological deficiency or inferiority by despising, dreading and dismissing the mysterious power of music. Perhaps his disregard for and denigration of music was Freud's way of trying to compensate for what his contemporary, Alfred Adler (1870–1937), referred to as this shameful "organ inferiority."

Not all music is art. Much of it can be banal and pedestrian, or just plain bad, especially when composed or played by unskilled, untalented, uninspired musicians. Consider common karaoke, for instance. Or the type of lousy lounge music parodied by comedians like Bill Murray. At its best, music conveys feelings and emotions more purely and powerfully than most other art forms. At its worst, it can be banal, offensive, insipid, prosaic, soul-less or simply boring. (Perhaps it was sometimes such vapid background noise or what we today pejoratively call "elevator" music that Freud found so offensive.) But even then, music can be entertaining to listen to and see being performed. And it can be even more fun for the musicians themselves. Playing music for others and with others is like no other experience. It is a heady mixture of team sport, interpersonal communication, and collective painting or sculpture combined. It provides the opportunity to express ourselves through a musical instrument, often non-verbally, in ways which we could never do otherwise. Which is what makes music so potentially therapeutic.

Indeed, music has been employed in the healing of psychological or spiritual suffering for thousands of years, from its use by shamans, witch doctors, priests and exorcists, to professional "music therapists" today. Music is an archetypal, primal means of human communication and self-expression, one that has been practiced from time immemorial. Most of us are born with the innate capacity to be musical. Rhythm, played on drum-like instruments, may be the earliest and most primitive form of music. It is in our blood. Deep in our DNA. Every culture makes music of some sort. It can be inspired by tragedy, loss, love, joy, serenity, terror, war or rage. Music, at its height, like art in general, wrote Franz Kafka, "must be the axe for the frozen sea inside us." This is what the best music can do, and music may do it better than most other art forms. It may be that most of all, Freud unconsciously feared this liberating axe. Perhaps he sought to prevent the frozen sea of feelings inside him from freely flowing and potentially inundating or overpowering his ego, terrified of triggering some unstoppable affective tsunami. If so, this certainly seems antithetical to his own proclaimed psychoanalytic task: *Making the unconscious conscious.* Though this therapeutic goal cannot always be accomplished intellectually, via cognitive insight alone, sometimes necessitating emotional catharsis or *abreaction*, it does comport with Freud's comparatively negative view of the unconscious, the irrational, and the feminine as contrasted to that of Carl Jung. In fact, despite, like Freud, pretty much ignoring the subject in his collected writings, the mature Jung (1956) eventually concluded that "music should be an essential part of every analysis. This reaches deep archetypal material that we can only sometimes reach in our analytical work with patients." Can music substitute for psychotherapy? Not really. But music can take us places "talk therapy" cannot. It provides deep emotional catharsis for both creator and listener. And I would argue that the capacity to create and appreciate music and other expressive art forms can not only complement psychotherapy, but may, for some, become the best therapy once traditional treatment ends.

Finally, Freud's disdain not only of music, but, famously, of religion and spirituality, must also be considered. Are they connected? I would say so. For music has long been linked with spirituality and religion, the antithesis of science. And this is because music evokes spirituality, the *mysterium tremendum*, the transcendent, the ineffable, the awesome, the numinous, which is why it has been for millennia such an integral part of shamanic rituals, prayer and religious ceremonies in Judaism, Buddhism, Hinduism, Christianity, etc. Freud denied this "irrational" side of himself, his more mystical, spiritual leanings, his religiosity, and feared and rejected Jung's fascination with such esoteric and "occult" matters, fighting tenaciously to exclude them (and Jung) from his purely rationalistic "science" of psychoanalysis. But, as Jung rightly pointed out, that which we try to exclude from our conscious personality inevitably becomes part of the "shadow." Much like his patients' repressed sexuality, Freud's own repressed spirituality may have expressed itself negatively in his numerous "irrational," obsessive, superstitious thoughts and fears, including that of music. We could speculatively conclude that Freud feared the spiritual power of music because he dreaded and disowned the spiritual side of himself. By completely excommunicating spirituality from psychoanalysis and his own personal psyche in the sacred name of science, Sigmund Freud sacrificed his potential relationship to the enigmatic magic and majesty of music. But, then, great genius always has its price.

Understanding the Text

1. In paragraph 6, Diamond recounts the story of one of his patients. What specific idea or claim is the writer illustrating with this example?

2. According to Diamond, how can music augment or complement psychotherapy?

Reflection and Response

3. Diamond's essay is called "Why We Love Music," but he spends much of the essay discussing Sigmund Freud's *dislike* of music. Why do you think the writer chose this approach? How does Diamond's focus on Freud's antipathy further the essay's overall purpose?

4. The writer is a psychologist, so it is not surprising that he views music through the lens of his field and profession. For example, he writes: "The best music comes from and most purely expresses personal experiences, but arises and speaks also to what Jung called the 'collective unconscious.' It taps directly into our psyche at the deepest possible level and addresses archetypal and existential concerns about the human condition, ultimate concerns and universal experiences we all share" (9). Do you find this a useful approach to the topic? What are its strengths and weaknesses?

Making Connections

5. In his conclusion, Diamond writes that "music evokes spirituality, the mysterious . . . the transcendent, the ineffable, the awesome . . ." (15). How might Brad Mehldau (p. 21) respond to this characterization, especially the words "transcendent" and "ineffable" (an adjective that refers to something incapable of being expressed in language)?

6. The writer asserts: "At its best, music conveys feelings and emotions more purely and powerfully than most other art forms. At its worst, it can be banal, offensive, insipid, prosaic, soulless or simply boring" (13). Find one example of music at its "best" and one example at its "worst," and then explain your reasoning in making these choices.

Music and Consciousness

Leonid Perlovsky

In this dense, ambitious, and demanding essay that deftly covers the history of human consciousness and its relationship to Western music, physicist Leonid Perlovsky tries to account for music's perennial appeal, power, and hold on the human mind. He also investigates the evolutionary purpose of music. He anchors his analysis in a view of cognition in which humans constantly test and refine their internal models of how the world works against the actual experience of that world. This requires mechanisms of "differentiation" and "synthesis"; the interplay between these two processes accounts for the emotions aroused by music. However, Perlovsky moves outside this cognitive model to show how changes in cognition and culture have led to changes in music, as the medium works as a means of "mechanism of synthesis, a means of creating harmony and wholeness in the human soul."

Leonid Perlovsky is CEO of LP Information Technology and a professor in Northeastern University's Psychology Department. His broad interests include the language, cognition, aesthetics, philosophy, and physics of the mind. He is the author of *Neural Networks and Intellect: Using Model-Based Concepts* (2000) and several other books.

Is it not strange that sheep's guts should hale souls out of men's bodies?

—SHAKESPEARE[1]

Mystery of Music

Music is an enigma. Almost no one is indifferent to it—and many of us have a positive passion for it. Whether seated in concert halls or in our living rooms, attached to our iPods or trapped in elevators and waiting rooms, we spend countless hours of our lives listening to it or making it ourselves. It's big business too: the US exports more music than guns and cars. But why is music so important to us? What role does it play in our minds? What evolutionary purpose does it serve? Explanations range from bonding military regiments together to dissipating psychological tensions. But these are not explanations at all; they just 'pass the buck' to music's military or therapeutic uses.[2] They do not explain its unique ability to touch our souls. Anybody who loves music, Bach or Gregorian chant, Beatles or Eminem, knows that utilitarian explanations only scratch its surface. Aristotle struggled with the mystery of how "rhythms and melodies, just mere sounds, remind [us of] slates of soul."[3] The evolutionary psychologist Steven Pinker prosaically opined that "music is auditory cheesecake."[4]—an undeniable treat for the senses, but essentially non-nutritious and unnecessary. Even the great Kant, who so brilliantly explained the epistemology of the beautiful and the sublime, could not explain music: "[As for] the expansion of the faculties . . . in the judgment for cognition, music will have the lowest place among [the beautiful arts] . . . because it merely plays with senses."[5]

As far back as Pythagoras, musicians, philosophers, and physicists have ventured to elucidate the principles of harmony. In the nineteenth century Herman von Helmholtz[6] explained consonances and dissonances, majors and minors, with reference to similarities or dissimilarities among overtones. With minor modifications his theory is still applied to electronic musical instruments today. But to analyze music's acoustic qualities is not at all the same thing as to account for music's aesthetic qualities.

The Knowledge Instinct

This article proposes that the key to music's mysterious power lies in its unique relationship to the basic mechanisms of the mind. We understand the physical world in terms of ideas or concept models that reside in our mind. We have an inborn instinct to test our internal models against the external world[7]; since the world and our understanding of it are constantly changing, we are constantly refining and revising our models as well. When a mental model resonates convincingly with its real-world original, when an idea "fits," our instinct for knowledge is satisfied and we experience a sensation of esthetic pleasure. I call this cognitive mechanism "the knowledge instinct."

Two aspects of the knowledge instinct are *differentiation* and *synthesis*. In addition to concept-models of physical things, our minds contain archetypes—inborn, unconscious psychic structures, undifferentiated vague representations—emotions that are directly connected to our instincts. Before we can use these archetypes in thinking, they have to be differentiated and made conscious. This process takes millennia and its results are ingrained in language. Language models (words, phrases . . .) are accessible to consciousness, but they are most meaningful to us—emotionally related to life—when they are connected to concept-models and to archetypes of the unconscious. Following Carl Jung,[8] I call this process *synthesis*. Two examples of concept-models that are connected to undifferentiated archetypes: an American flag, a Star of David. Both concept models have explicit content; both are pregnant with unconscious emotional associations. It is in this all-important process of differentiation and synthesis that music plays its unique role.

When we hear music, two distinct parts of our brains are called into 5
play. On the one hand, music is perceived by evolutionary-old neural
centers and resonates with archetypes that are directly connected to
instincts in which emotions and concepts are inextricably intertwined.[9]
The instinct that imputes a martial character to trumpets and drums is
similar to that which associates the roar of a leopard with danger. On the
other hand, music is perceived by evolutionary-new brain centers in the
cortex, where music creates new and diverse emotions—the exaltation
we experience when listening to the final movement of Beethoven's
Ninth Symphony; the intellectual and emotional subtleties of "The
Goldberg Variations." Thus music serves a dual purpose: it evokes new
emotions: at the same time, by creating associations between conscious
emotions and unconscious archetypes, it promotes synthesis or wholeness in the human psyche. Music at once differentiates and creates
wholeness; it engages the human being as a whole.

As consciousness evolves, it moves along a razor's edge between differentiation and synthesis. When there is excessive differentiation, concepts lose their intuitive, emotional content and cease to engage the
heart (Catholic monks who'd lost their religious vocation used the word
acedia to describe this state of mind); when there is excessive synthesis,
emotionality nails language and thinking too firmly to traditional values and a culture ceases to change. In order for a culture to sustain its
creative momentum it must maintain this precarious balance. Changes
in music and consciousness parallel and complement each other: they
can be traced through Antiquity, the Middle Ages, the Renaissance, the
Reformation, Classicism, Romanticism, all the way up until the present
day. For the last two thousand years of Western culture, synthesis and
differentiation have maintained their equilibrium with the help of music,
which evolved along with it.

Differentiated Consciousness and Antiphonal Singing

The Old Testament prophet Isaiah foresaw an impending national
catastrophe in the 8th century BCE; this created tensions in his soul
which he experienced as antiphonal choruses of Seraphims.° This was
the first time that the principle of antiphony—split choruses answer-
ing each other back and forth—was mentioned in the Bible. It would
become a foundation of psalmody in Jewish and Christian divine service:
"One cried to another, and said, Holy, holy, holy is the Lord of hosts."[10]

Seraphims: Celestial beings, similar to angels.

"The words sung by the Seraphim entered the Jewish liturgy . . . and were later adopted by the Christian church."[11]

There are remarkable coincidences between the development of consciousness in Ancient Greece and Israel. In the 6th century BCE the first Greek philosopher Thales repudiated myths, demanded conscious thinking, and pronounced the famous formula "know thyself." In Israel, the prophet Zechariah forbade prophecy,[12] an outdated and already dangerous form of thinking, demanding conscious thinking in its stead. But conscious thinking created a discord between the personal and the unconscious-universal and led to a feeling of separateness from the world. Tensions appeared in the psyche, which, as we've seen, were objectified by antiphonal singing. Antiphon as an *accepted* form of divine service is mentioned in the Bible for the first time in the book of Nehemiah[13] in 445 BCE, just a century after Zechariah. Split choirs symbolized the differentiated nature of the highest principles; they brought the feel of the split in the psyche closer to consciousness.

Christianity forestalled the split in the human soul; its new symbol of a suffering God, both mortal and immortal, assimilated the fundamental contradiction of human nature (between the finiteness of matter and the infiniteness of spirit, between conscious and unconscious).

The Renaissance and Tonal Music

How could music still inspire, when mysticism was giving way to humanism, when human reason became the measure of all things? To restore synthesis in the human consciousness, newer and more diverse emotions were needed. Beginning in the Renaissance a musical system of *tonality* was developed for differentiation of emotions.[14] In the 15th century John Dunstable, according to witnesses, changed all "music high and music low," music became more consonant and euphonious,[15] the better to connect differentiated emotions with the sublime.

The Reformation and Bach

The Reformation transplanted the battleground between good and evil from the heights of Heaven and the depths of Hades into the heart of the human soul. Protestants had to decide within their own minds how to reconcile the perpetual contradictions between their material and spiritual needs. The autonomy of religious symbols was lost; their unconscious contents were partly transferred into consciousness. Tensions in the human soul reached high levels. At the same time, music became unprecedentedly expressive. New musical forms were perfected in works of Buxtehude° and then Bach. Polyphonic music acquired complex and sublime form in the fugue; it combined 'horizontal' melodies and 'vertical' harmonies in the space of sounds. When hearing Bach's fugues, one ceases to argue with oneself; one either turns to God or discovers unexpected heights in oneself.

The 21st century and Rap

Today a vast chasm yawns between the vast numbers of differentiated concepts that characterize our culture and individuals' capacities to assimilate them while preserving synthesis within their souls. The animalistic and satanic styles of some of our contemporary rockers and rappers could be better understood if we compare them to the wild choruses of satyrs in the days of the Ancient Greeks. The ecstatic dithyramb° was an ancient way of creating synthesis, of connecting the sublime with the bestial, unconscious bases of the human psyche. Rap is contemporary dithyramb, restoring the connection between the conscious and unconscious. As in Ancient Greece 2,500 years ago, so today many young people are losing their bearing. By shouting words along with primitive melody and rhythms, a human being may restore synthesis, the connection of the conscious unconscious—the Dionysian bursts into Apollonian° consciousness and reasserts itself; a riven internal world is restored to wholeness.

Consciousness, especially as it is reflected in language, strives to split the world into pieces. Music makes it whole again, in all its manifold emotionality. This is why "Music is so deeply understood by our inmost being." It is a mechanism of synthesis, a means of creating harmony and wholeness in the human soul.

> "Consciousness, especially as it is reflected in language, strives to split the world into pieces. Music makes it whole again, in all its manifold emotionality. This is why "Music is so deeply understood by our inmost being." It is a mechanism of synthesis, a means of creating harmony and wholeness in the human soul."

Buxtehude: Danish-German Baroque Composer Dieterich Buxtehude (c. 1737–1707).
dithyramb: ancient Greek song celebrating Dionysus.
Dionysion and Apollonian: philosophical and aesthetic opposition between emotion, ecstasy, and loss of self (represented by the Greek god of wine, Dionysus) and logic, reason, and individuality (represented by the Greek god of Sun, light, and truth, Apollo).

References

1. Shakespeare, *Much Ado about Nothing,* Act II Scene III. See in *Complete Works of William Shakespeare.* Gramercy, 1990.

2. Huron, David. Ernest Bloch Lectures, University of California, Berkeley. Department of Music, 1999.

3. Aristotle, *Topics.* IV BCE. in *The complete works. The revised Oxford translation,* edited by Jonathan Bames. Princeton University Press, 1995.

4. Pinker, Steven. *How the Mind Works.* Norton, 1997.

5. Kant, Immanuel. *Critique of Judgement,* 1790. Translated by J. H. Bernard. Macmillan & Co., 1914, pp. 170–74.

6. Helmholtz, Hermann. 1863, see in *On the Sensations of Tone.* Dover Publications, 1954.

7. Perlovsky, Leonid I. "Toward Physics of the Mind: Concepts, Emotions, Consciousness, and Symbols." *Physics of Life Reviews, vol.* 3, no. 1, Jan. 2006, pp. 23–55.

8. Jung, Carl G. *Psychological Types.* In the *Collected Works.* vol. 6, Bollingen Series XX. Princeton University Press, 1971.

9. Perlovsky, Leonid I. *Music – The First Principles.* 2006, www.ceo.spb.ru /libretto/kon_lan/ogl.shtml.

10. Bible. ls. 6, 1–4, New King James Version.

11. Weiss, Piero, and Richard Taruskin, *Music in the Western World.* Schirmer, Macmillan, 1984, p. 19.

12. Zech. 3–4.

13. Neh. 12, 27–43.

14. Weiss, Piero, and Richard Taruskin, p. 546.

15. Dunstable, John. English musician (1453). Weiss, Piero, and Richard Taruskin, p. 80.

Understanding the Text

1. Perlovsky tries to explain music's appeal, power, and relationship to human consciousness, in part, because previous attempts to do so are unsatisfying. Why do these explanations miss the mark, according to the writer?

2. According to the writer, a fundamental shift in spirituality and human consciousness occurred during the Reformation. How was this change expressed and reflected in music of the time?

Reflection and Response

3. In his account of the evolution of human consciousness and the development of music, Perlovsky focuses on religious history and spirituality. Does his explanation depend on his readers being religious or spiritual? For example, would it be persuasive to an atheist or an agnostic? Explain your answer.

4. Perlovsky writes about consciousness and music entirely in the context of Western culture; in the process, he ignores other regions, histories, and musical traditions (e.g., Asian music). Does this limit or undermine his argument and his claims about human consciousness? Why or why not?

Making Connections

5. The writer claims: "As in Ancient Greece 2,500 years ago, so today many young people are losing their bearings. By shouting words along with primitive melody and rhythms, a human being may restore synthesis, the connection of the conscious and the unconscious . . ." (12). How might Judy Berman (p. 98) make sense of this assertion? Does her analysis in "Concerning the Spiritual in Indie Rock" support and extend Perlovsky's analysis, or complicate it?

6. Perlovsky describes the way in which music can help listeners achieve unity and perhaps experience the sublime, as "the Dionysian bursts into Apollonian consciousness and reasserts itself; a riven internal world is restored to wholeness" (12). Here, the writer evokes an opposition between the "Dionysian" and the "Apollonian." Research the meaning of these two terms and their relationship. How are they related to different kinds of musical experience and expression?

From the Homily on the First Psalm

St. Basil

Born in what is now Kayseri, Turkey, in about 330 CE, St. Basil was an important preacher and theologian in the early development of the Church. He is known, in particular, for his contributions to creating monastic institutions and practices. Several denominations venerate St. Basil, including the Roman Catholic Church, the Eastern Orthodox Church, and the Anglican Church.

In this excerpt from his "Homily on the First Psalm," St. Basil provides an illuminating view of the Psalms from an early Church father — one skilled in the art of rhetoric. The Book of Psalms is a section of the Old Testament comprised of poetic lyrics, written to be sung. For the writer, this scriptural music is not only pleasurable but ennobling, educational, and spiritually healthful: "A psalm is the tranquility of souls, the arbitrator of peace, restraining the disorder and turbulence of thoughts . . ."

1. ALL SCRIPTURE is given by inspiration of God and is profitable* and was composed by the Holy Spirit to the end that, as in a common dispensary for souls, we may, all men, select each the medicine for his own disease. For the Scripture saith, "Medicine pacifieth great offenses."† The Prophets therefore teach certain things, the Histories others, the Law others, and the kind of counsel given in the Proverbs others. But the book of the Psalms embraces whatever in all the others is helpful. It prophesies things to come, it recalls histories to the mind, it gives laws for living, it counsels what is to be done. And altogether it is a storehouse of good instructions, diligently providing for each what is useful to him. For it heals the ancient wounds of souls and to the newly wounded brings prompt relief; it ministers to what is sick and preserves what is in health; and it wholly removes the ills, howsoever great and of whatsoever kind, that attack souls in our human life; and this by means of a certain well-timed persuasion which inspires wholesome reflection.

For when the Holy Spirit saw that mankind was ill-inclined toward virtue and that we were heedless of the righteous life because of our inclination to pleasure, what did He do? He blended the delight of melody with doctrines in order that through the pleasantness and softness of the sound we might unawares receive what was useful in the words, according to the practice of wise physicians, who, when they give the more bitter

---

*I Timothy 3:16.
†Ecclesiastes 10:4.

draughts to the sick, often smear the rim of the cup with honey. For this purpose these harmonious melodies of the Psalms have been designed for us, that those who are of boyish age or wholly youthful in their character, while in appearance they sing, may in reality be educating their souls. For hardly a single one of the many, and even of the indolent, has gone away retaining in his memory any precept of the apostles or of the prophets, but the oracles of the Psalms they both sing at home and disseminate in the market place. And if somewhere one who rages like a wild beast from excessive anger falls under the spell of the psalm, he straightway departs, with the fierceness of his soul calmed by the melody.

2. A psalm is the tranquillity of souls, the arbitrator of peace, restraining the disorder and turbulence of thoughts, for it softens the passion of the soul and moderates its unruliness. A psalm forms friendships, unites the divided, mediates between enemies. For who can still consider him an enemy with whom he has sent forth one voice to God? So that the singing of psalms brings love, the greatest of good things, contriving harmony like some bond of union and uniting the people in the symphony of a single choir.

A psalm drives away demons, summons the help of angels, furnishes arms against nightly terrors, and gives respite from daily toil; to little children it is safety, to men in their prime an adornment, to the old a solace, to women their most fitting ornament. It peoples solitudes, it chastens market places. To beginners it is a beginning; to those who are advancing, an increase; to those who are concluding, a support. A psalm is the voice of the church. It gladdens feast days, it creates the grief which is in accord with God's will, for a psalm brings a tear even from a heart of stone.

> "A psalm drives away demons, summons the help of angels, furnishes arms against nightly terrors, and gives respite from daily toil; to little children it is safety, to men in their prime an adornment, to the old a solace, to women their most fitting ornament."

A psalm is the work of the angels, the ordinance of Heaven, the 5 incense of the Spirit. Oh, the wise invention of the teacher who devised how we might at the same time sing and learn profitable things, whereby doctrines are somehow more deeply impressed upon the mind!

What is learned unwillingly does not naturally remain, but things which are received with pleasure and love fix themselves more firmly in our minds. For what can we not learn from the Psalms? Can we not learn the splendor of courage, the exactness of justice, the dignity of

self-control, the habit of repentance, the measure of patience, whatsoever good things that you may name? Here is perfect theology; here is
foretold the incarnation of Christ; here are the threat of judgement, the
hope of resurrection, the fear of punishment, the assurance of glory, the
revelations of mysteries; all things are brought together in the book of
Psalms as in some great and common storehouse.

   Although there are many musical instruments, the prophet made this
book suited to the psaltery°, as it called, revealing, it seems to me, the
grace from on high which sounded in him through the Holy Spirit, since
this alone, off all musical instruments, has the source of its sound above.
For the brass wires of the cithara and the lyre sound from below against
the plectrum, but the psaltery has the origins of its harmonious rhythms
above, in order that we may study to seek for those things which are on
high and not be drawn down by the pleasantness of the melody to the
passions of the flesh.* And I think that by reason of this structure of the
instrument the words of the prophet profoundly and wisely reveal to us
that those whose souls are attuned and harmonious have an easy path to
things above. But now let us examine the beginning of the Psalms.

Understanding the Text

1. According to St. Basil, what relationship does the book of the Psalms have
   with other books of the Bible?

2. The writer argues that the Psalms were created by the Holy Spirit. According
   to the writer, why were they created? What were they designed to do?

Reflection and Response

3. St. Basil writes about music in an explicitly religious context. What is the
   relationship between religious music in a religious context and secular music
   in a secular context? Do their purposes overlap in any way? Are the two
   categories mutually exclusive? Can religious music serve a secular purpose?
   Can secular music serve a religious or spiritual purpose? Explain your
   answer with specific reference to St. Basil's text.

psaltery: an ancient and medieval musical instrument like a dulcimer but played by
plucking the strings with the fingers or a plectrum.

*For this comparison and the various symbolic interpretations placed on it by the
   Church Fathers see Hermann Abert, Die Musikanschauung des Mittelalters (Halle,
   1905), pp. 215–218, and Thêodore Gêrold, Les Pêres de l'église et la Musique (Paris,
   1931), pp. 126–130.

4. According to the writer, the Psalms are especially suited to the psaltery, an ancient stringed instrument, because it "has the origins of its harmonious rhythms above, in order that we may study to seek for those things which are on high and not be drawn down by the pleasantness of the melody to the passions of the flesh" (7). What is St. Basil suggesting about the goals and effects of music in this passage? How does it connect with your own view of music?

Making Connections

5. In "Music and Consciousness" (p. 35), Leonid Perlovsky writes about the history of consciousness in a religious context. Do you see St. Basil's characterization of the Psalms corresponding to Perlovsky's account in any way? For example, do the Psalms seem designed to help ease "tensions" in the psyche or help synthesize or "connect differentiated emotions with the sublime"? Explain your answer with reference to both texts.

6. Among its other roles, St. Basil sees music as a useful means of instruction: it educates both minds and "souls." As he writes, "What is learned unwillingly does not naturally remain, but things which are received with pleasures and love fix themselves firmly in our minds" (6). What function do you think music should serve in contemporary education, at any level? Do you think it is essential? Do you think it is secondary to more practical fields of instruction? Explain.

Brainworms, Sticky Music, and Catchy Tunes

Oliver Sacks

Most of us have had the experience of a "brainworm" or an "ear worm": a catchy song or a fragment of a melody that gets lodged in our minds and plays incessantly. While we may find this phenomenon distracting, annoying, or even maddening, famed neurologist and author Oliver Sacks finds it a curiosity worthy of serious investigation: "What is happening, psychologically and neurologically, when a tune or jingle takes possession of one like this? What are the characteristics that make a tune or song 'dangerous' or 'infectious' in this way?" In seeking answers, Sacks explores the relationship between music and the hardwired mechanisms of human cognition.

Oliver Sacks was a physician and writer who taught and practiced at Yeshiva University's Albert Einstein College of Medicine, the New York University School of Medicine, and Columbia University Medical Center, among other institutions. He was also the author of many books, including *Awakenings* (1973), *The Man Who Mistook His Wife for a Hat* (1995), and *Musicophilia: Tales of Music and the Brain* (2007).

Sometimes normal musical imagery crosses a line and becomes, so to speak, pathological, as when a certain fragment of music repeats itself incessantly, sometimes maddeningly, for days on end. These repetitions—often a short, well-defined phrase or theme of three or four bars—are apt to go on for hours or days, circling in the mind, before fading away. This endless repetition and the fact that the music in question may be irrelevant or trivial, not to one's taste, or even hateful, suggest a coercive process, that the music has entered and subverted a part of the brain, forcing it to fire repetitively and autonomously (as may happen with a tic or a seizure).

Many people are set off by the theme music of a film or television show or an advertisement. This is not coincidental, for such music is designed, in the terms of the music industry, to "hook" the listener, to be "catchy" or "sticky," to bore its way, like an earwig, into the ear or mind; hence the term "earworms"—though one might be inclined to call them "brainworms" instead. (One newsmagazine, in 1987, defined them, half facetiously, as "cognitively infectious musical agents.")

A friend of mine, Nick Younes, described to me how he had been fixated on the song "Love and Marriage," a tune written by James Van Heusen.*

---

*An earlier generation will remember the tune of "Love and Marriage" as the Campbell's soup advertisement "Soup and Sandwich." Van Heusen was

A single hearing of this song—a Frank Sinatra rendition used as the theme song of the television show *Married . . . with Children*—was enough to hook Nick. He "got trapped inside the tempo of the song," and it ran in his mind almost constantly for ten days. With incessant repetition, it soon lost its charm, its lilt, its musicality, and its meaning. It interfered with his school-work, his thinking, his peace of mind, his sleep. He tried to stop it in a num-ber of ways, all to no avail: "I jumped up and down. I counted to a hundred. I splashed water on my face. I tried talking loudly to myself, plugging my ears." Finally it faded away—but as he told me this story, it returned and went on to haunt him again for several hours.*

Though the term "earworm" was first used in the 1980s (as a lit-eral translation of the German *Ohrwurm*), the concept is far from new.† Nicolas Slonimsky, a composer and musicologist, was deliberately inventing musical forms or phrases that could hook the mind and force it to mimicry and repetition, as early as the 1920s. And in 1876, Mark Twain wrote a short story ("A Literary Nightmare," subsequently retitled

---

a master of the catchy tune and wrote dozens of [literally] unforgettable songs—including "High Hopes," "Only the Lonely," and "Come Fly with Me"—for Bing Crosby, Frank Sinatra, and others. Many of these have been adapted for television or advertising theme songs.

*Since the original publication of *Musicophilia*, many people have written to me about ways of dealing with a brainworm—such as consciously singing or play-ing it to the end of the song, so that it is no longer a fragment circling round and round, incapable of resolution; or displacing it by singing or listening to another tune [though this may only become another brainworm in turn].

> Musical imagery, especially if it is repetitive and intrusive, may have a motor component, a subvocal "humming" or singing of which the person may be unaware, but which still may exact a toll. "At the end of a bad music-loop day," wrote one correspondent, "my throat is as uncomfort-able as it might have been had I sung all day." David Wise, another corre-spondent, found that using progressive relaxation techniques to relax the "muscular correlates to the hearing of music involving the tightening and movement of the speech apparatus . . . associated with auditory thinking" was efficacious in stopping annoying brainworms. While some of these methods seem to work for some people, most others have found, like Nick Younes, no cure.

†Jeremy Scratcherd, a scholarly musician who has studied the folk genres of Northumberland and Scotland, informs me that

> Examination of early folk music manuscripts reveals many examples of various tunes to which have been attributed the title "The piper's maggot." These were perceived to be tunes which got into the musician's head to irri-tate and gnaw at the sufferer-like a maggot in a decaying apple. There is one such tune in the [1888] *Northumbrian Minstrelsy*. . . . The earliest collection of pipe music penned in 1733 by another Northumbrian, William Dixon, and this along with other Scottish collections suggests that the "maggot" most probably appeared in the early 18th century. Interesting that despite the disparity of time the metaphor has remained much the same!

"Punch, Brothers, Punch!") in which the narrator is rendered helpless after encountering some "jingling rhymes":

They took instant and entire possession of me. All through breakfast they went waltzing through my brain. . . . I fought hard for an hour, but it was useless. My head kept humming. . . . I drifted downtown, and presently discovered that my feet were keeping time to that relentless jingle. . . . [I] jingled all through the evening, went to bed, rolled, tossed, and jingled all night long.

Two days later, the narrator meets an old friend, a pastor, and inad- 5
vertently "infects" him with the jingle; the pastor, in turn, inadvertently infects his entire congregation.

What is happening, psychologically and neurologically, when a tune or a jingle takes possession of one like this? What are the characteristics that make a tune or a song "dangerous" or "infectious" in this way? Is it some oddity of sound, of timbre or rhythm or melody? Is it repetition? Or is it arousal of special emotional resonances or associations?

My own earliest brainworms can be reactivated by the act of thinking about them, even though they go back more than sixty years. Many of them seemed to have a very distinctive musical shape, a tonal or melodic oddness that may have played a part in imprinting them on my mind. And they had meaning and emotion, too, for they were usually Jewish songs and litanies associated with a sense of heritage and history, a feeling of family warmth and togetherness. One favorite song, sung after the meal on Seder nights, was "Had Gadya" (Aramaic for "one little goat"). This was an accumulating and repetitive song, and one that must have been sung (in its Hebrew version) many times in our Orthodox household. The additions, which became longer and longer with each verse, were sung with a mournful emphasis ending with a plaintive fourth. This little phrase of six notes in a minor key would be sung (I counted!) forty-six times in the course of the song, and this repetition hammered it into my head. It would haunt me and pop into my mind dozens of times a day throughout the eight days of Passover, then slowly diminish until the next year. Did the qualities of repetition and simplicity or that odd, incongruous fourth perhaps act as neural facilitators, setting up a circuit (for it felt like this) that reexcited itself automatically? Or did the grim humor of the song or its solemn, liturgical context play a significant part, too?

Yet it seems to make little difference whether catchy songs have lyrics or not—the wordless themes of *Mission: Impossible* or Beethoven's Fifth can be just as irresistible as an advertising jingle in which the words are almost inseparable from the music (as in Alka-Seltzer's "Plop, plop, fizz, fizz" or Kit Kat's "Gimme a break, gimme a break . . .").

For those with certain neurological conditions, brainworms or allied phenomena—the echoic or automatic or compulsive repetition of tones or words—may take on additional force. Rose R., one of the post-encephalitic parkinsonian patients I described in *Awakenings,* told me how during her frozen states she had often been "confined," as she put it, in "a musical paddock"—seven pairs of notes (the fourteen notes of "Povero Rigoletto") which would repeat themselves irresistibly in her mind. She also spoke of these forming "a musical quadrangle" whose four sides she would have to perambulate, mentally, endlessly. This might go on for hours on end, and did so at intervals throughout the entire forty-three years of her illness, prior to her being "awakened" by L-dopa.

Milder forms of this may occur in ordinary Parkinson's disease. One 10 correspondent described how, as she became parkinsonian, she became subject to "repetitive, irritating little melodies or rhythms" in her head, to which she "compulsively" moved her fingers and toes. (Fortunately, this woman, a gifted musician with relatively mild parkinsonism, could usually "turn these melodies into Bach and Mozart" and play them mentally to completion, transforming them from brainworms to the sort of healthy musical imagery she had enjoyed prior to the parkinsonism.)

The phenomenon of brainworms seems similar, too, to the way in which people with autism or Tourette's syndrome or obsessive-compulsive disorder may become hooked by a sound or a word or a noise and repeat it, or echo it, aloud or to themselves, for weeks at a time. This was very striking with Carl Bennett, the surgeon with Tourette's syndrome whom I described in *An Anthropologist on Mars.* "One cannot always find sense in these words," he said. "Often it is just the sound that attracts me. Any odd sound, any odd name, may start repeating itself, get me going. I get hung up with a word for two or three months. Then, one morning, it's gone, and there's another one in its place." But while the involuntary repetition of movements, sounds, or words tends to occur in people with Tourette's or OCD or damage to the frontal lobes of the brain, the automatic or compulsive internal repetition of musical phrases is almost universal—the clearest sign of the overwhelming, and at times helpless, sensitivity of our brains to music.

There may be a continuum here between the pathological and the normal, for while brainworms may appear suddenly, full-blown, taking instant and entire possession of one, they may also develop by a sort of contraction, from previously normal musical imagery. I have lately been enjoying mental replays of Beethoven's Third and Fourth Piano Concertos, as recorded by Leon Fleisher in the 1960s. These "replays" tend to last ten or fifteen minutes and to consist of entire movements. They come, unbidden but always welcome, two or three times a day. But on one very tense and insomniac night, they changed character, so that I heard only a single rapid run on the piano (near the beginning of the Third Piano Concerto), lasting ten or fifteen seconds and repeated hundreds of times. It was as if the music was now trapped in a sort of loop, a tight neural circuit from which it could not escape. Toward morning, mercifully, the looping ceased, and I was able to enjoy entire movements once again.*

Brainworms are usually stereotyped and invariant in character. They tend to have a certain life expectancy, going full blast for hours or days and then dying away, apart from occasional afterspurts. But even when they have apparently faded, they tend to lie in wait; a heightened sensitivity remains, so that a noise, an association, a reference to them is apt to set them off again, sometimes years later. And they are nearly always fragmentary. These are all qualities that epileptologists might find familiar, for they are strongly reminiscent of the behavior of a small, sudden-onset seizure focus, erupting and convulsing, then subsiding, but always ready to reignite.

Certain drugs seem to exacerbate earworms. One composer and music teacher wrote to me that when she was put on lamotrigine for a mild bipolar disorder, she developed a severe, at times intolerable increase in earworms. After she discovered an article (by David Kemp et al.) about the increase of intrusive, repetitive musical phrases (as well as verbal phrases or numerical repetitions) associated with lamotrigine, she stopped the medication (under her physician's supervision). Her earworms subsided somewhat but have remained at a much higher level than before. She does not know whether they will ever return to their original, moderate level: "I worry," she wrote, "that somehow these pathways in my brain have become so potentiated that I will be having these earworms for the rest of my life."

Some of my correspondents compare brainworms to visual after- 15
images, and as someone who is prone to both, I feel their similarity, too. (We are using "afterimage" in a special sense here, to denote a much more prolonged effect than the fleeting afterimages we all have for a few seconds following, for instance, exposure to a bright light.) After reading EEGs intently for several hours, I may have to stop because I start to see EEG squiggles all over the walls and ceiling. After driving all day, I may see fields and hedgerows and trees moving past me in a steady stream, keeping me awake at night. After a day on a boat, I feel the rocking for

---

*The duration of such loops is generally about fifteen to twenty seconds, and this is similar to the duration of the visual loops or cycles which occur in a rare condition called palinopsia, where a short scene—a person walking across a room, for example, seen a few seconds before—may be repeated before the inner eye again and again. That a similar periodicity of cycling occurs in both visual and auditory realms suggests that some physiological constant, perhaps related to working memory, may underlie both.

hours after I am back on dry land. And astronauts, returning from a week spent in the near-zero-gravity conditions of space, need several days to regain their "earth legs" once again. All of these are simple sensory effects, persistent activations in low-level sensory systems, due to sensory overstimulation. Brainworms, by contrast, are perceptual constructions, created at a much higher level in the brain. And yet both reflect the fact that certain stimuli, from EEG lines to music to obsessive thoughts, can set off persistent activities in the brain.

There are attributes of musical imagery and musical memory that have no equivalents in the visual sphere, and this may cast light on the fundamentally different way in which the brain treats music and visions.* This peculiarity of music may arise in part because we have to *construct* a visual world for ourselves, and a selective and personal character therefore infuses our visual memories from the start—whereas we are given pieces of music already constructed. A visual or social scene can be constructed or reconstructed in a hundred different ways, but the recall of a musical piece has to be close to the original. We do, of course, listen selectively, with differing interpretations and emotions, but the basic musical characteristics of a piece—its tempo, its rhythm, its melodic contours, even its timbre and pitch—tend to be preserved with remarkable accuracy.

It is this fidelity—this almost defenseless engraving of music on the brain—which plays a crucial part in predisposing us to certain excesses, or pathologies, of musical imagery and memory, excesses that may even occur in relatively unmusical people.

There are, of course, inherent tendencies to repetition in music itself. Our poetry, our ballads, our songs are full of repetition. Every piece of classical music has its repeat marks or variations on a theme, and our

---

*And yet an earworm may also, more rarely, include a visual aspect, especially for those musicians who automatically visualize a score as they are hearing or imagining music. One of my correspondents, a French horn player, finds that when her brain is occupied by a brainworm,

> reading, writing, and doing spatial tasks like arithmetic are all disturbed by it. My brain seems to be pretty well taken up with processing the [brainworm] in various ways, mainly spatial and kinesthetic: I ponder the relative sizes of the intervals between the notes, I see them laid out in space, I consider the layout of the harmonic structure that they are a part of, I feel the fingerings in my hand, and the muscular movements required to play them, although I don't actually act these out. It's not a particularly intellectual activity; it's rather careless and I don't put any intentional effort into it; it just happens. . . .
>
> I should mention that these unbidden [brainworms] never interfere with physical activity or with activities that don't require visual thought, like engaging in normal conversation.

greatest composers are masters of repetition; nursery rhymes and the little chants and songs we use to teach young children have choruses and refrains. We are attracted to repetition, even as adults; we want the stimulus and the reward again and again, and in music we get it. Perhaps, therefore, we should not be surprised, should not complain if the balance sometimes shifts too far and our musical sensitivity becomes a vulnerability.

> "We are attracted to repetition, even as adults; we want the stimulus and the reward again and again, and in music we get it. Perhaps, therefore, we should not be surprised, should not complain if the balance sometimes shifts too far and our musical sensitivity becomes a vulnerability."

Is it possible that earworms are, to some extent, a modern phenomenon, at least a phenomenon not only more clearly recognized, but vastly more common now than even before? Although earworms have no doubt existed since our forebears first blew tunes on bone flutes or beat tattoos on fallen logs, it is significant that the term has come into common use only in the past few decades.* When Mark Twain was writing in the 1870s, there was plenty of music to be had, but it was not ubiquitous. One had to seek out other people to hear (and participate in) singing—at church, family gatherings, parties. To hear instrumental music, unless one had a piano or other instrument at home, one would have to go to church or to a concert. With recording and broadcasting and films, all this changed radically. Suddenly music was everywhere for the asking, and this has increased by orders of magnitude in the last couple of decades, so that we are now enveloped by a ceaseless musical bombardment whether we want it or not.

Half of us are plugged into iPods, immersed in daylong concerts of our own choosing, virtually oblivious to the environment—and for those who are not plugged in, there is nonstop music, unavoidable and often of deafening intensity, in restaurants, bars, shops, and gyms. This barrage 20

---

*It may be that brainworms, even if maladaptive in our own music-saturated modern culture, stem from an adaptation that was crucial in earlier hunter-gatherer days: replaying the sounds of animals moving or other significant sounds again and again, until their recognition was assured—as one correspondent, Alan Geist, has suggested to me:

> I discovered, by accident, that after five or six continuous days in the woods without hearing any music of any kind, I spontaneously start replaying the sounds that I hear around me, mainly birds. The local wildlife becomes "the song stuck in my head." . . . [Perhaps in more primitive times] a traveling human could more readily recognize familiar areas by adding his memory of sounds to the visual clues that told him where he was. . . . And by rehearsing those sounds, he was more likely to commit them to long-term memory.

of music puts a certain strain on our exquisitely sensitive auditory systems, which cannot be overloaded without dire consequences. One such consequence is the ever-increasing prevalence of serious hearing loss, even among young people, and particularly among musicians. Another is the omnipresence of annoyingly catchy tunes, the brainworms that arrive unbidden and leave only in their own time — catchy tunes that may, in fact, be nothing more than advertisements for toothpaste but are, neurologically, completely irresistible.

Understanding the Text

1. Sacks quotes and discusses Mark Twain's 1876 short story, "Punch, Brothers, Punch!" Why does he refer to this story? What points does it help him make, both when he first cites it and near the end of this essay?

2. According to Sacks, some people compare musical brainworms to visual "afterimages." In his view, how are these two phenomena similar and how are they different? How does the distinction between the two reflect differences in our visual and auditory senses?

3. Why are brainworms probably more common now than they were in the past? How does this prevalence suggest changes in the way we consume music — and in the role music plays in our lives and culture?

Reflection and Response

4. At several points in the essay, Sacks uses rhetorical questions. How does he use these questions to structure his discussion? Do you find this approach effective? Why or why not? Point to specific transitional moments in the text.

5. In what way is this a personal essay? In what way is it a piece of science writing, concerned with empirical data and conclusions? How does Sacks move between the two forms?

Making Connections

6. In "Why We Love Music — and Freud Despised It" (p. 26), Stephen A. Diamond writes about Sigmund Freud's apparent *melophobia*, or fear of music. What insight might Sacks's discussion and analysis of brainworms provide into Freud's aversion to music — and vice versa? Like Diamond and Sacks, Freud was a brain scientist. Do you find that these discussions of psychology, neuroscience, and cognition broaden and deepen our understanding of music, or reduce and oversimplify our view of it?

7. What is your own experience with brainworms, sticky music, and catchy tunes? Give specific examples. Are you susceptible to them? Do you find them pleasing? Oppressive? Do you have techniques, as Sacks discusses, for ridding your mind of musical brainworms?

The Most Beautiful Melody in the World

Jan Swafford

If the appeal of music can be enigmatic, perhaps the most mysterious element of the medium's allure can be melody — the "tuney" quality of a musical figure that, as composer and author Jan Swafford writes, has "a kind of independent there-ness. . . ." What makes a melody memorable, haunting, and emotionally resonant? And how is it related to other elements of music, like rhythm and mood? Using a wide range of examples and a conversational style, Swafford tries to pin down the essence of melody in composers ranging from Bach to the Beatles.

Jan Swafford's musical works include *After Spring Rain* (1981–82) and *They That Mourn* (2002). He is also the author of several books, including *Johannes Brahms: A Biography* (1999) and *Beethoven: Anguish and Triumph* (2014).

O K, I'm not actually proposing to name the most beautiful melody in the world — I'm not that arrogant or that dumb (though I do have some thoughts on the matter, which I'll share below). For now, I want to offer a small tour of some of the most beautiful and enduring melodies I happen to know, and talk about what makes them that way. Will we thereby find the eternal secret of great melody? Well, no. But it's one of those questions that can get you somewhere if you don't take it too seriously.

First, naturally, we have to define what a melody is. It's . . . oh jeez. All right, let's turn to the authoritative *Grove Dictionary of Music*: "Melody, defined as pitched sounds arranged in musical time in accordance with given cultural conventions and constraints, represents a universal human phenomenon. . . . While the exact causal relationships between melody and language remain to be established, the broad cultural bases of 'logogenic melody' are no longer in question." Um, moving right along . . .

The venerable *Harvard Dictionary of Music* is more slippery, and maybe for that reason more convincing: "A coherent succession of pitches. Here pitch means a stretch of sound whose frequency is clear and stable . . . succession means that several pitches occur; and coherent means that the succession of pitches is accepted as belonging together." In other words, a succession of notes that sounds to you like a tune is a tune. As goofy as that is, I can't think of anything better, because we're dealing with an exquisitely subjective and mysterious phenomenon, one universal yet elusive, like love and God and other enigmas. You know it when you hear it — according to how you've been conditioned by your culture and experience to hear it.

This means that the next person's idea of a tune may not be yours. We musicians know all about this. Somebody once congratulated Debussy for transcending melody, and he retorted in outrage that his music was nothing but melody. Both Beethoven and Brahms were accused of having no melody; so has modern jazz. When I hear some traditional African songs, I enjoy them but can't figure out how they remember them. The same goes for a good number of pop tunes.

Each culture has its own sense of melody, one that often seems 5 peculiar to the next culture. Some early Japanese tourists in the West had to be carried out of opera performances, they were laughing so hard. Westerners often struggle when listening to traditional Japanese singing, which tends on first acquaintance to sound a bit constipational. (Some of these mutual strangenesses have to do with vocal style, of course.)

With time and experience, new kinds of melody can become coherent. I had to learn how to listen to Schoenberg's themes, but now his music sounds fairly tuney to me, and ditto Bartók. I'm far from claiming, though, that strong melodies are necessary to a piece. Some of the most beautiful music I know is not based on melody at all; rather, the effect comes from mood, harmony, rhythm, color, and how those things on their own can reach the heartstrings.

I'm going to focus here on Western melodies, ones of a particular kind. People tend to call everything a "song" these days, even a symphony, but there are all kinds of songs, and not all of them have melody. On the whole, rock 'n' roll is not a particularly tuneful genre. I'm fond of the Beatles' "Come Together," for example, but its "tune" mostly jogs in place on three notes, with a little flight at the end of the phrase. What makes that song work is its sound, its atmosphere, its distinctive loping rhythm, its surreal words: "Here come old flattop, he come groovin' up slowly, he got juju eyeball, he one holy roller . . ." Many classic songs are founded on a catchy rhythm (Gershwin's "I Got Rhythm") or a striking chord progression ("All the Things You Are"). Dylan's sublime "Subterranean Homesick Blues" is a pitchless chant, as is a good deal of rap. Most of the time, symphonic themes are not particularly tuney, because they are made to unfold and develop over a long haul. As we'll see, though, in classical pieces there are notable exceptions to that rule.

The tunes I mainly want to talk about are ones you might whistle in the shower or sing around a campfire: melodies that have a kind of independent there-ness on their own, often memorable and distinctive even without accompaniment. I'll start with one of my favorite traditional American songs, "Wildwood Flower." It was the Bluegrass group Flatt & Scruggs' theme song, Joan Baez did a fine version, and it was made famous mainly by the Carter Family. Supposedly folk songs are a spontaneous product of folks, not written by any one person, but that's partly myth: Like "Wildwood Flower," a lot of them were first composed by professionals, then evolved through the generations. (At least, they evolved before recordings, which tend to fix any piece into a standard form.) Texts and melodies are fluid, new words written for old tunes.

"A successful tune needs to be "coherent." What makes a tune coherent? That too is an elusive matter, but there are some things that can be identified: A memorable tune has some consistent motifs and a satisfying shape."

A successful tune needs to be "coherent." What makes a tune coherent? That too is an elusive matter, but there are some things that can be identified: A memorable tune has some consistent motifs and a satisfying shape. The most obvious motif in "Wildwood Flower" is rhythmic: the dum dee-dee dum dee-dee that starts at the beginning and goes throughout. The main melodic motif is a three-note bit of descending or ascending scale that happens some dozen times in the tune, starting with its first three notes. As to the shape, this one has mostly the stepwise rise and fall of typical folk songs; it rises quickly to the fifth degree of the scale and drifts back down. For me the glory of the tune is what happens in the middle: an exhilarating leap up to its highest note that in every verse nicely underlines the words at that point ("and the myrtle so bright"). Then it sinks back down in an echo of the beginning.

We find the same kind of thing in what may be the oldest extant hit 10 song in the West, the 16th-century "Greensleeves," done in a cappella style by the King's Singers. There's an old legend that this was written by King Henry VIII for Anne Boleyn. It wasn't. The subject may be a prostitute, or not. The author is perhaps one Richard Jones, and in its first year (1580) there were half a dozen versions in print. Shakespeare mentions it in *The Merry Wives of Windsor*. More recent incarnations have included the sighing orchestral variations by Ralph Vaughan Williams and the melody of Jacques Brel's acid "Amsterdam." In the 1950s a straightforward version was a hit single alongside Elvis songs.

The engine of "Greensleeves" is the steady lilting rhythm in the style of the time's romanesca. It's got an A idea of two lines and a B idea likewise. The main melodic motifs are a four-note bit of scale that goes up and down throughout, and three notes descending a chord. The tune has an especially elegant, rolling contour, highlighted by the passionate and climactic B idea ("Greensleeves was all my joy") that starts on the melody's highest note.

So there's a tune that has been embraced by millions for going on over 400 years and counting. I'm not saying that all great tunes get to the point of being what we call "standards," and hardly were all of them written by well-known composers. One of the most famous "Haydn" tunes is the F major Serenade for string quartet. Except it isn't by Haydn, but by the largely forgotten Roman Hofstetter, who passed it off as Haydn's. It used to be a theme song of TV comedian Ernie Kovacs.

Being a tunesmith, a crafter of catchy melodies, is a distinctive and rare kind of musical talent. A good tune happens to you; you can refine it, but in the end it can't be created by work or by will. Schubert and Mozart had the gift in spades, Beethoven less so, and there was not much Beethoven could do about it (though he wrote his share of splendid tunes). This also reveals that you don't have to be a tunesmith to be a great classical composer. Lots of Beethoven does perfectly well without striking themes, and sometimes in his instrumental music Schubert's pretty, self-contained tunes get in the way of the ongoing musical dialogue.

The early-Baroque master Claudio Monteverdi was a fine tunesmith when he needed to be, and one of his most stunning moments appears to be the final love duet in his opera *The Coronation of Poppea*. In fact, while most of the opera is unquestionably Monteverdi, this stunner "Pur ti miro" may be a contribution by some anonymous composer in a moment of high inspiration, with or without Monteverdi's approval. In any case, the duet provides a ravishing and incomparably cynical finish for the story of Nero, who put aside his wife, condemned his mentor Seneca, and crowned the prostitute Poppea his Empress of Rome.

The myriad glories of J.S. Bach's music tend to obscure what a terrific 15 tunesmith he was. He could come up with both grand themes and little tunes that sound artless but aren't. For an example of the latter, there's his all too famous but still lovely "Sheep May Safely Graze," in which he begins with a lilting pastoral melody of his own, moves to a traditional Lutheran hymn, then combines the two in effortless counterpoint. It's been regularly arranged for various ensembles. Bach's epic *St. Matthew Passion* paints the death of Christ as a universal story of love, loss, and grieving. Here's an aria from that passion, "Mache dich, mein Herze, rein." What gives this aria about love and loss a place in my heart is a warmth and tenderness in the melody that is as secular as sacred, and its heart-tugging hook on the line Ich will Jesum selbst begraben — "I will myself bury Jesus."

Franz Schubert was one of the most spectacular born melodists. He wrote more than 600 songs, and any number of them testify to his singular gift. "Tränenregen" ("Rain of Tears") is part of his song cycle *Die Schöne Müllerin* (*The Beautiful Miller's Daughter*). Schubert virtually created the style of German art song for the rest of the Romantic century, based on a sophisticated transmutation of folk music. Notice the highly Schubertian turn to a minor key at the end: That's where the tears start, and the tragic denouement of the story is foreshadowed.

Not all beautiful tunes are sad, though a disproportionate number are, thanks to a universal human quirk: Sadness is more interesting than happiness, and thus more creatively productive. From the German 19th century let's move to an American tunesmith of that century, Stephen Foster, who set himself up as the first professional songwriter in the country. In an age long before mass media, Foster's tunes traveled around the world. Still, he didn't end well. He spent his pathetic last years virtually living in a saloon, writing tunes on a barrelhead for quick sale to buy whiskey. One of his most familiar is "Jeanie With the Light-Brown Hair," with its tone of gentle passion soaring upward on "borne like a vapor on the summer air." It has been championed by everybody from Jascha Heifetz to Spike Jones. As an example of its universality, there's a choral version by the National Taiwan University Chorus.

As noted above, symphonic themes tend to be less tuney, more open-ended, because what's important is what can be made of them, what happens to them over time. What I'm calling a tuney tune has a beginning, middle, and end, and in a long piece, what can you do but play it again louder, or something? Johannes Brahms produced one of the most ubiquitous melodies of all time with his "Lullaby," originally written for an old inamorata who'd gone on to have a kid with somebody else. Its accompaniment is based on a Viennese song the lady used to sing to him. Here and there in his instrumental music Brahms let fly with a stupendous tune, and one of them is the third movement of his Third Symphony. I suspect Brahms knew that with this one he had a hit on his hands. The movement is the theme over and over in changing orchestral garb, with a bit of B section. I have a theory that nobody forgets the first time they hear this uncannily beautiful, heartrending, sui generis music.

In American popular music, the superstar of the middle decades of the last century was George Gershwin, who wrote his first hit, "Swanee," in about 10 minutes at age 20, while riding a bus (or so he claimed). That song paid the rent for the rest of his life. He went on to a long row of tremendous songs, and meanwhile taught himself to be a symphonic composer as well. In his short life the climax of that development was *Porgy and Bess*, the greatest American opera and a timeless example of how to make a successful crossover, in this case between opera and Broadway. Its most famous aria is, of course, "Summertime," but the one that moves me most in this tale of a crippled beggar and his drug-addicted lover is "Bess, You Is My Woman Now," which is equally a true operatic aria at the service of the story, and a moving and unforgettable melody on its own. In both words and music, it manages to bring together powerful feeling and incipient heartbreak—it's a tragic love song. This clip is from the Trevor Nunn BBC production conducted by Simon Rattle.

That kind of crossover went in the other direction with the work of Kurt 20 Weill, a classically and Germanically trained composer who discovered a populist strain when he got involved with lefty playwright Bert Brecht. Their most celebrated collaboration was *The Three-Penny Opera*. Its leading tune, "Mack the Knife," was a hit in the '50s for Bobby Darin. I'm kind of flummoxed by my own affection for this song, because there's practically nothing to it: two simple little phrases mainly designed to project a long and nasty lyric. My favorite version of it is the scraggly and vital rendition, with equally scraggly pit band, by Lotte Lenya, Weill's wife, for whom the song was written. The words are a narrative of rapine and murder, set with bitter irony to a sweet pop tune—that being Brecht and Weill in a nutshell.

Finally we arrive at modern pop music. Here we run into my feeling that on the whole, our pop tunes, including ones I happen to like, are not particularly tuney. A semi-exception to that pattern are some songs of the Beatles—I suspect the ones that Paul McCartney was mainly responsible for. One of the few examples in the last half-century of a popular standard in the traditional sense is McCartney's "Yesterday." Here's a tuney tune par excellence. McCartney's own original version is interestingly straight-ahead and a bit brisk in tempo, given its theme of lost love. (The words, for me, are spotty at best, but the tune unforgettable.) George Martin's string-quartet arrangement gives it elegant support.

So what about the present, many of you will ask. I admit that in pop music I'm not much involved with the present, and new classical music these days is not much involved with tunes. My composer colleague Andy Vores maintains that true melodies are founded on traditional harmony, and when that harmony is put aside, as in much of today's concert music, melody in the traditional sense is impossible. I don't agree that it's impossible; even a tonally free, unaccompanied melody can work if it has a coherent pattern and some emotional center. But indeed, in the classical world there have not been a lot of tunes out there lately. Meanwhile, much pop of the last decades is founded on what has been called "performers' music," which means that you're into the performer and their image, and maybe the lyrics, and the notes as such don't matter so much.

But what about my title, the most beautiful melody in the world? Actually, I have a definition of that vaporous entity: The most beautiful melody in the world is the one that at the moment you can't get out of your head. Not in the sense of worming annoyingly into your mind, but rather of somehow capturing something important and moving to you in particular, which may or may not be something that moves the masses. For me, off and on for some time, it's been a relatively obscure Yiddish song from 1911: "Mayn rue Plats," which I find passionately, sadly, hauntingly beautiful. Also subtly ironic, because I don't ultimately believe in art that flaunts its politics, even when I agree with the politics. This is a high-leftist song by Morris Rosenfeld, who was known as "the sweat-shop poet." I always appreciate it when art violates my principles and still works. This one does. From the first time I heard it, I was transfixed. Like a haunting face, like love, that's what a great melody can do for you.

Understanding the Text

1. According to Swafford, music can be beautiful without being especially tuneful or melodic. In such cases, what other elements contribute to a song's appeal or charm? What examples does he provide to make his point?

2. What is Swafford's ultimate definition of the "most beautiful melody in the world"?

Reflection and Response

3. In paragraph 2, the writer quotes a definition of melody from the "authoritative" *Grove Dictionary of Music*. But immediately after quoting the entry, he writes: "Um, moving right along." Why does he do this? What is Swafford suggesting by not engaging or elaborating on this definition? How is this rhetorical move related to his overall purpose?

4. According to Swafford, "Not all beautiful tunes are sad, though a disproportionate number are, thanks to a universal human quirk: Sadness is more interesting than happiness, and thus more creatively productive" (17). Do you agree with this assertion? Can you provide examples that support the writer's view, or (alternately) examples that problematize or refute Swafford's claim?

Making Connections

5. In paragraph 5, Swafford writes, "Each culture has its own sense of melody, one that often seems peculiar to the next culture." Does Swafford's discussion of melody in this essay provide any insight into the curious status of the "Asian tune" in Kat Chow's "How The 'Kung Fu Fighting' Melody Came to Represent Asia" (p. 245)? Explain your answer.

6. In attempting to define and delimit melody, the writer focuses on "tuney" songs that "you might whistle in the shower or sing around a campfire: melodies that have a kind of independent there-ness on their own, often memorable and distinctive even without accompaniment" (8). In the following paragraph, he explicates the melodic quality of the song "Wildwood Flower." Choose your own "tuney" melody and provide a similar analysis. What gives the melody shape or structure, or constitutes its "independent there-ness"?

Beethoven's Kapow

Justin Davidson

While Justin Davidson writes about a particular performance of Beethoven's symphonies at Lincoln Center in New York, his discussion and his themes have much wider implications. They touch upon the nature of symphonies like the (once radical and unsettling, now safe and familiar) "Eroica," the purposes of live performance, the current status of audiences for orchestral and classical music, and the meaning of art and music over time: "Why do we reenact these rituals of revolution, when revolution is no longer at stake? How can an act of artistic radicalism retain the power to disturb after two centuries? What's left when surprise has been neutralized and influence absorbed?"

Justin Davidson is a Pulitzer Prize–winning critic of music and architecture. He writes about both topics for *New York Magazine*, where this article first appeared.

If I could crash any cultural event in history, it would be the night in April 1805 when a short man with a Kirk Douglas chin and a wrestler's build stomped onto the stage of the Theater an der Wien in Vienna. Ludwig van Beethoven, 34 years old and already well along the way to deafness, swiveled to face a group of tense musicians and whipped them into playing a pair of fist-on-the-table E-flat major chords (*blam!* . . . *blam!*), followed by a quietly rocking cello melody. If I listen hard enough, I can almost transport myself into that stuffy, stuccoed room. I inhale the smells of damp wool and kerosene and feel the first, transformative shock of Beethoven's Third Symphony, the "Eroica," as it exploded into the world.

Before it was a work of genius, the "Eroica" was a provocation, and I sometimes wonder how I would have reacted if I had been in the crowd on that night in 1805. I might have concurred with the critic who felt "crushed by a mass of unconnected and overloaded ideas and continuing tumult by all the instruments." The performance probably flirted with chaos. Beethoven himself conducted, and he was a volatile man who could barely hear. The band of musicians had never grappled with a score so mountainous and rugged, and the audience hadn't either. Someone yelled, "I'll give another kreutzer if the thing will only stop!" It's easy to dismiss that wag as a philistine, but the first performance, unlike most of the thousands upon thousands that followed, didn't take admiration for granted.

This week, Lincoln Center hosts the conductor Iván Fischer leading two ensembles — one period, the other modern — in a comparative festival of Beethoven's symphonies. The Orchestra of the Age of Enlightenment plays the "Eroica," plus Symphonies Nos. 1, 2, 5, and 8, just as they purportedly sounded 200 years ago. The Budapest Festival Orchestra performs the remaining symphonies in their plusher, louder, and more modern incarnation. The difference between those styles is usually framed as a distinction between music's authentic past and its dynamic present, between scholarship and technology, the latest framing of a 40-year movement that goes by various cumbersome and misleading titles: Original Instruments, Early Music, Authentic Performance Practice. But in truth both paths pursue the same illusion: that a certified masterpiece has just come blaring out of the composer's brain.

Why do we reenact these rituals of revolution, when revolution is no longer at stake? How can an act of artistic radicalism retain the power to disturb after two centuries? What's left when surprise has been neutralized and influence absorbed? Beethoven toyed with expectations we do not have and dismantled conventions that no longer guide us. As a result, the "Eroica," which emerged with such blinding energy that some of its first listeners thought its composer must be insane, sounds like settled wisdom to us. His contemporaries had never experienced such wild, loud, assaultive sounds outside of combat. Our ears are attuned to a rougher sonic landscape: The construction site that edges Lincoln Center is far more raucous than whatever goes on in the hall.

If the composer flailed against the constraints of his world, today's 5 Beethoven performers battle the legacy he bequeathed: the whole stultifying tradition of greatness. Conductors have various strategies for making even connoisseurs forget the scriptural familiarity of those notes. They can exaggerate idiosyncrasies or whisk up an irritatingly manic sense of excitement. They can buff the playing to a technocratic gleam and engineer an interpretation so faithful to the written score that it becomes fanatically neutral. Or they might emulate the corporate approach of Herbert von Karajan, who drew from his orchestras a rich, emulsified sound and treated Beethoven's symphonies as monuments to be gilded with fresh applications of elegance.

The most thrilling versions of the "Eroica" I've heard have felt like quests, crackling with desperate urgency. In the mid-nineties, John Eliot Gardiner led his private band, the Orchèstre Révolutionnaire et Romantique, in a complete cycle of Beethoven symphonies that enshrined their violent defiance. He achieved that effect through scrupulous historicism and tolerance for the technical imperfections inherent in period instruments. Natural horns occasionally bobbled a difficult passage. Gut-string violins struggled to balance wooden flutes that wandered out of tune. Even with a full-arm wallop, the timpanist could only eke a muffled thud from his early-nineteenth-century Viennese kettledrums. But those challenges added to the revolutionary élan, and to the exhilarating suspicion that at any moment the whole apparatus might fall apart.

Beethoven craved that sense of imminent collapse. As a pianist, he pummeled the keyboard and tried to force it into playing lower, higher, louder, and softer than it could. The "Eroica" rattled the Theater an der Wien, a grand and modern space by 1805 standards, but an ornate little shoebox when compared with, say, Carnegie Hall. There's a moment in the middle of the first movement, when the symphony shudders as if it were coming unglued. The pulse grinds down and the burbling theme stops short, overpowered by a chain of dissonant blasts that, in the first performance, must have ricocheted off the graceful walls and buzzed through the audience's bones. In the early nineteenth century, listening to orchestral music was a full-body experience.

But the epic scale of Beethoven's symphonies created a new, supersized infrastructure that gradually swallowed his music. Larger audiences and bigger orchestras required more spacious venues, where music reaches the ears only after picking up resonance and losing its edge. The most authentic, and exciting, way to hear Beethoven's symphonies would be in cramped rooms rather than in great, flattering halls. (The Lincoln Center concerts take place in the relatively cozy Alice Tully Hall.)

We can't unravel a history of listening, and the work can't easily slough off its encrustations of meaning. Beethoven's music comes to us at once impoverished by time and marinated in meanings: Wagner's analytic raptures, Schroeder's obsession in "Peanuts," the Morse code V-for-victory of the Fifth during the Battle of Britain, *A Clockwork Orange,* Bernstein's substitution of *Freiheit* (freedom) for *Freude* (joy) in the Ninth at the collapsing Berlin Wall, and so on. We also can't recapture the heat with which the nineteenth century debated the meaning of that cryptic subtitle. Is the hero Napoleon, the composer himself, or perhaps a more archetypal figure? A moral but unconventional loner? A vessel of humanity's most intense feelings? An artist-genius? It hardly matters now, when the whole notion of a hero-worshipping symphony seems impossibly hoary. What sort of figure would we enrobe in music of such complexity, fury, and moral struggle? Tiger Woods? David Petraeus?

For much of today's public, even the most thoroughly tilled sym- 10 phonic turf has become unexplored terrain. The orchestral Establishment treats that widespread musical illiteracy as a disaster, but it's also a chance to give works of "Eroica"-like stature an infinite number of premieres. The fact that many audience members have never heard the piece should be a bracing thought for the players on the stage: To dispense revelation is a daunting responsibility.

Classical-music neophytes often worry that they don't have enough background to appreciate a performance, but the opposite is often true: They're the ones who listen without preconceptions and who are primed for danger and unpredictability. The "Eroica" was the first symphonic psychodrama, a chronicle of a character's interior battles. Already in the opening seconds, the restless theme spins away from its expected course to go skating through patches of harmonic uncertainty, disruptive syncopations, and asymmetrical phrases. Moods change with mercurial quickness. Beethoven knits his structure out of conflict and unease, turning unpleasant states of mind into artistic virtues.

"The "Eroica" was the first symphonic psychodrama, a chronicle of a character's interior battles. Already in the opening seconds, the restless theme spins away from its expected course to go skating through patches of harmonic uncertainty, disruptive syncopations, and asymmetrical phrases."

If the first movement romanticizes anxiety, the second makes misery seem celestial. It is a funeral march, but the orchestration suggests it is an imagined event, a procession unfolding in the protagonist's mind. The sounds are softer, rounder, than a street parade. We hear no brass. Cellos and basses play the role of muffled drums. An oboe takes the place of a mournful bugle. The march coaxes intimate emotions into the public realm. If Beethoven's music still speaks to us now, it's because, like that roomful of startled Viennese two centuries ago, we want to hear suffering transfigured, too. Pain is ugly and joy fleeting, but each performance of the "Eroica" offers to shape everyday disorder of the mind into something luminous and sublime.

Whether the upcoming Beethoven festival does justice to Beethoven will not depend on the vintage of instruments or the historical purity of technique. Modern orchestras and period ensembles can both pluck excitement out of the past. What matters instead is whether Iván Fischer and his two groups are faithful to the intertwining of nuances and extremes. If the performers etch the contrasts between a lonesome horn and a full orchestral roar, if they savor the abyssal terror of a silence, snap off an accented chord before it becomes pillowy and fat, bring out the pleasurable sourness of dissonance, dispel complacency, and banish habit, then they just might summon the prickle and panic of that first night.

Understanding the Text

1. In describing the live premiere of Beethoven's Third Symphony, the "Eroica," in 1805, Davidson writes: "Someone yelled, 'I'll give another kreutzer if the thing will only stop!' It's easy to dismiss that wag as a philistine, but the first performance, unlike most of the thousands upon thousands that followed, didn't take admiration for granted" (2). What is a "philistine"? Why is the term important in the context of Davidson's essay?

2. What would be the most "authentic" and "exciting" way to hear Beethoven's symphonies, according to the writer?

3. While the orchestral establishment — presumably, the professional performers, curators, professors, and connoisseurs of classical music — regard "widespread musical illiteracy as a disaster," Davidson sees that general lack of fluency and knowledge as a positive opportunity. Why?

Reflection and Response

4. The writer focuses entirely on the experience of hearing live music in a concert hall. How is that experience different from listening to music on a device? Would it be possible for listeners to perceive the "blinding energy" of a song or symphony mediated through technology like an MP3 file, for example? What are the strengths and weaknesses of these two kinds of musical consumption?

5. In paragraphs 11 and 12, Davidson writes about Beethoven's symphony in terms of its formal qualities and the emotions it evokes in listeners (for example, "Beethoven knits his structure out of conflict and unease, turning unpleasant states of mind into artistic virtues"). Find a recording of the "Eroica" online or elsewhere and listen to it. Do you find Davidson's interpretation accurate, perceptive, or helpful? How would you interpret or describe the symphony and its effect on you?

Making Connections

6. In paragraph 9, the writer asserts: "We can't unravel a history of listening, and the work can't easily slough off its encrustations of meaning." What does he mean by this? How does he support this claim? Can you think of other musical examples whose history or "encrustations of meaning" cannot be sloughed off or ignored?

7. Davidson writes about attempts to create intensity, excitement, and even (perhaps) "panic" during live performances. How would you compare his evocation of live symphonic music with Judy Berman's (p. 98) descriptions of performances — and audiences — at shows by Dan Deacon and Animal Collective? Do Davidson's and Berman's views overlap in their sensibility and aesthetic values, or do they present contrasting views of musical performance?

2

How Does Music Express and Shape the Self?

For many of us, music is an early means of expression, whether we are singing songs as toddlers or learning to play instruments as children. Likewise, listening to music may be one of our earliest experiences, as parents sing lullabies or play recorded music for their babies. Those experiences may even be prenatal: some research suggests that exposure to music in the womb can have lasting cognitive benefits for children. Our musical habits, preferences, and inclinations continue to shape our identities as we grow older, too — particularly during adolescence, which is such a crucial moment in the formation of ourselves. Because of its cultural, developmental, and other benefits, musical instruction has long been part of early education in the United States and elsewhere. But our strongest personal bonds with music probably evolve less formally: from the artists we love; from the social connections we create through shared musical passions; from the sense that certain songs or bands "speak" to — or for — us in some way. All these factors are likely more intense for those who play music as well as consume it.

The writers in this chapter approach the intersections of music and identity from different perspectives. In his evocative personal narrative "Left of the Dial," music critic Rob Sheffield recounts his infatuation with the indie-rock band the Replacements as a young adult making a "bold move into manhood." Writing over two thousand years prior to the sloppy post-punk of the Replacements, Greek philosopher Aristotle (excerpted from his *Politics*) reflects on the value of music and its role in education. In an excerpt from *My Bondage and My Freedom*, ex-slave and abolitionist Frederick Douglass meditates on the significance of slave songs: music that expressed profound collective suffering, even as it was profoundly misunderstood. In "Lady Day," literary scholar and jazz critic Robert O'Meally sheds light on jazz singer Billie Holiday as both an original individual vocalist *and* as a voice of twentieth-century racial anguish. Laina Dawes ("Hardcore Persona") writes about the tension between her deep affinity for heavy metal music and the perception that the genre's subculture is, somehow,

photo: Flashpop/Getty Images

unsuitable for a black woman. Judy Berman ("Concerning the Spiritual in Indie Rock") highlights the spiritual and metaphysical preoccupations of bands such as Animal Collective and Neutral Milk Hotel, suggesting that their music might "fill a void left by organized religion." In "Country Music, Openness to Experience, and the Psychology of the Culture War," Will Wilkinson examines how contemporary country music mirrors the politics and psychology of its fans. For Jeff Ousborne ("Songs of Myself? Not Quite"), the songwriting process leads to reflections on the centrality of form — in poetry, music, and other arts — even if formal or stylistic demands supplant factual truth or self-expression. In "Humble Trappings: Blue-collar Hip-Hop and Recasting the Drug Dealer's Myth," Zach Moldof writes about the possibility that hip hop music might shift its emphasis from excess and grandiosity to the lives of ordinary people. Finally, in "I Listen to Everything, Except Rap and Country Music," Jeremy Gordon traces the surprising parallels between hip hop and country music.

Left of the Dial

Rob Sheffield

In this brief but revealing personal narrative, music critic Rob Sheffield recalls his first summer living on his own "with a houseful of hippies" in New Haven, Connecticut. Music is at the center of his recollection — particularly, the legendary post-punk indie-rock band the Replacements, who "blasted out of the speakers" of his "boom box" every day as he woke up at noon. But the band serves as much more than just a background soundtrack for the writer, as he reveals.

Rob Sheffield is a longtime music critic, editor, and contributor to magazines such as *Rolling Stone, Blender, Spin,* and *Details.* He is the author of *Love Is a Mix Tape* (2007), *Talking to Girls about Duran Duran* (2010), and *Turn Around Bright Eyes: The Rituals of Love and Karaoke* (2013).

The bus came every afternoon, right on time. Every forty minutes, the New Haven city bus rumbled down Whalley Avenue and I could see it from my bedroom window. The billboard on the side had Judge Wapner's face and the tag line "Today Is Judgment Day!" I never got on the bus — I just waited to see that billboard as it rolled past my block. Proof that the world never runs out of trivial omens for ominously inclined adolescents, which is another thing the world never runs out of. Omens like this were a dime a dozen, and I was the sucker with the pocketful of dimes.

I was living with a houseful of hippies in New Haven, sleeping on a futon in the corner of my friend Bob's room. It was the first time I was living on my own, paying rent. It felt like a bold move into manhood. On Saturday afternoons, Bob and I would make Jell-O in the kitchen, and our housemates crowded around to watch. Bob stirred the liquid Jell-O as they stared into the bowl. It was the first time I began to get a vague sense of what drugs were.

It was a busted-up neighborhood with a lot of winos, who would hang around the corner liquor store and leave empty Thunderbird bottles around. One car down the street had a bumper sticker depicting a black Jesus who looked a lot like Prince. It read, MY PRINCE MAKES RAINBOWS . . . NOT PURPLE RAIN! My housemates mostly lounged on couches playing bongos or guitar while I made us all peanut butter sandwiches and wrote tortured love letters to a red-haired girl in Nova Scotia.

I had a job at the library shelving books, living on my daily bread of two Wawa dogs with extra cheese and a thirty-two-ounce Coke ($1.69). Every day around noon, I woke up, rolled over and pressed play on the boom box by my futon, drowsily contemplating the day ahead of me as the Replacements blasted out of the speakers. Before work, I would laze away the afternoon under a tree, reading St. Augustine's *Confessions.* That spring, I had read *Ulysses* and *Portrait of the Artist* for the first time, and they had really shaken up my Irish Catholic applecart. I was full of questions about God and the universe. The answers, obviously, were all there in my boom box.

The Replacements made me feel a little less scared, because they made 5 good imaginary friends. They looked like a band that would actually be fun to be in. Some bands just lend themselves to that fantasy, like Lynyrd Skynyrd or Earth, Wind & Fire—they looked like you could just drop in and they wouldn't even notice you were hanging around for at least two albums. Jonathan Richman once said he formed a band because he was lonely. The Replacements were imaginary friends who I could practice on while I was learning to have actual friends.

> "They looked like a band that would actually be fun to be in. Some bands just lend themselves to that fantasy, like Lynyrd Skynyrd or Earth, Wind & Fire — they looked like you could just drop in and they wouldn't even notice you were hanging around for at least two albums."

At night, everybody would gather on the couch to watch TV with the sound down, through a haze of bong smog, flipping channels while listening to Laurie Anderson. The goal was to find cosmic random synchronicities in the airwaves of the collective unconscious. One night, they flipped to a Superman cartoon during "O Superman." Everybody freaked and ran out of the room. There was another hippie house on our block with some guys who called their band Acidemix. The only song they knew was "Bela Lugosi's Dead," but they could play it for hours.

The neighborhood kids hung out in our yard, mainly because of Nick, who had a boa constrictor in his room. Once Nick let the kids come up to see Bo, we had the most popular house on the block. They lined up every evening for Bo's dinner. Nick would bike home from Woolworth's with a mouse in a cardboard box. The front of the box read, I'VE FOUND A HOME! The other side of the box read, SOMEBODY REALLY LOVES ME! The cover photo showed a boy and girl happily frolicking with their new hamster.

"Is he gonna eat that thing?"

"Damn."

"Is he gonna kill it first?" 10

"Is the mouse dead?"

"I can see him."

"He's got to be dead now."

After the snake had chowed down on the mouse, and the kids had finished screaming, Nick tossed the empty box out into the hallway, where they piled up and formed a little memorial pyramid. Every night, I came home from work and tiptoed to my room, stepping over the pile of I'VE FOUND A HOME! boxes.

I did a lot of things for the first time that summer: signed a lease, drank beer, drank coffee, gave myself a haircut, smoked pot, smoked Play-Doh (it took us all evening to realize it wasn't really hash). I learned to wash dishes and make pasta. I drew the line at sex and hacky sack. One roommate, Matt, lost his virginity while I slept through the whole thing. Jorge Luis Borges died the night I smoked pot for the first time. There I was the morning after, groggily sitting in the backyard, lost in the circular ruins of Catholic guilt, and I read in the paper that one of my all-time literary idols had died overnight and I felt certain that God was punishing the whole world for my transgression.

Everybody in the house played music. We'd sit out on the porch all night, with Jeffrey and James on guitar, Nick on bongos and David on flute. Jeffrey and I wrote poetic ballads of torment and squalor (sample title: "My Baby's Sleeping in a Burning House"). Jeffrey tried to teach me guitar, since I was desperate to join their jam sessions, but my fingers would not obey the merciless lashings of my muse. My burning desire to be the new Bob Dylan was severely hampered by the fact that I couldn't even master the chords to "Love Stinks."

Occasionally they took off to follow the Dead's summer tour, after Jerry got out of his coma. I went to the Dylan show at Madison Square Garden, a massive pilgrimage for me. His backing band was Tom Petty and the Heartbreakers, who didn't seem to know any of his songs, so every song sounded exactly like Billy Idol's "White Wedding." But what the hell—I got to see Dylan. We also decided to make a pilgrimage to every spot in New York that was mentioned in a Lou Reed song. We started out at Union Square but chickened out on the walk up to Lexington 1-2-5.

I also went to see the Replacements in Providence. It was the best night of my life up to that point, no question. It was an all-ages show at the Living Room. The opener was a local hard-core band called That'll Learn Ya. Paul Westerberg and Bob Stinson were out on the floor, watching the band. That was the first time I'd ever seen the guys in the headlining band come out to stand in the crowd with the rest of us. They didn't blend in, though. Paul Westerberg had these big, stripey, '70s dork pants on. Bob Stinson was wearing a toga.

15

While Westerberg was sitting over at the bar, my roommate nudged me and we went over to say hi. I froze up and couldn't utter a word, but he smiled and shook our hands, then said, "Well, gents, I'm gonna finish my Kool." When he headed backstage, I eyeballed the butt in the ashtray. I only hesitated a second before I pounced. I carried that crushed Kool filter in my pocket all night like an amulet.

I had a wad of cotton I'd saved from aspirin bottles. Up front by the stage, I stuffed some cotton in my ears and passed it to the girl next to me, who took some and passed it on. She smiled. I smiled back. The Replacements came on and started with "Hold My Life." It was pure noise, pure destruction. Everybody was pushing and thrashing and jumping—I was too. Paul Westerberg howled through his hair about small-town losers and big-town vices. Tommy Stinson sucked in his cheeks and preened for the ladies. Bob Stinson kept telling us, "Ya gotta boo!" The dude next to me kept throwing elbows and screaming for "Take Me Down to the Hospital."

The Replacements jumped from one song to another—"Left of the Dial," "I Will Dare," "Bastards of Young." They did the first verse of "Kiss Me on the Bus," then got bored and trailed off. Paul said, "Okay, you sissies, this is an Aerosmith song," and ripped into "My Fist Your Face." They did the *Green Acres* theme, with Paul as Eddie Albert and Tommy as Eva Gabor. They started messing around and switching instruments, with Paul playing drums for "Waitress in the Sky." They lurched offstage, leaving Bob alone to do a solo version of "What Is and What Should Never Be." When none of them were left standing, the Young Fresh Fellows came onstage, took their instruments and finished the show. "We're the replacements for the Replacements," the singer announced. They sucked. It was awesome.

I couldn't even describe what a great night that was. I felt indestructible, or at least undestroyed, more alive than I'd ever been. I walked out of the show feeling like I could do anything, dare anything, just jump into anything. Us against the world. I was used to feeling "me against the world," but "us against the world" was a lot more fun. My ears rang all the way home and I didn't want them to stop. It made me want to go start something. It was the greatest punk rock show I had ever seen.

I still had the Kool butt I stole from Paul Westerberg's ashtray. I took it home. The next day I mailed it to the girl in Nova Scotia. She wrote back, "It stinks to high heaven." Clearly, she and I were not meant to be. But the Replacements and I? Meant to be. *So* meant to be.

Understanding the Text

1. Why does the band the Replacements make the writer "feel a little less scared"? What key quality do they have for Sheffield — and what do they allow him to do?

2. What artifact does Sheffield take from the Replacements's Paul Westerberg? What does the writer do with it and what does it ultimately reveal to him?

Reflection and Response

3. In the essay, Sheffield refers to his religious background and sensibility. Does it seem important to his narrative? How does religion shape or color his perceptions?

4. The writer makes a point of referring to the reading he was doing before and during the summer: St. Augustine's *Confessions,* James Joyce's *Portrait of the Artist as a Young Man* and *Ulysses.* How are these texts related to his affinity for the Replacements, a sloppy indie-rock group? Is there continuity between the novelists and the band, or contrast?

5. In recalling the Replacements (21) concert, Sheffield writes that they played until "none of them were left standing." Then another band, the Young Fresh Fellows, came on stage to finish the show: "They sucked. It was awesome." How do you reconcile these two contrasting claims within the context of the essay? What do you think Sheffield is trying to communicate?

Making Connections

6. In "Concerning the Spiritual in Indie Rock" (p. 98), Judy Berman writes about concert-going in a spiritual context, as well as about indie-rock performers who strive "to eliminate the I-thou relationship between musician and fan." Does this description seem to correspond to Sheffield's experience at the Replacements show — and to his relationship with the band, generally? Explain your answer.

7. Sheffield describes the Replacements concert as the "best night" of his life: "I walked out of the show feeling like I could do anything, dare anything, just jump into everything." Have you ever had a musical experience like this — particularly with regard to a live performance? What was it like? How did the music affect you?

from *Politics*

Aristotle

In this excerpt from book VII of *Politics*, the Greek thinker Aristotle assesses the role of music in the education of citizens; ultimately, he approves of it, as both a means of pleasure and instruction. But note that his exploration of the topic is rooted in inquiry: "It is not easy to determine the nature of music, or why any one should have a knowledge of it. Shall we say, for the sake of amusement and relaxation . . . Or shall we argue that music conduces to virtue, on the ground that it can form our minds and habituate us to true pleasures . . . ? Or shall we say that it contributes to the enjoyment of leisure and mental cultivation . . . ?" If you find certain elements of his analysis difficult or ambiguous, keep in mind that philosophers, scholars, and translators have been arguing about Aristotle's works for well over two thousand years.

Aristotle is a foundational figure in Western philosophy. His range of inquiry and knowledge included mathematics, physics, biology, logic, metaphysics, ethics, agriculture, medicine, dance, theatre, and politics. He founded the Lyceum, a school in Athens.

Concerning music there are some questions which we have already raised; these we may now resume and carry further; and our remarks will serve as a prelude to this or any other discussion of the subject. It is not easy to determine the nature of music, or why any one should have a knowledge of it. Shall we say, for the sake of amusement and relaxation, like sleep or drinking, which are not good in themselves, but are pleasant, and at the same time "make care to cease," as Euripides° says? And for this end men also appoint music, and make use of all three alike—sleep, drinking, music—to which some add dancing. Or shall we argue that music conduces to virtue, on the ground that it can form our minds and habituate us to true pleasures as our bodies are made by gymnastic° to be of a certain character? Or shall we say that it contributes to the enjoyment of leisure and mental cultivation, which is a third alternative? Now obviously youths are not to be instructed with a view to their amusement, for learning is no amusement, but is accompanied with pain. Neither is intellectual enjoyment suitable to boys of that age, for it is the end, and that which is imperfect cannot attain the perfect or end. But perhaps it may be said that boys learn music for the sake of the amusement which they will have when they are grown up. If so, why should

---

Euripides (ca. 480–ca. 406): ancient playwright of tragedies.
Gymnastic: physical exercise and training.

they learn themselves, and not, like the Persian and Median kings, enjoy the pleasure and instruction which is derived from hearing others? (for surely persons who have made music the business and profession of their lives will be better performers than those who practice only long enough to learn). If they must learn music, on the same principle they should learn cookery, which is absurd. And even granting that music may form the character, the objection still holds: why should we learn ourselves? Why cannot we attain true pleasure and form a correct judgment from hearing others, like the Lacedaemonians?° — for they, without learning music, nevertheless can correctly judge, as they say, of good and bad melodies. Or again, if music should be used to promote cheerfulness and refined intellectual enjoyment, the objection still remains — why should we learn ourselves instead of enjoying the performances of others? We may illustrate what we are saying by our conception of the Gods; for in the poets Zeus does not himself sing or play on the lyre. Nay, we call professional performers vulgar; no freeman would play or sing unless he were intoxicated or in jest. But these matters may be left for the present.

The first question is whether music is or is not to be a part of education. Of the three things mentioned in our discussion, which does it produce? — education or amusement or intellectual enjoyment, for it may be reckoned under all three, and seems to share in the nature of all of them. Amusement is for the sake of relaxation, and relaxation is of necessity sweet, for it is the remedy of pain caused by toil; and intellectual enjoyment is universally acknowledged to contain an element not only of the noble but of the pleasant, for happiness is made up of both. All men agree that music is one of the pleasantest things, whether with or without songs; as Musaeus° says:

"Song to mortals of all things the sweetest."

> "For innocent pleasures are not only in harmony with the perfect end of life, but they also provide relaxation. And whereas men rarely attain the end, but often rest by the way and amuse themselves, not only with a view to a further end, but also for the pleasure's sake, it may be well at times to let them find a refreshment in music."

Hence and with good reason it is introduced into social gatherings and entertainments, because it makes the hearts of men glad: so that on this ground alone we may assume that the young ought to be trained in it. For innocent pleasures are not only in

---

Lacedaemonians: inhabitants of the Greek city Sparta.
Musaeus: ancient Greek musician, prophet, poet, and philosopher.

harmony with the perfect end of life, but they also provide relaxation. And whereas men rarely attain the end, but often rest by the way and amuse themselves, not only with a view to a further end, but also for the pleasure's sake, it may be well at times to let them find a refreshment in music. It sometimes happens that men make amusement the end, for the end probably contains some element of pleasure, though not any ordinary or lower pleasure; but they mistake the lower for the higher, and in seeking for the one find the other, since every pleasure has a likeness to the end of action. For the end is not eligible for the sake of any future good, nor do the pleasures which we have described exist for the sake of any future good but of the past, that is to say, they are the alleviation of past toils and pains. And we may infer this to be the reason why men seek happiness from these pleasures.

But music is pursued, not only as an alleviation of past toil, but also   5
as providing recreation. And who can say whether, having this use, it may not also have a nobler one? In addition to this common pleasure, felt and shared in by all (for the pleasure given by music is natural, and therefore adapted to all ages and characters), may it not have also some influence over the character and the soul? It must have such an influence if characters are affected by it. And that they are so affected is proved in many ways, and not least by the power which the songs of Olympus exercise; for beyond question they inspire enthusiasm, and enthusiasm is an emotion of the ethical part of the soul. Besides, when men hear imitations, even apart from the rhythms and tunes themselves, their feelings move in sympathy. Since then music is a pleasure, and virtue consists in rejoicing and loving and hating aright,° there is clearly nothing which we are so much concerned to acquire and to cultivate as the power of forming right judgments, and of taking delight in good dispositions and noble actions. Rhythm and melody supply imitations of anger and gentleness, and also of courage and temperance, and of all the qualities contrary to these, and of the other qualities of character, which hardly fall short of the actual affections, as we know from our own experience, for in listening to such strains our souls undergo a change. The habit of feeling pleasure or pain at mere representations is not far removed from the same feeling about realities; for example, if any one delights in the sight of a statue for its beauty only, it necessarily follows that the sight of the original will be pleasant to him. The objects of no other sense, such as taste or touch, have any resemblance to moral qualities; in visible objects there is only a little, for there are figures which are of a moral character, but only to a slight extent, and

aright: correctly.

all do not participate in the feeling about them. Again, figures and colors are not imitations, but signs, of moral habits, indications which the body gives of states of feeling. The connection of them with morals is slight, but in so far as there is any, young men should be taught to look, not at the works of Pauson, but at those of Polygnotus,° or any other painter or sculptor who expresses moral ideas. On the other hand, even in mere melodies there is an imitation of character, for the musical modes differ essentially from one another, and those who hear them are differently affected by each. Some of them make men sad and grave, like the so-called Mixolydian, others enfeeble the mind, like the relaxed modes, another, again, produces a moderate and settled temper, which appears to be the peculiar effect of the Dorian; the Phrygian inspires enthusiasm. The whole subject has been well treated by philosophical writers on this branch of education, and they confirm their arguments by facts. The same principles apply to rhythms; some have a character of rest, others of motion, and of these latter again, some have a more vulgar, others a nobler movement. Enough has been said to show that music has a power of forming the character, and should therefore be introduced into the education of the young. The study is suited to the stage of youth; for young persons will not, if they can help, endure anything which is not sweetened by pleasure, and music has a natural sweetness. There seems to be in us a sort of affinity to musical modes and rhythms, which makes some philosophers say that the soul is a tuning, others, that it possesses tuning.

Understanding the Text

1. Aristotle uses Zeus, the king of the gods in Greek mythology, to illustrate the answer to a question. What is the question and what is the answer? How does Aristotle seem to regard professional musicians in this passage?

2. According to Aristotle, why is music "introduced into social gatherings and entertainments" (4)?

Reflection and Response

3. Aristotle asks: "Or shall we argue that music conduces to virtue, on the ground that it can form our minds and habituate us to true pleasures as our bodies are made by gymnastic to be of a certain character?" (1). What analogy is he making here? How would you make the argument that Aristotle refers to?

Pauson . . . Polygnotus: Aristotle compares the ancient painter Pauson, who drew caricatures, with Polygnotus, who painted more ideal forms.

4. Near the end of this excerpt, Aristotle writes, "Enough has been said to show that music has a power of forming the character, and should therefore be introduced into the education of the young" (5). Do you agree? Does his argument have enough evidence and support? Why or why not?

Making Connections

5. While Aristotle discusses music generally and St. Basil focuses on the Psalms (p. 42), both of them write explicitly about music's effects on — and influence over — the "soul." How are their views of this influence similar? How are they different? Explain your answer.

6. Aristotle believes music can shape listeners emotionally and intellectually. He writes: "Rhythm and melody supply imitations of anger and gentleness, and also of courage and temperance, and of all the qualities contrary to these, and of the other qualities of character, which hardly fall short of the actual affections, as we know from our own experience, for in listening to such strains our souls undergo a change" (5). How might Leonid Perlovsky (p. 35) interpret the process Aristotle describes here? For example, does music seem to function as a means to (in Perlovsky's terms) maintain an equilibrium between "synthesis and differentiation"? Does music, as Aristotle describes it, make us conscious of the inborn "archetypes" in our minds?

from *My Bondage and My Freedom*

Frederick Douglass

Born into slavery, Frederick Douglass escaped to become a leading abolitionist, writer, social reformer, and political activist. He also wrote several well-known autobiographical works, including *Narrative of the Life of Frederick Douglass, an American Slave* (1845) and *My Bondage and My Freedom* (1855). In this selection from the latter book, Douglass recalls the plaintive power and meaning of the songs of slaves, even in their lingering memory as he writes: "The mere recurrence, even now, afflicts my spirit, and while I am writing these lines, my tears are falling. To those songs I trace my first glimmering conceptions of the dehumanizing character of slavery" (2). He also identifies their subversive quality of the lyrics — "jargon to others, but full of meaning to [the slaves] themselves" (1).

I have already referred to the business-like aspect of Col. Lloyd's plantation. This business-like appearance was much increased on the two days at the end of each month, when the slaves from the different farms came to get their monthly allowance of meal and meat. These were gala days for the slaves, and there was much rivalry among them as to who should be elected to go up to the great house farm for the allowance, and, indeed, to attend to any business at this (for them) the capital. The beauty and grandeur of the place, its numerous slave population, and the fact that Harry, Peter and Jake the sailors of the sloop — almost always kept, privately, little trinkets which they bought at Baltimore, to sell, made it a privilege to come to the great house farm. Being selected, too, for this office, was deemed a high honor. It was taken as a proof of confidence and favor; but, probably, the chief motive of the competitors for the place, was, a desire to break the dull monotony of the field, and to get beyond the overseer's eye and lash. Once on the road with an ox team, and seated on the tongue of his cart, with no overseer to look after him, the slave was comparatively free; and, if thoughtful, he had time to think. Slaves are generally expected to sing as well as to work. A silent slave is not liked by masters or overseers. "Make a noise," "make a noise," and "bear a hand," are the words usually addressed to the slaves when there is silence amongst them. This may account for the almost constant singing heard in the southern states. There was, generally, more or less singing among the teamsters, as it was one means of letting the overseer know where they were, and that they were moving on with the work. But, on allowance day, those who visited the great house farm were peculiarly excited and noisy. While on their way, they would make the dense old woods, for miles around, reverberate with their wild notes. These were not always merry because they were wild. On the contrary, they were mostly of a plaintive cast, and told a tale of grief and sorrow. In the most boisterous outbursts of rapturous sentiment, there was ever a tinge of deep melancholy. I have never heard any songs like those anywhere since I left slavery, except when in Ireland. There I heard the same wailing notes, and was much affected by them. It was during the famine of 1845-6. In all the songs of the slaves, there was ever some expression in praise of the great house farm; something which would flatter the pride of the owner, and, possibly, draw a favorable glance from him.

I am going away to the great house farm,
O yea! O yea! O yea!
My old master is a good old master,
O yea! O yea! O yea!   5

This they would sing, with other words of their own improvising — jargon to others, but full of meaning to themselves. I have sometimes thought, that the mere hearing of those songs would do more to impress truly spiritual-minded men and women with the soul-crushing and death-dealing character of slavery, than the reading of whole volumes of its mere physical cruelties. They speak to the heart and to the soul of the thoughtful. I cannot better express my sense of them now, than ten years ago, when, in sketching my life, I thus spoke of this feature of my plantation experience:

I did not, when a slave, understand the deep meanings of those rude, and apparently incoherent songs. I was myself within the circle, so that I neither saw or heard as those without might see and hear. They told a tale which was then altogether beyond my feeble comprehension; they were tones, loud, long and deep, breathing the prayer and complaint of souls boiling over with the bitterest anguish. Every tone was a testimony against slavery, and a prayer to God for deliverance from chains. The hearing of those wild notes always depressed my spirits, and filled my heart with ineffable sadness. The mere recurrence, even now, afflicts my spirit, and while I am writing these lines, my tears are falling. To those songs I trace my first glimmering conceptions of the dehumanizing character of slavery. I can never get rid of that conception. Those songs still follow me, to deepen my hatred of slavery, and quicken my sympathies for my brethren in bonds. If any one wishes to be impressed with a sense of the soul-killing power of slavery, let him go to Col. Lloyd's plantation, and, on allowance day, place himself in the deep, pine woods, and there let him, in silence, thoughtfully analyze the sounds that shall pass through the chambers of his soul, and if he is not thus impressed, it will only be because "there is no flesh in his obdurate heart."

The remark is not unfrequently made, that slaves are the most contented and happy laborers in the world. They dance and sing, and make all manner of joyful noises—so they do; but it is a great mistake to suppose them happy because they sing. The songs of the slave represent the sorrows, rather than the joys, of his heart; and he is relieved by them, only as an aching heart is relieved by its tears. Such is the constitution of the human mind, that, when pressed to extremes, it often avails itself of the most opposite methods. Extremes meet in mind as in matter. When the slaves on board of the "Pearl" were overtaken, arrested, and carried to prison—their hopes for freedom blasted—as they marched in chains they sang, and found (as Emily Edmunson tells us) a melancholy relief in singing. The singing of a man cast away on a desolate island, might be as appropriately considered an evidence of his contentment and happiness, as the singing of a slave. Sorrow and desolation have their songs, as well as joy and peace. Slaves sing more to make themselves happy, than to express their happiness.

> "The songs of the slave represent the sorrows, rather than the joys, of his heart; and he is relieved by them, only as an aching heart is relieved by its tears. Such is the constitution of the human mind, that, when pressed to extremes, it often avails itself of the most opposite methods."

Understanding the Text

1. Douglass writes that he has only heard the plaintive melancholy like the American slave songs in one other place and time. Where and when did he hear similar "wailing notes" (1)?

2. The writer implies that people often misunderstand the mood and attitude of slaves from their songs. What is the misunderstanding?

Reflection and Response

3. According to Douglass, a "silent slave is not liked by masters or overseers" (1). Why do you think that was the case? Why would masters and overseers want slaves to "make a noise"?

4. Douglass claims that slave songs always included "something which would flatter the pride of the owner" (1). He then quotes specific lyrics to make his point, noting: "This they would sing, with other words of their own improvising — jargon to others, but full of meaning to themselves" (6). How do you interpret the double meaning behind these words? How might "truly spiritual-minded men and women" hear them?

Making Connections

5. Douglass concedes: "I did not, when a slave, understand the deep meanings of those rude, and apparently incoherent songs. I was myself within the circle, so that I neither saw or heard as those without might see and hear. They told a tale which was then altogether beyond my feeble comprehension; they were tones, loud, long and deep, breathing the prayer and complaint of souls boiling over with the bitterest anguish" (7). Does his delayed understanding of these songs seem in line with Brad Mehldau's (p. 21) view of musical meaning, musical wisdom, and the way in which "musical expression [can] arrive before the depth of experience it seems to convey"? Where does the meaning of the slave songs come from? Where is the source of their wisdom? The singers? The listeners? Both?

6. Aristotle writes, "Since then music is a pleasure, and virtue consists in rejoicing and loving and hating aright, there is clearly nothing which we are so much concerned to acquire and to cultivate as the power of forming right judgments." How did music help Douglass "cultivate" his "power of forming right judgments"?

Lady Day

Robert O'Meally

In this illuminating essay on the art of Billie Holiday, writer and literary critic Robert O'Meally evokes the powerful and idiosyncratic voice of perhaps the greatest female American jazz singer. He pays special attention to her signature song, the anti-lynching lament "Strange Fruit." But he also addresses her skill as a stylistic interpreter and a cultural icon of the blues and beyond — a figure who transcended music and "became a story." Robert O'Meally is the Zora Neale Hurston Professor of English at Columbia University, as well as the founder and former director of the Center for Jazz Studies. His works include *Lady Day: The Many Faces of Billie Holiday* (author) (1989) and *Uptown Conversation: The New Jazz Studies* (editor) (2003).

Billie Holiday's greatest achievement was the unfolding of a distinctive and dramatically alluring style. She was born in Philadelphia in 1915, grew up in Baltimore, and died in New York City in 1959 — born into poverty, she grew up subjected to rape and juvenile detention and prostitution (one might call many of the singer's business arrangements with manager-boyfriends a form of prostitution), and she died under house arrest and police guard in the hospital, where she was being treated for liver failure. One cannot pin down, in her life, a single specific history-making moment of action in the way we can, say, a declaration of war or a vote of Congress.

Hers was an art of understatement: a mode of creation that Zora Neale Hurston called "dynamic suggestion" and "compelling insinuation." Space, timing, and the shaping of words were definitive. Holiday's first studio recordings, made in 1933 when she was eighteen, and her appearance with Duke Ellington's band in the short film *Symphony in Black*, made two years later, already reveal a storyteller's voice, with a graininess that gave it a been-there-and-gone authority. Her voice itself was thin, her pitch sometimes uncertain, her range narrow — and then narrower and lower with the years. She was one of the only great black American singers of the twentieth century who did not emerge from the Baptist church (Holiday's family was Catholic); her voice did not evoke the gospel setting. And yet sometimes her song "God Bless the Child" is sung in a black church setting. "The blues to me," she told a TV

> "Hers was an art of understatement: a mode of creation that Zora Neale Hurston called "dynamic suggestion" and "compelling insinuation." Space, timing, and the shaping of words were definitive."

interviewer, "is like being very sad, very sick, going to church, being very happy." Listening to these words, one can perhaps find one moment, not beyond but focusing others, when Holiday reached a verge, when she made her own event.

Holiday first recorded the anti-lynching song "Strange Fruit" in 1939; she performed it for the rest of her life. The story of the song is now well known: it was composed by Abel Meeropol, a member of the Communist Party who wrote under the name Lewis Allan and taught for many years at DeWitt Clinton High School in the Bronx (Meeropol and his wife adopted the two young sons of Julius and Ethel Rosenberg after their parents' execution in 1953 for treason). After seeing Holiday at Café Society, one of the only integrated nightclubs in Manhattan, Meeropol offered her the song, and her presentation of the piece there caused a sensation and a scandal. Seeking to record the song, Holiday was refused by her label, Columbia, and even by her producer, John Hammond, himself once a jazz critic for the *New Masses*; it was the small label Commodore that was willing to risk such a forthrightly political song. The words Meeropol wrote and Holiday sang have become part of American literature.

...

Black bodies swinging in the southern breeze
Strange fruit hanging from the poplar trees

...

Although the song was Meeropol's and was not, as Holiday often claimed, written especially for her, as art—as American speech—Holiday came to own "Strange Fruit," and she made plain her displeasure when others presumed to sing it. Comparisons of the original sheet music with Holiday's various recordings make clear that she painstakingly disassembled and then rebuilt the song in her own style—just as she routinely undid and redid songs from Broadway or Tin Pan Alley. For the first recording of "Strange Fruit," Holiday compressed the song's melody and slowed its pace to increase its searing power. Recordings from the 1940s and '50s show that, increasingly, she intensified the drama of the weighted language by extending the silences between phrases—spaces for the audience to take in the meaning, to reflect. A television clip of a performance in the mid-1950s shows, too, how she twists and extends the vowel sounds of certain words ("drop," "crop") until they become a mournful, accusatory wail. She cuts short the final, full-throated cry of "crop"; she does so with a suddenness that leaves her audience no room for sentimentality or self-pity, but instead confronts it with a void of silence—before the nervous applause—that is almost unbearably charged.

Holiday was an improvising jazz artist who recomposed or co-composed   5
not only "Strange Fruit" but everything she sang. The pianist Teddy
Wilson reported that, contrary to all stories, she rehearsed at length with
him for their landmark recording dates in the mid- to late-1930s, running over the melodies of new songs until she could begin to shape them
to her own purposes. Wilson presented Holiday as an improvising soloist whose statements of the melody made up each work's central solo
invention — and Holiday's inventions made up one event after another.
Consider her two recordings of "These Foolish Things," from 1936 and
1952. In the later recording, her once-buoyant and youthful voice has
become dark and oracular: the foolish things have become at once more
foolish than ever, foolish beyond description, as well as more mightily
alluring: beautiful but tragically lost forever. Close to the meaning of
the blues.

Despite the title of her autobiography, *Lady Sings the Blues*, Holiday
was not primarily a blues singer, but she could take songs that were not
framed in the blues form per se and charge them with the spirit of the
blues. Sometimes this had to do with the technical ability to flatten certain notes or to swing the music in the train-travel/dance-beat manner
associated with the blues. ("Billie could swing you into bad health," said
Carmen McRae.) But most significant of all was her ability to make a
Broadway song, or a cabaret torch song, yield a complexity of meaning
that elevated it beyond its original setting, and made it part of a narrative
of love, trouble, confrontation, and triumph. Ralph Ellison's 1945 essay
"Richard Wright's Blues" is pertinent:

> *The blues is an impulse to keep the painful details and episodes of a brutal*
> *experience alive in one's aching consciousness, to finger its jagged grain, and*
> *to transcend it, not by the consolation of philosophy but by squeezing from it*
> *a near tragic, near comic lyricism. As a form, the blues is an autobiographical*
> *chronicle of personal catastrophe expressed lyrically . . . they at once express*
> *both the agony of life and the possibility of conquering it through sheer tough-*
> *ness of spirit. They fall short of tragedy only in that they provide no solution,*
> *offer no scapegoat but the self.*

Ellison ends by noting that imperatives for social action are implied in
Wright's work, and, by extension, in the blues. "Nowhere in America
today is there social or political action based upon the solid realities of
Negro life depicted in *Black Boy*; perhaps that is why, with its refusal to
offer solutions, it is like the blues."

The subject of the blues, wrote James Baldwin in 1964 in "The Uses of the Blues," is that as a human being you are born to suffer. But the blues also record the life of a black American: "I am talking about what happens to you if, having barely escaped suicide, or death, or madness, or yourself, you watch your children growing up and no matter what you do, no matter what you do, you are powerless, you are really powerless against the forces of the world that are out to tell your child that he has no right to be alive." This was one of the stories Holiday told.

She herself became a story; save John Coltrane, no jazz musician appears as often in the pages of American writing as Billie Holiday. Frank O'Hara's poem "The Day Lady Died" records in stark language the shock of learning, via a newspaper's bald headline, that Holiday was gone. Langston Hughes's "Song for Billie" speaks of the power of her music to purge feelings of despair, and yet there is no satisfactory resolution:

> What can purge my heart
> Of the sadness
> Of the song?

There are striking appearances by Holiday in *The Autobiography of* 10 *Malcolm X* and Maya Angelou's *Heart of a Woman*. Malcolm uses his friendship with Holiday in the mid-1940s, as she teeters on the brink of decline into serious drug addiction, to indicate how, once, as the hustler Detroit Red, he was part of the world of Lady Day, the queen of the night herself. Malcolm presents her not only as a marker of his own decline — against which he would measure his rise, once he is saved, through Islam — but also as a singer in an ancient Greek chorus, calling out to the lost. Onstage at a club on 52nd Street, Holiday spots Malcolm walking in: "Her white gown glittered under the spotlight, her face had that coppery, Indianish look, and her hair was in that trademark ponytail. For her next number she did the one she knew I always liked so: 'You Don't Know What Love Is' — 'until you face each dawn with sleepless eyes · · · until you've lost a love you hate to lose.'" Holiday had unearthed a blues message in the middle of the ballad, and as James Baldwin would write, it warned of a society spun out of control: of helplessness, misery, and hunger. Malcolm goes on to present the tragedy of Holiday's own circumstances and early death to suggest a larger historical drama of race and nation: "She's dead; dope and heartbreak stopped that heart as big as a barn and that sound and style that no one successfully copies. Lady Day sang with the soul of Negroes from the centuries of sorrow and oppression. What a shame that proud, fine, black woman never lived where the true greatness of the black race was appreciated!"

Maya Angelou presents Holiday just months before the end, an unsteady old lady (forty-four years old), picking her way across the room in Angelou's home in Los Angeles. She surprises Angelou (and the reader) by spending so much time with Guy, Angelou's twelve-year-old son, to whom she sings an a cappella lullaby each night—but one incident Angelou offers is a parable about the artist as an oracle, telling more of the truth than her listeners are quite ready to take in. When Guy asks Holiday to define the words "pastoral scene" in "Strange Fruit," which she sings to him on her last night in the house, the answer she gives him is frightening:

Billie looked up slowly and studied Guy for a second. Her face became cruel, and when she spoke her voice was scornful. "It means when the crackers are killing the niggers. It means when they take a little nigger like you and snatch off his nuts and shove them down his goddam throat. That's what it means." The thrust of rage repelled Guy and stunned me.

Billie continued, "That's what they do. That's a goddam pastoral scene."

This is one voice in which Billie Holiday, who sang in many voices, sang the blues.

Bibliography

Angelou, Maya. *The Heart of a Woman*. 1981.

Baldwin, James. "The Uses of the Blues." *Playboy,* Jan. 1964.

Ellison, Ralph. "Richard Wright's Blues." *Living with Music: Ralph Ellison's Jazz Writings*, edited by Robert O'Meally, 2001.

Malcolm, X. *The Autobiography of Malcolm X with the Assistance of Alex Haley.* 1965.

Margolick, David and Hilton Als. *Strange Fruit: The Biography of a Song.* 2001.

Understanding the Text

1. While "Strange Fruit" became one of Holiday's most famous songs, why did she have to release it on a small record label, rather than her own label, Columbia?

2. Holiday grew up in a Catholic family. Why does this background make her unusual among "great black American singers of the twentieth century" (2)?

3. What was Holiday's most significant ability or talent as a singer, according to O'Meally?

Reflection and Response

4. O'Meally writes, "Holiday was an improvising jazz artist who recomposed or co-composed not only 'Strange Fruit' but everything she sang" (5). What do you think he means by this? What does it suggest about the relationship between songs and singers, as well as between songwriters and performers?

5. According to the writer, "Holiday was not primarily a blues singer, but she could take songs that were not framed in the blues form per se and charge them with the spirit of the blues" (6). How do you understand the "spirit of the blues"? Does O'Meally define it? In what ways does its meaning emerge in the text?

6. O'Meally claims that "no jazz musician appears as often in the pages of American writing as Billie Holiday" (9). He then includes references to — and textual passages from — writers such as Langston Hughes, Malcolm X, and Maya Angelou. What do these references add to his discussion and argument? How do they contribute to his portrait of Billie Holiday?

Making Connections

7. O'Meally refers to several literary texts in this essay, including Frank O'Hara's poem "The Day Lady Died." Read the O'Hara poem. Does it seem to be about Billie Holiday or her music? How do you interpret its meaning in the context of her death?

8. "Consider her two recordings of 'These Foolish Things,' from 1936 and 1952," writes O'Meally. "In the later recording, her once-buoyant and youthful voice has become dark and oracular: the foolish things have become at once more foolish than ever, foolish beyond description, as well as more mightily alluring: beautiful but tragically lost forever" (5). Listen to both of these recordings, which are available online. Do you agree with O'Meally's "reading" of the two songs? Can you hear the contrast he describes? Explain your answer.

Hardcore Persona

Laina Dawes

In this sharp essay that blends personal narrative and reflection with perceptive cultural analysis, Laina Dawes writes about the dilemma and bind of being a black, female heavy metal fan: "A black metalhead can be perceived not only as an affront to the past and present struggles black people have endured, but as a personal insult to those closest to them." Placing her struggle in the context of other fans and social critics, Dawes strives to reconcile the power and obligation of a collective identity with the need to be true to her own aesthetic sensibility and "persona."

Music critic and writer Laina Dawes is the author of *What Are You Doing Here?: A Black Woman's Life and Liberation in Heavy Metal* (2013).

Talking to people for the first time about my favorite music, I catch myself preparing for the inevitable. I mentally rehearse my replies before the questions about my musical preference arise. I find the process stressful—and wonder if I am being paranoid for thinking I will have to defend myself. "I call it parochial blackness," says Mashadi Matabane from Emory University in Georgia, author of a blog on black women guitarists from the blues era to today. "It's something that infects our minds and our decision-making process, because it forces you to always think, 'What are they thinking about me now?'"

Many of the women in this book discussing their lives in the metal, hardcore, and punk scenes felt the threat of losing their black cultural identity. They worried about being perceived as wanting to distance themselves from their culture or race. Believe it or not, blacks and nonblacks both commonly assume that black people get into heavier musical genres to shed their blackness—that we do not like ourselves and, worse, that we do not like others who look like us. Nothing could be further from the truth.

When I first met Pisso, a beautiful black woman with a proud Afro and a vast knowledge of punk and Oil music. I was stunned that she was once involved in the skinhead scene in Chicago. She just looked very different from the stereotype I had in my head. But being involved in the skinhead scene didn't necessarily mean that you were a racist, white-power Nazi. From a Caribbean family, Pisso is fluent in German and explains some of her experiences in Berlin, where she moved after graduating from college. "A big part of West Indian culture is to present yourself in a nice way: always clean, nice clothes. When I switched from punk to being a skinhead, my mom definitely noticed when I shaved my head. I had gone over to a friend's house to do it, and when

I got home, she freaked out. She was very upset, like I had shaved *her* hair.

"With my dad, it was definitely more of a problem," she adds. "He actually stopped talking to me from the time I was 15 until I was like twenty-something. He eventually told me that he didn't like that I was into that 'punk stuff'."

"I started hanging out with the skinheads," she continues, "and I felt 5 that I had a place. I always had to work, as I was going to school, and they respected that. They respected my heritage from the West Indies and they loved the music. I would hang out with them when I was 18, and I started college and we eventually grew apart and I started growing out my hair again. Since then, I've found myself longing to belong to a group again."

Writing this book, I found other black women who had felt rejected by friends, family members, or their communities because of their musical preferences. At one point, I distributed a mass questionnaire, and nearly three-quarters of the replies described negative reactions to listening to heavy metal.

Many of the replies were predictable: "Many people say the style of music I like isn't really music; it's just loud noise. Or that I'm not black because I like rock or punk music."

Others were encouraging: "Especially when I say I like rock, they think it's like devil or white music. I find it hilarious. I revel in my musical tastes and find audio joy wherever I can."

Some were unfortunate: "When I was younger, I was criticized for listening to 'white' music and told I was weird and [that] there was something wrong with me for being a black girl listening to rock 'n' roll. . . . [Then] I learned that black folks actually *created* it."

And many stories were downright infuriating: "Especially when I 10 was in my teens and twenties, comments from some family and friends if I was listening to rock or punk music were like: 'Why you listening to that white shit?' I once dated a white guy who grew up in a black neighborhood, and was trying to be 'down,' and he yelled at me for listening to Led Zeppelin: 'Don't you listen to any black music? What do you listen to that white music for?'—the funniest thing I ever heard. Now that I'm in my forties, I don't tend to associate with anyone who is so narrow-minded about me or my tastes in life."

A black metalhead can be perceived not only as an affront to the past and

> "A black metalhead can be perceived not only as an affront to the past and present struggles black people have endured, but as a personal insult to those closest to them."

present struggles black people have endured, but as a personal insult to those closest to them. "Some people, especially older people, feel that you are indifferent to being black because you are not listening to or respecting 'our' music," says Sameerah Blue. "They think you're indifferent to your culture, you're indifferent to being a black person."

Every black person in North America is somewhat aware of prevailing societal assumptions and must struggle to rise above them. Sharing certain commonalities — like dialect, dress, dating, and music preferences — signifies to other blacks that you show pride in who you are as a black person. For anyone who chooses not to adopt those cultural signifiers for whatever reason, the choice is seen as a rejection, even an insult.

In the 1903 essay "Of Our Spiritual Strivings," from *The Souls of Black Folk*, W. E. B. DuBois wrote about the polarization between blacks and whites at that time. He identified the danger of people trying to change their identities to conform to how others perceive them, abandoning what they know to be their true selves. He described this process as a loss that leads to self-doubt, depression, and isolation. Perceptions of black people already led to sweeping generalizations about the entire population, limiting creative and professional opportunities and hindering them from developing their individual identities. Why impose limits from within?

As DuBois wrote, and Patricia Hill Collins later redefined explicitly for black women, we live with a "dual consciousness" that reconciles how we perceive the outside world with how the outside world perceives us. "The effort to interact with those who [see] you as inferior to them while remaining expressionless was and is an arduous task," wrote Collins. "Behind the mask of behavioral conformity imposed on African-American women, acts of resistance, both organized and anonymous, have long existed." She specifies that black women struggle to leave stereotypes about their sexuality, physicality, and intelligence at the threshold when they come home every night.

Collins credits the arts as one of the only places where a black woman 15 may be above criticism, whether she chooses to be a performer, a writer, or a visual artist. Instead of wallowing in self-pity, Collins suggests creating an emotional and psychological vehicle to get yourself out of the mental oppression that can hinder your life. Thinking of this creative channel in terms of heavy metal is a great way to explain Keidra Chaney's upbringing as a metal fan on the south side of Chicago. In her essay "Sister Outsider Headbanger," written for *Bitch* magazine in 2000, she says:

I buried my metal affection at first, not wanting to seem like too much of a freak to my friends, sneaking Metallica songs in between Salt-N-Pepa and Digital Underground on mixtapes. What could I possibly find appealing about heavy metal, seeing as how it didn't reflect my life experience or cultural identity in any tangible way? And yet I think that contradiction was what appealed to me in the first place . . . allowed me to imagine myself as . . . someone who wouldn't take shit from anyone and didn't give a fuck about rules.

When I first read Chaney's essay, I thought she could have been writing about me. Even a decade after her piece was published, Chaney still occasionally gets e-mails from young black women relieved to discover someone else out there like themselves. "The fact that we are still dealing with that in this day and age is ridiculous," she says.

Chaney admits that she didn't really know any white people until she was in university. "It was very difficult to find other people into [heavy metal]," she says. "There was the band Living Colour, and Living Colour was the only common language I could pull out for people at my school. They were like: 'Well, they can do some shit with their guitars so I guess it's all right.' But it was difficult. I still liked hip hop, R&B, and new jack swing and all that, but I had this love for metal that I had to keep hidden. I could listen to it but not get too excited from it in case someone wanted to kick my ass or call me 'that white chick' or whatever."

From a historical standpoint, black people have sometimes depended on community for survival, such as when warning others of impending danger, or banding together as powerless people during the civil rights era in mass demonstrations and boycotts to become a unified force for social and political change. Our elders sometimes had to put their own needs and desires aside in order to work as a collective. In that context, black identity can exert a powerful pressure.

"Black people have a certain type of trauma, anxiety, and fear of being consumed by white American culture," says journalist and musician Greg Tate. "There is a certain basis for it because it goes back to the slave experience. It just has a hysterical dimension to it, this late in the day, the twenty-first century. I just think it's from people not being fundamentally secure in who they are, in their ability to move freely in the society. People cling to things that they are familiar with, and things that are unfamiliar represent limits that they have imposed within their own lives."

Ignoring negativity based on racial stereotypes is difficult when one is faced every day with perceived racial slights. In *Color Conscious: The Political Morality of Race.* Amy Gutmann writes "We can neither reflectively 20 choose our color identity nor downplay its social significance simply by willing it to be unimportant . . . but our color no more binds us to send a predetermined group message to our fellow human beings than our language binds us to convey predetermined thoughts." Amen.

Some of our parents told us that conforming was the only way to make it in North American society. "My mother's generation and my parents' generation was about making black people who were very prim and proper," says singer Camille Atkinson. "People who were very light skinned or very dark skinned, as they were, made sure that they never went out of the hue, made very good babies, and spread the good word of Catholicism. They didn't know that a couple of generations later, they were going to have queers, they were going to have punks, they were going to have feminists who were going to go to school for thirty years before they were going to have kids, so it shifted everyone's expectations. What it means to be black is constantly being redefined."

But for Tamar-kali, hardcore punk was a path to blackness. She looked at her family roots and stopped worrying about being accepted or rejected by her community. "I took the next step and started becoming aware of race in general and my history and my path in terms of being a descendant of enslaved Africans," she says. "I was interested in the history, and the hardcore scene really suited the emotions that I was experiencing and the things that I was finding out. So there was definitely a lock and a seal on me really embracing the music, and leading me emotionally. The sound of hardcore matched my emotions."

Among black women heavy metal and punk fans, there is a quiet movement to build allegiances, or at least a desire that I hope becomes reality before much longer. In the meantime, the general disapproval is strong enough to dissuade women who want to become involved from participating, and that is just sad. Rejection by friends or even family members, as Pisso mentioned, adds another layer of angst to the same trials and tribulations experienced by the white kid from the suburbs whose parents threaten to send him to private school over his Slayer and Gwar posters.

"In high school, a lot of my friends were these long-haired freaks listening to nothing but death, black metal, and rock music," says Ashley Greenwood, singer and guitarist for the New Jersey–based hard-rock band Rise from Ashes. "The other black kids didn't understand who I was as a person. This one girl called me the devil because I was listening to Black Sabbath. I said, 'How can you call me the devil and say that I'm an evil person and that I'm going to hell, when you are having premarital sex with your boyfriend? Doesn't God say that you're not supposed to do that? Who's the hypocrite?' She got very upset about that."

Figure 2.1 "You wanna change who I am": Alexis Brown, lead singer of Metalcore band Straight Line Stitch. Roger Kisby/Getty Images

The need to find a place to fit in is universal, and many black women 25
experience painful emotions when they are made to feel ashamed of
metal, punk, and hardcore scenes—the only places where they truly feel
they belong.

* * *

In early 2009, Afronerd.com invited director Raymond Gayle, creator of
the documentary *Electric Purgatory: The Fate of the Black Rocker*, to talk
about the contemporary state of black rock artists. I was pleased when
Gayle and the host expressed confusion as to why black rock, punk, and
metal artists cannot do what they do, reaching across racial lines however
they wish. "Music is music," the host exclaimed, recounting a story about
being rejected by an international film festival because the board that
reviewed films for the festival was perplexed by the subject matter, "Why
can't people just write the lyrics and play the music that they want?"

I understand a little resistance to loud, pounding music that incorporates screaming and yelling and references to the devil and hell. But I am
outraged by the classism that stereotypes metal as music for angry, racist,
sexist white men and the snobbery that questions the racial authenticity
and legitimacy of the black heavy metal fan. Are black heavy metal fans
supposed to be ashamed of their taste—or should the music establishment be ashamed of their own ignorance about where heavy metal came
from?

"We are simply going to say. 'This is what it is. This is what I enjoy.'
Lay down the law," says Tamar-kali. "Whenever somebody says no, we
have got to stand on our core experiences of being women of color. We
can't separate any of this. We can't compartmentalize things because people are not used to women of color and how we live our lives. We have
to set the tone of how we understand ourselves. We have to create our
own framework of understanding ourselves and how we function in the
world. We know our reality."

Understanding the Text

1. According to Dawes, what do people commonly assume about black people
   who "get into heavier musical genres"?

2. Citing the iconic civil rights activist and reformer W. E. B. DuBois, as well as
   the sociologist Patricia Hill Collins, Dawes refers to the concept of a "dual
   consciousness." What does this term mean? Why is it important to her
   essay?

Reflection and Response

3. Paraphrasing Patricia Hill Collins, Dawes writes: "Collins credits the arts as one of the only places where a black woman may be above criticism, whether she chooses to be a performer, a writer, or a visual artist . . . [she] suggests creating an emotional and psychological vehicle to get yourself out of the mental oppression that can hinder your life." How can music, in particular, serve as an "emotional and psychological vehicle" for those who want to escape "mental oppression"? Can you think of examples?

4. According to Dawes, "Our elders sometimes had to put their own needs and desires aside in order to work as a collective (18). In that context, black identity can exert a powerful pressure." What is Dawes's view of this community "pressure"? (18) In what ways is it a positive force? In what ways is it a negative force?

Making Connections

5. Dawes quotes the writer (and black, female heavy metal fan) Keirda Chaney: "What could I possibly find appealing about heavy metal, seeing as how it didn't reflect my life experience or cultural identity in any tangible way?" How might Brad Mehldau ("Blank Expressions: Brad Mehldau and the Essence of Music," p. 21) answer this question, particularly in light of his claims about "musical wisdom"? Are there forms of music you find appealing and resonant, even though they do not "reflect" your identity and experience "in any tangible way"? What might account for their allure?

6. In "Black Rhythm, White Power" (p. 193), Samantha Ainsley writes about "the ethics of cross-cultural musical appropriation." Is her topic and argument similar to Dawes's? How do you think she might respond to Dawes's argument? Explain your answer.

Concerning the Spiritual in Indie Rock

Judy Berman

In this selection from *The Believer,* Judy Berman reflects on the spiritual inclinations and obsessions of bands such as Neutral Milk Hotel, Yeasayer, Animal Collective, and Arcade Fire. For Berman, indie rock has a complex "metaphysical fixation" that seems to "grab for our souls." She frames her argument with the artist Wassily Kandinsky's 1911 essay, "Concerning the Spiritual in Art," a scaffolding that helps her define the "spiritual" as encompassing "both the enormity of the cosmos and the bottomless depths of the human psyche."

Judy Berman is the editor-in-chief of Flavorwire, a pop culture website. Her work has appeared in *Slate,* the *Atlantic,* the *Los Angeles Times,* and other publications. A former editor at *Salon,* she coedits (with Niina Pollari) *It's Complicated,* a 'zine that features feminist writers writing about the "artists whose misogynist work we love."

In his strange, dazzling 1911 essay "Concerning the Spiritual in Art," Wassily Kandinsky wrote, "Music has been for some centuries the art which has devoted itself not to the reproduction of natural phenomena but rather to the expression of the artist's soul." As he saw it, analyzing earthly minutiae that would soon become irrelevant was less important than pushing against the boundaries of consciousness and expanding the scope of mankind's experience. "Literature, music and art are the first and most sensitive spheres in which this spiritual revolution makes itself felt," as artists "turn away from the soulless life of the present toward those substances and ideas which give free scope to the non-material strivings of the soul." By "spiritual," Kandinsky meant both the universal and the emotional—accessing both the enormity of the cosmos and the bottomless depths of the human psyche.

Kandinsky's is an uncompromising standard. But what does it tell us about Animal Collective's latest single? Among the immediate forerunners of indie rock's current metaphysical fixation, Neutral Milk Hotel's 1998 *In the Aeroplane Over the Sea* is perhaps the most widely cherished. The album combines Middle Eastern and South Asian devotional music and Christian prayer, sometimes within the same song, to conjure the dream-story of the singer's mournful, soul-consuming obsession with Anne Frank.

This potentially disastrous conceit somehow yields a mysterious, ruminative, and profoundly affecting album. Hundreds of years of history melt together in a feverish heap of images. Without ever mentioning Frank's full name, Neutral Milk Hotel's singer and songwriter, Jeff Mangum, projects onto her ghostly figure a lifetime of anxieties about youth and aging, love and sex, birth and death and rebirth. We see his heroine buried alive only weeks before her liberators would have come, and then reincarnated as a "little boy in Spain playing pianos filled with flames." Mangum idealizes childhood and its chaste, innocent love affairs. Adult sexuality, with its insidious reminders of mortality, both attracts and repels him; the album bursts at the seams with bodily fluids and putrefying flesh.

Mangum's lyrics are strong enough that they could work on the page as poetry, but it's the arrangements that propel the songs heavenward. Violently plucked folk guitar amplifies the singer's ardor, and the antiquated instruments of rural musicians—banjo, singing saw, flugelhorn—get caught in the swells of miniature symphonies. Tapes, radios, and filters add another dimension, as layers of sound swell and then fade into the distance. Mangum's vocal cords are the most expressive instruments of all, allowing him to embody the roles of lover, child, and mystic. At moments he sounds messy and frantic, a holy fool receiving revelations in the desert; his voice stretches and quivers as he sings funeral dirges for his lost love. On "King of Carrot Flowers Pts. Two & Three," Mangum strains to reach a higher register, chanting, "I love you, Jesus Christ"—in nasal tones reminiscent of a Muslim call to prayer.

As if to cement *Aeroplane*'s mythic impact, the cryptic and fragile 5 Mangum abandoned his band before Neutral Milk Hotel could begin to lead a movement. Today's cadre of spiritually oriented musicians finds its de facto leadership in Animal Collective, a group that has spent nearly a decade chipping away at the barrier between earth and heaven. The incantatory single "My Girls," from the band's newest album, *Merriweather Post Pavilion,* is a glittering whirlpool of synthetic sound. Harmonic elements merge, divide, and disappear like cells gone wild, only to resurface, transformed, a verse or two later.

Animal Collective is only one of many bands striving for something more resonant than a catchy melody. At their most potent, these artists make big, constantly evolving sounds that redraw the universe around us in deep Kandinsky colors. Harmonies build, choruses climax with eye-dilating intensity, and, if we're lucky, time and space get disrupted.

In "My Girls," Animal Collective's chanted vocals become mantra-like,

"At their most potent, these artists make big, constantly evolving sounds that redraw the universe around us in deep Kandinsky colors. Harmonies build, choruses climax with eye-dilating intensity, and, if we're lucky, time and space get disrupted."

as the repetition itself becomes more important than the words being uttered. And while repetition is a hallmark of just about all popular music, the particular ways in which these musicians use it recall Zen meditation more than Top 40 choruses. Drone, a technique derived from southwest Asian music in which a single sound remains constant throughout a composition, permeates the album. Although it has been a hallmark of Western experimental music for decades, from La Monte Young's minimalist classical pieces to the shrieking violin compositions of Burning Star Core's C. Spencer Yeh, drone is fairly new to indie rock. Dirty Projectors bassist and vocalist Angel Deradoorian, who uses it on her recent solo EP, *Mind Raft,* has become fascinated with the way drone lends itself to subtle variations on a fixed theme.

Music may also make a grab for our souls by recalling the sounds or harmonic structures of devotional songs, thus reawakening our collective memory of what faith and worship feel like. Arcade Fire's *Neon Bible* (2007) was recorded for the most part in a converted church and reverberates with the deep groan of organs. Ezra Buchla of Gowns believes that his band's brittle harmonies have a similar effect to gospel music. ("If people have souls, that's the way to activate them," he says.) The band's 2007 album, *Red State,* shaped by layers of drone, amplifier static, and vocals that range from soft and dejected to harried and screaming, doesn't sound like church-choir material. But the tension between these elements sets up its own kind of call-and-response pattern; the feedback becomes a voracious chorus, always threatening to devour the soloist.

If many of these bands traffic in twenty-first-century head music, another contingent thrives on a polymorphously perverse brand of physical rapture. The title of Ponytail's most recent album, *Ice Cream Spiritual* (2008), perfectly captures the band's sugar-high, wonder-stricken noise-punk. Singer Molly Siegel's high-pitched shrieks and her bandmates' wild, experimental take on the classic guitar-bass-drum combination recall nothing more than childhood playtime. For Siegel, childhood and spirituality are about both exploding boundaries between ourselves and the universe and the "ecstasy in losing yourself" that creates. Such moments are explicitly communal for Los Angeles spazz-core outfit the Mae Shi, who build to moments of regressive, holy-rolling exhilaration, complete with contagious hand claps and delirious screams. And Ponytail's friend and fellow Baltimorean Dan Deacon shapes the sounds of childhood (video games, cartoons) into ebullient electronic music that's been dubbed "future shock."

Deacon often begins shows by asking everyone to grab their neighbors' hands and repeat a nonsensical chant ("Ethan Hawke, Ethan Hawke") whose only purpose is to transform groups of strangers into a united, 10

Figure 2.2 "Indie rock's predominantly young, urban, and irreligious audience kneels to worship at the foot of a stage": Arcade Fire performs at St. John's Church in London. Jim Dyson/Getty Images

if temporary, gathering of friends. Seeking to eliminate the I-thou relationship between musician and fan, he insists on setting up his array of
neon-accented keyboards, sound mixers, and microphones in the middle
of the audience. Ponytail's performances conjure the group-wide fervor of
Easter Sunday at an evangelical church where both minister and congregation are hyperactive preschoolers. Band and audience members fuse into
an army of true believers, baptized in sweat and whinnying in tongues.

Rather than break a performance's spell, Animal Collective and a
handful of like-minded bands seamlessly segue from one song to the
next. Their sets often include moments of quiet, but the absence of complete silence means there is no designated time for applause. Instead of
clapping politely as the rock stars onstage indulge in inane banter that
breaks the spell of a good concert, we cheer when Animal Collective's
music soars to its all-consuming zenith. Rather than detracting from the
power of the moment, this nearly involuntary applause intensifies it.

Devotional lyrics can't redeem a spiritually lifeless track, but, like those
that fill *In the Aeroplane Over the Sea,* they can focus our reveries. Set in
the harsh, natural world of the Dakotas in winter, Gowns' *Red State* summons its visual power from what Erika Anderson and Buchla call "visions."
Like recurring, waking dreams, these vivid images—of a soldier's empty
basement bedroom, of the American flag hanging in its window—meld
together on the album with memories of characters and scenes from Anderson's rural youth. Rather than elevating us to beatitude, *Red State* envelops
us in its stark desolation. We don't just empathize with the spiritual hunger
that comes from living in the middle of nowhere, with no one around to
listen but God; we feel it gnawing at our own stomachs, in Anderson's and
Buchla's searching voices and static snowdrifts ten feet high.

Gowns' lyrics brim with Christian imagery, oscillating between
an earthly hell — chained-up dogs and teenage rapists who huff
gasoline—and distant glimpses of heaven. On "Fargo," Anderson lists
the pharmaceuticals her narrator has been consuming, then makes a sudden, echo-laden break for the transcendent: The sun shines through the
window, and the days ahead reach out to eternity. Images of light from
above become glimmers of hope trailing the album's characters. A sav-
ior slides down the mountainside. "I've seen the sound of angels," sings
Anderson. "I've heard the sound, their wings / He said that I was judgment / You know I'm everything."

A few artists, such as Sufjan Stevens and Danielson's Daniel Smith
(who sometimes performs dressed as a tree bearing the nine fruits of
the Holy Spirit), are outspokenly Christian, and often weave their faith
into lyrics and song titles. But many others, like ex-Catholic Anderson
and lifelong non-believer Buchla, have more complicated relationships
to religion. Deradoorian, the Dirty Projectors bassist and vocalist, has

an ongoing fascination with religion that began in junior high, when she was "born again" in a youth-group parking lot. A few years later, she rejected fundamentalist Christianity and began practicing a nondenominational form of meditation. Members of the Mae Shi have wildly divergent takes on religion. While some have never believed in God, others are devout Christians. The songs on last year's *HLLLYH* (pronounced "hell yeah," or "hallelujah") fuse biblical imagery with *Dawn of the Dead* gore. But because the songwriters' standpoints clash, the tracks careen from fire and brimstone to deep-seated doubt.

Some bands are even leery of secular spirituality. Yeasayer's 2007   15 debut, *All Hour Cymbals,* traces its influences to a complex, global web of secular and devotional music. Haunting Middle Eastern psychedelia crosses paths with Bollywood soundtracks and African chants in a heady, hypnotic collage that only distantly resembles any one of its forebears. Critics pegged their music as cosmic and even "tribal," but the band members are avowed skeptics who understand mysticism's potential to mislead and anesthetize. Chris Keating, who sings and plays keyboards, calls *All Hour Cymbals* a nonbeliever's attempt to understand what devotion and awe might feel like. The album, he says, strives to awaken through art the feelings others go to church seeking.

These days, mainstream religion feels largely divorced from metaphysics. The language of good and evil has been co-opted in the service of countless holy wars, and Christian leaders spend more time railing against gay marriage than debating the nature of the human soul. Those of us who can't buy into these crusades must find other marvels to contemplate. As Keating recognizes, art may help to fill a void left by organized religion: Indie rock's predominantly young, urban, and irreligious audience kneels to worship at the foot of a stage. Bible study is replaced by ritualistic listening and re-listening to tease out the meaning or simply bask in the bliss of favorite albums.

Perhaps this is why Kandinsky exhorted artists to turn their attentions away from the sordidness of life on earth toward the "nonmaterial" realm. But these musicians are not as detached as he prescribed. In fact, many bring spirituality to bear on the physical realm. The mantra that pervades Animal Collective's "My Girls" has nothing to do with God or redemption. Noah "Panda Bear" Lennox sings—in words so sincere and conversational they are almost embarrassing—about wanting to protect his wife and daughter: "I don't mean to seem like I care about material things like a social status / I just want four walls and adobe slats for my girls." And Gowns uses religious imagery to talk about politics; Anderson goes so far as to say that the carefully titled *Red State* was a protest album, lamenting everything from rural poverty and drug dependence to South Dakota's proposed abortion ban.

From the very first listen, *In the Aeroplane Over the Sea* hooks us with its blaring horn section, singing saw solos, and Mangum's yowls. But what keeps us up at night, as our minds obsess over snatches of lyrics, is the mournful longing at the album's core, the way it makes Anne Frank and the horrors that befell her resonate. Kandinsky saw the spiritual and the earthly as opposites, but for indie rock's spiritual explorers, they are inextricably linked. This music doesn't suffer from the communion but originates in the space where they meet.

Understanding the Text

1. In the essay, Berman cites Chris Keating, a keyboardist and singer in the band Yeasayer. What is the goal of Yeasayer's album, *All Hour Cymbals,* according to Keating? How does this example support Berman's thesis?

2. Berman writes, "These days, mainstream religion feels largely divorced from metaphysics" (16). What does she mean by this? According to her, how have "Christian leaders" contributed to this disconnect?

Reflection and Response

3. Berman begins her essay by briefly summarizing a 1911 essay by the Russian painter Wassily Kandinsky. Why do you think she begins a discussion about contemporary indie rock in this way? How does Kandinsky's intellectual framework inform her own analysis?

4. Writing about one performer, Berman claims that he "seek[s] to eliminate the I-thou relationship between musician and fan." How does this contrast with a more conventional view of performers and their audiences? In what ways does it connect with themes of spirituality and religion?

Making Connections

5. Berman suggests that rock music can aspire to the highest aspirations of art and religion. According to her, it may even "help to fill a void left by organized religion." Does her analysis seem limited to a subgenre of indie rock, or is it applicable to other genres of music? Do you expect your own favorite bands or performers to be "spiritual explorers"? Or do you want something else from the music you love? Explain your answer with specific examples.

6. St. Basil (from "The Homily on the First Psalm," p. 42) is also deeply concerned with the religious and metaphysical aspects of music. While he writes in the fourth century about Psalms and Berman writes about contemporary bands, is there any overlap in their claims about music's purpose? For example, Berman writes that for metaphysically minded indie rockers, "the spiritual and the earthly" are "inextricably linked." How does this compare or contrast with St. Basil's views?

Country Music, Openness to Experience, and the Psychology of Culture War

Will Wilkinson

In this article, which originally appeared on the bigthink.com website, Will Wilkinson connects the powerful appeal of country music to listeners with specific temperamental tendencies, cognitive styles, political convictions, and group identifications. As he writes, for its fans, country music is a "bulwark against cultural change, a reminder that 'what you see is what you get,' a means of keeping the charge of enchantment in 'the little things' that make up the texture of the everyday. . . ."

Writer Will Wilkinson has held positions at the libertarian Cato Institute, George Washington University's Mercatus Center, and the Institute for Humane Studies. His work has appeared in the *Atlantic*, the *Economist*, *Slate*, *Reason*, and many other outlets.

In the car, I listen to country music. Country has an ideology. Not to say country has a position on abortion, exactly. But country music, taken as a whole, has a position on life, taken as a whole. Small towns. Dirt roads. Love at first sight. Hot-blooded kids havin' a good ol' time. Gettin' hitched. America! Raisin' up ruddy-cheeked scamps who you will surely one day worry are having too good a hot-blooded time. Showing up for Church. Venturing confused into the big wide world only to come back to Alabama forever since there ain't a damn single thing out there in the Orient or Paris, France, what compares to that spot by the river under the trembling willows where first you kissed the girl you've known in your heart since second grade is the only girl you would ever truly love. Fishin'! How grandpa, who fought in two wars, worked three jobs, raised four kids, and never once complained, can't hardly wait to join grandma up in heaven, cuz life just ain't no good without her delicious pies.

Last night, on my way to fetch bok choy, I heard Collin Raye's classic "One Boy, One Girl," a song that takes the already suffocating sentimentality of the FM-country weltanschauung and turns it up to fourteen. The overwhelming force of this song's manufactured emotion led me unexpectedly to a conjecture about conservative psychology and the stakes of the "culture wars."

Now, conservatives and liberals really do differ psychologically. Allow me to drop some science:

Applying a theory of ideology as motivated social cognition and a "Big Five" framework, we find that two traits, Openness to New Experiences and Conscientiousness, parsimoniously capture many of the ways in which individual differences underlying political orientation have been conceptualized . . .

We obtained consistent and converging evidence that personality differences between liberals and conservatives are robust, replicable, and behaviorally significant, especially with respect to social (vs. economic) dimensions of ideology. In general, liberals are more open-minded, creative, curious, and novelty seeking, whereas conservatives are more orderly, conventional, and better organized. (Carney et al. 807)

Full disclosure: I score very high in "openness to experience" and worryingly low in "conscientiousness." (When I was first diagnosed with ADD, my very concerned psychiatrist asked, "Do you have a hard time keeping jobs?") This predicts that I'm extremely liberal, that my desk is a total mess, and that my bedroom is cluttered with books, art supplies, and "cultural memorabilia." It's all true.

Is country music really conservative music? It's obvious if you listen to 5 it: Peter Rentfrow and Samuel Gosling's fascinating paper "The Do Re Mi's of Everyday Life: The Structure and Personality Correlates of Music Preferences" helps identify country as the most "upbeat and conventional" genre of music. A preference for "upbeat and conventional" music is negatively correlated with "openness" and positively correlated with "conscientiousness," and so, as you would then expect, self-described conservatives tend to like "upbeat and conventional" music (more than any other kind), while self-described liberals tend to like everything else better.

"More generally, country music comes again and again to the marvel of advancing through life's stations, and finds delight in experiencing traditional familial and social relationships from both sides."

Again, those low in "openness" are less likely to visit other countries, try new kinds of food, take drugs, or buck conventional norms generally. This would suggest that most conservatives aren't going to seek and find much intense and meaningful emotion in exotic travel, hallucinogenic ecstasy, sexual experimentation, or challenging aesthetic experience. The emotional highlights of the low-openness life are going to be the type celebrated in "One Boy, One Girl": the moment of falling in love with "the one," the wedding day, the birth [of] one's children (though I guess the song is about a surprising ultrasound). More generally, country music comes again and again to the marvel of advancing through life's stations, and finds delight in experiencing traditional familial and social relationships from both sides. Once I was a girl with a mother, now I'm a mother with a girl. My parents took care of me, and now I take care of them. I was once a teenage boy threatened by a girl's gun-loving father, now I'm a gun-loving father threatening my girl's teenage boy. And country is full of assurances that the pleasures of simple, rooted, small-town, lives of faith are deeper and more abiding than the alternatives.

My conjecture, then, is that country music functions in part to reinforce in low-openness individuals the idea that life's most powerful, meaningful emotional experiences are precisely those to which conservative personalities living conventional lives are most likely to have access. And it functions as a device to coordinate members of conservative-minded communities on the incomparable emotional weight of traditional milestone experiences.

Yesterday's *Washington Post* features a classic "conservatives in the mist" piece on the conservative denizens of Washington, OK, and their sense that their values are under attack. Consider this passage about a fellow named Mark Tague:

"I want my kids to grow up with values and ways of life that I had and my parents had," he says, so his youngest son tools around the garage on a Big Wheel, and his oldest daughter keeps her riding horse at the family barn built in 1907, and they buy their drinking milk from Braun's because he always has. "Why look for change?" he says. "I like to know that what you see is what you get." (Saslow)

Country music is for this guy.

But why would you want your kids to grow up with the same way of 10
life as you and your grandparents? My best guess (and let me stress *guess*) is that those low in openness depend emotionally on a sense of enchantment of the everyday and the profundity of ritual. Even a little change, like your kids playing with different toys than you did, comes as a small reminder of the instability of life over generations and the contingency of our emotional attachments. This is a reminder low-openness conservatives would prefer to avoid, if possible. What high-openness liberals feel as *mere* nostalgia, low-openness conservatives feel as the baseline emotional tone of a recognizably decent life. If your kids don't experience the same meaningful things in the same way that you experienced them, then it may seem that their lives will be deprived of meaning, which would be tragic. And even if you're able to see that your kids will find plenty of meaning, but in different things and in different ways, you might well worry about the possibility of ever really understanding and relating to them. The inability to bond over profound common experience would itself constitute a grave loss of meaning for both generations.

Figure 2.3 **"But country music, taken as a whole, has a position on life, taken as a whole. Small towns. Dirt roads. Love at first sight. Hot-blooded kids havin' a good ol' time. Gettin' hitched. America!"** Matt Cowan/Getty Images

So when the culture redefines a major life milestone, such as marriage, it trivializes one's own milestone experience by imbuing it [with] a sense of contingency, threatens to deprive one's children of the same experience, and thus threatens to make the generations strangers to one another. And what kind of monster would want that?

Country music is a bulwark against cultural change, a reminder that "what you see is what you get," a means of keeping the charge of enchantment in "the little things" that make up the texture of the everyday, and a way of literally broadcasting the emotional and cultural centrality of the conventional big-ticket experiences that make a life a life.

A lot of country music these days *is* culture war, but it's more bomb shelter than bomb.

Works Cited

Carney, Dana, et al. "The Secret Lives of Liberals and Conservatives: Personality Profiles, Interaction Styles, and the Things They Leave Behind." *Political Psychology*, vol. 29, no. 6, 2013, pp. 807–40.

Rentfrow, Peter J., and Samuel D. Gosling. "The Do Re Mi's of Everyday Life: The Structure and Personality Correlates of Music Preferences." *Journal of Psychology and Social Psychology*, vol. 84, no. 6, 2003, pp. 1236–56.

Saslow, Eli. "To Residents of Another Washington, Their Cherished Values Are Under Assault." *Washington Post*, 1 Mar. 2012. 29 Dec. 2014.

Understanding the Text

1. How would you state Wilkinson's thesis in your own words?

2. According to the writer, "Country has an ideology" (1). What does the word "ideology" mean in this context?

3. Wilkinson writes that country music celebrates the "emotional highlights of the low-openness life" (6). What are these "highlights"? How does country music "celebrate" them, according to the writer?

4. Near the end of his essay, Wilkinson writes, "A lot of country music these days *is* culture war, but it's more bomb shelter than bomb" (12). What does "culture war" mean? What distinction is the writer making with this "bomb shelter" metaphor — and why is it important for his argument?

Reflection and Response

5. Wilkinson is often self-referential. For example, he notes that he listens to country music while going to "fetch bok choy," and that he scores "very high in 'openness to experience' and worryingly low in 'conscientiousness'" (4). What does he gain by inserting himself into the essay in this way? How does it support or problematize his argument? Do you find this rhetorical strategy effective? Why or why not?

6. According to the writer, country music "functions as a device to coordinate members of conservative-minded communities on the incomparable emotional weight of traditional milestone experiences" (7). How do musical genres and subcultures serve to "coordinate" members of like-minded "communities"? For example, can you name other types of music that perform this social, cultural, or political function for their listeners? Or is country music unique in this role?

Making Connections

7. In "Concerning the Spiritual in Indie Rock" (p. 98), Judy Berman writes about the ways in which indie bands like Neutral Milk Hotel and Animal Collective have taken on the role of creating, shaping, and providing an opportunity for spiritual response — and spiritual community — from their fans: "Indie rock's predominantly young, urban, and irreligious audience kneels to worship at the foot of a stage. Bible study is replaced by ritualistic listening and re-listening to tease out the meaning or simply bask in the bliss of favorite albums." (16) In what ways does Berman's argument overlap with Wilkinson's? For example, do fans of country music and fans of indie rock share similar anxieties and fears about modernity encroaching on faith, community, spirituality, and other values? How do Berman's and Wilkinson's arguments diverge?

8. Do Wilkinson's assertions, insights, and categories apply to your own experiences, tastes, and views? Does the music you listen to have an "ideology"? Do his claims match your observations of other people and their relationships with their favorite musical genres?

Songs of Myself? Not Quite

Jeff Ousborne

In this personal essay, which originally appeared in the online magazine *Talking Writing,* Jeff Ousborne begins with a quotation from the English critic Walter Pater: "All art constantly aspires to the condition of music." Reflecting on his own experiences reading, teaching, and writing pop songs, Ousborne comes to a deeper understanding of Pater's aphorism — particularly in the context of art's "suavity," "charm," and style. He argues that too much emphasis on questions of representation and content — that is, what a song or poem is "about" — can "block the grace of art, and encourage us to view form and style as merely decorative."

Jeff Ousborne earned a PhD in English at Boston College and teaches at Suffolk University. A former music editor at *Details* magazine, he is the editor of *Reading Pop Culture: A Portable Anthology* and the author of *Critical Reading and Writing: A Spotlight Rhetoric.* His writing has appeared in the *Boston Phoenix*, *Entertainment Weekly*, *CMJ Music Monthly*, *Studies in Popular Culture*, *Clues: A Journal of Detection*, and other publications.

"All art constantly aspires to the condition of music"

—WALTER PATER, "THE SCHOOL OF GIORGIONE" (1877)

Whether you think it's true or not, Victorian critic Walter Pater's statement has an oracular quality that sounds like the truth. I first marveled at his work when I was in graduate school, especially after I read his disciples like Gerard Manley Hopkins and Oscar Wilde. But since I began writing songs a few years ago—both on my own and with my bandmates—Pater's claim about art and music strikes me viscerally as well as intellectually.

My songs are scratchy pastiches of the sloppy guitar pop from my teenage years, as well as twice-baked homages to earlier confections by the Velvet Underground, the Byrds, and Big Star. My rudimentary music does not aspire to the condition of "art"; it barely achieves the condition of "music." But it does force me to reflect on the relationship between form, content, and meaning. And that's Pater's subject.

For Pater, art should not aim to represent reality or explain some ostensible subject. It *may* do those things; it may even have a "legitimate function in the conveyance of a moral or political aspiration," as he writes in his essay "The School of Giorgione" (1877). Ideally, though, poetry and the other arts should not be "about" anything separable from their own formal aspects.

More than any other medium, then, music achieves that perfect union of form and content. Which makes sense: What are Bach's "Goldberg Variations" *about*, anyway? What is the "subject" of Miles Davis's *Kind of Blue*?

Similarly, I can't fully explain the meaning of Hopkins' "The 5 Windhover" or Wallace Stevens' "The Emperor of Ice Cream." The words transcend their function as the building blocks of "meaning" or "reference" and flare into pure energy. I love their crunch in my mouth, their flicker in my inner eye, and that dizzying twist I feel, somewhere in my guts, when I hear or read them.

The best writers reach us in ways beyond our conscious understanding of their subjects, even if doing so means deliberate vagueness, the necessary smudge, the ruthless suppression of "facts." That principle applies to purveyors of modest, three-minute pop songs, too. John Lennon once said of his enigmatic "Norwegian Wood," "I was trying to write about an affair without letting me wife know I was writing about an affair, so it was very gobbledygook." That's a good thing, too: no gobbledygook, no song.

> "The best writers reach us in ways beyond our conscious understanding of their subjects, even if doing so means deliberate vagueness, the necessary smudge, the ruthless suppression of "facts.""

In my case, it was only after I stopped trying to write songs "about" things that I was able to write them at all. On the rare occasions when people ask about the meaning behind my slapdash music and lyrics, I think of the questions I have asked over the years as a reader, scholar, and teacher: What is this or that poem "about"? Is this one about Robert Frost's marriage? Does that one reflect the importance of commerce in the 18th century?

Teaching poetry to undergraduates, I wince at the compulsion—my own included—to turn literature into philosophy, biography, history, sociology, psychology, or self-help—evasions that can keep us from talking about the words and sounds, the shape of the thing, the Möbius strip of meaning and structure at the center of so many literary texts.

Of course, novels, plays, movies, poems, paintings, and even songs of all kinds are "about" things—subjects, people, ideas, places. The Kinks' "Waterloo Sunset" evokes a miniature, melancholy cityscape in its clockwork chime: a minor miracle, turning at 45 R.P.M.

Even Pater concedes that poetry "deals, most often, with a definite   10
situation." I am not arguing otherwise, nor am I proposing a strict
Seinfeldian° doctrine of art-that-is-about-nothing.

But my amateur songwriting reminds me that too much emphasis on "content" may block the grace of art, and encourage us to view
form and style as merely decorative. Intuitively, we know they are not.
Countless forgotten poets have written about time, love, death, sex, and
art, but we read Shakespeare's sonnets (which happen to be about these
things) because of his deftness with the form, his alchemy of music and
perception.

Similarly, we don't listen to candied old pop songs primarily for their
repetitive, if timeless, subject matter: *I love my baby; My baby left me; My
baby still loves me; I'm leaving my baby; Why doesn't my baby love me?* We
listen to them (in Pater's words) for the "suavity" and "charm" that's
"caught from *the way in which they are done, which gives them a worth in
themselves.*" (emphasis added).

Suavity and charm: two underused and understated words when we
consider the highest aspirations of art. Yet both suggest an effortless,
seamless, maybe even magical embodiment of style—in a quicksilvered
paragraph from *The Great Gatsby*, in those terraced arches at the top of
the Chrysler Building, in the alternating lights and shadows of *Double
Indemnity,*° or in the filigreed verse of an Elvis Costello song.

My own songs are primarily about themselves and their own creation:
they aspire to form and style. I have no urge to "say" anything in particular, only a desire to give myself over to the hook with a twist; the rhyme,
surprising or predictable; the variation on a familiar chord change or
inversion of an old melody; that rigid corset of *verse-chorus-verse-chorus-
bridge-chorus* designed decades ago. I know if I can get the shape and the
sound right, secondary concerns like meaning and truth will take care of
themselves.

What do the songs "mean"? What are they "about"? Are they "true" to   15
life? I don't know, but I try to make them true to themselves. Pater writes
that the best art gives "one single effect to the 'imaginative reason.'"

Or to put it another way: it's only rock and roll, but I like it.

Seinfeldian: refers to the television situation comedy *Seinfeld,* a show that strived to be
about "nothing."
***Double Indemnity*:** a 1944 film noir thriller, based on 1943 novel by James M. Cain.

Understanding the Text

1. According to Ousborne, how do the "best writers reach us" (6)?

2. What connection does the writer make between Shakespeare's sonnets and pop songs?

Reflection and Response

3. As the writer implies, popular music often relies on songs that adhere to rigid and predictable forms and thematic content. Why would such repetition be appealing? How does Ousborne account for their appeal? Do you agree with him?

4. Ousborne writes that "suavity" and "charm" are worthy aspirations of art, as they suggest an almost "magical embodiment of style" (13). He then provides some examples. What examples would you add to his?

Making Connections

5. In "Blank Expressions: Brad Mehldau and the Essence of Music" (p. 21), pianist and composer Brad Mehldau writes, "Essentialist tropes are every-where in discussions about music, smugly short circuiting further inquiry, maintaining: 'We cannot put in words what is essential about music'" (2). Do you think Ousborne falls into this "essentialist" trap in his discussion of music and art? Does his argument "short circuit further inquiry"? Why or why not?

6. Ousborne refers to poems by Gerard Manley Hopkins and Wallace Stevens, acknowledging that while he cannot fully "explain their meaning," they affect him viscerally. Are you familiar with this experience of literature, music, or some other art form that affects you on a gut level, even if you cannot fully "explain" your reaction? What examples would you give from your own life? How would you describe them?

Humble Trappings: Blue-Collar Hip-Hop and Recasting the Drug Dealer's Myth

Zach Moldof

Zach Moldof is a San Francisco–based writer and indie hip-hop artist who performs under the stage name Zachg. His albums include *Sonter Masic* (2012) and *South Florida Mountains* (2014). He is the founder of Rad Reef, a "lifestyle collective" and record label of hip-hop artists; he is also the founder of Good Beach, a company that focuses on the distribution of music through streaming. His music writing has appeared on *Noisey, The 405,* and *Wax Poetics,* where the following essay was published.

In "Humble Trappings," Moldof suggests an alternative to the "exorbitance" of contemporary rap and hip-hop: a version of the genre that mythologizes "the life we're living in real time." He asks, what if rap and rap artists were less preoccupied with "gargantuan exploits," and more concerned with the prosaic compromises that underlie our daily survival?

One thing that has made rap music inaccessible in recent times—in spite of its relentless pursuit of ubiquity—is exorbitance. Exorbitance takes on many forms, but exaggeration is perhaps the most pervasive as it exists independent of material exorbitance. The influence of exaggeration is truly comprehensive washing over every element of an artist's reality—be it accomplishments, possessions, lawlessness, or any of the possible topics of a song—turning that reality into hopeful fodder for small scale traveling amusement parks, and life size action figure franchises. It's a shitty business, and while no one has to do it, more than plenty are inclined to step up to the plate and propagate a world of lies, or a vastly eroded depiction of the truth in order to make some quick cash. I'm not saying these folks are wrong for what they're doing, and I won't even go so far as to say they shouldn't be doing it. But, I will say that the degree to which this posturing and lie-parading has grown makes it tough to not point out that most of the current emperors of rap are in fact, all stark nude in the same fashion.

We know it's false because the current mantra of rap music is: "I became part of the one percent by breaking the rules. I do not have to worry about money. I get to do whatever I want. I am not bound to a life of labor, or the laws of this land." It's not that the mantra itself is untrue, it's just that the people who are saying it aren't actually living it. There isn't enough one percent to go around for all the folks who are bragging about being part of it. And being an outlaw is not something that successful outlaws brag about. So what's the alternative? Well, blue-collar rap music, of course. Music created by people whose survival is not guaranteed. Music filled with tales about being alive another day, even though you're not living the life you want to live. Tales about selling drugs to supplement your income, not supplant your employment. Essentially, contemporary artists mythologizing the life we're living in real time, and giving it back to us in a way that refreshes our seemingly ordinary surroundings.

> "So what's the alternative? Well, blue-collar rap music, of course. Music created by people whose survival is not guaranteed. Music filled with tales about being alive another day, even though you're not living the life you want to live."

Artists like New York's Black Dave, Moe Green in Vallejo (Bay Area), or Fourth Planet, the Huntsville crew made up of Sortahuman, Dizzy D, and Jhi Ali, further expand on one of the ideas I posed in the recent Tree profile. That is, that you can be outside of the accepted without being in flagrant defiance of it. We can find palpable dissent not only in the gargantuan exploits of Rick Ross°, but also in the skillfully rendered strokes of those who depict what is common amongst all of us. Smoking a joint and skateboarding in Washington Square park is enough to get you or Black Dave arrested, as Black Dave reminds us. Fourth Planet recount the very real ways that grinding for a piece to come up on is a full-time commitment, even if you're an artist. Moe Green offers existential summations of the working-class struggles that aren't weighed down by accounts of hefty exploits, instead, like all the other works mentioned, it is grounded in modest approachable reality.

You can do things that you'd rather not do in order to survive without corrupting your entire existence. And that is a reality that we all deal with in this day and age, whether you're buying goods made in sweatshops, skimming money out of the insurance pool, selling drugs to survive, cheating on tests, speeding in a school zone, scamming old people out of their money, labeling raw macadamias as roasted peanuts when you buy bulk nuts—whatever you're doing, we're all invariably compromising ourselves in this vast web of displaced violence, and disenfranchised bodies where a creeping web of laws further ensnares us every day. It's easy to see ourselves in relief against that, and imagine a better fantasy world when we listen to artists like Rick Ross whose exaggerations reach proportions which rival the architectural monuments of human history. But, what if the compromise isn't breaking the law? Can we still find something there if the compromise is working a shitty job that starts at 3 AM? If the only illegal money

---

Rick Ross: rapper and entrepreneur who founded Maybach Music Group.

you make is $2,000 a month are you a viable rapper in this economy? Is the quality of a musician's work determined by their financial standing relative to your own? Can you hang with a rapper who drives a two-year-old Lexus and parks it in the garage of a modest three-bedroom home?

Understanding the Text

1. In his opening paragraph, Moldof argues that "exorbitance" has made rap music "inaccessible in recent times." What do you think he means by this? What connotations does the word "exorbitance" have? Why would it make hip hop "inaccessible"?

2. What is the "current mantra of rap music," according to Moldof? What is the problem with it? Explain his reasoning.

Reflection and Response

3. For the writer, contemporary hip-hop propagates a "world of lies," composed of exaggeration and false mythology. Do you agree with this negative interpretation of rap culture? Explain your answer. Why might such "exorbitance" be so appealing?

4. According to Moldof, "whatever you're doing, we're all invariably compromising ourselves in this vast web of displaced violence, and disenfranchised bodies where a creeping web of laws further ensnares us every day" (4). Do you agree with this? Why or why not?

Making Connections

5. In "It's a Hip-Hop World" (p. 251), Jeff Chang writes about rap and hip-hop in a global context. He writes about the tensions in the genre, for example, as they have emerged in Kenyan hip-hop. Do you see any parallels between these tensions in other countries and the ones Moldof describes in the United States? What role do you think commercialism plays in both contexts?

6. Will Wilkinson considers the appeal of country music to those who have "low openness" to new experiences and find more meaning in the representation of the familiar and everyday. Does Wilkinson's argument about country music seem similar to Moldof's argument about rap, in which he proposes "a blue-collar rap music" that is "grounded in modest approachable reality" and everyday struggles? Explain your answer.

I Listen to Everything, Except Rap and Country Music

Jeremy Gordon

In this perceptive essay from *Pacific Standard*, Jeremy Gordon looks at the parallel and intersecting paths of country music and hip-hop. He finds the collaborations between — and name-checking among — artists like Nelly and Florida Georgia Line "not as weird as you might think." While the genres have always evoked divergent racial contexts and connotations, a key commercial imperative unites them: "[T]here's money to be made, and no point in ignoring a constantly growing audience thirsting for both rap and country."

Jeremy Gordon is the deputy news editor of Pitchfork Media. His writing has appeared in the *Wall Street Journal*, *Vice*, and *GQ*, among other publications.

No less an intellect than David Foster Wallace once remarked, "I have the musical tastes of a 13-year-old girl." You don't necessarily learn that much about someone by asking, "What type of music do you like?" But you can learn about someone through the music they don't like . . . and when I was in high school in Chicago, when people I knew were asked to describe their music tastes, no answer sprung up more than "everything but rap and country." (Metal was sometimes substituted for one or the other.) It's impossible to quantify, but I'm positive I wasn't alone in this experience. Googling "everything but rap and country" returns 449,000 results, ranging from the parodic to those earnestly describing this preference as some badge of honor. Open disdain of two genres with such contextually racial and socioeconomic backgrounds is a strange thing to proudly claim — and I wonder what my classmates might be thinking today.

If you turned on the radio in 2013, you would've eventually heard the Nelly-starring remix of Florida Georgia Line's "Cruise," which shattered sales records to become one of the biggest country singles of all time. You also might have heard Luke Bryan's "That's My Kind of Night," which casually mentioned throwing on some T-Pain as a way to set the mood, or Florida Georgia Line's "This Is How We Roll," which name-drops Hank Williams and Drake in the same line. That follows collaborations within the last decade between Jason Aldean and Ludacris, Willie Nelson and Snoop Dogg, Tim McGraw and Nelly — drops in the bucket, but new ground considering the stereotypes associated with each genre. For if rap is historically black and country is historically Southern white, how could the two styles co-exist? Why would they want to?

> "It's not as weird as you might think. They're both genres that began as regionally focused outsiders, battled with identity issues of how to be accepted by the greater world while still retaining their heart, and eventually wound up as two un-budging commercial forces."

It's not as weird as you might think. They're both genres that began as regionally focused outsiders, battled with identity issues of how to be accepted by the greater world while still retaining their heart, and eventually wound up as two un-budging commercial forces.

Country originated as the natural evolution from traditional forms like gospel and vaudeville, becoming a conduit for the Southern way of life through artists like Hank Williams, the Carter Family, and Johnny Cash (to briefly name a few). In the '60s, the encroaching influence of teen culture through rock 'n' roll helped popularize the "Nashville sound" with singers like Chet Atkins and Patsy Cline, who took a more mainstream, producer-driven approach to the traditional song forms.

In the late '70s and progressing through the early '80s, a broader, more romantic image of the country-associated lifestyle was spread by shows like *Dallas*, movies like *Urban Cowboy*, and so-called "countrypolitan" singers like Glen Campbell, Dottie West, and Lynn Anderson, who further combined the genre's traditional underpinnings with a more modern, pop-focused sound. More traditional artists like Dolly Parton and Willie Nelson weren't afraid of dipping their toes in this mainstream direction, either. As Chet Atkins famously remarked when asked what typified the Nashville sound, "It's the sound of money."

As the market is fickle, the proliferation of such a sound made country fans a little restless. The countrypolitan sound became less appealing as the '80s wore on, beginning with the rise of the "neotraditionalists" like Reba McEntire and Wynonna Judd, who appealed to the genre's atavistic heart. Writing in *Country Music: A Cultural and Stylistic History*, Jocelyn Neal remarks that the "essence" of the neotraditionalists was "a concerted effort on the part of the musicians and fans alike to reclaim the past of country music for the present, to rekindle traditions that they felt had been lost."

It's not altogether dissimilar from what you might say rap is going through right now, as the genre's outlaw heart has been somewhat tamed by the massive amounts of money to be had. Kanye West is credited with being the first modern rapper to show that you didn't have to be "gangsta" to appeal to big audiences—without him, it's impossible to see rappers like Drake, who openly raps about super-specific emotions usually found in teenaged Livejournals, finding any kind of chart traction.

But the pendulum has arguably swung from criminal and past Kanye into the deracialized, inauthentic pop that cannibalized country in the '80s. Where the mainstream norm was once ringtone rappers like Kid Hurricane and J-Kwon blazing on the charts for a brief moment, old schoolers like Ludacris and Busta Rymes, respectively, guesting on songs by Justin Bieber and the Pussycat Dolls, or Nicki Minaj pandering to her pop fans, it's now Macklemore: a rapper described by Jon Caramanica of the *New York Times* as the "first contextually post-black pop-star rapper," which means none of his success is owed to rap's traditional power structures. Macklemore's appeal as the soberest cheerleader at the turn-up function is obvious, but his meteoric rise to the top presages a souring from "real hip-hop fans," who aren't so enthused that the genre they spent an entire life learning the ways of is now being co-opted by fans with less patience for tradition.

Of course, such complaints end up not mattering in the long run. For as much righteous complaint as there's to be made that the white-washing of rap—a historically black genre—is bundled with America's tendency toward doing things how they've always been done, it's inexorably true that rap has become less of a market curio and more of the entrenched norm. (Certainly, no local news station would ever run a segment on rap as the latest, hottest craze kids are into. They'd rather save their energy for molly and Skrillex.) You could say the same of country, which rebounded from the post-'80s cold snap with mega-stars like Garth Brooks, Tim McGraw, and Faith Hill, who helped solidify pop-country as a way of life and paved the road for acts like Luke Bryan and Florida Georgia Line to come through. After country sales and radio control exploded in the '90s because of those stars, things leveled off to a point that was still far above the '70s boom.

What's more important is that each genre's more traditional prac- 10 titioners don't appear to have any interest in being too harsh about the way things are now, at least not in public. Famously, Macklemore received pretty much no criticism from any of his fellow nominees when he ended up winning the Grammy for Best Rap Album over more artistically deserving albums by Kendrick Lamar, Kanye West, and Drake. (Jay-Z was also nominated.) Of those four, Drake came the closest to a rebuke when he remarked: "This is how the world works: He made a brand of music that appealed to more people than me, Hov, Kanye and Kendrick. Whether people wanna say it's racial, or whether it's just the fact that he tapped into something we can't tap into. That's just how the cards fall."

Similarly, a country singer like Zac Brown hedged his words in criticizing the modern sound pushed by singers like Bryan—he wasn't hating on the sinner, but the sin. To do so would be hypocritical, as though any singer with enough ego to make a full-time career of it isn't trying to get as big as possible—as though it's more ethical to make a Sprite commercial than a song like "Thrift Shop."

The point of all of this is that there's money to be made, and no point in ignoring a constantly growing audience thirsting for both rap and country. Some fans and artists may be battling with those identity issues of how to remain authentic while getting bigger, but the definition of "authentic" continues to shift. Who can decide what "selling out" means in 2014? It's much easier to have fun.

"I think those collaborations came to be because the industry now understands that country music consumers are not a music fan of only one type of music," Karen Stump, senior director of consumer insights at the Country Music Association, told me. "You're not country only or rap only; people like both. I think that's been there for some time, but we recognize it now, so collaborations work well, and the reverse is they help grow the interests of artists and music as a crossover." She points to interior data suggesting that today's modern country fan is, essentially, anyone: young and old, rich and poor, college-educated and not. As the popularity of the music has grown, so has its audience. New York City, the pinko progressive capital of the world, even opened up a country music radio station last year, Nash 94.7, after 17 years without one.

Not every collaboration is destined for success. Florida Georgia Line and Nelly may have hit the top of the charts, but Brad Paisley and LL Cool J weren't received so warmly when they collaborated on the ill-titled, ill-advised, ill-everything'd "Accidental Racist." They were honestly trying to ameliorate lingering tensions (real or imagined) between their respective fan bases, but it came off as a little too on-the-nose. Conversely, the "Cruise" remix succeeded because the subject matter was so remarkably unambitious—it's a song about cruising and having a good time. The world hasn't totally spun around—Tim McGraw aside, it's still more likely to see a rapper on a country song, not the other way around—but we're getting closer. In the end, the promise of the market evens everything out. If you're still proud to not listen to rap or country, you're suddenly in the minority.

Understanding the Text

1. In paragraph 2, Gordon provides a series of examples. What general claim does he support with them?

2. Beginning in paragraph 3 and throughout the rest of the essay, the writer traces parallels between country music and rap music. What are they? Identify three.

Reflection and Response

3. According to Gordon, "You don't necessarily learn that much about someone by asking, 'What type of music do you like?' But you can learn about someone through the music they don't like . . ." (1). Do you agree with these two statements? Why or why not? What can you learn about others from their tastes in music?

4. Gordon writes: "Open disdain of two genres with such contextually racial and socioeconomic backgrounds is a strange thing to proudly claim . . ." (1) What does he mean by this? What "contextually racial and socioeconomic backgrounds" is he referring to?

Making Connections

5. Consider the meaning of the phrase "selling out." The writer claims that for some people, "it's more ethical to make a Sprite commercial than a song like [the Macklemore and Ryan Lewis hit] 'Thrift Shop'" (10). What distinction is he making here? Do you agree with his assertion? Gordon then asks, "Who can decide what 'selling out' means in 2014? It's much easier to have fun" (11). What does "selling out" mean to you? Do you think of music in these terms?

6. In "A Paler Shade of White" (p. 208), Sasha Frere-Jones writes about indie rock's estrangement from black popular music. But he claims that the "most important reason for the decline of musical miscegenation, however, is social progress." Does the recent cross-pollination between country and rap music complicate Frere-Jones's argument in any way? Is it also evidence of "social progress"? Why or why not?

Flashpop/Getty Images

3 | How Do We Make and Consume Music?

For many people, learning to play an instrument at home, or participating in a school band, is a childhood rite of passage. In doing so, they engage in an ancient human activity. For thousands of years, the only way to hear music was to make it yourself or listen to others make it in a live setting. Thomas Edison's 1877 invention of the phonograph changed that: the mechanical reproduction of sound vastly increased access to music, which could now be recorded. Indeed, one story of the last century has been the widening availability of music. From tinfoil and wax cylinders, to vinyl records, magnetic tapes, compact disks, and digital files — it has become easier to listen with each advance in technology. And Americans *are* listening to lots of music. More than 90 percent consume it on a regular basis; on average, they spend $152 on it every year. Much of that spending (52 percent) goes toward live events, but people get their music through a variety of platforms: from commercial radio to increasingly popular streaming services. Technological developments have been integral to the evolution of musical expression as well as musical consumption. That principle is applicable to the development of instruments, for example, whether in the form of ancient flutes fashioned out of bones, electric guitars, or contemporary pitch-correction devices in a recording studio.

From different perspectives, the writers in this chapter explore how we create and listen to music. In "Stop Forcing Your Kids to Learn a Musical Instrument," Mark Oppenheimer challenges the conventional wisdom that learning to play instruments is inherently worthwhile. In a direct response to Oppenheimer, Gracy Olmstead ("Loving Through the Pain: Why Learning an Instrument Matters") defends the value of musical training in childhood. Meghan Daum's witty personal narrative ("Music Is My Bag") recounts her youthful experience as an oboist; her real focus, however, is the eccentric subculture of musically committed children and parents who spontaneously harmonize while singing happy birthday and attend "six-hour rehearsal[s] of the New Jersey All State Band or Orchestra." In "Seduced by Perfect

photo: Flashpop/Getty Images

Pitch: How Auto-Tune Conquered Pop Music," Lessley Anderson offers a perceptive take on the famous pitch-correction effect Auto-Tune, which has become so common during the last two decades. Read "On the Efficiency of AC/DC: Bon Scott versus Brian Johnson" with a sense of irony: in this comic send-up of academic discourse, economist Robert Oxoby appears to settle an old debate in the history of rock music. In "When Things Look Dark, Country Music Gets Sunnier," Tom Jacobs summarizes recent social psychology research on the relationship between economic circumstances and the thematic content of country and pop music. The last two selections, Damon Krukowski's "Making Cents" and George Howard's "Why Artists Should Stop Chasing Spotify's Pennies and Focus on Top Fans," take opposing viewpoints on the changing nature of the music business in the age of streaming.

Stop Forcing Your Kids to Learn a Musical Instrument

Mark Oppenheimer

In this wry and witty essay from the *New Republic*, Mark Oppenheimer upends the conventional wisdom that aspirational activities like music lessons and ballet classes have lasting value for children as they grow up. Indeed, he suspects that in the case of his daughter — and most other cases, as well — such instruction is "pointless." Along the way, he provides an illuminating social history of the "complicated reasons" that caused Americans to take up musical instruments, "or force their children to."

Mark Oppenheimer writes for the *New York Times*, the *Believer*, *Salon*, and many other publications. He is the author of several books, including *Knocking on Heaven's Door: American Religion in the Age of Counterculture* (2003) and *Wisenheimer: A Childhood Subject to Debate* (2010).

Our daughter Rebekah, who is in second grade, takes three after-school classes every week. On Monday there is violin; on Wednesday, Hebrew; and on Thursday, ballet. One of these classes connects her to a religious tradition going back three thousand years. Two of them are pretty well pointless.

I don't mean that as a bad thing. Pointlessness rules, as far as I am concerned. Lots of great activities have little or no point, at least beyond the fact that somebody likes to do them. My annual viewing of *Dazed and Confused* is pointless (it's not as if I didn't get all the nuance by the fifteenth time around). Candy corn is pointless. Watching local Pentecostal preachers on public-access cable is pointless. Hobbies are all the better for having no point beyond the fun they provide. Rebekah enjoys her violin and ballet classes, both after-school at New Haven's terrific Neighborhood Music School. She loves her teachers, and she is proud when she makes progress. That's good enough for me.

But that's not good enough for some parents, who make claims for the utility of music and dance lessons that are, I think, unfounded and overblown. Lessons are fine, and I think it's especially important that all public schools offer music and other arts in their curricula—both for their educational value, and so arts instruction does not become the province only of Americans who can afford to pay for after-school classes. But Americans' emphasis on certain kinds of lessons—like ballet and classical instruments—are just accidents of history, entirely contingent. And if we look closely at why we encourage our children to study music and dance, and what the real benefits are, we will see that our children are taking the wrong lessons, and for the wrong reasons.

So why are so many children taking ballet, violin, piano? Lately, I have been asking my fellow middle-class urbanite parents that question. About dance, they say things like, "Ballet teaches them poise," or, "Ballet helps them be graceful." And about violin or piano they say, "It will give them a lifelong skill," or, "They'll always enjoy listening to music more."

It does not take a rocket scientist, or a Juilliard-trained cellist, to see   5 the flaws in these assertions. First, as to ballet, I propose a test. Imagine we took ten girls (or boys) who had studied ballet from the ages of five to twelve, and then quit, and mixed them in with ten girls (or boys) who had never taken dance. Let's say that we watched these twenty tweens move around their schools for a day: around the cafeteria, the library, the gym, passing notes, sneaking out behind the middle school for a smoke, all the stuff tweens do. Does anyone really believe we could spot the ones who had spent seven years in weekly or biweekly ballet class?

I do not doubt that a ballet teacher or dance aficionado might spot some tell-tale moves—a slip into first position here or there, a certain elegance in a jump during a game of ultimate frisbee. And probably one or two of the ballet students, the best of them, really would appear more graceful than the others. But for the general mass of kids, the dance classes will not have had much impact on how they move. If you don't believe me, then please visit a middle school in a wealthy town, watch children in the lunch line, and try to pick out which ones had studied ballet.

As for the enduring value of music lessons, I propose an even simpler test. Go on Facebook and ask your friends to chime in if, when they were children, they took five years or more of a classical instrument. Then ask all the respondents when they last played their instrument. I tried a version of this at a dinner party recently. There were about ten adults present; I was the only one who had not played an instrument for many years as a child. All of them confessed that they never played their instrument. Whatever it was—violin, piano, saxophone—they had abandoned it. The instrument sat lonely in a closet somewhere, or in the attic of their childhood home. Or their parents off-loaded it in a tag sale years ago.

And the music that these friends listen to as adults—klezmer, Indigo Girls, classic rock—is in each case quite far from what their parents paid for them to study. Their studies of cello had not made them into fans of Bach. And unless I am mistaken, Shinichi Suzuki didn't include Rush in his violin books.

Now it is clearly the case that if *nobody* studied ballet or violin, we would have no professional orchestras or ballet companies. That would be a great loss. But for such art forms to persist, it is only necessary that the most eager and gifted students persist in their studies. I'm all for lots of children trying classical music or dance, but we no more need millions of fourth-year violin students than we need millions of fourth-year origami students. We all love paper cranes, I think, but we aren't rushing to give our children to the cause.

Before the twentieth century, there was a good reason for anyone to   10
study music: If you couldn't make the music yourself, then you would rarely hear it. Before the radio and the phonograph, any music in the house was produced by the family itself. So it made sense to play fiddle, piano, jug, whatever. And before urbanization and the automobile, most people did not have easy, regular access to concerts. Of course, small-town people could come together for occasional concerts, to play together or to hear local troupes or traveling bands. Growing up in the sticks, you still might see Shakespeare performed, and a touring opera company could bring you Mozart. But very infrequently. If music was to be a part of your daily life, it had to be homemade.

But there were other, more complicated reasons that people took up instruments, or forced their children to. As the historian Susie Steinbach writes in *Understanding the Victorians*, in the mid-nineteenth-century the piano, which had always been handmade and tended to reside in upper class parlors, became an accessible, middle-class status symbol, as fit for a tradesman's house as for Emma Woodhouse's. "By the 1850s and 1860s many pianos were manufactured in Germany and in the United States as well as in Britain," Steinbach writes, "and were made by machine; both changes made pianos less expensive."

Changes in financing helped, too: The advent of the installment plan brought pianos to people who did not have vast capital. As the price of instruments dropped, music lessons became the burden of the well-bred girl, or of the girl whose parents hoped to massage some breeding into her.

By the 1880s, when the United States began filling up with unwashed immigrants, a whole class of do-gooder, piano-taught ladies believed that one way to acculturate the new immigrants was to offer them, especially the children, musical instruction. The institutions of the settlement-house movement, as it became known, offered much more than music classes; they provided instruction in English, the trades, home economics, and many arts. But music was everywhere seen as one important key to the cabinet of proper, middle-class ways.

That belief helped animate the founders of the Educational Alliance, Henry Street Settlement, and Third Street Music School Settlement, all founded in downtown New York City between 1889 and 1894; Settlement Music School in Philadelphia (1908); the settlement houses that became Community Music Center of Boston (1910); Neighborhood House, which became New Haven's Neighborhood Music School (1911); and the Cleveland Music School Settlement (1912). Not all of those schools were founded specifically to teach music, but even those that were not, and many like them across the country, quickly included music classes in their offerings.

The schools have stayed, even as the nationality of the immigrants 15 has changed. At the Educational Alliance, where my wife took piano lessons as a child, the clientele used to be mainly Jewish; more recently, it's Chinese, Latino, and much else besides. But the music classes go on, the product of a couple centuries of parents' aspirations for their own children and others'. The schools have long grown beyond their initial mission of acculturating immigrants, and are now educating the middle-class children and grandchildren of the first waves of students.

The classes are not a bad thing. Studying music or dance over a long time teaches perseverance and can build self-confidence. But then again, studying *anything* over a long time teaches perseverance and can build self-confidence. There is no special virtue in knowing how to play the violin, unless you have a special gift for the violin. Otherwise, you're learning the same valuable lessons that you'd get from karate class, or from badminton. Or from endless hours of foosball.

I am not saying that children should stop learning stuff outside of school (although some days, when I see how overscheduled some children are, that's precisely what I want to say). We just need to sign them up for classes that make more sense, given that it's 2013, not 1860, and that I don't need a violin-playing daughter to cement my class status. Look, I love the Mendelssohn Violin Concerto, but one could make the argument that Rebekah would be better off learning to play the Lumineers' "Ho Hey" on guitar. That skill would certainly be more of an asset at summer camp.

> "The classes are not a bad thing. Studying music or dance over a long time teaches perseverance and can build self-confidence. But then again, studying *anything* over a long time teaches perseverance and can build self-confidence."

We can probably all agree that it's worthwhile for children (as well as their parents) to try new activities, and that there is virtue in mastering difficult disciplines. So what challenges should we be tackling, if not ballet and classical music? How about auto repair? At least one Oppenheimer should be able to change the oil, and it isn't me. It may as well be one of my daughters. Sewing would be good. And if it has to be an instrument, I'd say bass or guitar. The adults I know who can play guitar can actually be seen playing their guitars. And as any rock guitarist will tell you, there is a shortage of bassists.

But I do not believe that all artistic pursuits, or all disciplines that one studies, should be judged for their usefulness. The sublimity of art is tied, after all, to its uselessness (cf. *Dazed and Confused*). More than anything, I want children to find pursuits, whether useful or not, that they can take with them into adulthood. For a while, a number of children in my neighborhood were taking ukulele lessons. I don't much like the ukulele, and I think I successfully kept my daughters from knowing what their playmates were up to. But I was heartened by the whimsy of it all, and I kind of wish that the little gang of kids had stuck with it. Before too long, they might have gotten pretty good. At the very least, it might have kept them away from ballet.

As it happens, a trend like what I am advocating may be under way. My friend Noah Bloom, a trumpeter who works at Neighborhood Music School and used to be at Church Street School for Music and Art, in Lower Manhattan, told me that at Church Street there were "as many electric guitarists and young singers wanting to be Green Day or some hot pop artist as there were kids wanting to be classical pianists." He also told me about School of Rock, a chain with dozens of franchised schools and camps, here and abroad, offering lessons geared specifically to aspiring kiddie-rockers. The School of Rock only teaches guitar, bass, keyboards, vocals, and drums. "They're our competition," Bloom said.

Rebekah, for her part, will continue with ballet. And violin. Periodically, we ask her if she'd like to quit, and she always says no. That's good enough for us. If she finds a lifelong pursuit, that's great. But if one evening, at her usual practice hour, she decides enough is enough, maybe I'll suggest the guitar. Or maybe I'll just ask if she wants to sit with me on the couch and watch *Dazed and Confused*.

Understanding the Text

1. Oppenheimer writes, "Before the twentieth century, there was a good reason for anyone to study music" (10). What was the reason?
2. According to Oppenheimer, in what ways are contemporary piano and violin lessons for children a legacy of social and immigration history, as well as class aspiration?

Reflection and Response

3. In paragraph 5, the writer proposes a test to determine the enduring value of ballet lessons for children. What is the test? Does it seem like a good way to determine the value of ballet? Why or why not?

4. Oppenheimer claims: "There is no special virtue in knowing how to play the violin, unless you have a special gift for the violin. Otherwise, you're learning the same valuable lessons that you'd get from karate class, or from badminton. Or from endless hours of foosball" (16). Do you agree? Are all these activities equal, in terms of "valuable lessons"? Explain your answer.

Making Connections

5. The writer makes several claims about the lasting value of learning a musical instrument or taking dance as a child. How would you respond to his arguments? How do your own experiences with (or without) music or dance lessons shape your response? Has your early training — or lack thereof — affected your life in any important ways?

6. In "Music Is My Bag" (p. 136), Meghan Daum recalls her childhood and teenage years as a committed oboist. At the age of twenty-one, she stopped playing the instrument. Does her example support Oppenheimer's argument? Does it refute it or problematize it? Explain your answer.

Loving through the Pain: Why Learning an Instrument Matters

Gracy Olmstead

Writing for the *American Conservative*, Gracy Olmstead responds to Mark Oppenheimer's essay ("Stop Forcing Your Kids to Learn a Musical Instrument"). Arguing for the enduring value of classical music training, she recalls her own experiences as she learned the piano and the violin: "Through hours of repetition with a metronome, practicing specific bowing techniques, perfecting my vibrato, and listening to Anne-Sophie Mutter, classical music became my own. It became part of me." Ultimately, Olmstead suggests the connection between the experience of difficulty and the nature of "true passion."

Gracy Olmstead is a senior writer at the *American Conservative*. Her work has also appeared in the *Washington Times*, *Humane Pursuits*, the *Federalist*, and other publications.

Mark Oppenheimer started a conversation over at the *New Republic* on whether parents ought to force their children to learn a classical instrument. He contended that, despite arguments for the education's lifelong value, his grown associates have experienced few benefits from their former musical training:

> All of them confessed that they never played their instrument. Whatever it was — violin, piano, saxophone — they had abandoned it. The instrument sat lonely in a closet somewhere, or in the attic of their childhood home. Or their parents off-loaded it in a tag sale years ago. And the music that these friends listen to as adults — klezmer, Indigo Girls, classic rock — is in each case quite far from what their parents paid for them to study. Their studies of cello had not made them into fans of Bach.

In light of this, Oppenheimer argues that only the inspired student should delve into classical training. Although he sees the benefit of the perseverance and self-confidence learned, he notes, "Studying anything over a long time teaches perseverance and can build self-confidence. There is no special virtue in knowing how to play the violin, unless you have a special gift for the violin. Otherwise, you're learning the same valuable lessons that you'd get from karate class, or from badminton. Or from endless hours of foosball."

Oppenheimer is right: many of the lessons learned from the practice room are also inculcated on the basketball court, tennis field, or machine shop. Why should students be forced to pursue classical music? Paul Berman, a Senior Editor at *TNR*, responded to this question on Friday. He contended that the study of classical music is, in his words, "a spiritual enterprise": "I do not mean to say that classical music is better than other kinds of music," he writes, ". . . But I do think that classical music is, in some respect, bigger than other kinds of music. The music has been going on for five hundred years as a self-conscious tradition, dedicated to an extended meditation on a series of musical structures so limited as nearly to be arithmetical."

This is true of my experience with classical music, as well: it is the   5 "mother art." When you pour your heart and soul into learning her quirks and essence, she rewards you immensely—not just in the classical strain, but in every other realm of musical study. Those trained classically usually find other genres easy to pick up. I've met several classically trained guitarists whose jazz and rock solos put others to shame. They learned the "mother art," and her demanding rigor made other styles accessible.

I began piano lessons at age seven. Though auditory memorization came naturally to me, sight-reading was a long and painstaking process. I wonder at times whether building that reflex also enhanced my speed-reading. Early on in my classical training, I developed a love for Romantic music—especially Debussy, Brahms, and Beethoven. During one of my first competitions, I played a simple romantic-era waltz. I was so in love with the piece, I forgot where I was. I forgot anything and everything—except those soulful, otherworldly notes. Indeed, I was so swept up in the moment, I almost forgot how to end the piece. But after the song's conclusion, when I turned around, the judge was smiling at me. Despite my trance-induced memory hiccup, he awarded me the highest prize for my age group. I think he knew I was in love with the music.

My love of baroque music didn't come until I played violin and began lessons with a wonderfully gifted Bulgarian violinist. She was the most demanding, detailed, and brilliant teacher I've ever had. Through her rigor and attention to detail, Bach came alive. I saw the beauty in his Sonatas and Partitas, the complexity and artistry blossoming in every note. I realized the truth Berman describes, how

> If you study Bach with sufficient ardor, instrument in hand, you ought to be able to discover that, at moments, you and Bach have merged. You ought to discover that Bach's inquiries into mathematical figures are your own inquiries, and Bach's ecstasies are yours, as well. Bach was a genius, and you, too, are a genius, when you

perform his work—even if some person listening to you trample clumsily over the score may conclude that you are an oaf. Your purpose in playing is not to impress anyone else, though, nor to entertain.

"Through hours of repetition with a metronome, practicing specific bowing techniques, perfecting my vibrato, and listening to Anne-Sophie Mutter, classical music became my own. It became part of me."

Through hours of repetition with a metronome, practicing specific bowing techniques, perfecting my vibrato, and listening to Anne-Sophie Mutter, classical music became my own. It became part of me. Although I do not play seriously anymore, I still enjoy performing with friends. I don't constantly listen to classical, but I still enjoy it—and believe its artistry taught me to hunt for jazz, rock, and even pop music that employs similar complexity.

But we must return to the question of force: did my parents force   10
me to play piano or violin? No, they did not. There were times when I wanted to stop playing: for instance, in the first few months of violin, when everything still sounded squeaky and dissonant, or when my months of vibrato practice still resulted in sickening see-saw sounds.

But whenever I went to my father and said I wanted to quit, he responded with this story: "You know, my parents wanted me to play piano and signed me up for lessons. But after only a short time, I told them I wanted to quit. They let me—and I've regretted it my whole life." He would always ask me to "give it one more month, just to see if it gets better."

I would always agree. And lo and behold—after one month, everything felt better. My tone had improved, the vibrato had finally crystallized, the painfully difficult piece was becoming a personal favorite. In my opinion, this lesson served me better than any force would have: my father taught me that what we want is not always clear in the present moment. Our emotions are rather fickle, but true love is built through perseverance: if we persist through the moment of distaste, we may develop a true passion.

Understanding the Text

1. The writer describes classical music as the "mother art" (5). What does she mean by this? What implications does the claim have for her overall argument?

2. How has Olmstead's musical training remained with her, even though she no longer plays "seriously"?

Reflection and Response

3. In paragraph 8, Olmstead states that when you perform the works of a composer like Bach, your "purpose in playing is not to impress anyone else, though, nor to entertain." But does Olmstead ever state or imply a performer's true "purpose in playing"? What purpose do you infer from the essay?

4. In paragraph 10, she writes: "But we must return to the question of force: did my parents force me to play piano or violin? No, they did not." Why is this such a key question? How does she answer it?

Making Connections

5. Olmstead writes explicitly in response to Mark Oppenheimer's essay "Stop Forcing Your Kids to Learn a Musical Instrument" (p. 126). How would you compare her voice and tone, as a writer, with Oppenheimer's? How might their stylistic differences reflect their different views of training in classical music?

6. In her conclusion, Olmstead writes, "Our emotions are rather fickle, but true love is built through perseverance: if we persist through the moment of distaste, we may develop a true passion" (12). Do you agree that "true passion" emerges in this way? Can you narrate or describe an experience from your own life that supports her contention?

Music Is My Bag

Meghan Daum

In this sharply observed personal narrative, which originally appeared in *Harper's*, writer Meghan Daum recalls and reflects upon her — and her family's — immersion in "the unmistakable world of Music Is My Bag": a peculiar culture of pre-adolescent amateurish obsession, strongly marked by "a sense that the enthusiasm developed at a time when the person was lacking in some significant area of social or intellectual life." But the trappings of this subculture ultimately alienated her from the passion for music that Music Is My Bag is supposed to sustain.

Meghan Daum is a columnist for the *Los Angeles Times*. She has written for the *New Yorker*, *Vogue*, the *Atlantic*, and other publications. Her books include *Life Would Be Perfect If I Lived in That House* (2010) and *The Unspeakable: And Other Subjects of Discussion* (2014).

The image I want to get across is that of the fifteen-year-old boy with the beginning traces of a mustache who hangs out in the band room after school playing the opening bars of a Billy Joel song on the piano. This is the kid who, in the interests of adopting some semblance of personal style, wears a fedora hat and a scarf with a black-and-white design of a piano keyboard. This is the kid who, in addition to having taught himself some tunes from the *Songs from the Attic* sheet music he bought at the local Sam Ash, probably also plays the trombone in the marching band, and experienced a seminal moment one afternoon as he vaguely flirted with a not-yet-kissed, clarinet-playing girl, a girl who is none too popular but whose propensity for leaning on the piano as the boy plays the opening chords of "Captain Jack" give him a clue as to the social possibilities that might be afforded him via the marching band.

If the clarinet-playing girl is an average student musician, she carries her plastic Selmer in the standard-issue black plastic case. If she has demonstrated any kind of proficiency, she carries her Selmer in a tote bag that reads "Music Is My Bag." The boy in the piano-key scarf definitely has music as his bag. He may not yet have the tote bag, but the hat, the Billy Joel, the tacit euphoria brought on by a sexual awakening that, for him, centers entirely around band, is all he needs to be delivered into the unmistakable realm that is Music Is My Bagdom.

I grew up in Music Is My Bag culture. The walls of my parents' house were covered with framed art posters from musical events: The San Francisco Symphony's 1982 production of *St. Matthew's Passion*, The Metropolitan Opera's 1976 production of *Aida*, the original Broadway production of *Sweeney Todd*. Ninety percent of the books on the shelves were about music, if not actual musical scores. Childhood ceramics projects made by my brother and me were painted with eighth notes and treble clef signs. We owned a deck of cards with portraits of the great composers on the back. A baby grand piano overtook the room that would have been the dining room if my parents hadn't forgone a table and renamed it "the music room." This room also contained an imposing hi-fi system and a $300 wooden music stand. Music played at all times: Brahms, Mendelssohn, cast recordings of Sondheim musicals, a cappella Christmas albums. When my father sat down with a book, he read musical scores, humming quietly and tapping his foot. When I was ten, my mother decided we needed to implement a before-dinner ritual akin to saying grace, so she composed a short song, asking us all to contribute a lyric, and we held hands and sang it before eating. My lyric was, "There's a smile on our face and it seems to say all the wonderful things we've all done today." My mother insisted on harmonizing at the end. She also did this when singing "Happy Birthday."

Harmonizing on songs like "Happy Birthday" is a clear indication of the Music Is My Bag personality. If one does not have an actual bag that reads "Music Is My Bag" — as did the violist in the chamber music trio my mother set up with some women from the Unitarian Church — a $300 music stand and musical-note coasters will more than suffice. To avoid confusion, let me also say that there are many different Bags in life. Some friends of my parents have a $300 dictionary stand, a collection of silver bookmarks, and once threw a dinner party wherein the guests had to dress up as members of the Bloomsbury Group. These people are Literature Is My Bag. I know people who are Movies Are My Bag (detectable by key chains shaped like projectors, outdated copies of *Halliwell's Film Guide*, and one too many T-shirts from things like the San Jose Film Festival), people who are Cats Are My Bag (self-explanatory), and, perhaps most annoyingly, Where I Went To College Is My Bag (Yale running shorts, plastic Yale tumblers, Yale Platinum Plus MasterCard, and, yes, even Yale screensavers — all this in someone aged forty or more, the perennial contributor to the class notes).

Having a Bag connotes the state of being overly interested in something, and yet, in a certain way, not interested enough. It has a hobbyish quality to it, a sense that the enthusiasm developed at a time when the enthusiast was lacking in some significant area of social or intellectual life. Music Is My Bag is the mother of all Bags, not just because in the early 1980s some consumer force of the public radio fund-drive variety distributed a line of tote bags that displayed that slogan, but because its adherents, or, as they tend to call themselves, "music lovers," give off an aura that distinguishes them from the rest of the population. It's an aura that has to do with a sort of benign cluelessness, a condition that, even in middle age, smacks of that phase between prepubescence and real adolescence. Music Is My Bag people have a sexlessness to them. There is a pastiness to them. They can never seem to find a good pair of jeans. You can spot them on the street, the female French horn player in concert dress hailing a cab to Lincoln Center around seven o'clock in the evening, her earrings too big, her hairstyle unchanged since 1986. The fifty-something recording engineer with the running shoes and the shoulder bag. The Indiana marching band kids in town for the Macy's Thanksgiving Day Parade, snapping photos of each other in front of the Hard Rock Cafe, having sung their parts from the band arrangement of *Hello Dolly* the whole way on the bus, thinking, knowing, that it won't get better than this. Like all Music Is My Bag people, they are a little too in love with the trappings. They know what their boundaries are and load up their allotted space with memorabilia, saving the certificates of participation from regional festivals, the composer-a-month calendars, the Mostly Mozart posters. Their sincerity trumps attempts at snideness. The boys' sarcasm only goes a fraction of the way there, the girls will never be great seducers. They grow up to look like high school band directors even if they're not. They give their pets names like Wolfgang and Gershwin. Their hemlines are never quite right.

I played the oboe. This is not an instrument to be taken lightly. The oboist runs a high risk of veering into Music Is My Bag culture, mostly because to get beyond the entry level is to give oneself over to an absorption with technique that can make a person vulnerable to certain vagaries of a subcategory, the oboe phylum. This inevitably leads to the genus of wind ensemble culture, which concerns itself with the socio-political infrastructure of the woodwind section, the disproportionate number of solo passages, a narcissistic pride in sounding the A that tunes the orchestra. Not many people play the oboe. It's a difficult instrument, beautiful when played well, horrifying when played poorly. I was self-conscious about playing the oboe, mostly because so many people confuse it with the bassoon, its much larger, ganglier cousin in the double-reed family. The act of playing the oboe, unlike the graceful arm positions of the flute or the violin, is not a photogenic one. The embouchure puckers the face into a grimace; my childhood and adolescence is documented by photos that make me look slightly deformed—the lipless girl. It's not an instrument for the vain. Oboe playing revolves almost entirely around saliva. Spit gets caught in the keys and the joints and must be blown out using cigarette rolling paper as a blotter (a scandalous drugstore purchase for a twelve-year-old). Spit can accumulate on the floor if you play for too long. Spit must constantly be sucked out from both sides of the reed.

The fragile, temperamental reed is the player's chronic medical condition. It must be tended to constantly. It must be wet but never too wet, hard enough to emit a decent sound, but soft enough to blow air through. The oboist must never stray far from moisture; the reed is forever in her mouth, in a paper cup of water that teeters on the music stand, being doused at a drinking fountain in Parsippany High School at the North Jersey Regional Band and Orchestra Audition. After a certain age, the student oboist must learn to make her own reeds, build them from bamboo using knives and shavers. Most people don't realize this. Reed-making is an eighteenth-century exercise, something that would seem to require an apprenticeship before undertaking solo. But oboists, occupying a firm, albeit wet, patch of ground under the tattered umbrella of Music Is My Bag, never quite live in the same era as everyone else.

Though I did, at one point, hold the title of second-best high school player in the state of New Jersey, I was a mediocre oboist. My discipline was lacking, my enthusiasm virtually nil, and my comprehension of rhythm (in keeping with a lifelong math phobia) held me back considerably. But being without an aptitude for music was, in my family, tantamount to being a Kennedy who knows nothing of politics. Aptitude was something, perhaps even the only thing, I possessed. As indifferent to the oboe as I was—and I once began an orchestra rehearsal without noticing that I had neglected to screw the bell, which is the entire bottom portion, onto the rest of my instrument—I managed to be good enough to play in the New Jersey All State High School Orchestra as well as a local adult symphony. I even gained acceptance into a music conservatory. These aren't staggering accomplishments unless you consider the fact that I rarely practiced. If I had practiced with any amount of regularity, I could have been, as my parents would have liked me to be, one of those kids who was schlepped to Juilliard on Saturdays. If I had practiced slightly more than that, I could have gone to Juilliard for college. If I had practiced a lot I could have ended up in the New York Philharmonic. This is not an exaggeration, merely a moot point. I didn't practice. I haven't picked up the oboe since my junior year in college, where, incidentally, I sat first chair in the orchestra even though I did not practice once the entire time.

I never practiced and yet I always practiced. My memory is always of being unprepared, yet I was forced to sit in the chair for so many hours that I suspect something else must have been at work, a lack of consciousness about it, an inability to practice on my own. "Practice" was probably among the top five words spoken in our family, the other four probably being the names of our family members. Today, almost ten years since I've practiced, the word has lost the resonance of our usage.

I now think of practice in terms of law or medicine. There is a television show called *The Practice*, and it seems odd to me that I never associate the word sprawled across the screen with the word that wove relentlessly throughout our family discourse. For my entire childhood and adolescence, practicing was an ongoing condition. It was both a given and a punishment. When we were bad, we practiced. When we were idle, we practiced. Before dinner and TV and friends coming over and bedtime and a thousand other things that beckoned with the possibility of taking place without all that harrowing noise, we practiced. "You have practicing and homework," my mother said every day. In that order. My father said the same thing without the homework part.

Much of the reason I could never quite get with the oboe-playing program was that I developed, at a very young age, a deep contempt for the Music Is My Bag world. Instead of religion, my family had music, and it was the church against which I rebelled. I had clergy for parents. My father: professional composer and arranger, keyboard player and trombonist, brother of a high school band director in Illinois. My mother: pianist and music educator of the high school production of *Carousel* genre. My own brother a reluctant Christ figure. A typically restless second child in youth (he quit piano lessons but later discovered he could play entirely by ear), my brother recently completed the final mix of a demo CD of songs he wrote and performed—mid-eighties pop, late Doobie Brothers groove. His house is littered with Billy Joel and Bruce Hornsby sheet music, back issues of *Stereo Review*, the liner notes to the digital remastering of John Williams's score for *Star Wars*. Music is the Bag.

I compose songs in my sleep. I can't do it awake. I'll dream of song- 10 writers singing onstage. I'll hear them perform new songs, songs I've never heard, songs I therefore must have written. In childhood I never put one thought toward composing a song. It would have been like composing air, creating more of something of which there was already quite enough. Wind players like flutists and saxophonists need as much air as they can get. Oboists are always trying to get rid of air. They calibrate what they need to get the reed to vibrate, end up using even less, and dispense with the rest out the corners of their mouths. It's all about exhaling. On an eighth rest, they're as likely to blow air out as they are to steal a breath. There's always too much air for oboists, too much of everything, too many bars when they're not playing and too many bars where there's hardly anyone playing but them, too many percussion players dropping triangles on the floor, too many violinists playing "Eleanor Rigby" before the rehearsal starts. Orchestras have only two oboists, first chair and second chair, pilot and copilot, though the "co" in this case is, like all "co's," a misnomer. The second oboist is the perpetual backup system, the one on call, the one who jumps in and saves the other when his reed dries up in the middle of a solo, when he misses his cue, when he freezes in panic before trying to hit a high D. I've been first oboist and I've been second oboist and, let me tell you, first is better, but not by much. It's still the oboe. Unlike the gregarious violinist or the congenial cellist, the oboist is a lone wolf. To play the oboe in an orchestra is to complete an obstacle course of solos and duets with the first flutist who, if she is hard-core Music Is My Bag, will refer to herself as a "floutist." Oboe solos dot the great symphonies like land mines, the pizzicati that precede them are drumrolls, the conductor's pointing finger an arrow for the whole audience to see: Here comes the oboe, two bars until the oboe, now, now. It's got to be nailed, one flubbed arpeggio, one flat half note, one misplaced pinky in the middle of a run of sixteenth notes, and everyone will hear, everyone.

My parents' presence at a high school orchestra concert turned what should have been a routine event into something akin to the finals of the Olympic women's figure skating long program. Even from the blinding, floodlit stage I could practically see them in the audience, clucking at every error, grimacing at anything even slightly out of tune. Afterwards, when the other parents — musically illiterate chumps — were patting their kids on the head and loading the tuba into the station wagon, I would receive my critique. "You were hesitating in the second movement of the Haydn Variations." "You over-anticipated in the berceuse section of the Stravinsky." "Your tone was excellent in the first movement but then your chops ran out." My brother, who was forced for a number of years to play the French horn, was reduced to a screaming fight with our father in the school parking lot, the kind of fight only possible between fathers and sons. He'd bumbled too many notes, played out of tune, committed some treasonous infraction against the family reputation. My father gave him the business on the way out to the car, eliciting the alto curses of a fourteen-year-old, pages of music everywhere, an instrument case slammed on the pavement.

This sort of rebellion was not my style. I cried instead. I cried in the seventh grade when the letter telling me I'd been accepted to the North Jersey regional orchestra arrived three days late. I cried in the tenth grade, when I ended up in the All State Band instead of the orchestra. I cried when I thought I'd given a poor recital (never mind that the audience thought I was brilliant — all morons), cried before lessons (under-prepared), cried after lessons (sentenced to a week of reviewing the loathsome F-sharp étude). Mostly I cried during practice drills supervised by my father. These were torture sessions wherein some innocent tooting would send my father racing downstairs from his attic study, screaming "Count, count, you're not counting! Jesus Christ!" Out would come a pencil—if not an actual conductor's baton—hitting the music stand, forcing me to repeat the tricky fingerings again and again, speeding up the tempo so I'd be sure to hit each note when we took it back down to real time. These sessions would last for hours, my mouth muscles shaking from atrophy, tears welling up from fatigue and exasperation. If we had a copy of the piano part, my mother would play the accompaniment, and together my parents would bark commands. "Articulate the eighth notes more. More staccato on the tonguing. Don't tap your foot, tap your toe inside your shoe." The postman heard a lot of this. The neighbors heard all of it. After practicing we'd eat dinner, but not before that song—"There's a smile on our face, and it seems to say all the wonderful things . . ." "Good practice session today," my mother would say, dishing out the casserole, WQXR's *Symphony Hall* playing over the kitchen speakers. "Yup, sounding pretty good," my father would say. "How about one more go at it before bed?"

My mother called my oboe a "horn." This infuriated me. "Do you have your horn?" she'd ask every single morning. "Do you need your horn for school today?" She maintained that this terminology was technically correct, that among musicians, a "horn" was anything into which air was blown. My oboe was a $4,000 instrument, high-grade black grenadilla with sterling silver keys. It was no horn. But such semantics are a staple of Music Is My Bag, the overfamiliar stance that reveals a desperate need for subcultural affiliation, the musical equivalent of people in the magazine business who refer to publications like *Glamour* and *Forbes* as "books." As is indicated by the use of "horn," there's a subtly macho quality to Music Is My Bag. The persistent insecurity of musicians, especially classical musicians, fosters a kind of jargon that would be better confined to the military or major league baseball. Cellists talk about rock stops and rosin as though they were comparing canteen belts or brands of glove grease. They have their in-jokes and aphorisms, "The rock stops here," "Eliminate Violins In Our Schools."

I grew up surrounded by phrases like "rattle off that solo," "nail that lick," and "build up your chops." Like acid-washed jeans, "chops" is a word that should only be invoked by rock and roll guitarists but is more often uttered with the flailing, badly timed anti-authority of the high school clarinet player. Like the violinist who plays "Eleanor Rigby" before rehearsal, the clarinet player's relationship to rock and roll maintains its distance. Rock and roll is about sex. It is something unloved by parents and therefore unloved by Music Is My Bag people, who make a vocation of pleasing their parents, of studying trig and volunteering at the hospital and making a run for the student government even though they're well aware they have no chance of winning. Rock and roll is careless and unstudied. It might possibly involve drinking. It most certainly involves dancing. It flies in the face of the central identity of Music Is My Baggers, who chose as their role models those painfully introverted characters from young adult novels—"the klutz," "the bookworm," "the late bloomer." When given a classroom assignment to write about someone who inspires her, Music Is My Bag will write about her grandfather or perhaps Jean-Pierre Rampal. If the bad-attitude kid in the back row writes about AC/DC's Angus Young, Music Is My Bag will believe in her heart that this student should receive a failing grade. Rock and roll is not, as her parents would say when the junior high drama club puts on a production of *Grease*, "appropriate for this age group." Even in the throes of adolescence, Music Is My Bag will deny adolescence. Even at age sixteen, she will hold her ears when the rock and roll gets loud, saying it ruins her sense of overtones, saying she has sensitive ears. Like a retiree, she will classify the whole genre as nothing but a bunch of noise, though it is likely she is a fan of Yes.

During the years that I was a member of the New Jersey All State 15 Orchestra I would carpool to rehearsals with the four or so other kids from my town who made All State every year. This involved spending as much as two hours each way in station wagons driven by people's parents and, inevitably, the issue would arise of what music would be played in the car. Among the most talented musicians in school was a freshman who, in addition to being hired by the Boston Symphony Orchestra at age twenty-two, possessed, as a fifteen-year-old, a ripe enthusiasm for the singer Amy Grant. This was back in the mid-1980s when Amy Grant's hits were still relegated to the Christian charts. Our flute-playing carpool-mate loved Amy Grant. Next to Prokofiev and the Hindemith Flute Sonata, Amy Grant occupied the number-one spot in this girl's studious, late-blooming heart. Since her mother, like many parents of Baggers, was devoted solely to her daughter's musical and academic career, she did most of the driving to these boony spots—Upper Chatham High School, Monmouth Regional, Long Branch Middle School. Mile after New Jersey Turnpike mile, we were serenaded by the wholesome synthesizers of songs like "Saved By Love" and "Wait for the Healing," only to spill out of the car and take no small relief in the sound of twenty-five of New Jersey's best student violinists playing "Eleanor Rigby" before the six-hour rehearsal.

To participate in a six-hour rehearsal of the New Jersey All State Band or Orchestra is to enter a world so permeated by Music Is My Bagdom that it becomes possible to confuse the subculture with an entire species, as if Baggers, like lobsters or ferns, require special conditions in order to

"To participate in a six-hour rehearsal of the New Jersey All State Band or Orchestra is to enter a world so permeated by Music Is My Bagdom that it becomes possible to confuse the subculture with an entire species, as if Baggers, like lobsters or ferns, require special conditions in order to thrive."

thrive. Their ecosystem is the auditorium and the adjacent band room, any space that makes use of risers. To eat lunch and dinner in these venues is to see the accessories of Badgom tumble from purses, knapsacks, and totes; here more than anyplace are the real McCoys, actual Music Is My Bag bags, canvas satchels filled with stereo Walkmen and A.P. math homework and Trapper Keeper notebooks featuring the piano-playing Schroeder from the *Peanuts* comic strip. The dinner break is when I would embark on oboe maintenance, putting the reed in water, swabbing the instrument dry, removing the wads of wax that, during my orthodontic years, I placed over my front teeth to keep the inside of my mouth from bleeding. Just as I had hated the entropy of recess back in my grade-school years, I loathed the dinner breaks at All State rehearsals. To maximize rehearsal time, the wind section often ate separately from the strings, which left me alone with the band types. They'd wolf down their sandwiches and commence with their jam session, a cacophonous white noise of scales, finger exercises, and memorized excerpts from their hometown marching band numbers. During these dinner breaks I'd generally hang with the other oboist. For some reason, this was almost always a tall girl who wore sneakers with corduroy pants and a turtleneck with nothing over it. This is fairly typical Music Is My Bag garb, though oboists have a particular spin on it, a spin characterized more than anything by lack of spin. Given the absence in most classical musicians of a style gene, this is probably a good thing. Oboists don't accessorize. They don't wear buttons on their jackets that say "Oboe Power" or "Who Are You Going to Tune To?"

There's high-end Bagdom and low-end Bagdom, with a lot of room in between. Despite my parents' paramilitary practice regimes, I have to give them credit for being fairly high-end Baggers. There were no piano-key scarves in our house, no "World's Greatest Trombonist" figurines, no plastic tumblers left over from my father's days as director of the Stanford University Marching Band. Such accessories are the mandate of the lowest tier of Music Is My Bag, a stratum whose mascot is P.D.Q. Bach, whose theme song is "Piano Man," and whose regional representative is the kid in high school who plays not only the trumpet but the piano, saxophone, flute, string bass, accordion, and wood block. This kid, considered a wunderkind by his parents and the rest of the band community, plays none of these instruments well, but the fact that he knows so many different sets of fingerings, the fact that he has the potential to earn some college money by performing as a one-man band at the annual state teacher's conference, makes him a hometown hero. He may not be a football player. He may not even gain access to the Ivy League. But in the realm of Music Is My Bag, the kid who plays every instrument, particularly when he can play Billy Joel songs on every instrument, is the Alpha Male.

The flip side of the one-man-band kid are those Music Is My Baggers who are not musicians at all. These are the kids who twirl flags or rifles in the marching band, kids who blast music in their rooms and play not air guitar but air keyboards, their hands fluttering out in front of them, the hand positions not nearly as important as the attendant head motions. This is the essence of Bagdom. It is to take greater pleasure in the reverb than the melody, to love the lunch break more than the rehearsal, the rehearsal more than the performance, the clarinet case more than the clarinet. It is to think nothing of sending away for the deluxe packet of limited-edition memorabilia that is being sold for the low, low price of one's entire personality. It is to let the trinkets do the talking.

I was twenty-one when I stopped playing the oboe. I wish I could come up with a big, dramatic reason why. I wish I could say that I sustained some kind of injury that prevented me from playing (it's hard to imagine what kind of injury could sideline an oboist—a lip strain? Carpal tunnel?) or that I was forced to sell my oboe in order to help a family member in crisis or, better yet, that I suffered a violent attack in which my oboe was used as a weapon against me before being stolen and melted down for artillery. But the truth, I'm ashamed to say, has more to do with what in college I considered to be an exceptionally long walk from my dormitory to the music building, and the fact that I was wrapped up in a lot of stuff that, from my perspective at the time, precluded the nailing of Rachmaninoff licks. Without the prodding of my parents or the structure of a state-run music education program, my oboe career had to run on self-motivation alone—not an abundant resource—and when my senior year started I neither registered for private lessons nor signed up for the orchestra, dodging countless calls from the director imploring me to reassume my chair.

Since then, I haven't set foot in a rehearsal room, put together a fold- 20 ing music stand, fussed with a reed, marked up music, practiced scales, tuned an orchestra or performed any of the countless activities that had dominated my existence up until that point. There are moments every now and then when I'll hear the oboe-dominated tenth movement of the Bach Mass in B Minor or the berceuse section of Stravinsky's *Firebird* and long to find a workable reed and pick up the instrument again. But then I imagine how terrible I'll sound after eight dormant years and put the whole idea out of my mind before I start to feel sad about it. I can still smell the musty odor of the inside of my oboe case, the old-ladyish whiff of the velvet lining and the tubes of cork grease and the damp fabric of the key pads. Unlike the computer on which I now work, my oboe had the sense of being an ancient thing. Brittle and creaky, it was vulnerable when handled by strangers. It needed to be packed up tight, dried out in just the right places, kept away from the heat and the cold and from anyone stupid enough to confuse it with a clarinet.

What I really miss about the oboe is having my hands on it. I could come at that instrument from any direction or any angle and know every indentation on every key, every spot that leaked air, every nick on every square inch of wood. When enough years go by, the corporeal qualities of an instrument become as familiar to its player as, I imagine, those of a long-standing lover. Knowing precisely how the weight of the oboe was distributed between my right thumb and left wrist, knowing, above all, that the weight would feel the same way every time, every day, for every year that I played, was a feeling akin to having ten years of knowledge about the curve of someone's back. Since I stopped playing the oboe, I haven't had the privilege of that kind of familiarity. That's not an exaggeration, merely a moot point.

Understanding the Text

1. Daum writes, "I never practiced and yet I always practiced" (8). How does she explain this apparent contradiction?

2. The writer is "infuriated" that her mother calls her oboe a "horn" (13). What does this terminology reveal, according to Daum?

Reflection and Response

3. The writer includes many reminiscences and descriptions of her parents. How do her mother and father come across in the essay? How do you respond to them, as a reader?

4. Why is a rock and roll musical so unsettling and antithetical to Music Is My Bag culture, according to Daum? How is this antipathy related to the "sexlessness" (5) that she ascribes to Music Is My Bag people?

Making Connections

5. How might you read Gracy Olmstead's "Loving Through the Pain: Why Learning an Instrument Matters" (p. 132) through the lens of Daum's essay? Does Olmstead match the image of a Music Is My Bag person? Why or why not?

6. Daum writes, "Having a Bag connotes the state of being overly interested in something, and yet, in a certain way, not interested enough" (5). Do you or your family have a "Bag"? Are you a "Bagger" of any sort? If you are not, are you aware of other people in your life who are? Do you see the qualities and tendencies Daum describes? Explain.

Seduced by "Perfect" Pitch: How Auto-Tune Conquered Pop Music

Lessley Anderson

In this article from The *Verge*, a website and network devoted to technology news, writer Lessley Anderson explores the ubiquitous studio pitch-correction effect Auto-Tune, which has become prevalent in popular music over the last two decades. But the implications of the device go well beyond the confines of sound-boards and production studios to issues of musical authenticity and humanity: "The Auto-Tune or not Auto-Tune debate always seems to turn into a moralistic one . . ."

Lessley Anderson is a San Francisco–based writer whose work has appeared in *SFGate*, the *San Francisco Chronicle*, *Fast Company*, *Vanity Fair*, the *New York Times*, and other publications.

In January of 2010, Kesha Sebert, known as 'Ke$ha' debuted at number one on Billboard with her album, *Animal*. Her style is electro pop-y dance music: she alternates between rapping and singing, the choruses of her songs are typically melodic party hooks that bore deep into your brain: "Your love, your love, your love, is my drug!" And at times, her voice is so heavily processed that it sounds like a cross between a girl and a synthesizer. Much of her sound is due to the pitch correction software, Auto-Tune.

Sebert, whose label did not respond to a request for an interview, has built a persona as a badass wastoid, who told *Rolling Stone* that all male visitors to her tour bus had to submit to being photographed with their pants down. Even the bus drivers.

Yet this past November on the *Today Show*, the 25-year-old Sebert looked vulnerable, standing awkwardly in her skimpy purple, gold, and green unitard. She was there to promote her new album, *Warrior*, which was supposed to reveal the *authentic* her.

"Was it really important to let your voice be heard?" asked the host, Savannah Guthrie.

"Absolutely," Sebert said, gripping the mic nervously in her fingerless 5 black gloves.

"People think they've heard the Auto-Tune, they've heard the dance hits, but you really have a great voice, too," said Guthrie, helpfully.

"No, I got, like, bummed out when I heard that," said Sebert, sadly. "Because I really can sing. It's one of the few things I can do."

Warrior starts with a shredding electrical static noise, then comes her voice, sounding like what the *Guardian* called "a robo squawk devoid of all emotion."

"That's pitch correction software for sure," wrote Drew Waters, Head of Studio Operations at Capitol Records, in an email. "She may be able to sing, but she or the producer chose to put her voice through Auto-Tune or a similar plug-in as an aesthetic choice."

So much for showing the world the authentic Ke$ha. 10

Since rising to fame as the weird techno-warble effect in the chorus of Cher's 1998 song, "Believe," Auto-Tune has become bitchy shorthand for saying somebody can't sing. But the diss isn't fair, because everybody's using it.

For every T-Pain—the R&B artist who uses Auto-Tune as an over-the-top aesthetic choice—there are 100 artists who are Auto-Tuned in subtler ways. Fix a little backing harmony here, bump a flat note up to diva-worthy heights there: smooth everything over so that it's perfect. You can even use Auto-Tune live, so an artist can sing totally out of tune in concert and be corrected before their flaws ever reach the ears of an audience. (On season 7 of the UK *X-Factor*, it was used so excessively on contestants' auditions that viewers got wise, and protested.)

Indeed, finding out that all the singers we listen to have been Auto-Tuned does feel like someone's messing with us. As humans, we crave connection, not perfection. But we're not the ones pulling the levers. What happens when an entire industry decides it's safer to bet on the robot? Will we start to hate the sound of our own voices?

Cher's late '90s comeback and makeover as a gay icon can entirely be attributed to Auto-Tune, though the song's producers claimed for years that it was a Digitech Talker vocoder pedal effect. In 1998, she released the single, "Believe," which featured a strange, robotic vocal effect on the chorus that felt fresh. It was created with Auto-Tune.

> "As humans, we crave connection, not perfection. But we're not the ones pulling the levers. What happens when an entire industry decides it's safer to bet on the robot?"

The technology, which debuted in 1997 as a plug-in for Pro Tools (the 15 industry standard recording software), works like this: you select the key the song is in, and then Auto-Tune analyzes the singer's vocal line, moving "wrong" notes up or down to what it guesses is the intended pitch. You can control the time it takes for the program to move the pitch: slower is more natural, faster makes the jump sudden and inhuman sounding. Cher's producers chose the fastest possible setting, the so-called "zero" setting, for maximum pop.

"Believe" was a huge hit, but among music nerds, it was polarizing. Indie rock producer Steve Albini, who's recorded bands like the Pixies and Nirvana, has said he thought the song was mind-numbingly awful, and was aghast to see people he respected seduced by Auto-Tune.

"One by one, I could see that my friends had gone zombie. This horrible piece of music with this ugly soon-to-be cliché was now being discussed as something that was awesome. It made my heart fall," he told the *Onion AV Club* in November of 2012.

The Auto-Tune effect spread like a slow burn through the industry, especially within the R&B and dance music communities. T-Pain began Cher-style Auto-Tuning all his vocals, and a decade later, he's still doing it.

"It's makin' me money, so I ain't about to stop!" T-Pain told DJ Skee in 2008.

Kanye West did an album with it. Lady Gaga uses it. Madonna, too. 20 Maroon 5. Even the artistically high-minded Bon Iver has dabbled. A YouTube series where TV news clips were Auto-Tuned, "Auto-Tune the News," went viral. The glitchy Auto-Tune mode seems destined to be remembered as the "sound" of the 2000s, the way the gated snare (that dense, big, reverb-y drum sound on, say, Phil Collins songs) is now remembered as the sound of the '80s.

Auto-Tune certainly isn't the only robot voice effect to have wormed its way into pop music. In the '70s and early '80s, voice synthesizer effects units became popular with a lot of bands. Most famous is the Vocoder, originally invented in the 1930s to send encoded Allied messages during WWII. Proto-techno groups like New Order and Kraftwerk (ie: "Computer World") embraced it. So did American early funk and hip hop groups like the Jonzun Crew.

'70s rockers gravitated towards another effect, the talk box. Peter Frampton (listen for it on "Do You Feel Like We Do") and Joe Walsh (used it on "Rocky Mountain Way") liked its similar-to-a-vocoder sound. The talk box was easier to rig up than the Vocoder—you operate it via a rubber mouth tube when applying it to vocals. But it produces massive amounts of slobber. In Dave Tompkins' book, *How to Wreck a Nice Beach*, about the history of synthesized speech machines in the music industry, he writes that Frampton's roadies sanitized his talk box in Remy Martin Cognac between gigs.

The use of showy effects usually have a backlash. And in the case of the Auto-Tune warble, Jay-Z struck back with the 2009 single, D.O.A., or "Death of Auto-Tune."

That same year, the band Death Cab for Cutie showed up at the Grammys wearing blue ribbons to raise awareness, they told MTV, about "rampant Auto-Tune abuse."

The protests came too late, though. The lid to Pandora's box had been 25 lifted. Music producers everywhere were installing the software.

"I'll be in a studio and hear a singer down the hall and she's clearly out of tune, and she'll do one take," says Drew Waters of Capitol Records. That's all she needs. Because they can fix it later, in Auto-Tune.

There is much speculation online about who does—or doesn't—use Auto-Tune. Taylor Swift is a key target, as her terribly off-key duet with Stevie Nicks at the 2010 Grammys suggests she's tone deaf. (Label reps said at the time something was wrong with her earpiece.) But such speculation is naïve, say the producers I talked to. "Everybody uses it," says Filip Nikolic, singer in the LA-based band, Poolside, and a freelance music producer and studio engineer. "It saves a ton of time."

On one end of the spectrum are people who dial up Auto-Tune to the max, a la Cher/T-Pain. On the other end are people who use it occasionally and sparingly. You can use Auto-Tune not only to pitch correct vocals, but other instruments too, and light users will tweak a note here and there if a guitar is, say, rubbing up against a vocal in a weird way.

"I'll massage a note every once in a while, and often I won't even tell the artist," says Eric Drew Feldman, a San Francisco—based musician and producer who's worked with The Polyphonic Spree and Frank Black.

But between those two extremes, you have the synthetic middle, 30 where Auto-Tune is used to correct nearly every note, as one integral brick in a thick wall of digitally processed sound. From Justin Bieber to One Direction, from The Weeknd to Chris Brown, most pop music produced today has a slick, synth-y tone that's partly a result of pitch correction.

However, good luck getting anybody to cop to it. Big producers like Max Martin and Dr. Luke, responsible for mega hits from artists like Ke$ha, Pink, and Kelly Clarkson, either turned me down or didn't respond to interview requests. And you can't really blame them.

"Do you want to talk about that effect you probably use that people equate with your client being talentless?"

Um, no thanks.

In 2009, an online petition went around protesting the overuse of Auto-Tune on the show *Glee*. Those producers turned down an interview, too.

The artists and producers who would talk were conflicted. One indie 35 band, The Stepkids, had long eschewed Auto-Tune and most other modern recording technologies to make what they call "experimental soul music." But the band recently did an about face, and Auto-Tuned their vocal harmonies on their forthcoming single, "Fading Star."

Were they using Auto-Tune ironically or seriously? Co-frontman Jeff Gitelman said,

"Both."

"For a long time we fought it, and we still are to a certain degree," said Gitelman. "But attention spans are a certain way, and that's how it is . . . we just wanted it to have a clean, modern sound."

Hanging above the toilet in San Francisco's Different Fur recording studios—where artists like the Alabama Shakes and Bobby Brown have recorded—is a clipping from *Tape Op* magazine that reads: "Don't admit to Auto-Tune use or editing of drums, unless asked directly. Then admit to half as much as you really did."

Different Fur's producer/engineer/owner, Patrick Brown, who hung 40 the clipping there, has recorded acts like the Morning Benders, and says many indie rock bands "come in, and first thing they say is, 'We don't tune anything,'" he says.

Brown is up for ditching Auto-Tune if the client really wants to, but he says most of the time, they don't really want to. "Let's face it, most bands are not genius." He'll feel them out by saying, with a wink-wink-nod-nod: "Man, that note's really out of tune, *but that was a great take*." And a lot of times they'll tell him, go ahead, Auto-Tune it.

Marc Griffin is in the RCA-signed band 2AM Club, which has both an emcee and a singer (Griffin's the singer.) He first got Auto-Tuned in 2008, when he recorded a demo with producer Jerry Harrison, the former keyboardist and guitarist for the Talking Heads.

"I sang the lead, then we were in the control room with the engineer, and he put 'tune on it. Just a little. And I had perfect pitch vocals. It sounded amazing. Then we started stacking vocals on top of it, and *that* sounded amazing," says Griffin.

Now, Griffin sometimes records with Auto-Tune on in real time, rather than having it applied to his vocals in post-production, a trend producers say is not unusual. This means that the artist hears the tuned version of his or her voice coming out of the monitors while singing.

"Every time you sing a note that's not perfect, you can hear the fre- 45 quencies battle with each other," Griffin says, which sounds kind of awful, but he insists it "helps you hear what it will really sound like."

Singer/songwriter Neko Case kvetched about these developments in an interview with online music magazine, *Pitchfork*. "I'm not a perfect note hitter either but I'm not going to cover it up with auto tune. Everybody uses it, too. I once asked a studio guy in Toronto, 'How many people don't use Auto-Tune?' and he said, 'You and Nelly Furtado are the only two people who've never used it in here.' Even though I'm not into Nelly Furtado, it kind of made me respect her. It's cool that she has some integrity."

That was 2006. This past September, Nelly Furtado released the album, *The Spirit Indestructible*. Its lead single is doused in massive levels of Auto-Tune.

Somebody once wrote on an online message board that the guy who created Auto-Tune must "hate music." That could not be further from the truth. Its creator, Dr. Andy Hildebrand, AKA Dr. Andy, is a classically trained flautist who spent most of his youth playing professionally, in orchestras. Despite the fact that the 66-year-old only recently lopped off a long, gray ponytail, he's no hippie. He never listened to rock music of his generation.

"I was too busy practicing," he says. "It warped me."

The only post-Debussy artist he's ever gotten into is Patsy Cline.   50

Hildebrand's company—Antares—nestled in an anonymous looking office park in the mountains between Silicon Valley and the Pacific Coast, has only ten employees. Hildebrand invents all the products (Antares recently came out with Auto-Tune for Guitar). His wife is the CFO.

Hildebrand started his career as a geophysicist, programming digital signal processing software which helped oil companies find drilling spots. After going back to school for music composition at age 40, he discovered he could use those same algorithms for the seamless looping of digital music samples, and later for pitch correction. Auto-Tune, and Antares, were born.

Auto-Tune isn't the only pitch correction software, of course. Its closest competitor, Melodyne, is reputed to be more "natural" sounding. But Auto-Tune is, in the words of one producer, "the go-to if you just want to set-it-and-forget-it."

In interviews, Hildebrand handles the question of "is Auto-Tune evil?" with characteristic dry wit. His stock answer is, "My wife wears makeup, does that make her evil?" But on the day I asked him, he answered, "I just make the car. I don't drive it down the wrong side of the road."

The T-Pains and Chers of the world are the crazy drivers, in   55 Hildebrand's analogy. The artists that tune with subtlety are like his wife, tasteful people looking to put their best foot forward.

Another way you could answer the question: recorded music is, by definition, artificial. The band is not singing live in your living room. Microphones project sound. Mixing, overdubbing, and multi-tracking allow instruments and voices to be recorded, edited, and manipulated separately.

There are multitudes of effects, like compression, which brings down loud sounds and amplifies quiet ones, so you can hear an artist taking a breath in between words. Reverb and delay create echo effects, which can make vocals sound fuller and rounder.

When recording went from tape to digital, there were even more opportunities for effects and manipulation, and Auto-Tune is just one of many of the new tools available. Nonetheless, there are some who feel it's a different thing. At best, unnecessary. At worst, pernicious.

"The thing is, reverb and delay always existed in the real world, by placing the artist in unique environments, so [those effects are] just mimicking reality," says Larry Crane, the editor of music recording magazine, *Tape Op*, and a producer who's recorded Elliott Smith and The Decemberists. If you sang in a cave, or some other really echo-y chamber, you'd sound like early Elvis, too. "There is nothing in the natural world that Auto-Tune is mimicking, therefore any use of it should be carefully considered."

"I'd rather just turn the reverb up on the Fender Twin in the troubling place," says Arizona indie rock pioneer Howe Gelb, of the band Giant Sand. He describes Auto-Tune and other correction plug-ins as "foul" in a way he can't quite put his finger on. "There's something embedded in the track that tends to push my ear away."

Lee Alexander, one time boyfriend of Norah Jones and bass player and 60 producer for her country side project, The Little Willies, used no Auto-Tune on their two records, and says he doesn't even own the program.

"Stuff is out of tune everywhere . . . that to me is the beauty of music," he wrote in an email.

In 2000, Matt Kadane of the band The New Year, and his brother, Bubba covered Cher's "Believe," complete with Auto-Tune. They did it in their former Texas Slo-Core band, Bedhead. Kadane told me he hated the original "Believe," and had to be talked into covering it, but had surprisingly found that putting Auto-Tune on his vocals "added emotional weight." He hasn't, however, used Auto-Tune since.

"It's one thing to make a statement with hollow, disaffected vocals, but it's another if this is the way we're communicating with each other," he says.

For some people, I said, it seems that Auto-Tune is a lot like dudes and fake boobs. Some dudes see fake boobs, they know they're fake, but they get an erection anyway. They can't help themselves. Kadane agreed that it "can serve that function."

"But at some point you'd say 'that's fucked up that I have an erec- 65 tion from fake boobs!'" he says. "And in the midst of experiencing that, I think ideally you have a moment that reminds you that authenticity is still possible. And thank *God* not everything in the world is Auto-Tuned."

Does your brain get rewired to expect perfect pitch?

The concept of pitch needing to be "correct" is a somewhat recent construct. Cue up the Rolling Stones' *Exile on Main St.*, and listen to what Mick Jagger does on "Sweet Virginia." There are a lot of flat and sharp notes, because, well, that's characteristic of blues singing, which is at the roots of rock and roll.

"When a (blues) singer is 'flat' it's not because he's doing it because he doesn't know any better. It's for inflection!" says Victor Coelho, Professor of Music at Boston University.

Blues singers have traditionally played with pitch to express feelings like longing or yearning, to punch up a nastier lyric, or make it feel dirty, he says. "The music is not just about hitting the pitch."

Of course that style of vocal wouldn't fly in Auto-Tune. It would get 70 corrected. Neil Young, Bob Dylan, many of the classic artists whose voices are less than pitch perfect—they probably would be pitch corrected if they started out today.

John Parish, the UK-based producer who's worked with PJ Harvey and Sparklehorse, says that though he uses Auto-Tune on rare occasions, he is no fan. Many of the singers he works with, Harvey in particular, have eccentric vocal styles—he describes them as "character singers." Using pitch correction software on them would be like trying to get Jackson Pollock to stay inside the lines.

"I can listen to something that can be really quite out of tune, and enjoy it," says Parish. But is he a dying breed?

"That's the kind of music that takes five listens to get really into," says Nikolic, of Poolside. "That's not really an option if you want to make it in pop music today. You find a really catchy hook and a production that is in no way challenging, and you just *gear it up*!"

If you're of the generation raised on technology-enabled perfect pitch, does your brain get rewired to expect it? So-called "supertasters" are people who are genetically more sensitive to bitter flavors than the rest of us, and therefore can't appreciate delicious bitter things like IPAs and arugula. Is the Auto-Tune generation likewise more sensitive to off key-ness, and thus less able to appreciate it? Some troubling signs point to "yes."

"I was listening to some young people in a studio a few years ago, and 75 they were like, 'I don't think The Beatles were so good,'" says producer Eric Drew Feldman. They were discussing the song "Paperback Writer." "They're going, 'They were so sloppy! The harmonies are so flat!'"

John Lennon famously hated his singing voice. He thought it sounded too thin, and was constantly futzing with vocal effects, like the overdriven sound on "I Am the Walrus." I can relate. I love to sing, and in my head, I hear a soulful, husky, alto. What comes out, however, is a cross between a child in the musical *Annie*, and Gretchen Wilson: nasal, reedy, about as soulful as a mosquito. I'm in a band and I write all the songs, but I'm not the singer: I wouldn't subject people to that.

Producer and editor Larry Crane says he thinks lots of artists are basically insecure about their voices, and use Auto-Tune as a kind of protective shield.

"I've had people come in and say I *want* Auto-Tune, and I say, 'Let's spend some time, let's do five vocal takes and compile the best take. Let's put down a piano guide track. There's a million ways to coach a vocal. Let's try those things first,'" he says.

Recently, I went over to a couple-friend's house with my husband, to play with Auto-Tune. The husband of the couple, Mike, had the software on his home computer—he dabbles in music production—and the idea was that we'd record a song together, then Auto-Tune it.

We looked for something with four-part harmony, so we could all 80 sing, and for a song where the backing instrumental was available online. We settled on Boyz II Men's "End of the Road." One by one we went into the bedroom to record our parts, with a mix of shame and titillation not unlike taking turns with a prostitute.

When we were finished, Mike played back the finished piece, without Auto-Tune. It was nerve wracking to listen to, I felt like my entire body was cringing. Although I hit the notes OK, there was something tentative and childlike about my delivery. Thank God these are my good friends, I thought. Of course they were probably all thinking the same thing about their performances, too, but in my mind, *my* voice was the most annoying of all, so wheedling and prissy sounding.

Then Mike Auto-Tuned two versions of our Boys II Men song: one with Cher/T-Pain style glitchy Auto-Tune, the other with "natural" sounding Auto-Tune. The exaggerated one was hilariously awesome—it sounded just like a generic R&B song.

But the second one shocked me. It sounded like us, for sure. But an idealized version of us. My husband's gritty vocal attack was still there, but he was singing on key. And something about fine-tuning my vocals had made them sound more confident, like smoothing out a tremble in one's speech.

The Auto-Tune or not Auto-Tune debate always seems to turn into a moralistic one, like somehow you have more integrity if you don't use it, or only use it occasionally. But seeing how really innocuous-yet-lovely it could be, made me rethink. If I were a professional musician, would I reject the opportunity to sound, what I consider to be, "my best," out of principle?

The answer to that is probably no. But then it gets you wondering. 85 How many insecure artists with "annoying" voices will retune themselves before you ever have a chance to fall in love?

Understanding the Text

1. In interviews, Auto-Tune's creator has used two metaphors to answer the question: "Is Auto-Tune evil?" What are they?

2. Anderson concludes her article, in part, by narrating an account of using Auto-Tune on her own vocals in a studio. What happens? What insight does her experience give her?

Reflection and Response

3. Anderson writes that "finding out that all the singers we listen to have been Auto-Tuned does feel like someone's messing with us" (13). Do you agree? Does Auto-Tune inhibit or interfere with your connection to music? Explain.

4. As the writer notes, "recorded music is, by definition, artificial. The band is not singing live in your living room. Microphones project sound. Mixing, over-dubbing, and multi-tracking allow instruments and voices to be recorded, edited, and manipulated separately" (56). How does this perspective affect your view of Auto-Tune? Is it merely another element of that artifice? Or is it artificially different in some way? Explain your answer.

Making Connections

5. Several of the readings in this book touch upon or explore the notion of "authenticity" in music, from Justin Davidson's ("Beethoven's Kapow," p. 61) recollection of a performance of Beethoven's "Eroica" with technically-imperfect period instruments, to Jeremy Gordon's ("I Listen to Everything, Except Rap and Country Music," p. 117) discussions of authenticity in country music and hiphop. How important is the notion of "authenticity" to your own experience and appreciation of music? What makes music "authentic"? Do music's medium or recording process matter? Or can music have an essential authenticity, independent of its production? Explain your answer.

6. Anderson quotes music producer John Parish, who discusses "character singers": vocalists with imperfect or "eccentric" vocal styles. Parish says, "I can listen to something that can be really quite out of tune, and enjoy it" (72). Do you appreciate "character singers"? Can you give examples of eccentric singers or performers whose music might be diminished by pitch correction?

On the Efficiency of AC/DC: Bon Scott versus Brian Johnson

Robert J. Oxoby

In this ironic article from the peer-reviewed scholarly journal *Economic Inquiry*, behavioral economist Robert J. Oxoby uses "tools from experimental economics to address the age-old debate": Who was a better lead singer for the venerable Australian hard rock band AC/DC, Bon Scott or Brian Johnson? The paper was meant as a joke. According to Oxoby, a former graduate student was studying the effects of music on behavior; during the two sessions for the experiment, however, two different AC/DC songs were played by mistake. Oxoby used the data from that experiment to write this tongue-in-cheek article. Yet, it might lead readers to consider not only the ostensible topic — music's effects on mood and behavior — but the nature of academic discourse, as well.

The author of many articles on behavioral and experimental economics, political economy, microeconomics, and other related fields, Robert J. Oxoby is a professor in the Department of Economics at the University of Calgary and director of the university's Behavioral and Experimental Economics Laboratory.

We use tools from experimental economics to address the age-old debate regarding who was a better singer in the band AC/DC. Our results suggest that (using wealth maximization as a measure of "better") listening to Brian Johnson (relative to listening to Bon Scott) resulted in "better" outcomes in an ultimatum game. These results may have important implications for settling drunken music debates and environmental design issues in organizations. (*JEL* C7, C9, D6, Z1)

I. Introduction

The band AC/DC is considered one of the most influential hard rock bands, often compared to Led Zeppelin and Black Sabbath in influencing many subsequent hard rock and heavy metal bands. Indeed Christie (2003) argues that AC/DC was a "key common denominator" in the new wave of heavy metal emerging from Britain in the 1970s and influencing all genres of rock & roll through the 1980s and 1990s. The band was formed in 1973 by Angus and Malcolm Young, who took the band's moniker from the back of their sister's sewing machine.

In its 35-year history, the band has sold more than 150 million albums, including 42 million copies of the 1980 album *Back in Black*, making *Back in Black* the highest selling album by any rock band. Of the 19 albums the band released, Eddy (1991) classifies eight of these albums in the top 500 heavy metal albums in the universe and in 2003 the band was inducted into the Rock & Roll Hall of Fame. Given all this, it is no wonder that AC/DC has such a rabid fan base and, as discussed below, faces an epic debate regarding its lineup.

Among musicologists, researchers of popular culture, and rock and roll lovers of all ages there exists a common debate. That is, with respect to the rock band AC/DC, who is the better vocalist: Bon Scott or Brian Johnson? The band's original vocalist, Scott, performed on seven of the band's albums (excluding live albums and compilations) before dying in 1980. Brian Johnson joined the band in 1980, serving as vocalist on nine albums (excluding live albums and compilations). Since 1980, there has been near-constant contention regarding who was the better singer.[1]

In this paper, we explore this issue. Since it is difficult to ascertain which vocalist was better given the heterogeneity of musical tastes, our analysis does not focus on the aural or sonic quality of the vocalists' performances. Rather, using tools from the field of experimental economics, we consider which vocalist results in individuals arriving at more efficient outcomes in a simple bargaining game. Our results suggest that having participants listen to songs by AC/DC in which Brian Johnson served as vocalist results in participants realizing more efficient outcomes. Thus, in terms of a singer's ability to implement efficient behavioral outcomes among listeners, our results suggest that Brian Johnson was a better vocalist than Bon Scott.[2]

"Since it is difficult to ascertain which vocalist was better given the heterogeneity of musical tastes, our analysis does not focus on the aural or sonic quality of the vocalists' performances."

---

[1]Masino (2007) and Walker (2001) document (and fall on opposite sides) of this debate.

[2]Our research also follows important research conducted by Blinder (1974) on oral hygiene, McAfee (1983) on the invincibility of America, and Snower (1982) on the role of the undead in macroeconomic policy making.

MAO: Minimum Acceptable Offer

Figure 3.1 "The question as to who was a better singer, Bon Scott or Brian Johnson, may never truly be resolved": AC/DC's Bon Scott. Erica Echenberg/ Getty Images

Figure 3.2 "The question as to who was a better singer, Bon Scott or Brian Johnson, may never truly be resolved": AC/DC's Brian Johnson. Chris Walter/ Getty Images

By focusing on the effects of music on outcomes, our research follows previous research in physiology, psychology, and sociology. For example, Bernardi, Porta, and Sleight (2006) document how different styles of music can induce cardiovascular, respiratory, and cerebrovascular changes in listeners. In psychology, Lesuik (2005) has documented how the use of music in the workplace can result in positive mood changes and enhanced productivity. Finally, Bryson (1996) has demonstrated how music (particularly heavymetal) can contribute to reinforcing symbolic boundaries between individuals and Stack and Gundlach (1992) have documented how listening to country music increases the incidence of suicide.

II. Experimental Design

In our experiment we utilize a common procedure from experimental economics entitled the ultimatum game (see Roth, 1995). In this game, individuals are randomly paired and assigned the roles of either proposer or responder. Proposers are allocated a sum of money from which they must choose an amount to extend as an offer to the responder. The responder, upon learning of this offer, can either accept or reject the offer. If she accepts the offer, the responder receives the offer (in cash), and the proposer is given the original sum of money less the offer. If the offer is rejected, both participants receive nothing.

Under the assumption that individuals have preferences over only their own wealth, the predicted game theoretic outcome (the subgame-perfect Nash equilibrium) is that in which the proposer extends the smallest possible offer and the responder (weakly) accepts any offer greater than (or equal to) zero. Such an outcome is efficient in the sense that no resources are lost in the bargaining process (i.e., the resources are not lost via a decision to reject the offer). However, experiments have shown that proposers typically offer between 20% and 50% of the wealth available in the experiment and responders, on average, reject offers below 30% (see Camerer 2003). These results suggest that individuals not only value their own wealth, but also the wealth of others and the fairness of an allocation. This has fostered new models of economic behavior incorporating inequity aversion, cooperation, and reciprocity (e.g., Bolton and Ockenfels 2000; Charness and Rabin 2002; Fehr and Schmidt 1999).

In our experiment, participants were paired and told the structure of the game. Each pair was endowed with $10 to use in the game (i.e., $10 from which the proposer must choose an offer to extend the responder) and offers were restricted to integer values (i.e., whole dollars). Prior to learning his or her role as proposer or responder, each participant provided the offer they would extend were they assigned the role of proposer and, for each possible offer (i.e., for each offer between $0 and $10), whether they would accept or reject the offer were they assigned the role of responder. After all individuals had provided this information, the roles of proposer and responder were randomly assigned within each pair and the indicated offer (from the proposer) and the respective accept/reject decision (from the responder) were implemented.[3] The corresponding payoffs were paid in cash to each participant.

Our treatment variable in the experiment was the type of music played while individuals made decisions. As demonstrated by Bernardi, Porta, and Sleight (2006), different musical styles can have different physiological effects in individuals. These effects, along with emotional responses, may result in different patterns of decision-making regarding distributing money between oneself and another. In our Bon Scott treatment, participants listened to "It's a Long Way to the Top" (featuring Bon Scott on vocals) from the album *High Voltage* (AC/DC 1976). In our Brian Johnson treatment, participants listened to "Shoot to Thrill" (featuring Brian Johnson on vocals) from the album *Back in Black* (AC/DC 1980). These songs were chosen in order to avoid preconceived preferences for the band's most popular singles (e.g., "Highway to Hell," "You Shook Me All Night Long").[4]

III. Results

A total of 36 participants from a large Canadian university took part in the experiment (two sessions of 18 individuals each). In one session, "It's a Long Way to the Top" was played while participants made their decisions; in the other session "Shoot to Thrill" was played while participants made their decisions. To maintain anonymity among subjects and bargaining pairs, participant pairings were made by computer and decisions were entered via computers located in separated experimental stations.[5]

10

---

[3]Oxoby and McLeish (2004) demonstrate that this manner of elicitation yields results that are indistinguishable from assigning roles prior to eliciting decisions.
[4]In a similar research design, Kirchsteiger, Rigotti, and Rustichini (2006) used films (Spielberg's *Schindler's List* and Chaplin's *City Lights*) to induce mood in subjects playing a gift-giving game. Their results suggest that watching *Schindler's List* yields greater reciprocity while watching *City Lights* yields greater generosity.
[5]The experiments were programmed using the software by Fischbacher (2007).

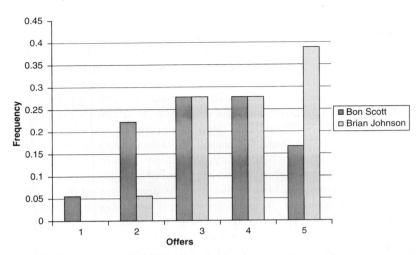

Figure 1   The distributions of offers in the Bon Scott and Brian Johnson treatments.

To analyze the results, we compared the offers extended by participants across each treatment. For each participant we also calculated their minimum acceptable offer (MAO; the lowest offer a participant would accept) and compared these across treatments. Note that in any participant pair, an efficient outcome (i.e., an offer that was not rejected) was more likely in the presence of a higher offer and a lower MAO.

When the music of Bon Scott was played, participants extended offers with mean (standard deviation) of 3.28 (1.18) whereas participants in the Brian Johnson treatment extended offers with mean (standard deviation) of 4.00 (0.97). The distributions of offers in each treatment are presented in Figure 1. Using nonparametric Wilcoxon rank–sum tests, we can reject the hypothesis that the distribution of offers across treatments are the same ($p = .064$).

In terms of MAOs, participants in the Bon Scott treatment had minimum acceptable offers with mean (standard deviation) of 3.94 (0.87) while participants in the Brian Johnson treatment had minimum acceptable offers with mean (standard deviation) of 3.17 (1.25). The distributions of MAOs are presented in Figure 2. Again, using nonparametric Wilcoxon rank–sum tests, we can reject the hypothesis that the distribution of MAOs in each treatment are the same ($p = .050$). Thus, offers were lower and MAOs were higher when participants heard the music of Bon Scott. This suggests that

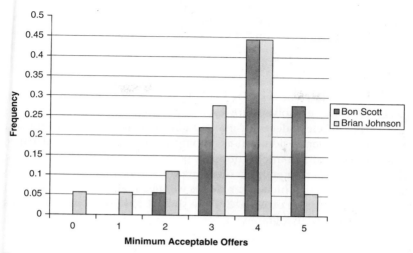

Figure 2   The distributions of MAOs in the Bon Scott and Brian Johnson treatments.

more offers would be rejected when listening to Bon Scott than when listening to Brian Johnson.[6]

In terms of the actual number of pairs in which offers were rejected, we observed five rejections (four acceptances) in the Bon Scott treatment as opposed to three rejections (six acceptances) in the Brian Johnson treatment. As suggested by our analysis above, we observed a higher rate of rejection and hence less efficient outcomes when the music of Bon Scott was played during participants' decision making. It is interesting to note that 14 of 16 participants in the Brian Johnson treatment would have accepted their own offers (i.e., their offers were greater than or equal to their MAO). On the other hand, only 50% of participants in the Bon Scott treatment would have accepted their own offer. It is natural to consider this type of "internal" consistency (accepting one's own offer) as an aspect of rationality or proper understanding of the dynamic structure of the game. Thus our analysis potentially sheds light on the cognitive

---

[6]We considered extending this research to shed light on the Van Halen debate. Unfortunately, we were unable to obtain ethics clearance to play Gary Cherone in our lab. While we attempted to restrict our analysis to the comparison of Van Halen vocalists David Lee Roth and Sammy Hagar, a research assistant thought we were exploring the Roth/Hagar debate and played Sammy Hagar's "Why Can't This Be Love" along with a pre-recorded lecture by noted economist Al Roth. The results from this experiment are obvious and not discussed here.

states and cognitive costs that are induced by listening to Brian Johnson and Bon Scott. We leave this for future research.

IV. Conclusions

The question as to who was a better singer, Bon Scott or Brian Johnson, may never truly be resolved. However, our analysis suggests that in terms of affecting efficient decision-making among listeners, Brian Johnson was a better singer. In addition to helping settle many barroom debates, our analysis has direct implications for policy and organizational design: when policy makers or employers are engaging in negotiations (or setting up environments in which other parties will negotiate) and are interested in playing the music of AC/DC, they should choose from the band's Brian Johnson era discography.[7]   15

References

AC/DC. "It's a Long Way to the Top If You Want to Rock and Roll." *High Voltage*. ATCO, 1976.

AC/DC. "Shoot to Thrill." *Back in Black*. Altantic, 1980.

Bernardi, L., C. Porta, and P. Sleight. "Cardiovascular, Cerebrovascular, and Respiratory Changes Induced by Different Types of Music in Musicians and Non-Musicians: The Importance of Silence." *Heart*, vol. 92, 2006, pp. 445–52.

Blinder, A.S. "The Economics of Brushing Teeth." *Journal of Political Economy*, vol. 82, 1974, pp. 887–91.

Bolton, G.E., and A. Ockenfels. "A Theory of Equity, Reciprocity, and Competition." *American Economic Review*, vol. 30, 2000, pp. 166–93.

Bryson, B. "Anything but Heavy Metal: Symbolic Exclusion and Musical Dislikes." *American Sociological Review*, vol. 61, 1996, pp. 884–99.

Camerer, C.F. *Behavioral Game Theory*. Princeton University Press, 2003.

Charness, G., and M. Rabin. "Understanding Social Preferences with Simple Tests." *Quarterly Journal of Economics*, vol. 117, 2002, pp. 817–69.

Christie, I. *Sound of the Beast: The Complete Headbanging History of Heavy Metal*. Harper Collins, 2003.

Eddy, C. *Stairway to Hell: The 500 Best Heavy Metal Albums in the Universe*. Harmony Books, 1991.

Fehr, E., and K. Schmidt. "A Theory of Fairness, Competition, and Cooperation." *Quarterly Journal of Economics*, vol. 114, 1999, pp. 817–68.

Fischbacher, U. "z-Tree: Zurich Toolbox for Ready-Made Economic Experiments." *Experimental Economics*, vol. 10, 2007, pp. 171–78.

---

[7]A secondary implication of this research is on the role of the internet in information dissemination. See Wright and Jinman (2007).

Kirchsteiger, G., L. Rigotti, and A. Rustichini. "Your Morals Might Be Yours Truly, Moods." *Journal of Economic Behavior and Organization*, vol. 59, 2006, pp. 155–73.

Lesuik, T. "The Effect of Music Listening on Work Performance." *Psychology of Music*, vol. 33, no. 2, 2005, pp. 173–91.

Levitt, S.D. "There Is Hope for Economics: The AC/DC Paper Was a Joke." NY Times Blog, August 21, 2007, http://freakonomics.blogs.nytimes.com/2007/08/21/ there-is-hope-for-economics-the-acdc-paper-was-a-joke/.

Masino, S. *The Story of AC/DC: Let There Be Rock*. Omnibus Press, 2007.

McAfee, P. "American Economic Growth and the Voyage of Columbus." *American Economic Review*, vol. 73, 1983, pp. 735–40.

Oxoby, R.J., and K.N. McLeish. "Specific Decision and Strategy Vector Methods in Ultimatum Bargaining: Evidence on the Strength of Other-Regarding Behavior." *Economics Letters*, vol. 84, 2004, pp. 399–405.

Roth, A.E. "Bargaining Experiments." *Handbook of Experimental Economics*, edited by J.H. Kagel and A.E. Roth, Princeton University Press, 1995.

Snower, D.J. "Macroeconomic Policy and the Optimal Destruction of Vampires." *Journal of Political Economy*, vol. 90, 1982, pp. 647–55.

Stack, S., and J. Gundlach. "The Effect of Country Music on Suicide." *Social Forces*, vol. 71, no. 1, 1992, pp. 211–18.

Walker, C. *Highway to Hell: The Life and Times of AC/DC Legend Bon Scott*. Verse Chorus Press, 2001.

Wright, G., and R. Jinman. "This Is TNT: Bon Wasn't Best Front-Man." *Sydney Morning Herald*, 22 Aug. 2007.

Understanding the Text

1. In experimental settings, how do the actual results of ultimatum games differ from the "predicted game theoretic outcome" (7)? What does that difference suggest, according to the author?

2. According to the author, what are this study's "direct implications for policy and organizational design" (15), however tongue-in-cheek those "implications" are?

Reflection and Response

3. Do you find this article funny? Why or why not? If you do, can you point to specifics in the text that create comic effects? What clues are there that the author is joking?

4. What do you think Oxoby's purpose was in writing this article? Do you think he is trying to mock academic discourse? Is he trying to inform his readers on any level? What does he presume about his audience that might shed light on his goal?

Making Connections

5. In paragraph 5, Oxoby points to other serious research on the "effects of music on outcomes" in physiology, psychology, and sociology. Do you listen to music when you work? Why or why not? How does listening to music affect your own productivity?

6. Despite his own comic approach, the author cites several serious academic papers, including "The Effect of Country Music on Suicide" by Steven Stack and Jim Gundlach and "The Effect of Music Listening on Work" by Teresa Lesiuk. Using selected sources from Oxoby's references section, as well as selections from this text (for example, Stephen A. Diamond's "Why We Love Music – and Freud Despised It," p. 26, and Tom Jacobs's "When Things Look Dark, Country Music Gets Sunnier," p. 169), write an annotated bibliography on the topic of music's psychological, emotional, and sociological influences and effects. You might then use the annotated bibliography to begin research for your own related topic and paper.

When Things Look Dark, Country Music Gets Sunnier

Tom Jacobs

In this short article from *Pacific Standard*, writer Tom Jacobs discusses recent research by sociologist Jason Eastman and psychologist Terry Pettijohn that looks at a curious difference between pop music and country music. According to these researchers, in hard times, popular music gets more serious and downbeat, while country music becomes more upbeat and positive. This cuts against assumptions and expectations, as country music is "stereotypically thought to focus almost exclusively on the darker and depressing aspects of life." For their part, Eastman and Pettijohn offer class-based explanations for this difference, which may call for further scrutiny. Jacobs provides a good introduction to the article, and it might best be used as an entry to the research itself.

Tom Jacobs is a journalist who, has written for the *Los Angeles Daily News*, the *Los Angeles Times*, the *Chicago Tribune*, *Alternet*, and other publications.

In tough times, do happy or sad songs top the charts? Do we prefer music that reflects our fears and hardships, or tunes that allow us to temporarily forget our troubles?

Newly published research suggests the answer varies dramatically by genre. Pop fans reflexively gravitate to music that mirrors their emotions, while country devotees go for escapism.

In an analysis of the most popular country songs over six decades, Jason Eastman and Terry Pettijohn II of Coastal Carolina University find top hits are "lyrically more positive, musically upbeat, and use more happy-sounding major chords during difficult socioeconomic times."

> "Newly published research suggests the answer varies dramatically by genre. Pop fans reflexively gravitate to music that mirrors their emotions, while country devotees go for escapism."

In contrast, previous research on best-selling pop songs found that, in times of societal stress, those numbers "are longer, slower, more lyrically meaningful, and in more somber-sounding keys."

"Even though country music is often stereotypically thought to focus almost exclusively on the darker and depressing aspects of life, *Billboard* country songs of the year are less likely to lyrically incorporate negative emotions during difficult social and economic times."

In the journal *Psychology of Popular Media Culture,* Eastman, a 5
sociologist, and Pettijohn, a psychologist, looked at the 63 songs that
topped the *Billboard* magazine country music chart each year from 1946
to 2008. The music and lyrics of each was analyzed, along with the age
and gender of the performer(s).

This information was then compared with how the nation was faring
in the year of its release, as determined by Pettijohn's General Hard Time
Measure. It uses a variety of statistics, including the rates of unemployment, divorce, suicide, and homicide, plus the consumer price index
and "changes in disposable personal income," to create "a measure of
society-wide well-being."

The results: "Even though country music is often stereotypically
thought to focus almost exclusively on the darker and depressing aspects
of life, *Billboard* country songs of the year are less likely to lyrically incorporate negative emotions during difficult social and economic times."

Songs released in these periods also tended to have more upbeat tem-
pos and a larger proportion of major chords. All of those trends are the
mirror opposite of pop music.

This likely reflects the differing attitudes held by members of various socioeconomic groups, according to Eastman and Pettijohn, who
note that the audience for country music remains predominantly
working class.

"Middle-class parents socialize their children to take control and mas- 10
ter their environment," they write. "As the primary consumers of pop
music, this audience likely seeks out sadder, more serious songs in bad
socioeconomic times to match the negative emotions and anxieties they
personally feel, but are ultimately confident they will overcome."

"In contrast, working-class parents are less secure because of their lack
of power and resources, and thus socialize their children to be accepting
of life's hardships," they add. This attitude leads them to seek out "songs
that offer temporary relief from stress and anxiety they believe is inevitable, and inescapable."

While that's a reasonable and compelling analysis, it's worth pointing out that recessions don't hit all socioeconomic groups with equal
force. The most recent downturn, which does not figure into this study,
is essentially over for college-educated pop fans, but is very much still a
fact of life for the working-class country crowd.

So over the next few years, upbeat songs may be particularly popular
in both genres—for opposite reasons.

Understanding the Text

1. According to the authors, during economic downturns and recessions, pop music gets sadder and more serious, while country music tends to be more upbeat and positive. What explanations do the researchers give for this contrast?

2. How does Jacobs question and complicate the explanations of the researchers?

Reflection and Response

3. What is Jacobs's purpose in writing this article? To inform? To persuade? To critique? Explain your answer.

4. Jacobs quotes Eastman and Pettijohn as they generalize about middle-class and working-class people. How do you respond to these generalizations? Do they seem valid? Why or why not?

5. Jacobs asks, "Do we prefer music that reflects our fears and hardships, or tunes that allow us to temporarily forget our troubles?" (1). How would you answer that question? Do your responses support the research? Explain.

Making Connections

6. In "Country Music, Openness to Experience, and the Psychology of Culture War" (p. 105), Will Wilkinson writes about the appeal of country music to people with particular psychological, economic, and political profiles. Does this recent research seem to support Wilkinson's thesis? To answer the question, you may want to access Jason Eastman and Terry Pettijohn's original article, "Gone country: An investigation of *Billboard* country songs of the year across social and economic conditions in the United States," from the April 2015 issue of *Psychology of Popular Media Culture*.

7. For their study, Eastman and Pettijohn used the *Billboard* magazine country music chart each year from 1946 to 2008 to analyze songs. What does this seem to assume about country music and its fan base? Is that assumption reasonable? Why or why not? To answer this question, you will want to look at Eastman and Pettijohn's methodology.

Making Cents

Damon Krukowski

"I'm sure each generation of musicians feels they've lived through a time of tremendous change," writes musician and songwriter Damon Krukowski. But as he points out, the changes in technology, the music business, and the commercial distribution of music have been "extraordinary" over the last three decades. They include the shift from music pressed onto vinyl records and sold in stores to music in the form of streaming audio provided by services like Pandora and Spotify. Krukoswski writes from the perspective of an artist, frustrated with a new financial model that seems exploitative and even irrational. But his reflections as an artist may have implications for listeners and consumers, too, as music fans may want to consider the wider context — economic and ethical — of their listening.

Damon Krukowski is a musician, writer, and poet. His books include *Afterimage* (2011). His written work has appeared in *Artforum* and *Bookforum*, as well as in Pitchfork Media, where this article first appeared.

I'm sure each generation of musicians feels they've lived through a time of tremendous change, but the shifts I've witnessed in my relatively short music career—from morphing formats to dissolving business models—do seem extraordinary. The first album I made was originally released on LP only, in 1988—and my next will likely only be pressed on LP again. But in between, the music industry seems to have done everything it could to screw up that simple model of exchange; today it is no longer possible for most of us to earn even a modest wage through our recordings.

Not that I am naively nostalgic for the old days—we weren't paid for that first album, either. (The record label we were signed to at the time, Rough Trade, declared bankruptcy before cutting us even one royalty check.) But the ways in which musicians are screwed have changed qualitatively, from individualized swindles to systemic ones. And with those changes, a potential end-run around the industry's problems seems less and less possible, even for bands who have managed to hold on to 100% of their rights and royalties, as we have.

Consider Pandora and Spotify, the streaming music services that are becoming ever more integrated into our daily listening habits. My BMI royalty check arrived recently, reporting songwriting earnings from the first quarter of 2012, and I was glad to see that our music is being listened to via these services. Galaxie 500's "Tugboat," for example, was played 7,800 times on Pandora that quarter, for which its three songwriters were paid a collective total of 21 cents, or seven cents each. Spotify pays better: For the 5,960 times "Tugboat" was played there, Galaxie 500's songwriters went collectively into triple digits: $1.05 (35 cents each).

To put this into perspective: Since we own our own recordings, by my calculation it would take songwriting royalties for roughly 312,000 plays on Pandora to earn us the profit of one—*one*—LP sale. (On Spotify, one LP is equivalent to 47,680 plays.)

> "To put this into perspective: Since we own our own recordings, by my calculation it would take songwriting royalties for roughly 312,000 plays on Pandora to earn us the profit of one — *one* — LP sale. (On Spotify, one LP is equivalent to 47,680 plays.)" [5]

Or to put it in historical perspective: The "Tugboat" 7" single, Galaxie 500's very first release, cost us $980.22 for 1,000 copies—including shipping! (Naomi kept the receipts)—or 98 cents each. I no longer remember what we sold them for, but obviously it was easy to turn at least a couple bucks' profit on each. Which means we earned more from every one of those 7"s we sold than from the song's recent 13,760 plays on Pandora and Spotify. Here's yet another way to look at it: Pressing 1,000 singles in 1988 gave us the earning potential of more than 13 million streams in 2012. (And people say the internet is a bonanza for young bands . . .)

To be fair, because we are singer-songwriters, and because we own all of our rights, these streaming services end up paying us a second royalty, each for a different reason and each through a different channel. Pandora is considered "non-terrestrial radio," and consequently must pay the musicians who play on the recordings it streams, as well as the songwriters. These musicians' royalties are collected by SoundExchange, a non-profit created by the government when satellite radio came into existence. SoundExchange doesn't break our earnings down by service per song, but it does tell us that last quarter, Pandora paid a total of $64.17 for use of the entire Galaxie 500 catalogue. We have 64 Galaxie 500 recordings registered with them, so that averages neatly to one dollar per track, or another 33 cents for each member of the trio.

Pandora in fact considers this additional musicians' royalty an extraordinary financial burden, and they are aggressively lobbying for a new law—it's now a bill before the U.S. Congress—designed to relieve them of it. You can read all about it in a series of helpful blog posts by Ben Sisario of the *New York Times*, or if you prefer your propaganda unmediated, you can listen to Pandora founder Tim Westergren's own explanation of the Orwellian Internet Radio Fairness Act.

As for Spotify, since it is not considered radio, either of this world or any other, they have a different additional royalty to pay. Like any non-broadcast use of recordings, they require a license from the rights-holder. They negotiate this individually with each record label, at terms not made public. I'm happy to make ours public, however: It is the going "indie" rate of $0.005 per play. (Actually, when I do the math, that rate seems to truly pay out at $0.004611—I hope someone got a bonus for saving the company four-hundredths of a cent on each stream!) We didn't negotiate this, exactly; for a band-owned label like ours, it's take it or leave it. We took it, which means for 5,960 plays of "Tugboat," Spotify theoretically owes our record label $29.80.

I say theoretically, because in practice Spotify's $0.004611 rate turns out to have a lot of small, invisible print attached to it. It seems this rate is adjusted for each stream, according to an algorithm (not shared by Spotify, at least not with us) that factors in variables such as frequency of play, the outlet that channeled the play to Spotify, the type of subscription held by the user, and so on. What's more, try as I might through the documents available to us, I cannot get the number of plays Spotify reports to our record label to equal the number of plays reported by the BMI. Bottom line: The payments actually received by our label from Spotify for streams of "Tugboat" in that same quarter, as best I can figure: $9.18.

"Well, that's still not bad," you might say. (I'm not sure who would really say that, but let's presume someone might.) After all, these are immaterial goods—it costs us nothing to have our music on these services: no pressing, no printing, no shipping, no file space to save a paper receipt for 25 years. All true. But immaterial goods turn out to generate equally immaterial income. 10

Which gets to the heart of the problem. When I started making records, the model of economic exchange was exceedingly simple: make something, price it for more than it costs to manufacture, and sell it if you can. It was industrial capitalism, on a 7" scale. The model now seems closer to financial speculation. Pandora and Spotify are not selling goods; they are selling access, a piece of the action. Sign on, and we'll all benefit. (I'm struck by the way that even crowd-sourcing mimics this "investment" model of contemporary capitalism: You buy in to what doesn't yet exist.)

But here's the rub: Pandora and Spotify are not earning any income from their services, either. In the first quarter of 2012, Pandora—the same company that paid Galaxie 500 a total of $1.21 for their use of "Tugboat"—reported a net loss of more than $20 million dollars. As for Spotify, their latest annual report revealed a loss in 2011 of $56 million.

Leaving aside why these companies are bothering to chisel hundredths of a cent from already ridiculously low "royalties," or paying lobbyists to work a bill through Congress that would lower those rates even further—let's instead ask a question they themselves might consider relevant: Why are they in business at all?

The answer is capital, which is what Pandora and Spotify have and what they generate. These aren't record companies—they don't make records, or anything else; apparently not even income. They exist to attract speculative capital. And for those who have a claim to ownership of that capital, they are earning millions—in 2012, Pandora's executives sold $63 million of personal stock in the company. Or as Spotify's CEO Daniel Ek has put it, "The question of when we'll be profitable actually feels irrelevant. Our focus is all on growth. That is priority one, two, three, four and five."

Growth of the music business? I think not. Daniel Ek means growth   15
of his company, i.e., its capitalization. Which is the closest I can come to understanding the fundamental change I've witnessed in the music industry, from my first LP in 1988 to the one I am working on now. In between, the sale of recorded music has become irrelevant to the dominant business models I have to contend with as a working musician. Indeed, music itself seems to be irrelevant to these businesses—it is just another form of information, the same as any other that might entice us to click a link or a buy button on a stock exchange.

As businesses, Pandora and Spotify are divorced from music. To me, it's a short logical step to observe that they are doing nothing for the business of music—except undermining the simple cottage industry of pressing ideas onto vinyl, and selling them for more than they cost to manufacture. I am no Luddite—I am not smashing iPhones or sabotaging software. In fact, I subscribe to Spotify for $9.99 a month (the equivalent of 680,462 annual plays of "Tugboat") because I love music, and the access it gives me to music of all kinds is incredible.

But I have simply stopped looking to these business models to do anything for me financially as a musician. As for sharing our music without a business model of any kind, that's exactly how I got into this—we called it punk rock. Which is why we are streaming all of our recordings, completely free, on the Bandcamp sites we set up for Galaxie 500 and Damon & Naomi. Enjoy.

Understanding the Text

1. According to Krukowski, what was the "model of exchange" (11) for making and selling music when he began his career? How has it changed?

2. Given that Pandora and Spotify are not earning income from their services, Krukowsk asks, "Why are they in business at all?" (13). What is his answer?

Reflection and Response

3. After explaining how much his band earns from streaming music, he anticipates a response: "'Well, that's still not bad,' you might say. (I'm not sure who would really say that, but let's presume someone might.)" (10). How do you respond to his account of his band's earnings? Do you think his complaints are justified? Why or why not?

4. In paragraph 16, Krukowski asserts, "I am no Luddite." What is a "Luddite"? Why do you think he includes this assertion? What point does it help him make?

5. In his conclusion, the author asserts: "But I have simply stopped looking to these business models to do anything for me financially as a musician. As for sharing our music without a business model of any kind, that's exactly how I got into this — we called it punk rock" (17). What does he mean by this, specifically in the context of "punk rock"? What relationship between art and commerce does his statement imply?

Making Connections

6. In "Why Artists Should Stop Chasing Spotify's Pennies and Focus on Top Fans" (p. 177), George Howard writes that artists' complaints about streaming services is its own writing genre, as they all have the same basic elements. He then lists them. Does this seem like an accurate description and fair assessment of Krukowski's argument? Why or why not?

7. Krukowski writes, "The first album I made was originally released on LP only, in 1988 — and my next will likely only be pressed on LP again" (1). Indeed, the last several years have seen a resurgence of vinyl LPs, as even big, mainstream stars such as Taylor Swift and Justin Bieber have released music on traditional records. How would you account for this return to an earlier technology? Do you buy records? Do they seem like a better model for distributing music, whether for consumers or musicians, than streaming or MP3 files? Compare and contrast the experience of music — whether making it or listening to it — on records versus streaming services (or other, more ephemeral digital forms).

8. The legendary punk rock musician and producer Steve Albini has argued: "Record labels, which used to have complete control, are essentially irrelevant . . . The process of a band exposing itself to the world is extremely democratic and there are no barriers. Music is no longer a commodity, it's an environment, or atmospheric element. Consumers have much more choice and you see people indulging in the specificity of their tastes dramatically more. They only bother with music they like." How do you respond to these claims? How do you think Krukowski would respond to them? Where might he agree with Albini? Where might he disagree?

Why Artists Should Stop Chasing Spotify's Pennies and Focus on Top Fans

George Howard

For some artists, consumers, and observers, streaming and other new media models of music distribution are exploitative; for others, the apparent decline of the traditional music industry production-and-distribution model provides promising artistic and commercial opportunities. Writing in *Forbes*, George Howard falls mainly into the latter category, as he responds to artists' complaints about their work being devalued: "As is so often the case with stories that seem to suck just about everyone into their vortex, they often are full of sound and fury, but signify nothing." But Howard does more than criticize: he suggests a different way for artists to think about streaming services to distribute their work — and ultimately, get compensated for their music.

George Howard is associate professor of music business/management at Berklee College of Music in Boston. He is co-founder of Music Audience Exchange, one of the original founders of TuneCore, and the former president of Rykodisc.

Nary a day goes by when we don't hear from an artist with a variant on the following: "My song was streamed on Spotify/Pandora [insert "large" number here], and I was only paid [insert "small" number here]."

These stories make for good fodder in that they highlight a perceived inequity with respect to an artist's work being devalued. They have all the right elements: there's the David and Goliath trope; the not-so-subtle dystopian inference that our society is going to hell because it's over-valuing corporate greed to the detriment of artistry; and the fact that, because it's music—something that plays some sort of role (however large or small) in most peoples' lives, we're all vaguely complicit in these inequities.

As is so often the case with stories that seem to suck just about everyone into their vortex, they often are full of sound and fury, but signify nothing. Such is the case with the hubbub around payments (or lack thereof) from Spotify, et al. to artists.

This is not to say that what Spotify and other music services is or isn't paying artists is right or just. Rather, it's irrelevant. In fact, not only does this debate have zero bearing on artists (not to mention consumers), but by its very nature it serves as a distraction with respect to what artists should really be focusing on.

Certainly, the payments to artists from streaming services are immate-   5
rial to the artists. This does not mean that these services aren't paying out some, *prima facie*, big numbers to certain artists. It's just that even if, for instance, Pandora pays out a million dollars to Jay Z, this amount, when compared to the money Jay Z earns from other ventures, is immaterial. It works the same way for a new artist who gets a payment of $0.25 from Spotify; it's immaterial when compared to what they got paid for playing a club gig or selling a t-shirt. Same deal for mid-level and heritage artists.

Is this "right"? Hard to say. Right now customers are the prime beneficiaries of this windfall of historically deeply discounted music. Any song ever recorded for — at most — around $10/month is hard to argue with, and even harder to change; customers have now been conditioned that this is what music costs, and, the vast majority of customers are not going to ever pay more for it. The services who are now forced to price their subscriptions at this price point argue that if they raise their payments to artists they will go out of business; Pandora actually intimates that if they don't pay *less* to artists they will go out of business, because 50% of their revenue is going to artists royalties. Of course, rather than reducing artist payments to lower this percentage, the other way to reduce this percentage is to *increase revenue!* But, again, Pandora doesn't want to do this because they fear customer revolt if, for example, they run more ads per hour to increase revenue.

All of this is of course outside the artists' hands. No matter how many Facebook posts artists make discussing the real or perceived inequities regarding payments the chances of the rates going up are slim, and, again, even if they do the payments will still be immaterial.

Artists must therefore recalibrate not only their expectations with respect to payments (they should expect nothing), but also their approach generally. Here's how.

We can loosely lump music consumers into three basic clumps: Casual Fans, Active Fans, and Passionate Fans. This grouping nicely corresponds with the Customer Journey as created by the auto industry (but applicable to pretty much everything) that states that customers follow the same path: Awareness, Consideration, Trial, Purchase, and Re-Purchase.

Overlapping these two we see that the streaming services fall neatly   10
into this trajectory. For instance, the first stages of the Customer Journey, Awareness and Consideration, line up well with the Casual music listener. That is, someone who doesn't know what they want, but has a felt need for music might turn to a non-interactive streaming service such as

Pandora, Songza, or a web-radio station. These non-interactive streaming services allow for Casual Fans to hear an array of music.

Given that the core competency of Pandora is to customize a listening experience to your likes, it stands to reason that the Casual Fan could discover something they like that moves them to the Active Fan level. This stage aligns with the Consideration/Trial stage of the customer journey. Here the customer might turn to Spotify or one of the other interactive streaming services (the difference between non-interactive and interactive services is that interactive services allow you to select specific tracks, and listen to them repeatedly; non-interactive services do not allow this). The customer has discovered something in the casual stage and is now considering it/trying it by actively selecting it on Spotify to listen to it a number of times to see if there is resonance.

While the payout to artists increases exponentially when a customer goes from causally discovering their music on a non-interactive source to actively selecting and playing it on interactive service, the payout remains immaterial.

It's only when the customer, after truly resonating with an artist, moves from an Active Fan to a Passionate Fan that the artist stands a chance of making money. This is because this Passionate Fan aligns with the Purchase and (more importantly) Re-Purchase stage of the customer journey. Here the artist can finally unshackle from the contingency of payments from the streaming services, and instead make material money via things like sale of tickets, vinyl, merchandise, membership/subscription modes to their own site for exclusive content, direct sales from their website of downloads of non-album tracks (live performances, demos), etc.

> "It's only when the customer, after truly resonating with an artist, moves from an Active Fan to a Passionate Fan that the artist stands a chance of making money."

These items (recordings of live shows, tickets, etc.) are *only* of interest to Passionate Fans, of course, and thus the importance of using these services like Spotify and Pandora for all their worth to drive more potential Passionate Fans into the funnel in order for the percentage of Passionate Fans to grow.

As seen as a potential catalyst to herd more casual and active fans—fans who may become Passionate Fans—into this funnel, these services take on a real value. This value *far* exceeds any direct financial payment (whether that number goes up or down 10%). To this end, the artists must learn to use these services and benefit from them in the same way the artists are being used by and benefiting these services. 15

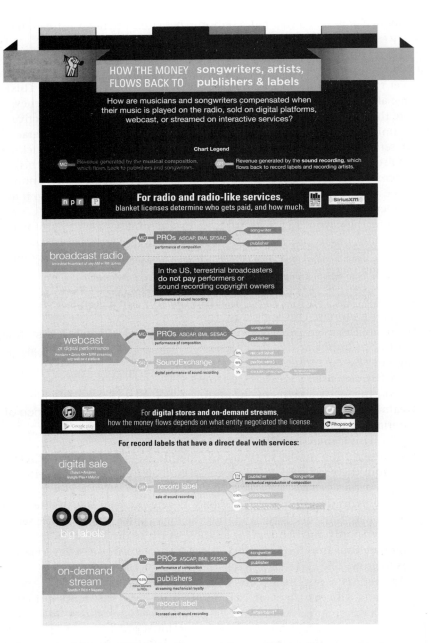

Figure 3.3 Following the money: How musicians and songwriters are paid when their music is played on the radio, sold on digital platforms, presented in a webcast, or streamed on interactive services. Future of Music Coalition, © 2016, http://futureofmusic. org/moneyflow

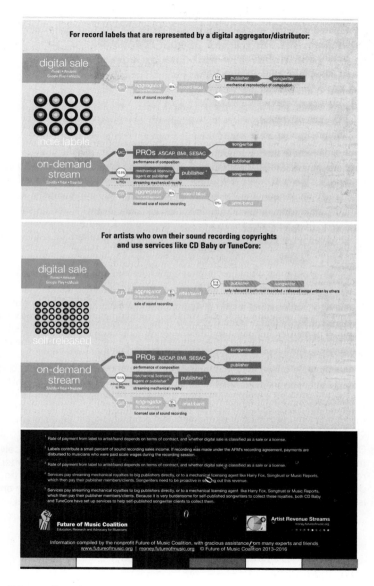

Figure 3.3 *continued*

Understanding the Text

1. Howard considers debates about streaming services' payments to artists a "distraction." Why? What are they a distraction from, in his view?

2. According to the writer, who currently benefits the most from low-priced streaming music?

Reflection and Response

3. After describing the current model of compensating artists, Howard asks, "Is it 'right'?" (6). Why do you think he puts the word "right" in quotation marks? Does he see this issue as a matter of ethics? Do you agree with him? Why or why not?

4. For the purposes of his analysis, Howard writes, "We can loosely lump music consumers into three basic clumps: Casual Fans, Active Fans, and Passionate Fans" (9). Does this seem like an accurate and useful framework for categorizing listeners? Does he exclude any group of listeners? Explain. How do you fit into these categories as a music consumer?

Making Connections

5. As part of his advice to artists who make their work available on streaming services, Howard writes: "Artists must . . . recalibrate not only their expectations with respect to payments (they should expect nothing), but also their approach generally" (8). This assertion provoked many responses from readers and musicians — so much so that Howard posted a follow-up article (available online) to clarify his meaning. Read some of the responses online, as well as Howard's clarification. After considering these different viewpoints and arguments, including Damon Krukowski's "Making Cents," what is your view of the issue? For example, which side — or *sides* — of this debate seem the most persuasive? How would you stake out your own position on the controversy?

6. Do you use streaming services? Do you use any "free" services to receive music? Is payment to the artist a factor in your consumer choices? After reading Howard's and Krukowski's articles, as well as other sources, how do you answer this question? Have the writers changed your thinking on the issue? Will their argument affect your behavior? Explain your answers.

Flashpop/Getty Images

4

How Does Music Negotiate Race and Ethnicity?

A merican popular music has long been enmeshed in the country's complex relationship with racial and ethnic diversity. For example, we might view the course of musical genres such as jazz, rock and roll, and hip-hop in light of a persistent pattern: African Americans largely originate and develop a musical form, which makes it both attractive and frightening to broader, white audiences; white artists then both appropriate — and contribute to — the form, as its commercial possibilities and "crossover appeal" expand; in the process, the form moves from the margins to the mainstream. This account may be too reductive, but the ethics of racial and cultural appropriation are unquestionably problematic. As Samantha Ainsley asks in her essay "Black Rhythm, White Power": ". . . [W]hat, then, distinguishes the use of black music by white musicians from the continual borrowing and sharing of musical property upon which black music is built?" This "borrowing and sharing" goes beyond racial categories, too. As America is, in so many ways, a nation of immigrants, that history of influence, assimilation, and even exploitation applies to other ethnicities and forms, from Afro-Cuban jazz and Brazilian boss nova to Celtic-inflected music and Latino hip-hop: all have undergone cross-pollination in the United States.

In this chapter, the writers view music through the prism of race, ethnicity, and national identity. In "My Bill Evans Problem: Jaded Visions of Jazz and Race," Eugene Holley reflects on his ambivalence toward the legendary and beloved jazz pianist Bill Evans, a white musician who came to prominence in an African American musical form. Samantha Ainsley's provocative "Black Rhythm, White Power" looks unflinchingly at the cycle of the white appropriation and exploitation of black music in the twentieth century — as well as at the larger implications of this process for race relations, generally. Heben Nigatu pushes back against misguided, clichéd, and condescending responses to controversial hip-hop star Kanye West with her perceptive essay "In Defense of Kanye's Vanity: The Politics of Black Self-Love." If

photo: Flashpop/Getty Images

American popular music has so often engendered racial "miscegenation" across musical forms, Sasha Frere-Jones ("A Paler Shade of White: How Indie Rock Lost Its Soul") wonders why so many contemporary indie-rock bands seem to avoid African American influences. In "To Rock or Not to Rock: Cultural Nationalism and Latino Engagement with Rock 'n' Roll," Deborah Pacini Hernandez provides a comprehensive and scholarly exploration of Puerto Rican and Chicano responses to rock music in America. In "Latin Music Is American Music," Chris Kjorness views contemporary debates about immigration and assimilation in the context of America's diversity and the musical contributions of immigrant cultures. Kat Chow tries to discover the origins of a familiar, nine-note melody — one featured prominently in the 1970s hit novelty song "Kung Fu Fighting" — that has come to serve as a musical shorthand for "Asian." Finally, Jeff Chang's "It's a Hip-Hop World" investigates the profound reach of hip-hop as a musical, cultural, and political force in a global context.

My Bill Evans Problem: Jaded Visions of Jazz and Race

Eugene Holley

Here, writer Eugene Holley wrestles with a musical, racial, and cultural problem that preoccupied him for many years: "What was the problem? Bill Evans was white. And I am black." Bill Evans (1930–1980) was a legendary jazz pianist who collaborated with pioneers of the form such as Miles Davis and Charles Mingus. But Holley always felt ambivalent about his admiration for Evans's music. Ultimately, the writer develops a more nuanced view of race, jazz, and culture — one that allows space for his admiration for Evans without relegating "the music's black known and unknown bards to the back of the bus."

Eugene Holley is a writer and essayist whose work has appeared in the *New York Times Book Review*, *Wax Poetics*, *Vibe*, and other outlets. This essay originally appeared on *New Music Box*.

> I never experienced any racial barriers in jazz other than from some members of the audience.
>
> —BILL EVANS

In the early '80s, I was working in a Washington, D.C. record store when I heard *Kind of Blue*, Miles Davis's midtempo, modal masterpiece of an album that for me, and many others, was an initiation into the colors, cadences, and complexities of jazz. Transfixed by the many aural shades of the LP's blue moods, I made it a point to get every recording the musicians on the album had ever made. But it was the poetic and profound pianism of Bill Evans that haunted me the most. When I listened to Evans's studio LP *Explorations*—with drummer Paul Motian and bassist Scott LaFaro—my Evans-induced hypnotic trance deepened; and so did my problem.

What was the problem? Bill Evans was white. And I am black.

When I got into jazz, I was in my twenties. As a child growing up in the '60s and '70s, I was a beneficiary of the Civil Rights Movement, and, more importantly, I grew up in a period of American history when, thankfully, black pride was taken for granted. I had black history courses beginning in the first grade and continuing through middle school, and black contributions to world music were a natural extension of that education. I attended Howard University (the so-called Mecca of historically black colleges and universities). Throughout my life, it had been drilled into me that jazz was created by blacks and represented the apex of African-American musical civilization. I learned about the great jazz heroes—from Louis Armstrong and Duke Ellington to Dizzy Gillespie to Charlie Parker—and of America's refusal to give these Olympian musicians their proper due as the revolutionary artists the world knows them to be. I came to know something deeper: in many cases, white jazz musicians achieved more fame and were given more credit for the creation of the music.

There are enough examples of this in jazz history. Paul Whiteman was 5 the King of Jazz. Benny Goodman was the King of Swing. Duke Ellington knocked on Dave Brubeck's hotel door, to show the white pianist that he made the cover of *Time* magazine in 1954 before he did. (Brubeck, for the record, was hurt and embarrassed.) Then there was the 1965 Pulitzer Prize snub of Ellington. In the '70s, President Carter presented jazz on the White House lawn, with Dizzy Gillespie and Stan Getz as featured artists. President Carter asked Getz about how bebop was created, with Gillespie standing right there.

Against that historical backdrop, I also practiced a form of racial profiling of musicians. Though I was wrong about the racial identities of the Righteous Brothers, Average White Band, and Teena Marie, I knew what black musicians "sounded like" via Motown, Stax, and Philadelphia International records. Though no one stated it specifically, there was a "black sound" and a "white sound." To like a "white sound," or worse, a white musician who "sounded black," was cultural treason. Without realizing it at the time, this inhibited me on many levels, especially as a clarinetist and pianist in high school. When I was studying classical music, and I allowed myself to be moved by it, I feared that some of my black peers would see me as an Uncle Tom.

> "Though no one stated it specifically, there was a 'black sound' and a 'white sound.' To like a 'white sound,' or worse, a white musician who 'sounded black,' was cultural treason."

It was Bill Evans's love of, and application of, European classical styles, approaches, and motifs into jazz that was so attractive to my ears, as evidenced by the azure impressionism of "Blue in Green" on *Kind of Blue*, the intoxicating melodicism of "Israel" from *Explorations*, the lyrical logic of "Peace Piece" from *Portraits in Jazz*, and the chamber timbre of "Time Remembered" from Witt Symphony Orchestra.

So it was in that hot-house atmosphere of well-meaning—but ultimately immature and xenophobic attitudes about music and race—that my Bill Evans problem existed. The problem manifested itself in many ways. I would often hide Bill Evans albums when talking about jazz musicians with fellow black jazz fans for fear of being "outed" as a sellout, given a look of disapproval, or asked, "Why are you listening to that white boy?" The fact that Evans was lauded by white critics because he was white and his classical pedigree didn't help.

Slowly but surely, my perceptions about jazz and race began to evolve and change. As my jazz historical studies deepened, I learned that music is a cultural, not a racial phenomenon. Black Americans at the turn of the 20th century created jazz by combining elements of European classical instruments, harmonies, and song forms with African, Afro-Caribbean, and American rhythms and melodic structures. As Ralph Ellison noted, "blood and skin don't think." Or to put it a different way: jazz didn't come into existence because black people were simply black. Its creation was the result of history, geography, social conditions, and, most importantly, the will to create something of artistic human value. To believe anything else plummets us into the foul abyss of pseudo-racist demagoguery that still plagues us on so many levels today.

Specifically, I asked myself, "Why would Miles Davis, a proud, strong   10
black man, hire someone who was white like Evans?" The answer was simple: the artistry of the musician mattered more to him; not his or her color. Davis hired and collaborated with many white musicians throughout his career, from Gerry Mulligan and Lee Konitz in the historic *Birth of the Cool* sessions of the late '40s and his extremely popular mid-1950s recordings arranged by Gil Evans to his later fusion bands which included Keith Jarrett, Joe Zawinul, Chick Corea, and even British guitarist John McLaughlin. So Davis chose Bill Evans because (in his own words, as recounted in Peter Pettinger's biography *Bill Evans: How My Heart Sings*): "He can play his ass off." Davis was more specific in his autobiography (*Miles: The Autobiography*, co-written by Quincy Troupe): "Bill brought a great knowledge of classical music, people like Rachmaninoff and Ravel. He was the one who told me to listen to the Italian pianist Arturo Michelangeli, so I did and fell in love with his playing. Bill had this quiet fire that I loved on piano."

In addition to Davis, other black jazz superstars hired Evans. He recorded on bassist Charles Mingus's *East Coasting*, a superb and elegant recording from the '50s, and on alto saxophonist Oliver Nelson's '60s masterpiece *Blues and the Abstract Truth*, which also featured Eric Dolphy and Freddie Hubbard. Evans was the featured soloist on arranger/composer George Russell's arrangement of "All About Rosie," and on his third stream-meets-bop *Jazz Workshop* album. He also worked with bassist Ortiz Walton, the author of the book *Music: Black, White and Blue*. My further explorations revealed that Evans was not the lily-white suburban racial recluse I stereotyped him to be. He was heavily indebted to Nat "King" Cole and Bud Powell (Evans described Powell as "the most

Figure 4.1   "To like a 'white sound,' or worse, a white musician who 'sounded black,' was cultural treason": Bill Evans. AF Archive/Alamy

comprehensive talent of any jazz player I have ever heard presented on the jazz scene"). So much for being the "great white devil" or the "white hope" black and white critics made him out to be.

So what does my former Bill Evans problem say about jazz and race today? For one thing, it is firmly and correctly established in music education, and in society in general, that jazz is an African-American art form: blacks have gotten their due as the art form's primary creators. No credible critic, musician, or music curriculum would state otherwise. At the same time, it is equally true that white musicians have made and continue to make great contributions to jazz. While the role Evans and other whites have played should not be exaggerated to move the music's black known and unknown bards to the back of the bus, giving Caucasians appropriate acknowledgment does not threaten the African-American creation of the music.

If anything, jazz at the beginning of the 21st century is appropriately black, brown, and beige; with every global musical/cultural ingredient embellishing, extending, and enriching it. This is a good thing. More importantly, youth around the world—white youth included—want to play it, despite the fact that in the United States you barely see jazz on TV, radio stations that play it are shrinking, and print coverage of it is dwindling.

The declining significance of jazz in the media and marketplace has, in my opinion, increased the unfortunate crabs-in-a-bucket mentality that plagues the jazz infrastructure, which by default can cause the racial aspect to become more prominent. I see this in two distinctly different, but related aspects. The first is the notion of the "Crow-Jimmed" white musician who has been racially discriminated against by blacks, the record industry, and white critics who are guilt-tripped into adopting an "exclusionary" black agenda to support a kind of affirmative action for black musicians. This was the primary gist behind the 2010 publication of trumpeter Randy Sandke's controversial book, *Where the Dark and Light Folks Meet: Race and the Mythology, Politics, and Business of Jazz.* Sandke, a New York–based musician whom I first met when we shared a panel on Louis Armstrong at Hofstra University in 2001, sees today's jazz scene as a retreat into a cult of racial exclusionism that betrays the integration of black and white musicians who played together in the same groups going back to the 1930s. It was a phenomenon which lessened in the '60s and which was largely forgotten during the so-called "Young Lions" era of the '80s when young, African-American musicians such as the Marsalis brothers rose to prominence.

"Having once been in the vanguard, jazz has fallen prey to the same 15 racial divisions that have plagued the rest of American society," Sandke writes. "The overwhelming racialization of jazz has not only denied outside musical influences, stifled creativity, and pitted group against group: it has also overlooked the crucial role that white audiences and presenters have played in disseminating and promoting the music."

I think, with all due respect, Sandke overdramatizes the plight of the white jazz musician. Yes, the Young Lions phenomenon was overwhelmingly black and young, and Sandke is partially right about the market-driven motives of record executives who wanted to hype black musicians to an extent, but their actions pale in comparison to how whites have promoted musicians of a paler shade for centuries. In the end, there is a big difference between the jazz intelligentsia's attempt to right a historical wrong and the willful promotion of a reverse apartheid for white musicians. Sandke's views are ironic, because many black jazz musicians and writers complain that African Americans—who, according to the 2010 CENSUS, are 12% of the population—do not frequent jazz venues in sizable numbers.

On the other end of the spectrum, there is Nicholas Payton: a New Orleans–born trumpet player and son of bassist Walton Payton. Payton has enjoyed a critically acclaimed career, earning a Grammy for his 1997 collaboration with the great Doc Cheatham. In the past decade, he has recorded two challenging and creative CDs: *Sonic Trance* and *Into the Blue*. Now Payton feels straitjacketed as a jazz musician, and he has created #BAM—Black American Music—in response, a movement that is "about setting straight what has been knocked out of alignment by mislabeling and marketing strategies," according to his website. What started out as a provocative essay from "On Why Jazz Isn't Cool Anymore" has degenerated in some posts and tweets into finger pointing and name calling that advances nothing. To be fair to Payton, he is not saying that you have to be black to appreciate or play #BAM. "Black American Music just acknowledges the culture from which it sprung forth. You don't have to be Black to appreciate and play it any more than you have to be Chinese to cook and eat noodles," he writes on his website.

While, as an African American I have some sympathy for Payton's views, I have the same reservations about his conclusions as I do Sandke's views. Payton suggests that black jazz musicians cannot change the status quo of their current stature if they call their music jazz. Payton also ignores or diminishes the fact that, as I stated earlier, everyone in the jazz infrastructure acknowledges blacks as the creators of jazz. Yes, jazz artists are hampered by market-driven definitions, but that is nothing special to them. Every musician regardless of genre complains about this.

Just as my Bill Evans problem obscured my early development in my appreciation of the music, adopting verbatim the thoughts and opinions of musicians like Sandke and Payton could do the same for young people just getting into the music, whether as musicians or as fans. It would be quite Pollyannaish of me to tell someone to "simply ignore race." I (and we) live in a racialized world, and jazz is a part of that world. But if the music teaches us anything, it teaches us that we can keep racial distinctions and distortions at bay.

Understanding the Text

1. What is it, specifically, about Bill Evans's playing that appeals to Holley?
2. The writer tries to understand his "Bill Evans problem," in part, through questioning. He asks himself, "Why would Miles Davis, a proud, strong black man, hire someone who was white like Evans?" How does Holley answer that question?

Reflection and Response

3. Holley writes, "Slowly but surely, my perceptions about jazz and race began to evolve and change. As my jazz historical studies deepened, I learned that music is a cultural, not a racial phenomenon." What does he mean? How do you understand the difference between "cultural" and "racial" in this context?
4. According the writer, "in the United States you barely see jazz on TV, radio stations that play it are shrinking, and print coverage of it is dwindling." How do you account for (in Holley's words) the "declining significance of jazz"? Do you consider jazz a vital contemporary musical form? Is a form's significance or vitality a function of its general popularity? Explain.

Making Connections

5. In "Black Rhythm, White Power" (p. 193), Samantha Ainsley explores the "mainstream absorption of black musical forms," and the cultural appropriation (and misappropriation) of these forms by white artists. How do you think she would understand Holley's "Bill Evans problem"? How do you think she would resolve it?
6. Holley asks, "So what does my former Bill Evans problem say about jazz and race today?" Are his insights into race, culture, and jazz applicable to other musical forms rooted in racial and cultural "blackness," such as hip-hop and rock and roll? For example, can Holley's approach help us better understand and contextualize figures such as Elvis Presley or Macklemore?

Black Rhythm, White Power

Samantha Ainsley

In this sharp, well-researched, and closely argued essay, Ainsley examines the history and ethics of the white appropriation of black musical forms in American popular culture, from jazz to hip-hop. Her goal is to "discover why the Elvises and Eminems are able to reap the glory of African-American cultural innovation." In the process, she explores the notion of the "gift economy," as well as the way in which art becomes commodified and, as a result, emotionally inert. Ultimately, she takes a sobering view of interracial and cross-cultural musical influence, particularly with regard to contemporary hip-hop's popularity with its white audience.

Samantha Ainsley is a graduate of Columbia University. She is currently a PhD candidate in computer science at the Massachusetts Institute of Technology. This essay originally appeared in the *Morningside Review*, an online journal published by the Undergraduate Writing Program at Columbia University.

Introduction and All that Jazz

The lights went down at the Miller Theater, but not a note was played. Then a voice rose above the muffled sounds of the crowd, followed by another, and then another: Martin Luther King, Jr.'s "I Have a Dream" speech, interlaced with words by Malcolm X and Muhammad Ali. The three men's tones resonated with the rhythm of the African djembe beating in the backdrop. Soon, Christian McBride's anticipated bass riff joined the refrain. The great speeches faded along with the drum line, and the jazz took hold, as was permissible since the foundation had been laid: Jazz is a music, a history, a culture. That is, African-American culture is intrinsic to jazz.

The music has its roots in post-Reconstruction New Orleans, at a time when Jim Crow laws lumped Creoles and blacks into one marginalized subgroup. Jazz evolved as a synthesis of "African-derived rhythmic, tonal, and improvisational senses" and French-inspired Creole string ensembles (Hall 36). The word "jazz," in fact, derives from the Creole jass, a slang term for sex. Granted, Creoles are light-skinned and hardly black in the usual sense of the word. To that Perry Hall, director of African American studies at the University of North Carolina at Chapel Hill, adds, "Creole participation in jazz came directly as a result of the discovery by Creole musicians of their Blackness" (47). In other words, Creoles began to play jazz after relocation to and degradation in the United States made them party to the black experience. Yet when jazz gained mainstream popularity in 1917, its face was neither black nor Creole. The first jazz record released to the masses was that of the self-proclaimed "Original Dixieland Jass Band," a group of five white musicians (Hall 38). In the years that followed, a white musician by the name of Paul Whiteman enjoyed great success performing "symphonic jazz," a style that tamed the "primitive rhythms" of original jazz and therein became "more acceptable to white audiences" (Hall 38). In uprooting jazz from its African-American culture, Whiteman grossed one million dollars in a single year in the 1920s and was dubbed the "King of Jazz" (Hall 39).

Hail to the Thief

Paul Whiteman's success arguably lacked merit, but it was hardly unique. Since Whiteman, white men have perpetually sat atop the thrones of black music. For example, in the 1930s, Benny Goodman, a white man, became the "King of Swing" (Hall 31). Decades later, Elvis Presley was crowned the "King of Rock 'N' Roll." In 2003, *Rolling Stone* declared Justin Timberlake the "King of R&B" (Kitwana 156). And of course there's Eminem, who continues to be revered as "the Elvis of hip-hop" (Kitwana 139). How can a white man be the face of black music?

To answer this question, we must examine the long-standing tradition of mainstream absorption of black musical forms (Hall 32). Beginning with jazz and leading up to hip-hop, white America has appropriated black music as its own. When whites cannot stake claims to black music—as in the case of hip-hop—the nature of the relationship between mainstream society and African-American culture is simply exploitative. This essay will examine the ethics of cross-cultural musical appropriation in an attempt to discover why the Elvises and Eminems are able to reap the glory of African-American cultural innovation.

Gillespie, Gifts-Giving, and Genocide

"You can't steal a gift. Bird gave the world his music, and if you can hear 5 it you can have it," Dizzy Gillespie declared in defense of Phil Woods, a white saxophonist who had been accused of poaching Charlie "the Bird" Parker's style (Lethem 70). Jonathan Lethem, in his essay "The Ecstasy of Influence: A Plagiarism," draws inspiration from Gillespie in criticizing copyrights and exploring the concept of a "gift economy" (65). According to Lethem, works of art exist in such an economy, which is rooted in the poignancy of the product (65–66). This gift economy is independent of the market economy in which art and music are commoditized because "a gift conveys an uncommodifiable surplus of inspiration" (Letham 66).

No doubt black musical forms—as is true of all art—function in such an economy both in giving and receiving. To a greater extent, rock 'n' roll connoisseur Theodore Gracyk questions whether there was ever an African-American musical form "that wasn't already the result of miscegenation and hybridization" (86). For example, as noted earlier, the first jazz musicians drew inspiration from both "the French tradition of military marching bands" and the European-style string orchestra (Hall 36). As Lethem would argue for any art, the making of music is a continual process of borrowing and sharing. Thus, Gillespie and Gracyk are right to say that black artists cannot claim exclusivity to black music. But what, then, distinguishes the use of black music by white musicians from the continual borrowing and sharing of musical property upon which black music is built?

In truth, the gift analogy is oversimplified. You certainly cannot "steal" a gift if it has been given to you, but you can misuse it. When appropriating black musical forms, white artists such as Paul Whiteman often reshape and redefine the styles to "minimize their association with 'Blackness'" (Hall 32). This type of cultural appropriation is less an exchange of gifts than "a virtual stripping of Black musical genius and aesthetic innovation" (Hall 33). To Gracyk, the very process of reshaping is what grants "those engaged in appropriation . . . some right to claim ownership of the music they perform" (107). Thus, symphonic jazz can be appreciated independently of the black musical style from which it is derived, and its creation gives whites some cultural ownership of jazz. Yet Gracyk fails to recognize the effect of appropriation on the original musical form, which distinguishes unethical appropriation from the harmless inspiration that Lethem supports. In the most basic sense, a gift can be considered "misused" when it is damaged through usage. As is often the case when mainstream America whitewashes black cultural property and then claims it as its own, the result is what philosopher Amiri Baraka, one of the greatest voices of "spoken word" jazz, describes as a "cultural genocide" (quoted in Gracyk 110).

Gracyk rejects this notion of cultural genocide. According to Gracyk, "the analogy with genocide hinges on the thesis that, were it not for the nonreciprocal behavior of the cultural imperialist, the 'dominated' culture would not have changed" (110). Because African-American culture would have evolved independently of white influence, white America's reshaping of black musical forms, he claims, simply gives rise to a "legitimate transformation" (110). Gracyk depicts this instance of cultural appropriation as natural, yet black musical forms have tended to evolve unwillingly. New forms emerge in hopes of reestablishing "the distinctiveness of Black music in a given sociohistorical context" (Hall 32).

What is particularly unnatural is the continual need for African Americans to reassert their cultural autonomy. For example, when rock music became more closely associated with Elvis than Chuck Berry, black musicians such as Ray Charles and Sam Cooke fused rhythm and blues with "gospel-inflected harmonies" to create what became known in the 1960s as "soul" (Hall 44). Such innovation is less the result of dynamism than of marginalization. Cultural genocide arises when the art is separated from the people (Hall 31). The heavily consumed, appropriated forms are "ineffective as expressions and affirmations of the unique cultural experiences from which they arise" (Hall 32). Cultural meanings are thereby often erased (Hall 35), as happened when whites appropriated soul music—which spoke to black emotion and struggle during the Civil Rights Movement—and called it "disco" (Hall 45). When whites appropriate black music, the art is stripped not only of its cultural identity but also of its ability to function in the gift economy. Although Lethem agrees that one cannot steal a gift, he argues that one can destroy it: "Where there is no gift there is no art, [thus] it may be possible to destroy a work of art by converting it into a pure commodity" (66). When black musical forms are completely dissociated from their emotional foundation—as in the case of soul's devolution into disco—the result is no longer a work of art but a mere commodity, which Lethem defines by its inability to create a genuine emotional connection (66). However, the mainstream need not appropriate black music in order to commoditize it. We see this in the case of hip-hop. Though rap has been reinterpreted by a myriad of races, including whites, it is nevertheless identified with African-American culture—a culture that is now bought and sold.

Back Yard DJs to NWA: Origins of Hip Hop

Rap in general dates all the way back to the motherland, where tribes would use call-and-response chants. In the 1930s and 1940s you had Cab Calloway pioneering his style of jazz rhyming. The sixties you had the love style of rapping, with Isaac Hayes, Barry White, and the poetry style of rapping with the Last Poets, the Watts poets and the militant style of rapping with brothers like Malcolm X and Minister Louis Farrakhan.

—AFRIKA BAMBAATAA, 1993 (QUOTED IN PERKINS 2)

Rap is revolutionary as a black musical form because every path traces its lineage back to an element of African-American culture. Granted, today there are countless cultural varieties of hip-hop from Asian to Hispanic rap; still, all of these styles are indisputably derived from black music.

So far, hip-hop has inspired imitations but it has nevertheless resisted cultural genocide. That is not to say, however, that it has escaped exploitation.

Hip-hop was born in the South Bronx in the mid 1970s as the product of the yard culture of West Kingston brought to New York by Jamaican immigrants in the late '60s: "Yard DJs brought huge speakers and turntables to the slums, where they rapped over the simple bass lines of the ska and reggae beats . . . The DJ ruled during hip hop's early days, and it was the DJ who established the foundations for the lyricist (MC)" (Perkins 6). In the 1980s, black middle-class rappers L.L. Cool J and the group Run DMC, both from suburban Queens, were representative of the first wave of hip hop artists to achieve mainstream success (Perkins 15) — that is, until their minimalist style gave way to controversial "gangsta" rap in the 1990s (Perkins 18). "The gangsta was epitomized by the now defunct group NWA (Niggas with Attitude), which consisted of the MCs Dr. Dre, Ezy-E, Ice Cube, MC Ren . . . and Ice-T" (Perkins 18). Then came the "message rap" of artists such as Long Island's Public Enemy, which was followed by the much less political "booty rap" of groups like 2 Live Crew (Perkins 19–20). Rap's decades-long transformation exemplifies the natural cultural dynamics about which Gracyk theorizes. Its cultural autonomy remained intact at this point. Then, in the late 1990s, a white rapper from Detroit emerged on the scene and started down the path to becoming hip-hop's Elvis.

The Blue-Eyed Baller

> "If I have a cup of coffee that is too strong for me because it is too black, I weaken it by pouring cream into it."(2)
>
> —MALCOLM X, 1963.

In 2003, a well-established hip-hop magazine, *The Source,* acted on a per-   10
sonal vendetta against the industry's most successful artist of the time, white rapper Eminem. In an attempt to derail the rapper's carrier, *The Source* published lyrics from unreleased tracks by Eminem that featured blatantly racist attacks on black women: "Girls I like have big butts/no they don't, 'cause I don't like that nigga shit . . . Black and whites they sometimes mix/But black girls only want your money/cause they be dumb chicks"(quoted in Kitwana 136). After a public apology in which Eminem attributed his racist remarks to teenage angst and bitter resentment toward an African-American ex-girlfriend, Eminem's success and popularity were unaffected (Kitwana 141). But *The Source's* crusade against

the white rapper did not end there; the magazine's greatest concern was not that rap's most successful artist was racist, but that he was white and that hip-hop rightly belonged to a black youth subculture (Kitwana 136). Granted, Eminem was not first white rapper to enjoy mainstream success. In fact, the first No.1 hip-hop album was the all white hip-hop group the Beastie Boys' 1986 *License to III* (White 201). Similarly, the first hip-hop single to top the charts was Vanilla Ice's "Ice, Ice Baby" in 1991 (Perkins 37). But the most successful white rappers often parodied the genre, which led some listeners to write them off as "wiggers." Eminem's music was revered as genuine hip-hop, and *The Source* feared the familiarity of his success. Countless times, owners of *The Source* declared that Eminem was on "the fast track to becoming hip-hop's Elvis" (Kitwana 136). That is, as had happened with Elvis, yet another black musical form would be more closely identified with an iconic white artist than with black artists.

In the early 1950s, Sam Phillips—the Sun Records executive who helped Elvis rise to stardom—proclaimed, "If I could find a white man who had the Negro sound and the Negro feel, I could make a billion dollars" (quoted in Perkins 38). Unlike his wannabe predecessors, Eminem can produce rap with that very "Negro feel." His lyrics have thematic similarities to some black rap because Eminem grew up in the marginalized class of impoverished white Americans. Hence, his music preserves the emotional aspect of the hip-hop gift. Perhaps Eminem's music exemplifies hip-hop's ability to function as a gift economy. After all, whereas Elvis' stardom catalyzed rock 'n' roll to become the predominately white musical form it is today, Eminem's success has not given hip-hop a white face. Has the music industry evolved beyond racial exploitation, or is the mainstream interested in keeping hip-hop black?

Mr. Ambassador at the Minstrel Show

In late 2002, the *New York Times Magazine* ran a cover story on hip-hop's cultural bandit, Marshall Mathers, a.k.a. Eminem, and titled it "Mr. Ambassador" (Kitwana 160). The astute title was fitting for the rap superstar who had previously been labeled the "king" of hip-hop, for Eminem is just that: the envoy of white America to the hip-hop nation. Eminem has attracted many mainstream listeners to hip-hop essentially because he looks like they do. Before Eminem, true hip-hop—which excludes the whitewashed works of Vanilla Ice and the Beastie Boys—was exclusively black and therefore incomprehensible to most white audiences. It does not follow, however, that Enimem is the white man's rapper. Quite the contrary: "although rap is still proportionately more popular among blacks, its primary audience is white and lives in the suburbs" (Samuels, quoted in Kitwana 82). In February 2004, *Forbes* reported that of an estimated 45 million hip-hop consumers between the ages of 13 and 34, eighty percent are white (Kitwana 82). This begs the question: Why do white people love hip-hop, that is, hip-hop in its true form? According to pop journalist Arnold White, "Rap flourished into corporate-sponsored hip hop because of the symbiosis that held whites enthralled to Blacks and kept Blacks indentured" (183). White America's embrace of hip-hop culture is hardly a move toward racial acceptance and cultural understanding. Rather, it is the product of "white supremacy (i.e. black kids selling black images of black criminality and inferiority and white kids buying them to reinforce their superiority)" (Kitwana 103). Hip-hop perpetuates the American tradition of minstrelsy, except that rather than whites painting their faces black, black artists have succumbed to stereotypes of themselves. In the case of hip-hop, white supremacy is enforced not through imitation but consumption of the "minstrel portrait" of black "dehumanization" (Baraka 328). In the eyes of the mainstream, hip-hop reinforces conventions and stereotypes of blackness that foster white power.

Though Eminem may honor hip-hop as a gift, the mainstream renders it a commodity. A commodity fails to establish an emotional connection between two people (Lethem 66). Though rap music showcases black suffering, mainstream America receives it not with compassion but with mockery—white supremacy prevents an emotional connection. Previous musical generations saw white artists destroying the gift of black music by failing to recreate its poignancy; the hip-hop generation sees poignancy destroyed through direct commoditization. In the case of hip-hop, whites are able to reap the power and profits of black culture not by marginalizing black ingenuity but by exploiting it. Simply put: whites couldn't do it better themselves.

Why Deny the Obvious, Child?

Hip-hop may have broken the appropriative trend between mainstream America and black music, but it has done little to end the marginalization of African Americans. It seems that the key issue is not so much the act of appropriation as the driving force behind it. Incidentally, when discussing mainstream absorption of black music, few scholars aside from Theodore Gracyk acknowledge its contributions. We cannot deny that "rock could not exist without appropriation" (Gracyk 97), nor can we blame individual artists for acts of appropriation.

Take, for example, Paul Simon's *Graceland*, which is often criticized for   15
Simon's arguably exploitative use of a group of South African folk singers
to enhance the tone of the album and, ultimately, his own success. The
accusation runs: "Visually and aurally, Simon appears as the white master
who exerts a benign rule over his black subjects" (Mitchell, quoted
in Gracyk 91). Yet to suggest that Simon's work with the South African
choir had imperialistic motives is excessive. In truth, he was motivated
by "a genuine love of South African music" (Gracyk 98); we cannot criticize
him for that. Concomitantly, the South African tribal leader Joseph
Shabalala praised Simon for "the opportunity to disclose [their] music
all over the world" (quoted in Gracyk 105). Though not Simon's fault,
Graceland failed to inspire interest in South African music. Most people I
know who own the album admit to skipping the only track that features
the South African choir almost exclusively. The only music *Graceland* successfully
promoted was that of Paul Simon—just as when Keith Richards
and Mick Jagger started the Rolling Stones, in Richard's words, "to turn
other people on to" African-American blues artist Muddy Waters (quoted
in Gracyk 15), they really only turned people on to the Rolling Stones.

> "The crime, then, is not the use of black musical gifts but the bigotry that often leads to their commoditization."

The crime, then, is not the use of
black musical gifts but the bigotry that
often leads to their commoditization.
The success of *Graceland* and the Rolling
Stones speaks to whites' lack of interest
in the black experience and their
desire not simply to steal black music,
but more basically to de-contextualize it—that is, to avoid establishing
emotional connections. Appreciation of black music goes hand in hand
with appreciation of black people, except in the case of hip-hop through
which blacks have allowed themselves to be dehumanized. That is not to
say that non-hip-hop black musicians enjoy no mainstream success—we
know that to be untrue. Rather, mainstream America tends to depreciate
black music, for connecting emotionally with such works of art might
bring about an understanding of black suffering that would undermine
white supremacy. Moreover, the commoditization of black music continues
to foster white power by granting financial success to those who
control the music industry: whites. The power disparity between whites
and blacks in music industry suggests that the music is another tool the
mainstream uses to perpetuate black marginalization. As Amiri Baraka has
observed, "The laws once openly stated blacks inferior. Now it is the relationship
these laws uphold that maintain the de facto oppression" (329).
In the shift from de jure to de facto racism, mainstream America reshaped

bigotry in much the same way it did black music — through the simple process of whitewashing.

Note

1. An allusion to Radiohead's 2003 album.
2. From a speech by Malcolm X entitled "God's Judgment of White America (The Chickens Come Home to Roost)," delivered on December 4, 1963, in New York City.
3. An allusion to the title of a Paul Simon track from 1990's *Rhythm of the Saints*.

Works Cited

Baraka, Amiri. *The Music: Reflections on Jazz and Blues*. William Morrow, 1987.

Gracyk, Theodore. *I Wanna Be Me: Rock Music and the Politics of Identity*. Temple University Press, 2001.

Hall, Perry A. "African-American Music: Dynamics of Appropriation and Innovation." *Borrowed Power: Essays on Cultural Appropriation*, edited by Bruce Ziff and Pratima V. Rao, Rutgers UP, 1997, pp. 31–51.

Kitwana, Bakari. *Why White Kids Love Hip-Hop: Wankstas, Wiggers, Wannabes, and the New Reality of Race in America*. Basic Civitas Books, 2005.

Lethem, Jonathan. "The Ecstasy of Influence: A Plagiarism." *Harper's Magazine*, Feb. 2007, pp. 59–71.

Little, Malcolm (aka Malcolm X). "God's Judgment of White America (The Chickens Come Home to Roost)." Speech delivered in New York City on 4 Dec. 1963, http://www.blackcommentator.com/42/42_malcolm.html.

Perkins, William E. "The Rap Attack: An Introduction." *Droppin' Science: Critical Essays on Rap Music and Hip-Hop Culture*, edited by William E. Perkins, Temple University Press, 1996, pp. 1–45.

White, Armond. "Who Wants to See Ten Niggers Play Basketball?" *Droppin' Science: Critical Essays on Rap Music and Hip-Hop Culture*, edited by William E. Perkins, Temple University Press, 1996, pp. 182–210.

Understanding the Text

1. In the context of the "gift economy" that she discusses, how can a "gift" be "misused," according to Ainsley? In what ways has jazz been misused?
2. How does Ainsley explain the conception and development of "soul" music?
3. Why is rap distinctively "revolutionary" as a black musical form, according to the writer?

Reflection and Response

4. Borrowing the phrase from the poet and writer Amiri Baraka, Ainsley writes about the process of "cultural genocide" (6). What does this analogy mean? How do you respond to it, in the context of her essay?

5. For Ainsley, "White America's embrace of hip-hop culture is hardly a move toward racial acceptance and cultural understanding. . . . Appreciation of black music goes hand in hand with appreciation of black people, except in the case of hip-hop through which blacks have allowed themselves to be dehumanized" (12, 16). Do you agree with her view that the genre "is another tool the mainstream uses to perpetuate black marginalization" (16)? Why or why not?

Making Connections

6. In "A Paler Shade of White: How Indie Rock Lost Its Soul" (p. 208), Sasha Frere-Jones laments the genre's disengagement from "black" music, noting that during the 1990s, "black influences had begun to recede, sometimes drastically, and the term 'indie rock' came implicitly to mean white rock." How is Frere-Jones's reading of race and popular music similar to — and different from — Ainsley's? For example, do they share a similar view of transracial-racial musical borrowing and influence, or are their views incompatible?

7. Ainsley's article notes that hip hop's primary audience is white and suburban. What do you think accounts for its broad appeal, particularly in the context of race? Explain your answer.

In Defense of Kanye's Vanity: The Politics of Black Self-Love

Heben Nigatu

Over the last several years, perhaps no high-profile, mainstream hip-hop artist has been the subject of as much discussion and debate as Kanye West. In this essay from *Buzzfeed*, Heben Nigatu pushes back against the conventional wisdom that West is "crazy" — especially as this "boring" characterization relates to his supposedly outsized vanity. In its place, she provides a sophisticated, revealing, and provocative view of the rapper that highlights his "populist narcissism" and his underappreciated vulnerability. For her, his personal egotism is an inspiring political statement: "To assert that, despite the boundaries of a racist world that strangles your very view of what is possible, you are still going to be out here stuntin' on everyone, that you will love yourself and love yourself excessively, is powerful beyond measure."

Heben Nigatu is a former writer for *Buzzfeed* and current co-host of *Buzzfeed's Another Round* podcast. She is also a writer for *The Late Show with Stephen Colbert*.

Maybe it was the absurdly nonfunctional shutter shades or the audacious (and, let's be real, honest) Taylor Swift interruption, but at some point in pop culture, Kanye West became a punch line. When he sat down with *The New York Times'* Jon Caramanica for a rare, rather lengthy interview, the responses were predictable. Various media roundups* characterized his quotes as "ridiculous," "textbook-crazy," "obnoxious," and, well, you get the point.** All of this makes me wonder if anyone actually read the interview, because he talks about (and complicates) the very thing that others so boringly mock him for: his vanity. I'm not here to convince you to love Kanye's music or to love him as a figure. What I am interested in talking about, and what I think is often overlooked, is how race affects the way people perceive and respond to his vanity. Kanye is a part of a long tradition of black artists for whom self-love is a political act.

The concept of vanity is so rooted in the idea of a singular narcissist that it can be hard to catch that Kanye speaks almost from a populist perspective—a populist narcissism, if you will. Granted, the thematic focus on community vs. the personal has evolved from *College Dropout* to *Yeezus*, but take a second and remember the very first song on Kanye's first album. He has a chorus of children singing, "We wasn't supposed to make it past 25/Joke's on you, we still alive/Throw your hands up in the sky/And say we don't care what people say." If you chalk up his "we don't care what people say" attitude to simply his ego, then you have missed the point entirely. This isn't about ego; this is about boldly asserting yourself in a world that is not meant for you. This is a vanity that is rooted in bringing the community up with you. To the ire of some who are so wrapped up in the anxiety of respectability, the message he gives the kids (in front of all these white folks who are listening to his music!) is not to be modest but to unapologetically laugh in the face of a world that does not care about them. The joke's on you, white America. We made it, and we don't even have the decency to be grateful. We're laughing. We dare to laugh.

This is why it's so critical to really think about how and why folks are calling him "crazy." There's a great Dave Chappelle quote from his Inside the Actors Studio interview that really gets to the heart of this. In a conversation about the difficulties of black celebrity life, Chappelle explains, "The worst thing to call somebody is 'crazy.' It's dismissive. 'I don't understand this person. So they're crazy.' That's bullshit." To continuously label what Kanye says as "crazy" is to dismiss him as not worth understanding and to flatten his deeply complex work and complex personality. Kanye told *Rolling Stone* in 2004, "I'm the rap version of Dave Chappelle. I'm not sayin' I'm nearly as talented as Chappelle when it comes to political and social commentary, but like him, I'm laughing to keep from crying." "Laughing to keep from crying" is a tone that captures so much of both of their work, but it's also a survival mantra. Originating with Langston Hughes, this expression encapsulates a history of black artists who have used wit and satire to capture their exasperations and make light of the world's absurdities. The humor shouldn't be overlooked here; people seem to miss that Kanye is very tongue-in-cheek, that he is constantly making jokes. As *Vulture's* Jody Rosen puts it, "Anyone who gets riled up about 'I Am a God,' or about the album's title, is missing the joke—or rather, taking the bait. More than ever, West is aiming to provoke." Yes, and also, sometimes he's just making fun of you.

The jokes are fun, but the difficulty and power of his vanity cannot be emphasized enough. To assert that, despite the boundaries of a racist world that strangles your very view of what is possible, you are still going to be out here stuntin' on everyone, that you will love yourself and love yourself excessively, is powerful beyond measure. And as many black artists have said before, for black folks to love themselves is a political act. The poet Audre Lorde captures it best: "Caring for myself is not self-indulgence, it is self-preservation, and that is an act of political warfare." Kanye's "vanity" is meant to be inspiring; it is not a mindless arrogance but it is pointed and intentional. One of the most compelling things he says in his *Times* interview is that he views his work, in some ways, as an extension of the fight for justice of the activists and artists who came before him. In their traditions but also in his own way, he is fighting for justice: "I'm going to use my platform to tell people that they're not being fair . . . Justice. And when you say justice, it doesn't have to be war. Justice could just be clearing a path for people to dream properly."

Kanye's infatuation with the sartorial world is also important to con-   5
sider in the light of the black artists who came before him. As Monica Miller points out in the fascinating *Slaves to Fashion: Black Dandyism and the Styling of Black Diasporic Identity*, there is a long history of black artists who use fashion, art, and a couture-level interest in looking beautiful and self-fashioning as a powerful tool of self-actualization. From as far back as the slaves who dressed in their Sunday best to the black dandies of the English Enlightenment, from the luminaries of the Harlem Renaissance to the greats of the Jazz Age and to contemporaries like Andre 3000, black artists have used art and fashion to re-imagine the possibilities of what it means to be black, of what is possible and imaginable for black identities. This play with dandyism is both about an individual's self-image and about how they are regarded, it is personal and political, and it is within the community and about the dynamics outside it. Kanye is very aware of this history and this balance between the political and the beautiful has been characteristic of his discography. He tells the *Times*, "That's how I was raised. I am in the lineage of Gil Scott-Heron, great activist-type artists. But I'm also in the lineage of a Miles Davis—you know, that liked nice things also."

Conversations that take Kanye's vanity as a given annoyance obfuscate the fact that Kanye has helped change the game entirely for how black men are allowed to express their vulnerabilities in public. In the *Times* interview, he talks about how, in the public's imagination, "the idea of Kanye and vanity are like, synonymous." He goes on to explain, however: "But I've put myself in a lot of places where a vain person wouldn't put themselves in. Like what's vanity about wearing a kilt?" If you see him simply as a crazy egomaniac, you've taken away his right to be a dimensional human being. You miss the moments when he is so boldly asserting his vulnerabilities, his anxieties, his humanity—the times he is placing his bare self on the line as an artist. This bravado mixed with

> "Conversations that take Kanye's vanity as a given annoyance obfuscate the fact that Kanye has helped change the game entirely for how black men are allowed to express their vulnerabilities in public."

a deeply sincere self-reflectiveness has characterized his career from the very beginning. It began with the earnest confessions of his first single and grew to become an entire album where he sings—despite openly acknowleging he's a horrible singer—about heartbreak. It's hard to imagine the sappy crooning of Drake or the angsty emo rap of Kid Cudi existing if it weren't for Kanye. And, to return to the sartorial for a moment, notice how in that quote, he articulates his expression of vulnerability in terms of fashion choices, in terms of a leather kilt. He's keenly aware of the way black identity, and black masculinity in particular, is wedded to an image, a static image, and he purposefully plays with that.

All of this is obviously not to say that Kanye is immune from criticism or that I, myself, have never side-eyed things he has said or done. But ultimately, I am grateful for the space that his bold and unapologetically vain work has created for black artists, for black children, for dreamers. On a more fundamental level, this conversation begs the question, how much pride is allowed for one person? At what point does being proud of yourself turn into being "too vain"? Who decides? Kanye has just dropped *Yeezus*, an incredibly dense and complicated album that revels in a dark spiral of introspection mixed with the political articulations and sonic embellishing that is so characteristic of his canon. His work continues to refuse an easy reading, and this album boldly proclaims that he is someone you must pay attention to. You don't have to love it, but you will respect it.

Understanding the Text

1. Nigatu writes that she is not trying to convince her readers to love Kanye West's music or love him as a person. What is her purpose? What is her thesis?

2. From the writer's perspective, what is wrong or misleading about labeling West "crazy"?

Reflection and Response

3. According to the writer, West speaks from a "populist narcissism" (2). What does that phrase mean? How is it paradoxical? In what way does West resolve the paradox?

4. Nigatu's essay includes references to a range of figures such as comedian Dave Chappelle, Langston Hughes, and Audre Lorde, as well to the scholarly work of Barnard College English professor, Monica Miller. How are these references related to her purpose? What do they enable her to do?

Making Connections

5. In paragraph 2, Nigatu writes: "To the ire of some who are so wrapped up in the anxiety of respectability, the message he gives the kids (in front of all these white folks who are listening to his music!) is not to be modest but to unapologetically laugh in the face of a world that does not care about them." What does the "anxiety of respectability" mean? Research the meaning of this term, along with the phrase "respectability politics," in the context of contemporary discussions of race, politics, and social justice. How are figures like Kanye West, specifically, and hip-hop music, generally, linked to this notion of "respectability"?

6. The writer provides a brief analysis of West's 2013 album *Yeezus*: "*Yeezus*, an incredibly dense and complicated album that revels in a dark spiral of introspection mixed with the political articulations and sonic embellishing that is so characteristic of his canon. His work continues to refuse an easy reading, and this album boldly proclaims that he is someone you must pay attention to" (7). Do you agree with her evaluation and assessment of the album? What is your "reading" of it, regarding race, vanity, justice, and other issues discussed in Nigatu's essay?

7. Nigatu suggests that many critics and fans misunderstand Kayne West and his music, even as she places him in a tradition of other African American cultural figures. Likewise, in the excerpt from *My Bondage and My Freedom* (p. 80), Frederick Douglass writes about the ways in which many listeners misunderstood the songs of slaves. Do you think there are any parallels in these misunderstandings and "mis-hearings"? Explain your answer.

A Paler Shade of White: How Indie Rock Lost Its Soul

Sasha Frere-Jones

Critic and musician Sasha Frere-Jones has written for many publications, including The *Village Voice*, *Spin*, and the *New York Times*. He was a staff writer for *The New Yorker* magazine from 2004 to 2015.

He also served as executive editor of Genius.com and a critic for the *Los Angeles Times*. In this widely discussed *New Yorker* essay from 2007, Frere-Jones claims that rock and roll, "the most miscegenated popular music ever to have existed, underwent a racial re-sorting in the nineteen-nineties." While this musical form always benefited from a two-way influence and "miscegenation" (a process Frere-Jones traces), indie bands, in particular, have turned away from the signature elements and influences of African American music. This issue is thorny, as it touches on provocative questions of "appropriation, minstrelsy, or co-optation" that have haunted American music for decades. But Frere-Jones's analysis offers a perceptive take on the intersection of race, influence, and popular culture.

In May, I went with a friend to see the Canadian indie-rock band Arcade Fire perform at the United Palace, a gilded rococo church in Washington Heights that seats more than three thousand and doubles as a theatre. The band was playing to a noisily receptive crowd during what has been a very successful year. Arcade Fire's latest album, *Neon Bible*, which was released here in March, has sold more than three hundred thousand copies—an impressive number for an indie band during an industry-wide sales slump—and the group was on its second visit to New York in three months.

The band, six men and three women, shared the stage with half a dozen curved screens and slender red fluorescent lights, which encircled the musicians like a ring of candles. In January, at a less elaborate show in a small London church, the band's members had called to mind Salvation Army volunteers who had forgotten to go home after Christmas—their execution was ragged but full of brio—and I had spent the evening happily pressed against the stage. At the United Palace, even though the music was surging in all the right places, I was weary after six songs. My friend asked me, "Do they play everything in the same end-of-the-world style?"

Arcade Fire's singer and songwriter, Win Butler, writes lyrics that allude to big, potentially buzz-killing themes: guilt, rapture, death, redemption. And because, for the most part, he deals convincingly with these ideas, the band has been likened to older bands known for passion and gravitas, including the Clash. (On tour, Arcade Fire sometimes plays a cover of the Clash's anti-police-brutality anthem "Guns of Brixton.")

By the time I saw the Clash, in 1981, it was finished with punk music. It had just released Sandinista!, a three-LP set consisting of dub, funk, rap, and Motown interpretations, along with other songs that were indebted—at least in their form—to Jamaican and African-American sources. As I watched Arcade Fire, I realized that the drummer and the bassist rarely played syncopated patterns or lingered in the low registers. If there is a trace of soul, blues, reggae, or funk in Arcade Fire, it must be philosophical; it certainly isn't audible. And what I really wanted to hear, after a stretch of raucous sing-alongs, was a bit of swing, some empty space, and palpable bass frequencies—in other words, attributes of African-American popular music.

There's no point in faulting Arcade Fire for what it doesn't do; what's 5 missing from the band's musical DNA is missing from dozens of other popular and accomplished rock bands' as well—most of them less entertaining than Arcade Fire. I've spent the past decade wondering why rock and roll, the most miscegenated popular music ever to have existed, underwent a racial re-sorting in the nineteen-nineties. Why did so many white rock bands retreat from the ecstatic singing and intense, voicelike guitar tones of the blues, the heavy African downbeat, and the elaborate showmanship that characterized black music of the mid-twentieth century? These are the volatile elements that launched rock and roll, in the nineteen-fifties, when Elvis Presley stole the world away from Pat Boone and moved popular music from the head to the hips.

It's difficult to talk about the racial pedigree of American pop music without being accused of reductionism, essentialism, or worse, and such suspicion is often warranted. In the case of many popular genres, the respective contributions of white and black musical traditions are nearly impossible to measure. In the nineteen-twenties, folk music was being recorded for the first time, and it was not always clear where the songs—passed from generation to generation and place to place—had come from. The cadence of African slave hollers shaped the rising and falling patterns of blues singing, but there is still debate about the origins of the genre's basic chord structure—I-IV-V—and how that progression became associated with a singing style on plantations and in Southern prisons. In 1952,

> "It's difficult to talk about the racial pedigree of American pop music without being accused of reductionism, essentialism, or worse, and such suspicion is often warranted."

the record collector Harry Smith released *Anthology of American Folk Music*, a highly regarded compilation (and, later, a source for Bob Dylan), which showed that white "country" performers and black "blues" artists had recorded similar material in the nineteen-twenties and thirties, singing about common legends, such as "Stackalee," over similar chord progressions. Even the call-and-response singing that is integral to many African-American church services may have been brought to America by illiterate Scottish immigrants who learned Scripture by singing it back to the pastor as he read it to them.

Yet there are also moments in the history of pop music when it's not difficult to figure out whose chocolate got in whose peanut butter. In 1960, on a train between Dartford and London, Mick Jagger and Keith Richards, then teen-agers, bonded over a shared affinity for obscure blues records. (Jagger lent Richards an LP by Muddy Waters.) "Twist and Shout," a song that will forever be associated with the Beatles, is in fact a fairly faithful rendition of a 1962 R. & B. cover by the Isley Brothers. In sum, as has been widely noted, the music that inspired some of the most commercially successful rock bands of the sixties and seventies—among them Led Zeppelin, Cream, and Grand Funk Railroad—was American blues and soul.

The Beatles, especially in Paul McCartney's compositions, married blues and soul with the verse-chorus-bridge structure common to songs from the English music hall and Tin Pan Alley, and hooked teen-agers on a combination of Irving Berlin and Muddy Waters that previously would have been unthinkable. Similarly, when Mick Jagger stopped trying to imitate Bobby Womack he became, musically speaking, an original—a product of miscegenation. He sang with weird menace and charm, and with an accent that placed him in an unidentifiable neighborhood (with more than one bar) somewhere over the Atlantic Ocean. Jagger's knock-kneed dancing may have begun as an homage to Little Richard's exuberant hamming, but he eventually devised his own style—a bewitching flexion of knees and elbows.

The borrowing went both ways. Keith Richards wanted a horn section to play the main guitar riff in the Stones' 1965 single "(I Can't Get No) Satisfaction," on the theory that this would make the song sound like an American soul track. But the song was recorded without a horn section, and immediately became popular, inspiring several covers. One of the better ones was by Otis Redding. ("Otis Redding got it right," Richards said.)

Until Michael Jackson, another soul singer, achieved international 10 prominence, in the late seventies, however, some of the most successful venders of American black music were not black. MTV had been on the air for nearly two years before it got up the courage to play the video for Jackson's "Billie Jean," in 1983. (Jackson was the first black artist to appear on the channel, though it had played videos by the equally gifted white soul act Hall & Oates.) Jackson's 1982 album "Thriller" is the second-biggest-selling record of all time (after *Eagles: Their Greatest Hits 1971–1975*), but he alone could not alter pop music's racial power balance. Black and white musicians continued to trade, borrow, and steal from one another, but white artists typically made more money and received more acclaim. This pattern held until 1992, when the Los Angeles rapper and producer Dr. Dre released *The Chronic*, an album whose star performer was a new rapper named Snoop Doggy Dogg.

You could argue that Dr. Dre and Snoop were the most important pop musicians since Bob Dylan and the Beatles. There had already been several important hip-hop hits: the 1979 single "Rapper's Delight," by the Sugarhill Gang, which marked the genre's commercial début; the 1986 remake of "Walk This Way," a raplike song by the white seventies rock band Aerosmith that the group rerecorded with the black hip-hop trio Run-DMC (as pure an example of musical miscegenation as there can be); and the 1988 album *Straight Outta Compton*, by Dr. Dre's group N.W.A., which helped make sampling and sexually violent lyrics central to hip-hop's aesthetic.

The Chronic, which has sold more than five million copies, upended established paradigms. It presented rappers chanting over smooth funk played on live instruments, as well as over grainy digital samples of old records, and in doing so it changed hip-hop's sound. It started a conceptual migration, establishing the template for hip-hop from outside New York—especially in the South, a region that has recently come to dominate the genre. Hip-hop became music for driving; it was designed to soothe. (The heavy bass frequencies cause car seats to vibrate, literally massaging the passengers.) The menace was now limited to the lyrics, which featured increasingly explicit tales of gunplay and sex, creating a dissonance between sound and sense that typifies gangsta rap even today.

Videos of songs from *The Chronic* were broadcast on MTV, and Snoop, then a twenty-year-old former gang member from Long Beach, California, who delivered his grim narratives with laid-back aplomb, became the face of hip-hop for many people who had little experience with the genre. If young white musicians had been imitating black ones, it was partly because they had been able to do so in the dark, so to speak. In 1969, most of Led Zeppelin's audience would have had no idea that Robert Plant and Jimmy Page had taken some of the lyrics of "Whole Lotta Love" from the blues artist Willie Dixon, whom the band had already covered twice (with credit) on its début album. (After Dixon sued Led Zeppelin, the band credited him with the song.)

By the mid-nineties, the biggest rock stars in the world were rappers, and the potential for embarrassment had become a sufficient deterrent for white musicians tempted to emulate their black heroes. Who would take on Snoop, one of the most naturally gifted vocalists of the day? Of course, a few did — there have been white rappers and several commercial, if generally unappealing, blends of rock and rap. But, in the thirty years since hip-hop became widely available, there have been only three genuinely popular white rap acts: the Beastie Boys, whose biggest-selling album sold to kids who were more taken with the Led Zeppelin samples and the lewd jokes than with the rap music; Vanilla Ice, an anomaly who owes much of his success to his vertical hair and the decision to rap (in "Ice Ice Baby") over "Under Pressure," a song by David Bowie and Queen that has proved immune to destruction; and Eminem, the exception who proves the rule. A protégé of Dr. Dre's who spent part of his youth in Detroit, he had to be better than the local black competition simply in order to be accepted — a fascinating inversion of the racism that many blacks have encountered in the workplace.

In the mid- and late eighties, as MTV began granting equal airtime to videos by black musicians, academia was developing a doctrine of racial sensitivity that also had a sobering effect on white musicians: political correctness. Dabbling in black song forms, new or old, could now be seen as an act of appropriation, minstrelsy, or co-optation. A political reading of art took root, ending an age of innocent — or, at least, guilt-free — pilfering. This wasn't a case of chickens coming home to roost. Rather, it was as though your parents had come home and turned on the lights.

I've spent much of my life playing music, and on and off since 1990 I've been a member of a funk band called Ui. We've had six members, all white, though most of the musicians who inspire our sound are black (the New Orleans band the Meters; several artists who played with Miles Davis in the seventies; various Jamaican rhythm sections) or are white bands heavily indebted to black music (Led Zeppelin, the German band Can). We released our first record in 1993 — a vinyl EP available only in England, the first in a series of dubious marketing decisions — and the handful of reviews that it received were factually accurate, citing the bands I've mentioned as influences and recognizing that we were primarily interested in making instrumental funk, not in singing. The singing, what little there was, was my job, and it caused me to start thinking about musical miscegenation.

When we played our version of funk or dub reggae, or tried to make a synthesizer sound like a dolphin fixing a tractor (tough but doable), it felt natural. Most of our music didn't require singing, but a few pieces needed the sound of a human voice to round them out. Yet singing stumped me.

Except for a single, miraculous week when I was sixteen, I've never rapped successfully, and melodic singing was inappropriate for the jumpy, poly-rhythmic music we played. So I fudged, splitting the difference between singing, chanting, and rapping, each time with diminishing returns. (I can hardly stand to listen to these tracks now.) And the problem was clearly related to race. It seemed silly to try to sound "black," but that is what happened, no matter how hard I tried not to. In some ways, this was the result of a categorical confusion, the assumption that if I could use my hands to play a derivation of black music with any authority I could use my voice to do the same thing. Playing black music never felt odd, but singing it—a more intimate gesture—seemed insulting. By the time we recorded our last album, in 2003, I had given up singing alto-gether. It had become clear to me that, to understate the case wildly, I lacked the ability of Mick Jagger and Prince and any number of other great rockers to fuse disparate traditions into a sound that was obviously related but unique—a true offspring.

Many indie bands seemed to be having complex reactions of their own to musical miscegenation. The indie genre emerged in the early eighties, in the wake of British bands such as the Clash and Public Image Ltd., and originally incorporated black sources, using them to produce a new music, characterized by brevity and force, and released on independent labels. The Minutemen, a group of working-class white musicians from San Pedro, California, who were influential in the late eighties, wrote frantic political rants that were simultaneously jazz, punk, and funk, without sounding like any of these genres. But by the mid-nineties black influences had begun to recede, sometimes drastically, and the term "indie rock" came implicitly to mean white rock. Pavement, a group that the *Village Voice* rock critic Robert Christgau, in 1997, called "the finest rock band of the nineties—by critical acclamation," embodied this trajectory. The band's first drummer, Gary Young, had a strong sense of swing and a solid backbeat (at least, when he managed to stay on his drum stool), but after his departure, in 1993, Pavement began producing a flat-footed mixture of shaggy, improvi-sational rock and sylvan curlicues taken from obscure folk groups. During the same period, indie-band singers abandoned full-throated vocals and began to mumble and moan, and to hide their voices under noise. Lyrics became increasingly allusive and oblique. (From Pavement's 1995 song "Grave Architecture": "Am I just a bathtub waiting to be gripped or found on shady ground? And the lampshade's poised on the overwhelm. Drugs, and need the talent to breathe.") Several groups that experienced commer-cial success, such as the Flaming Lips and Wilco, drew on the whiter genres of the sixties—respectively, psychedelic music and country rock—and gradually Brian Wilson, of the Beach Boys, a tremendously gifted musician who had at best a tenuous link to American black music, became indie rock's muse. (Two currently popular indie acts, Panda Bear and Sufjan Stevens, are well schooled in Wilson's beatific, multi-tracked harmonies, which evoke the sound of glee clubs and church choirs.)

Wilco's 2002 album, *Yankee Hotel Foxtrot*, which won that year's Pazz and Jop national critics' poll in the *Village Voice*, is one of the most celebrated indie-rock records of the past five years. (It was released on Nonesuch, which was a subsidiary of the major label Atlantic—further evidence that "indie rock" has become an aesthetic description, and no longer has anything to do with labels.) Wilco, which formed in 1994, was initially an alt-country band, whose songwriter, Jeff Tweedy, demonstrated a knack for writing clipped, vernacular descriptions of relationships and emotional states. The band's 1996 album, *Being There*, is one of the few alt-country records that I play. It is indebted to a couple of readily identifiable sources—country (as the Rolling Stones played it) and bluegrass—and the music has a pleasing crackle. But after that Wilco and Tweedy, presumably under the influence of other indie bands, drifted from accessible songs toward atomization and noise. On *Yankee Hotel Foxtrot*, the lyrics are embarrassing poetry laid over plodding rhythms. ("Tall buildings shake, voices escape singing sad, sad songs, tuned to chords strung down your cheeks.") The album features synthesizer squeaks and echoey feedback, which fail to give shape to the formless music. A little more syncopation would have helped.

Other flagship indie bands—the Fiery Furnaces, the Decemberists, the 20 Shins—occasionally produce memorable hooks and moments of inspired juxtaposition. (The Fiery Furnaces have a constantly mutating lineup of instruments, which makes the band sound, at its best, like a jukebox on the fritz.) Grizzly Bear, the indie band that excites me most right now, is making songs with no apparent links to black American music—or any readily identifiable genre. (The band's sound suggests a group of eunuchs singing next to a music box on a sunken galleon.) But, in the past few years, I've spent too many evenings at indie concerts waiting in vain for vigor, for rhythm, for a musical effect that could justify all the preciousness.

How did rhythm come to be discounted in an art form that was born as a celebration of rhythm's possibilities? Where is the impulse to reach out to an audience—to entertain? I can imagine James Brown writing dull material. I can even imagine the Meters wearing out their fans by playing a little too long. But I can't imagine any of these musicians retreating inward and settling for the lassitude and monotony that so many indie acts seem to confuse with authenticity and significance.

The segregation occurred in both directions. Beginning in the late eighties, there were several high-profile lawsuits involving sampling. In

1991, a U.S. federal court ruled that the rapper Biz Markie's use on his album *I Need a Haircut* of a sample from a song by Gilbert O'Sullivan constituted willful infringement. (The album was withdrawn from stores and rereleased without the offending track.) A similar suit led to a decision by a federal appeals court, in 2004, that the use of even three notes from someone else's work could be a violation of copyright, making it difficult for all but the wealthiest rappers to use samples. For twenty years, beginning in the mid-eighties, with the advent of drum machines that could store brief digital excerpts of records, sampling had encouraged integration. (Think of De La Soul rhyming over an excerpt from the seventies educational cartoon series *Schoolhouse Rock!* or of Jay-Z rapping over a snippet from the Broadway musical *Annie*.) In practice, the ruling obliged hip-hop producers to write their own music, which left them with a larger share of royalties. And, as producers became as powerful and as well known as rappers, having a distinctive sound that wasn't associated with another genre or artist became an asset. Rap musicians, lacking incentives to appropriate other sounds, began to stress regional differences instead: in Atlanta, the rugged, spare sound of crunk; in the Bay Area, the whizzing, burping, synthesizer-dominated sound of the hyphy movement.

The most important reason for the decline of musical miscegenation, however, is social progress. Black musicians are now as visible and as influential as white ones. They are granted the same media coverage, recording contracts, and concert bookings, a development that the Internet, along with dozens of new magazines and cable shows devoted to celebrities, has abetted by keeping pop stars constantly in the public eye. Even unheralded musicians don't need Led Zeppelin to bring their songs to the masses anymore: an obscure artist can find an audience simply by posting an MP3 on MySpace. The Internet, by democratizing access to music—anybody, anywhere can post or download a song on MySpace—has also made individual genres less significant. Pop music is no longer made of just a few musical traditions; it's a profusion of strands, most of which don't intersect, except, perhaps, when listeners click "shuffle" on their iPods. Last month, in the *Times*, the white folk rocker Devendra Banhart declared his admiration for R. Kelly's new R. & B. album *Double Up*. Thirty years ago, Banhart might have attempted to imitate R. Kelly's perverse and feather-light soul. Now he's just a fan. The uneasy, and sometimes inappropriate, borrowings and imitations that set rock and roll in motion gave popular music a heat and an intensity that can't be duplicated today, and the loss isn't just musical; it's also about risk. Rock and roll was never a synonym for a polite handshake. If you've forgotten where the term came from, look it up. There's a reason the lights were off.

Understanding the Text

1. What does Frere-Jones notice is missing from Arcade Fire's music? What did he want to hear?

2. As a member of a funk band, what specifically spurred Frere-Jones to "start thinking about musical miscegenation"? Why?

Reflection and Response

3. How does Frere-Jones use rhetorical questions to structure his essay? Point to a specific example and explain how it helps further the writer's analysis.

4. In paragraph 15, the writer discusses the role "political correctness" may have played in inhibiting "musical miscegenation." What does he mean by "political correctness" in the context of musical appropriation? Do you agree with this analysis? Why or why not?

Making Connections

5. Frere-Jones writes, "The most important reason for the decline of musical miscegenation, however, is social progress" (23). How do you think Ainsley (p. 193) would respond to this claim — and to Frere-Jones's essay, generally?

6. Writing in 2007, Frere-Jones wondered about the retreat of white rock bands from "the ecstatic singing and intense, voicelike guitar tones of the blues, the heavy African downbeat, and the elaborate showmanship that characterized black music of the mid-twentieth century . . ." (5). A decade later, is Frere-Jones's analysis of this "racial re-sorting" still relevant?

To Rock or Not to Rock: Cultural Nationalism and Latino Engagement with Rock 'n' Roll

Deborah Pacini Hernandez

In this chapter from her book *Oye Como Va! Hybridity and Identity in Latino Popular Music* (2010), Deborah Pacini Hernandez writes about Latino "responses to developments in mainstream popular music" from the 1950s through the 1980s. She frames her analysis by comparing and contrasting Los Angeles Chicano engagements with rock and roll with their New York Puerto Rican counterparts on the East Coast. The result is a knowing history of Latino rock and pop traditions that includes well-known artists such as Tito Puente, Santana, Los Lobos, Ricky Martin, and Jose Feliciano, but also lesser-known figures like Ruben Guevara, Johnny Colon, and the band Chango (to name a few).

Deborah Pacini Hernandez is Professor Emeritus, Anthropology and American Studies, at Tufts University. She is co-editor of *Reggaeton* (2009) and the author of *Bachata: A Social History of a Dominican Popular Music* (1995), among other publications.

When Tito Puente[1] wrote his now-anthemic song "Oye Como Va!" in 1963, the United States was poised on the brink of profound social and cultural upheavals that, in the seven short years between Puente's original recording and Carlos Santana's 1970 rock version, would profoundly alter the context, nature, and meaning of Latino musical practices. In the early 1960s, thousands of economically displaced Puerto Ricans, including Puente's family, had arrived in New York in search of opportunity—just as the city was beginning to lose its manufacturing base, condemning many of the new arrivals and their mainland-born children to lives of chronic unemployment, poverty, and racial discrimination. Increasinglygly negative images of Puerto Ricans and their culture began appearing in the media, such as John Frankenheimer's 1961 film *The Young Savages* and the 1961 film *West Side Story* (based on the 1957 play). In this context, Puente's Cuban-inspired version of "Oye Como Va!" found receptive ears in New York's Puerto Rican community, but the

---

[1]**Tito Puente (1923–2000):** Legendary New York–born American musician and composer who was an influential figure in Afro-Cuban music, Latin jazz, and other popular genres.

rest of the nation was turning its back on the Spanish Caribbean mambos and cha-chas once synonymous with tropical festivity and cosmopolitan glamour, dancing instead to rock 'n' roll. Elsewhere in the Americas, the economic restructuring that anticipated (and prepared the way for) an increasingly globalized economy was setting in motion massive human displacements that would bring millions of Mexicans searching for better lives into the United States, among them Santana's family.

In 1963. however, these processes had not yet made themselves fully felt. The Vietnam War had not yet mobilized the nation's youths to rebel against authority, and young second-wave feminists were only beginning to issue calls for the end of patriarchy. Psychedelic drugs and alternative visions of how society could be organized had not yet caught the imaginations of young people around the globe. The Beatles were on the eve of their dramatic arrival in the United States but had not yet become global countercultural icons. The country's racist structures were being challenged by the civil rights movement, although the intersecting impacts of race and ethnicity later foregrounded by the Chicano and Puerto Rican movements in the 1970s had not yet surfaced, nor had these activists issued their manifestos calling on Latinos to resist assimilation and to retain their cultural heritage and distinct identities.

By 1970, in contrast, when Santana's version of "Oye Como Va!" burst onto the *Billboard* charts, these groundbreaking, paradigm-shaking transformations had been set in motion. Increasingly frustrated with their persistent marginality and inspired by cultural nationalism, young Latinos heeded the call to maintain and to celebrate their traditional Latin American cultural heritages. But at the same time, many of them, especially bilingual and bicultural Latino youths, continued to embrace the mainstream styles that had provided the soundtracks to their daily lives. As I argue in this chapter Latinos were not outsiders looking in or passive consumers of mainstream styles; they were active (if often unrecognized) participants in musical developments that incorporated, but went beyond, practices considered by cultural nationalists as appropriate for representing their ethnic identities.

There was nothing new, of course, about the layered quality of U.S. Latino musical practices, which have always been far more complex than surface-level correspondences—for example, between Puerto Ricans and salsa or Tejanos and conjunto—would suggest. U.S.-born Latinos, particularly in their youth, have routinely consumed their own communities' traditional musics as well as the same mainstream popular music and culture as their non-Latino contemporaries. Latino engagement with mainstream styles has encompassed jazz, swing, and Tin Pan Alley in the 1920s, 1930s, and 1940s; rock 'n' roll, pop, and various subgenres of rock in the 1950s, 1960s, and 1970s; and, since the 1980s, rap and hip-hop. Such engagements, however, were particularly fraught in the late 1960s and 1970s, when cultural nationalism stimulated by the African American, Chicano, and Puerto Rican civil rights movements rendered cultural hybridity, long vexing to a nation loath to acknowledge it, increasingly problematic to Latinos themselves as well as to non-Latinos trying to interpret their cultural productions.

Significantly, Latino responses to developments in mainstream pop- 5 ular music in the rock era, which coincided with the rise of cultural nationalism, have taken quite different forms; these different responses are the subject of this chapter. Chicanos have engaged with rock 'n' roll directly, consistently, and (relatively) successfully. Santana's version of "Oye Como Va!"—in which he blended two styles, Afro-Cuban cha-cha and guitar-based rock, neither of which was considered an authentically Mexican style—exemplified Chicanos' familiarity and comfort with cultural and musical hybridity. Many of Santana's New York Puerto Rican contemporaries, in contrast, were deliberately distancing themselves from mainstream, English-language rock in favor of music unambiguously rooted in Spanish Caribbean sonorities that were closer in spirit and aesthetics to Puente's original version.

Concepts and Comparisons: Historical Perspectives

In order to unravel the differences between West Coast Chicano and East Coast Puerto Rican engagement with rock 'n' roll, several variables must be considered: the groups' immigration histories; the characters of their most important receiving cities, Los Angeles and New York, including their residential patterns and demographic compositions; their relationships with local and national music industries; the position of each Latino community in the U.S. racial hierarchy, especially vis-à-vis African Americans; and, finally, their interactions with musical developments in the sending regions of Mexico and Puerto Rico.

At first glance, the positions of Chicanos and New York Puerto Ricans within U.S. society seem remarkably similar, even taking into consideration important differences, such as the fact that Chicanos trace their origins in what is now U.S. territory well back into the Spanish colonial period, centuries before California was seized from Mexico after the 1848 Mexican-American War; in contrast, Puerto Ricans did not begin migrating to New York in substantial numbers until after the 1898 Spanish-American War that brought the island under U.S. colonial rule. Both communities were relatively small at the turn of the century: Mexicans, for example, comprised only 5 percent of the population of Los Angeles in 1900, while Puerto Ricans in 1920 numbered only twelve thousand in the entire U.S. territory. Similarly, both communities became larger, better established, and more internally diverse after World War II thanks to the concurrent accelerations in processes of assimilation and immigration, making both of them the most culturally influential Latino group in each receiving city.

Some crucial differences between the two communities, however, influenced their identities and their musical practices. Mexican Americans' and Puerto Ricans' racial identities had evolved quite differently within the United States as a result of their distinct colonial histories. Mexican Americans are predominantly mestizos of mixed European and Amerindian heritage and have therefore fallen outside the long-standing U.S. racial binary. (Indeed, because they lacked clear and obvious African antecedents, at various points in U.S. history, Mexican Americans were able to lay legal claim to whiteness.) Puerto Ricans, in contrast, are the racial and cultural descendants of the Spanish colonizers, indigenous Tafnos, and the enslaved Africans brought to island. Many Puerto Ricans disavow their African heritage; nonetheless, as Juan Flores and others have pointed out, Puerto Ricans have unmistakable historical and cultural commonalities with African Americans that Mexican Americans do not share. Because of their mixed racial ancestries, both Mexican Americans and New York Puerto Ricans were subjected to racial discrimination, and they often resided in segregated neighborhoods in close proximity to African Americans. New York, however, has always been more spatially concentrated than Los Angeles, with its characteristic metropolitan sprawl; as a result, Puerto Ricans, particularly in Spanish Harlem and the South Bronx, lived and worked in closer physical proximity to African Americans than did Mexican Americans in Los Angeles, where Mexican American barrios have been comparatively more removed from African American neighborhoods (with some exceptions, such as Watts); for example, African Americans predominated in South Central Los Angeles, while Mexican Angelenos were concentrated in downtown and East Los Angeles.

As for the relationships between Chicanos and New York Puerto Ricans and musical developments in their respective homelands, particularly in regard to rock, both Mexico and the island of Puerto Rico developed active rock 'n' roll scenes as early as the 1950s. In both locations, rock 'n' roll was initially associated not with rebellious working-class youths but rather with lighter-skinned, upper-class young people, whose desire to participate in its associated modernity was perceived by nationalists as reflections of a colonized mentality. In Mexico, however, rock 'n' roll was indigenized when a working-class Mexican rock scene evolved in dialogue (albeit unequal and nearly one-sided) with developments in the United States (U.S. rockers took little interest in Mexican rock). In Puerto Rico, in contrast, rock 'n' roll—regardless of whether the musicians were African American or white—continued to be perceived as an intrusive and unwelcome product of U.S. imperialism, against which salsa became a symbolic bulwark. Given Puerto Ricans' equation of salsa with authenticity and nationalism, and rock 'n' roll with U.S. cultural imperialism, it is not surprising that aesthetic moves in the direction of rock were not received more enthusiastically within the working-class and intensely nationalistic New York Puerto Rican community. Chicano nationalists, in contrast, could look upon Mexico's vibrant rock scene with pride; no less a figure than Santana, whose career as a rocker began in Tijuana, was a product of that scene.

West Coast Mexican Americans and Rock 'n' Roll

As an expanding body of scholarship has made clear, the most import- 10 ant influences on Mexican American rock 'n' roll musicians were their African American neighbors, with whom they shared the experience of racial and economic oppression and segregated, marginalized urban spaces. African American groups routinely played in East Los Angeles venues, and they were familiar with Mexican American culture, which they incorporated into some of their music, much to the delight of their Mexican American fans. As far back as 1953, for example, Texas-born African American sax player Chuck Higgins wrote the song "Pachuko Hop" (referring to the zoot-suited Mexican American youths known as "pachucos"), which became enormously popular among Mexican American youths in Los Angeles. In the 1960s, the Penguins recorded a song called "Hey Senorita," and one of their later songs was entitled "Memories of El Monte," the East Los Angeles stadium where a mixed crowd of Mexican American, African American, and white teens saw their favorite rock 'n' roll groups. In the 1970s, the song "Low Rider" by the group War explicitly celebrated the customized cars so closely associated with Mexican Angelenos; indeed, the song has become an anthem to Mexican American lowriders.

Despite their affinities with African Americans, Mexican American forays into the rock 'n' roll arena were by no means limited to African American styles: Trini Lopez worked in the folk rock style, Chris Montez recorded soft pop ballads, and Bobby Espinosa started his career playing surf music with a group called Mickey and the Invaders before going on to become a founder of the 1970s group El Chicano. Rubén Guevara collaborated with avant-garde rocker Frank Zappa on Zappa's album *Cruising with Ruben and the Jets*, and Guevara later formed an actual neo-doo-wop group—as opposed to the fictitious one mocked on Zappa's album—called Ruben and the Jets. Even acid rock, so closely associated with white middle-class hippies, had important Mexican American participants, most notably Santana but also his brother Jorge's group Malo, and other groups, such as Sapo and Azteca.

Some scholars have suggested that Mexican American rockers developed a characteristic sound, attributed to their extensive use of the Farfisa organ sometimes used in conjunto ensembles—an intriguing suggestion, to be sure, although it does not account for the full range of styles played by Mexican Angelenos in which the Farfisa organ was not employed. Indeed, even when aesthetics from Mexican or other Latin/o American music were incorporated, the effects tended to be quite subtle, rendering scholar's efforts to describe the distinctiveness of Mexican American rock 'n' roll rather imprecise. Guevara, for example, explains the Mexican influences in the music of the self-identified 1950s Mexican American rocker L'il Julian Herrera (a Hungàrian American Jew raised by a Mexican American family) as follows: "It was very much in the black style, but something about it—the accent, the voice, the *attitude*—made it different." Matt Garcia is similarly vague in identifying a Mexican American sound in a more "intense" rhythmic pattern and the presence of a brass section, especially the saxophone. The point here is not that these characterzaions of Mexican American rock 'n' roll are incorrect but that most casual listeners would not likely have been able to identify the music as distinctively Mexican American.

Rock 'n' roll produced by Mexican Americans in the 1950s and 1960s was as remarkably successful as it was stylistically varied. Those who attained national hits included Cannibal and the Headhunters, whose "Land of a Thousand Dances" (1965) earned them the spot as openers for the Beatles on their second U.S. tour; Chris Montez with "Let's Dance" (1962), "Call Me" (1966), "The More I See You" (1966), and "There Will Never Be Another You" (1966); Trini Lopez (Texas-born but performing in Los Angeles when he was discovered) with his folk-rock version of "If I Had a Hammer" (1963), "Kansas City" (1963). "Lemon Tree" (1965), and "I'm Comin' Home Cindy" (1966); and the Premiers with "Farmer John" (1964). Dozens of other East Los Angeles bands, such as Rene and Ray, the Blendells, Thee Midniters, and the Romancers, charted locally or on the Top 100 chart nationally. These bands, whose song titles and lyrics often celebrated local cultural practices and geographies (the most famous example being Thee Midniters' 1965 song "Whittier Boulevard," named after Chicanos' favorite strip for cruising), enjoyed the support of a large and enthusiastic community of East Los Angeles teenage fans, who flocked to performances held in the city's largest venues, such as the Paramount Ballroom and the El Monte American Legion Stadium. Indeed, in Los Angeles, so much Mexican American rock was produced between the 1950s and 1970s that a term was coined to refer to it collectively—the so-called "East Side Sound."

Groups composed entirely or partially of Mexican Americans from other parts of the country also made the national charts during this period, demonstrating the vitality and range of Mexican American rock 'n' roll in the I 950s and 1960s. Texan Mexicans were particularly successful: Sunny and the Sunglows with "Talk to Me" (1963); Sam the Sham and the Pharaohs with "Woolly Bully" (1964), "Ju Ju Hand" (1965), "Ring Dang Doo" (1965), "Li'l Red Riding Hood" (1966), and "The Hair on My Chinny Chin Chin" (1966); the Sir Douglas Quintet with "She's About a Mover" (1965), "The Rains Came" (1966), and "Mendocino" (1969); and Rene and Rene with "Lo Mucho Que Te Quiero" (1968). Tejano musician Freddy Fender's English and Spanish versions of his rock 'n' roll songs "Mean Woman" "Que Mala" and "Holy One"/"Hay Amor" became local hits in the 1950s and he later scored four number-one hits on the national country charts, which then crossed over to the pop charts—although, with the exception of "Before the Next Teardrop Falls" (1975), to somewhat lower positions. The Detroit-based ? (Question Mark) and the Mysterians also made the national charts in 1966 with "96 Tears," followed the next year with "I Need Somebody."

While collectively Mexican Americans' successes are noteworthy, the 15
fact that their songs were largely sung in English and were aesthetically very similar to—if not indistinguishable from—mainstream rock 'n' roll enabled Mexican Americans to step into the mainstream popular music arena in the 1950s and 1960s. To be sure, included in the substantial body of Mexican American rock 'n' roll produced between the 1950s and 1970s were some remakes of Spanish-language songs; examples include Ritchie Valens's version of "La Bamba," based on a traditional Veracruzan folk song, and various versions of the classic Mexican bolero "Sabor a Mí." Nonetheless, in the 1960s, the mainstream music industry and the English-speaking public had lost their appetites for Latin American music.

The cultural nationalism inspired by the Chicano movement in the late 1960s and early 1970s, in contrast, stimulated Chicano rockers to ethnically mark their music by employing a variety of performance strategies—although they did not abandon the rock 'n' roll idiom in favor of more "authentically Mexican" styles. The group originally called the VIPs, for example, which played music ranging from the Beatles'

"Lady Madonna" to Eddie Floyd's "Knock on Wood," changed their name to El Chicano in 1969 but continued to play the same repertoire. Instrumentation was also employed to convey ethnicity, such as the prominent mariachi horns in Yaqui's bilingual song "Time for a Change (Es Tiempo Para un Cambio)" (1973). Other musicians released songs with Spanish titles, such as El Chicano's 1970 hit song "Viva Tirado," named after a Mexican bullfighter—despite the fact that the tune, written by Los Angeles jazzman Gerald Wilson, was an instrumental and had nothing to do with bullfighting. Album cover art also made explicit musicians' links to the ideology of the Chicano movement, a noteworthy example being the iconic image of an indigenous warrior and princess featured on the cover of Malo's 1972 eponymous recording, which invoked Chicanos' southwest homeland, the mythical Aztlán.

In response to the Chicano movement's emphasis on cultural roots, traditional Mexican music was imbued with additional value, particularly within the farm workers' struggle, where cultural activists such as Luis Valdéz employed Mexican *corridos* and conjunto music in their drive to unionize workers. Nonetheless, the sources many Chicano rockers drew on, even in this highly politicized period, were not Mexican but Spanish Caribbean, thereby invoking a more generalized pan-Latino identity. Santana's "Oye Como Va!" and "Evil Ways" are certainly the most famous examples of such Spanish Caribbean–infused Chicano rock, but other groups, such as Malo, Sapo, and Azteca, similarly blended rock with Spanish Caribbean aesthetics, particularly in the domain of percussion. Spanish Caribbean Latin music had always been popular in Los Angeles but it should be noted that those most responsible for developing the Afro-Latin rock style were Chicanos/Latinos from San Francisco. Significantly, Santana's first group, the Santana Blues Band, began, as its name clearly indicates, not as a rock band but as a blues band, specializing in Chicago-style blues; Latin percussion and stylings were introduced when conga player Mike Carabello joined the band and were later enhanced with the addition of José "Chepito" Areas and Pete and Coke Escovedo. Los Angeles Chicanos, in contrast, generally favored a more African American–oriented R & B/funk sound, although some gravitated to the new punk style that emerged in the l970s.

By the end of the 1970s, the Chicano movement, like other social movements originally stimulated by cultural nationalism and identity politics in the 1970s, was being modified by more nuanced views of ethnic identity generated by Latinos, especially feminists and gays, who contested essentialist, monolithic (and masculinist) constructions of what it meant to be Chicano. Ethnic identity and pride remained important, but the range of opportunities for articulating them through music expanded. Chicano punk rockers such as the Plugz and The Brat, for example, reflected the political tenor of the times by harshly critiquing the establishment. Other punk groups, such as Los Illegals, insisted on incorporating Spanish into their lyrics, but they rejected the heroic nationalism adopted by their predecessors in terms of their performance styles and the iconographies invoked in their cover art. The changing political environment can be observed in the trajectory of the rock group Los Lobos: They had begun playing rock 'n' roll in their youth, but when they formed the band in the early 1970s as the Chicano movement was in ascent, they turned to traditional Mexican music; they returned to English and the rock 'n' roll idiom in the 1980s; and since then, they have maintained a successful career based on their ability to play both traditional Mexican music *and* straight-up guitar rock as well as zydeco, blues, and country and western. Achieving national acclaim with their 1984 bilingual recording *How Will the Wolf Survive?* followed by their role in Luis Valdéz's successful 1987 biopic *La Bamba* (based on the life of Ritchie Valens), Los Lobos' command of the full range of U.S. and Mexican popular music styles — sometimes blending them, sometimes not — allowed them to sustain a fan base of both ethnic Mexican and mainstream audiences.

The career of Chicano Elvis impersonator El Vez (Robert Lopez), who began his musical career in the Los Angeles–based punk rock group the Zeros, similarly articulates Mexican Americans' increasingly creative and strategic use of their hybridity. El Vez's music is designed primarily for listeners who are bilingual, bimusical, and bicultural, all of which are necessary traits for understanding his unique brand of ironic humor and social commentary. Take, for example, his song "Nunca He Ido a España," from his CD *Fun in Español*. The song is a parody of Three Dog Night's 1972 hit "Never Been to Spain," in which El Vez subverts the original song's idea of Spain as an exotic travel destination: In his (Spanish) lyrics, he explains that since he has never been to Spain, he should not be called Hispanic, but since he *has* been to Mexico, he should be called Chicano. But his humor also functions at a musical level: After a few verses closely following the Three Dog Night original, the tune switches to a parody of George Harrison's 1973 song "Wah Wah." Here, El Vez substitutes the chorus of "wah wah" with the word "agua," the Spanish word for water, and lyrically switches his narrative to the consequences of Columbus's voyage across the ocean. The full richness of El Vez's commentary on Mexican and Mexican American identities depends on listeners who not only understand English and Spanish but also are thoroughly familiar with the rock 'n' roll canon. Monolingual and monocultural listeners might enjoy the music, but they will not get the jokes.

In summary, Mexican Americans, especially those from Los Angeles, 20 have a long, continuous, multifaceted engagement with rock 'n' roll and, by extension, with U.S. mainstream popular music. Although some of their musical productions have been bilingual and even fewer have been entirely in Spanish, the majority have been in English. Mexican American rockers certainly encountered barriers created by the disinterest (if not the racism) of the mainstream music industry, and artistic recognition and economic success eluded most of them, but enough of them achieved mainstream success that Mexican Americans must be considered coparticipants in the development of U.S. rock 'n' roll. Most germane to this discussion, however, is the idea that Mexican American rockers, whether or not they made the national charts, received consistent support from within the Mexican American community, because rock 'n' roll was perceived as their birthright.

New York Puerto Ricans and Rock 'n' Roll

On the East Coast, young New York Puerto Rican teens in the 1950s were, like their West Coast counterparts, listening avidly to rock 'n' roll as well as to their parents' Spanish Caribbean musics. As the subsequent decades unfolded, however, New York Puerto Rican musicians and fans did not dedicate themselves to rock 'n' roll with the same enthusiasm and consistency as their Mexican American counterparts. With the exception of the short-lived boogaloo and two Puerto Rican musicians, José Feliciano and Tony Orlando, New York Puerto Rican musicians' engagement with rock 'n' roll and the English-language mainstream popular music arena in general has been more tenuous and ambivalent, and, when it has taken place, it has been primarily with those styles at the African American end of the rock 'n' roll continuum. Indeed, other than Feliciano and Orlando (who are discussed further below), only two New York Puerto Rican musicians made the national charts between the 1950s and the late 1990s, when Ricky Martin and Jennifer Lopez burst onto the pop charts: Ray Barretto with "El Watusi" (1963) and Joe Cuba's boogaloo "Bang Bang" (1966). Significantly, Barretto's and Cuba's tunes, both hybrids of R & B with Spanish Caribbean styles, were, with the exception of some Spanish phrases, primarily instrumental.

The first step in unpacking New York Puerto Rican's relationship to rock 'n' roll is to emphasize to fact that, well before the 1950s, Puerto Rican musicians in New York had always engaged with U.S. popular music, albeit more often with African American styles than with the mainstream-oriented Tin Pan Alley music. Like their Mexican American counterparts, New York Puerto Ricans were victims of racial discrimination and shared with African Americans not only the same segregated neighborhoods but also often the same tenement buildings—and, as one New York Puerto Rican acerbically noted, the same cockroaches. Unlike Mexican Americans, however, many New York Puerto Ricans were of African ancestry, which, coupled with the spatial concentration of New York's minority neighborhoods—compared to Los Angeles's more ethnically specific neighborhoods and metropolitan sprawl—brought New York Puerto Ricans closer culturally and physically to their African American neighbors. Indeed, Flores has argued that the constant social and cultural interactions between these two groups in New York City encouraged New York Puerto Ricans to engage laterally with African American culture rather than assimilating into the dominant white mainstream culture. Nevertheless, New York Puerto Ricans' relationships with African Americans, if close, have not been unproblematic, as writer Piri Thomas and many others have observed: New York Puerto Ricans have resisted the effacement of their cultural distinctiveness when misidentified as African Americans, a confusion that was not experienced by Mexican Americans, who were more likely to be mestizos.

New York, the country's premier immigrant city and historically the center of the nation's recording industry, had long been a magnet for talented musicians from the Caribbean and Latin America as well as African Americans and whites from throughout the United States, rendering it fertile ground for musical exchanges and creative experimentation. When rock 'n' roll emerged in the 1950s, New York–based Puerto Rican musicians were enjoying the benefits of being embedded within a dynamic music scene solidly grounded in Spanish Caribbean styles as well as being in close proximity to the international music industry—both of which offered clear professional advantages to those musicians interested in working in Spanish Caribbean idioms. Given the dynamism of the local Latin music scene at the time, New York Puerto Rican musicians had less motivation to look beyond the boundaries of Spanish Caribbean repertoires, even when English-language R & B and doo-wop groups began routinely including Latin-tinged songs in their repertoires in the 1950s.

In addition to witnessing the florescence of mambo and cha-cha on the national stage, New York Puerto Rican teens in the 1950s were experiencing another quite distinct but extraordinarily vibrant musical moment: the eruption of rock 'n' roll, which was being performed live in venues across the city, including the Apollo Theater in Harlem, as well as on locally produced (but nationally broadcast) television variety shows, such as Ed Sullivan's. Young New York Puerto Ricans, most of whom had arrived as children during the surge of migration from

Puerto Rico in the 1940s, were among those who avidly embraced rock 'n' roll, especially doo-wop. Doo-wop, being primarily vocal, was an easily accessible musical style that required no instruments and could be performed by anyone, anywhere. Doo-wop's sentimental lyrics were particularly appealing to young New York Puerto Ricans raised in a culture that had long valued romantic music, the quintessential example being the bolero. Three Puerto Rican musicians achieved nationwide success in doo-wop, although in both cases they were assumed by most listeners to be black: Herman Santiago and Joe Negroni of Frankie Lymon and the Teenagers, and Harold Torres, who sang with the Crests (of "16 Candles" fame). Other New York Puerto Rican vocalists began their careers singing doo-wop in the 1950s. Jimmy Sabater, for example, sang with a doo-wop group called the Viceroys before later scoring a hit with Willie Torres's Latin soul ballad "To be with, You" and Joe Loco (a pianist who had performed with the legendary Afro-Cuban bandleader Machito) released a version of "Gee," which had been a major hit for the African American doo-wop group the Crows. (Loco's Latinized doo-wop song is considered to be the first Latinized R & B vocal, but it did not make headway in the market.)

Throughout the 1950s, Latin stylings continued to show up in rock 25 'n' roll music produced by both white (e.g., Bobby Darin) and African American artists (e.g., Betty Everett), but, by the end of the decade, the attraction of Latin music for mainstream audiences was on the wane. In part, this was due to the saturation of schlocky mambos and cha-chas that had flooded the marketplace, but more importantly, Latin music was displaced by the exploding popularity of the newer sounds of R & B and rock 'n' roll followed by Beatlemania and the so-called British Invasion in the early 1960s. Another blow to the Latin music scene in New York was the U.S. blockade of revolutionary Cuba, which abruptly cut off musical interactions with the island that for decades had served as an incubator of new rhythms and sounds. To older and well-established Puerto Rican and Cuban bandleaders accustomed to sophisticated and vibrant Latin musics rooted in their own communities, rock 'n' roll was of little interest, but they were unable to compete with its appeal to young people; instead, they continued to churnout mambos and cha-chas that did not comparably reflect the tumultuous new decade.

In the 1960s, some of New York's well-established Latino musicians attempted to revitalize Spanish Caribbean music by infusing it with new rhythms and energy, resulting in scores of flute- and violin-based *pachanga* and *charanga* recordings. Some of these cha-cha-inspired charangas and pachangas (such as Tito Puente's "Oye Como Va!") were solidly grounded in Spanish Caribbean aesthetics, although others (such as Johnny Pacheco's "Acuyuyé") had a subtle R & B rhythmic feel. It was precisely this combination of Latin and R & B sonorities that sent Ray Barretto's instrumental "El Watusi" to the top twenty on the national pop charts in 1963. That same year, Cuban-born percussionist Mongo Santamaría also made the charts with his R & B–inflected "Watermelon Man." These mainstream hits, however, did not reflect the sensibilities and preferences of that generation; indeed, Barretto is said to have been uncomfortable with the pressure to replicate the success of "El Watusi" and, instead, returned to more patenty Spanish Caribbean aesthetics in his 1964 recording *Guajira y Guanguancó* (which anticipated the more roots-oriented style he would develop with Fania a few years later).

However, a younger generation of New York–born or New York–bred Puerto Rican musicians, such as Johnny Colon, made more dramatic and sustained attempts to renovate what they perceived as their parents' old-fashioned "hick music" by mixing it with R & B, creating a new musical hybrid called "boogaloo," or *bugalu* (much of which was released on Goldner's Tico label. The boogaloo was based not on the complex 3-2 (or 2-3) Cuban clave rhythm that had underpinned most Spanish Caribbean Latin music but rather on rock 'n' roll's steadier 4/4 rhythms. The trap drums added to Spanish Caribbean percussion further expressed the musicians' layered experiences as Puerto Ricans and as urban U.S. teenagers who liked rock 'n' roll. Significantly, boogaloo was most heavily influenced by soul and funk—that is, the African American end of the rock 'n' roll spectrum—which is not surprising given the physical and cultural commonalities between the two communities, referred to above. Indeed, Flores sees the creation of the boogaloo as a deliberate attempt to get "Black Americans involved and onto the dance floor." The fact that most boogaloos were either in English or bilingual facilitated such crossovers, and in 1966 Joe Cuba's "Bang Bang" hit the mainstream charts at number 63. Other boogaloos, such as Pete Rodríguez's "I Like It Like That" (1966) and Colon's "Boogaloo Blues" (1966), did not chart nationally but became instant hits within New York.

Boogaloo's Latin percussion- and horn-based textures were noticeably closer to Spanish Caribbean dance music than to the electric guitar–based rock 'n' roll being produced at the same time in East Los Angeles by groups such as Cannibal and the Headhunters. However, a noteworthy point of convergence between East and West Coast Latino rock 'n' roll in the 1960s reflected how the spirit of the times was being articulated by young Latinos. Many of the recordings produced contemporaneously by Los Angeles Chicanos and New York Puerto Ricans featured raucous party sounds and celebratory shouts in the background that expressed the uninhibited informality of the 1960s and their refusal to conform to the constraints required of a well-defined "song." Indeed, Flores's description of the boogaloo sound as "a bawdy happening at the peak of its emotional and sexual energy, with instrumentals and vocals playing in full and wild association with the crowd" could just as well describe the Premiers' "Farmer John" (1964) or the Blendells' "La La La La" (1964). In this regard, the boogaloo and its West Coast counterparts expressed the liberatory spirit of the 1960s, in which conventions and boundaries were gleefully transgressed. Whether boogaloo could or should be categorized as a variant of rock 'n' roll is certainly open to debate, although it should be noted that Santana's Spanish Caribbean and rock hybrids—which are sung in Spanish—*are* considered to be rock. The boogaloo, however, preceded Santana's successful combinations of rock 'n' roll with Afro-Cuban music by several years.

Despite boogaloo's promising success in New York, New York Puerto Rican musicians in the 1960s were unable to achieve levels of national visibility in the mainstream arena comparable to those of Chicano rockers in that decade. One issue was that the boogaloo did not receive adequate support from New York's Latin music industry. On the contrary, despite Goldner's efforts to promote boogaloo on his Latin music–oriented Tico label, the genre faced active hostility from established bandleaders (including Tito Puente) who considered it musically primitive but were clearly threatened by the competition. More crucial to the fate of boogaloo, however, was the rise of Puerto Rican cultural nationalism and the contemporaneous emergence of salsa, a music that, unlike boogaloo, was deeply rooted in Spanish Caribbean musical traditions.

Salsa's intense symbolic importance to New York Puerto Ricans in the 30 1970s was directly related to the appalling social conditions and urban decay imposed on Latino and black neighborhoods as the first rumblings of economic globalization began to make themselves felt in New York. The city's manufacturing base was eroding as factories relocated to other locations with cheaper and more tractable labor, while changes in immigration policies in 1965 were opening tip the doors to hundreds of thousands of new immigrants from Latin America (and other parts of the globe). The flight of white middle-class residents to the suburbs drained city coffers just as the need for public services was rising, contributing to the decay of New York's once vital Puerto Rican neighborhoods. Inspired by the black and Chicano civil rights movements, militant Puerto Rican cultural nationalists, particularly the South Bronx—based Young Lords, sought to defend their communities not only by challenging the city's neglect but also by fostering community empowerment, urging their ethnic cohorts to rely on their own cultural resources as a source of strength and pride.

Salsa, drew upon multiple contemporary musical sources, including R & B, jazz, and other Latin American and Caribbean genres, but at its core it reinvigorated and celebrated the Spanish Caribbean musical aesthetics that had flourished in New York in the 1940s and 1950s. The music of young *salseros* such as Willie Colón could be differentiated from that of its Spanish Caribbean predecessors by its aggressive, busy energy and stinging lyrics that reflected the salseros' struggles growing up in New York's besieged barrios. However, notwithstanding its distinct New York flavor, salsa's aesthetic emphasis was solidly Spanish Caribbean—so much so that some of the older musicians performing it, such as Tito Puente, insisted they were simply playing existing Latin dance musics such as mambo and cha-cha under a new name. Musical mixings and innovations did take place in the 1970s, as salseros incorporated jazz and African American R & B stylings, but they drew little from the domain of guitar-based rock, at the time virtually synonymous with U.S. cultural imperialism.

To activists such as Felipe Luciano, a member of the Young Lords, salsa was the musical symbol of the Puerto Rican and Latino communities' political and cultural resistance. Performed by a dizzying number of talented musicians (many, but not all, of whom were Puerto Rican), salsa dominated the Latin dance scene throughout the 1970s, not only in New York but also in other U.S. cities, such as Los Angeles, with large Latino populations as well as throughout urban, working-class Latin America. Yet despite the polarizing rhetoric of the times, New York Puerto Rican musicians, including some of the older and well-established ones, made overtures in the direction of non-Latin mainstream styles and English-language vocals. Roberto Roena's 1969 recording *Apollo Sound*, for example, incorporates sounds reminiscent of the groups Blood, Sweat, and Tears and Chicago, although it is noteworthy that these groups were horn-based rather than electric guitar–based. Even Latin music stalwart Eddie Palmieri experimented by combining Spanish Caribbean sonorities with R & B in the 1970s. In 1973, Fania—salsa's premier record label—organized a Madison Square Garden concert featuring its biggest stars entitled *Salsa, Soul, Rock,* in which Jorge Santana, Carlos's brother and leader of the Chicano rock group Malo, played straight guitar-based rock in a duo with prominent Puerto Rican salsa singer Cheo Feliciano (although each in their own musical idiom). Nevertheless, these gestures were the exceptions rather than the rule; overall, salsa succeeded in pulling Spanish Caribbean music back to more traditional Spanish Caribbean aesthetics, insisting on a rhythmic grounding in the clave and rejecting the English lyrics and R & B rhythms used in boogaloo in favor of Spanish lyrics, Latin percussion (congas, bongos, and timbales), and the big brass sound of trumpets and trombones. As John Storm Roberts observed, "the prevailing rhetoric was of roots, purity, and a concept (related to the growth of Latino political awareness) of 'community music.'"

If salsa and cultural nationalism dominated the soundscape and imaginations of most New York Puerto Rican dancers and activists in the 1970s, a small handful of New York–based Latin rock bands did appear in the late 1960s, most of whose musicians were New York Puerto Rican: Harvey Averne's Barrio Band; Toro; Seguida; Benitez; and, from the town of Woodstock (an hour's drive north of New York), the group Chango. These groups recorded very little and did not achieve much commercial success; indeed, they would most likely be forgotten but for their inclusion in a 1988 compilation CD entitled *Chicano Power! Latin Rock in the USA 1968–1976*. As the liner notes explain in reference to the New York–based bands, "The problem was ironically a product of the fact that in New York there was already a strong latin [*sic*] music industry spearheaded by the Fania record company. Whilst Fania brilliantly manipulated New York latin music into a worldwide marketable commodity, giving it the term Salsa, latin rock was unfortunately not really understood by the people who controlled the industry . . . [and] . . . few salsa purists accepted latin rock." Interestingly, these New York Puerto Rican rock groups maintained aesthetic and personal connections with Chicano rockers as well as with their local Latin music counterparts. Harvey Averne's Barrio Band, for example, "featured the cream of New York's salsa musicians" (e.g., Andy González on bass and Hector Lavoe and Ismael Miranda on vocals), and one of their songs, "Cayuco," was covered by the West Coast bands El Chicano and Macondo.

Before concluding, it is necessary to address two New York Puerto Rican musicians who did achieve mainstream success in the 1960s but were not grounded in the New York Puerto Rican community in the same way that their counterparts performing salsa were. In the 1960s and 1970s, Tony Orlando (born in New York of a Puerto Rican mother and a Greek father) had a string of pop chart hits (either solo or with his backup vocal group, Dawn), the most famous of which were his 1961 version of "Halfway to Paradise," his 1970 hit songs "Candida" and "Knock Three Times," 1973's "Tie a Yellow Ribbon 'Round the Ole Oak Tree," and his 1975 version of "He Don't Love You (Like I Love You)." Between 1974 and 1976, he even had his own television variety show, *Tony Orlando and Dawn*. José Feliciano, born in Puerto Rico but raised in New York from the age of five, attended P.S. 57, a public high school famous for the number of successful salsa musicians trained in its music program. Feliciano took up the accordion and the guitar, and at the age of nine performed at South Bronx's Teatro Puerto Rico, but while he was in high school, his musical performances were in Greenwich Village coffee shops rather than salsa clubs. His first U.S. mainstream hit, which reached number 4 on the pop charts, was an acoustic version of the Doors' "Light My Fire" that lie recorded on the suggestion of his Los Angeles–based producer. The album it was on, *Feliciano!*, won two Grammys in 1968, one for Best New Artist and the other for Best Male Contemporary Pop Vocal Performance; it was also nominated for Album of the Year. That same year, Feliciano had another hit with his acoustic version of "High Heel Sneakers." Feliciano did not have any additional Top-40 hit singles, but throughout the 1970s he headlined several sold-out performing tours and sessioned with major artists, such as John Lennon and Joni Mitchell.

How do these two extraordinarily successful New York Puerto Rican 35 artists fit into the musical practices and preferences of the New York Puerto Rican community in the 1960s and 1970s? Feliciano was primarily a singer-songwriter-guitarist whose stylings were more indebted to jazz and folk than to rock, but his music, in content as well as in context, was unequivocally located within the mainstream rock 'n' roll arena. As for Orlando, thanks to such schmaltzy songs as "Tie a Yellow Ribbon Round the Ole Oak Tree," his particular strain of pop rock "had little street credibility," but seventeen of his songs charted in the Top 40, and numerous others made the Top-100 list—a feat that no Puerto Rican or Chicano musician has even come close to matching. In short, the achievements of these two musicians are noteworthy indeed, although they have often been overlooked by the journalists who gushed over Ricky Martin in the 1990s as if he were the first Puerto Rican artist to achieve mainstream success. Yet, in spite of Feliciano's and Orlando's undeniable importance in commercial terms, their music was not rooted in a local, community-based music scene, nor did they contribute to the development of an influential and recognizable style comparable to the East Side sound created and supported by West Coast Chicano musicians and their fans.

Concluding Thoughts

If both East and West Coast Latinos were inspired by cultural nationalism and identity politics in the 1970s, their musical responses and trajectories diverged dramatically. West Coast

"If both East and West Coast Latinos were inspired by cultural nationalism and identity politics in the 1970s, their musical responses and trajectories diverged dramatically."

Chicanos continued to perform guitar-based R & B and rock, although they devised a range of strategies to convey their ethnic consciousness within these idioms. Chicanos, like Puerto Ricans, demonstrated preferences for the horn- and percussion-heavy styles associated with African Americans, but they also routinely played the electric guitar–centered rock styles commonly associated with white groups. To be sure, the issues of assimilation and cultural nationalism raised by the Chicano movement in the late 1960s and early 1970s created a dilemma for young Chicano musicians sympathetic to their communities' efforts to celebrate their ancestral Mexican cultural traditions, but they did not thereby categorically reject rock 'n' roll and English because they were the idioms of their oppressors; rather, they sought to use these idioms to express their grievances, their resistance, and their ethnic pride. As George Lipsitz notes of the musical choices of Chicanos, "Mexican-American musicians could stick to Chicano musical forms like ranchera and cumbia musics and find recognition and reward within their own community. Or they could master Anglo styles and be assimilated into the mainstream without anyone being aware of their Chicano identity. But Los Angeles Chicano rock-and-roll artists have selected another path. They have tried to straddle the line between the two cultures, creating a fusion music that resonates with the chaos and costs of cultural collision. In short, Chicanos cannot be described as being more "assimilated" or less conscious of their ethnic identity, but, in terms of popular music in the United States, it is undeniable that, on the whole, they have been more willing to engage with rock than their New York Puerto Rican counterparts.

New York Puerto Ricans also engaged with a variety of non-Latin musical idioms, but their participation in the English-language mainstream popular music scene in the 1960s and 1970s was less consistent and less visible overall than that of their Chicano counterparts. Moreover, to the extent that they experimented with non-Latin styles, they tended to favor the African American end of the rock 'n' roll continuum. Significantly, in spite of a deep tradition of acoustic guitar music in Puerto Rico and elsewhere in the Spanish Caribbean, New York Puerto Rican musicians generally avoided the electric guitar that was so closely associated with rock 'n' roll. In contrast, cutting-edge Cuban dance bands in the 1970s such as Los Van Van routinely added the electric guitar and trap set as well as rock stylings to their ensembles, much to the delight of their young fans eager to hear updated versions of Cuban dance music. This is not to suggest that New York Puerto Ricans did not influence developments in mainstream popular music during this period—indeed, their contributions in this regard were significant; but their presence was more audible in terms of aesthetics rather than as visible center-stage participants.

Chicanos, in contrast, were far less influential on developments in the domain of commercial Latin music, domestically and internationally.

While this chapter has focused on comparing West Coast Mexican Americans' and East Coast New York Puerto Ricans' relationships with rock 'n' roll, it is important to note that the musical practices of Mexican Americans in Texas and other parts of the United States generally were comparable to those of their Los Angeles–based counterparts. Miami's Cuban Americans, in contrast, were too recently arrived in the 1960s and 1970s, and too obsessed with the possibility of returning to Cuba, to become involved in the civil rights movements marking that tumultuous era; moreover, they did not perceive themselves as members of racially or socioeconomically subordinated groups. Thus, even though second-generation Cuban Americans gravitated toward rock 'n' roll in the same period, the cultural implications of their choices were quite dissimilar.

In comparing Chicano and New York Puerto Rican musical practices in the 1960s and 1970s, it is important to emphasize that this is not an attempt to valorize one community's choices and to devalue the other's but rather to acknowledge and learn from the local specificities of each. New York, for example, has always been the site of extraordinary cultural creativity, and historically it has been more ethnically diverse than Los Angeles; nevertheless, as a city that values traditions and continuity, it has retained many of its long-standing physical and cultural contours. Los Angeles, in contrast, celebrates—indeed, prides itself—on its newness, its progressive modernity, its ability to reinvent itself, and its inhabitants' willingness to do likewise. In the most general contextual terms, then, New York has offered advantages to those musicians and fans seeking to maintain traditional repertoires, while Los Angeles has offered plenty of space for those seeking to reshape them.

But, ultimately, it is at the intersection of the historical, social, and 40 cultural forces shaping each community's urban experience that we can most productively seek explanations for these differences. Los Angeles Mexican American mestizos defy the United States' black or white binary, giving them some flexibility in forming their racial identities; New York Puerto Ricans, in contrast, were more likely to be confused with African Americans. Moreover, while Mexican Americans' national origins in sovereign Mexico have always been a source of pride, the post-Chicano movement generation insisted on a U.S.-based ethnic identity and accepted the distinctions between here and there. Rubén Guevara, for example, explained why he celebrates Los Angeles as his "home" in his song "Con Safos," which contains an extensive narrative about Chicano history and identity: "The inspiration . . . came from a jarring culture shock I experienced in 1974 on my first trip to Mexico in search of my indigenous roots and identity. . . . I came to the painful realization that my social culture was not Mexican. My ancestral cultural roots were, but not my social culture—it was and is Chicano. Regardless of whether one interprets Aztlán as myth or historical fact, its location in the Southwest provides Chicanos with a powerful symbolic basis for claims to national belonging and the rights of cultural citizenship.

New York Puerto Ricans' homeland, in contrast, was (and is) a colony, and even their U.S. citizenship, like their residence in New York, was perceived by many as the imposed and unwanted consequence of their colonial tragedy. New York Puerto Ricans commonly express the sentiment that no matter where they were born, no matter where they live, and no matter what language they might choose to speak, they are first, foremost, and always Puerto Rican. Nostalgic, loving images of Puerto Rico in New York Puerto Rican expressive arts are ubiquitous, while New York has often been rendered as cold, hostile, and unforgiving, or, at best, just a place to earn a living rather than a home. Despite their ambivalence toward New York, many New York Puerto Ricans have never lived on the island and no longer speak Spanish—or, at best, speak a New York–inflected Spanish/Spanglish that is scorned on the island—and they are fully established within the New York communities in which they live. Numerous mainland-based Puerto Rican observers, from novelist Piri Thomas to filmmaker Frances Negrón-Muntaner, have commented on New York Puerto Ricans' contradictory experiences of not fully belonging either to the United States or to the island homeland—yet, at the same time, being attached to both. This sense of in-betweenness seems to have produced more reluctance to lay similarly historical and celebratory claims to the geographical and cultural spaces of the United States among Puerto Ricans than among West Coast Chicanos.

The New York Puerto Rican community has relied more heavily on Spanish Caribbean–based cultural traditions as a steadying and unifying force, which is *not* to imply that they are backward-looking; indeed, their contributions to developments in Latin and mainstream styles, have been profound and significant. Nevertheless, many Puerto Ricans, particularly an older generation, still believe that their musical "essence" has been best expressed in salsa, whose most prominent and defining aesthetics are unequivocally Spanish Caribbean. For example, Ángel Quintero Rivera, referring to both Puerto Ricans on the island and on the mainland, sees the uninterrupted production of salsa for over thirty years as a victory over the threat of rock and the cultural impositions it is perceived to embody. He goes on to conclude that "the battle of 'resistance' seems to have been won" and notes that since rock is no longer a threat to salsa (and, by implication, to Puerto Rican identity), Puerto Ricans can now comfortably accept it. Such sentiments did not, I might note, spare Ricky Martin in the 1990s from accusations that he sold out his Puerto Rican culture by performing electric guitar–based music in English for the U.S. pop marketplace.

Although a strong adherence to tradition may have discouraged a more radical reshaping and reinvention of Spanish Caribbean musical styles and may have deterred New York Puerto Rican musicians from venturing into the more lucrative rock arena in the 1960s and 1970s, it undeniably helped the community maintain its cultural coherence and integrity in years when it was under intense social and economic pressures. It is important to acknowledge and understand that maintaining a strong sense of ethnic identity is not necessarily dependent on any particular mode of engagement with mainstream U.S. musical practices: Communities and individuals must decide for themselves when and where it is appropriate to participate and when and where it makes more sense to withdraw and resist.

Understanding the Text

1. While "the positions of Chicanos and New York Puerto Ricans" (7) may seem superficially similar, what are some of the crucial differences Pacini Hernandez identifies between their histories and communities? How are these differences reflected in their respective relationships toward rock 'n' roll music?

2. According to the writer, how does the musical and career trajectory of Los Angeles rock band Los Lobos reflect the "changing political environment" (18) of Chicanos?

3. In Pacini Hernandez's view, why was there more cultural overlap between Puerto Ricans and African Americans in New York City than between Mexican Americans and African Americans in Los Angeles?

Reflection and Response

4. The writer opens her essay by focusing on the song "Oye Como Va!" in both its 1963 and 1970 versions. Why do you think she uses this example? How does the song tie into — and allow her to introduce — her more general themes and analysis?

5. As the essay is structured, the writer devotes two final paragraphs in the main body of her text to the performers Tony Orlando and Jose Feliciano. Why do you think she writes separately about these two artists? How are they distinctive, from her perspective?

Making Connections

6. Pacini Hernandez writes that in the 1970s, the Chicano movement "was being modified by more nuanced views of ethnic identity generated by Latinos, especially feminists and gays, who contested essentialist, monolithic (and masculinist) constructions of what it meant to be Chicano" (18). Similarly, in "A Paler Shade of White: How Indie Rock Lost Its Soul" (p. 208), Sasha Frere-Jones claims, "It's difficult to talk about the racial pedigree of American pop music without being accused of reductionism, essentialism, or worse, and such suspicion is often warranted." What does the term "essentialism" mean in these contexts? What is the problem with "essentialist" views — and why would they be "contested"?

7. Pacini Hernandez provides a rich and nuanced account of Latino national, cultural, and musical identity in New York and Los Angeles. What specific insights about music, influence, and ethnicity do you find in her analysis? For example, does she complicate or problematize any of your assumptions about Latino music and culture in the United States?

Latin Music Is American Music

Chris Kjorness

While it is a cliché to characterize America as a "nation of immigrants," the issue of immigration remains a perennial source of political, social, and cultural controversy. And for some, immigrants and their cultural influence represent a threat to the United States. In this 2013 essay from *PopMatters*, writer Chris Kjorness addresses the issue from the perspective of popular music. Looking at the Latino influence on music "from ragtime to hip-hop," the writer tries to bring insight and perspective to those who (in his words) worry that America "is going to hell in a tamale wrapper because a kid in a mariachi suit sang the national anthem on TV."

Chris Kjorness is a writer, teacher, and musician whose work has appeared in *Popmatters*, *Reason*, and the *Richmond Times-Dispatch*. He is the founder and director of Da Vinci's Window, an out-of-school arts and academic enrichment program for children.

It's not every day that an 11-year-old boy gets blasted on Twitter. But last month, when Sebastian De La Cruz stepped into the spotlight to sing "The Star-Spangled Banner" before the third game of the NBA Finals series between the San Antonio Spurs and the Miami Heat, numerous viewers took to the internet to indignantly ask why an "illegal immigrant" was singing the national anthem. Cruz handled the vitriolic tweets with the same poise he uses to sing, and was invited back for a repeat performance two days later.

Even though he's a native San Antonian, Cruz's appearance (including full mariachi attire) stoked an underlying fear that motivates those who oppose immigration: Too many immigrants will adulterate the culture of the United States. Far from a fringe view, in a 2004 article for *Foreign Policy* ("The Hispanic Challenge"), the late Harvard Political Science professor Samuel P. Huntington called immigration from Latin America "the single most immediate and most serious challenge to America's traditional identity."

What these people fail to recognize is that for more than a century, immigrants—particularly those from Latin America—have helped forge the cultural identity of the United States. And nowhere is this more apparent than in popular music, where from ragtime to hip-hop, artists have frequently looked beyond the North American continent to find American music. As John Boehner and House Republicans try to suffocate the latest attempt to reform America's hopelessly broken immigration

Figure 4.2 Singer Sebastian De La Cruz, a San Antonio native featured on America's Got Talent, faced anti-immigrant vitriol after he sang "The Star-Spangled Banner" at an NBA Finals game in 2013. Andy Lyons/Getty Images

system, it's worth taking a look at just how deeply ingrained Latin culture is in "American" popular music.

At the dawn of the 20th century, rhythms from south of the border began showing up in the instrumental music of the North American mainland, most notably, the *tresillo,* a long-long-short rhythmic cell, and its logical extension, the *habanera,* where the *tresillo* is fit against an even, two-beat march. While variants of these rhythms are common to a number of African cultures and can be heard in the clapping and stomping of Alan Lomax's field recordings, the stateside suppression of slave drumming kept the rhythms from reaching their full fruition in the United States.

The self-proclaimed inventor of jazz, Jelly Roll Morton, called these 5 rhythms the "Spanish Tinge." Likely picked up by Morton from Cubans who immigrated to New Orleans after the Cuban Emancipation in 1886, the use of these rhythms became an integral element of Morton's distinctive, pioneering style. So essential was the "Spanish Tinge" to jazz that Morton asserted that musicians who could couldn't put tinges of Spanish in their music would "never be able to get the seasoning [for jazz] right."

It wasn't just Morton who found inspiration in Cuban music. The "Father of the Blues," W. C. Handy, who had spent time in Cuba during the 1900 US occupation of the island, wedged *ahabanera*-based tango section into his "Saint Louis Blues." Ever the businessman, Handy added the tango in hopes of currying favor with Manhattan dance mavens Paul and Irene Castle who having invented the fox-trot, were now teaching sophisticated Manhattanites to tango.

One need only read the title of Rudy Vallee's "When Yuba Plays the Rhumba on his Tuba" to realize these early flirtations with Latin music were fairly shallow, and full of ugly stereotypes. Still by 1923, the Victor Records catalog listed 146 Cuban recordings, making Cuban music (and by extension, music from Mexico and Central America) a growing force in American popular culture.

In the '50s, the exotic glamour of Cuba and Mexico began drawing in visitors from the United States, who were benefiting from a surging postwar economy. If there was one figure who epitomized Cuban music in the mid-'50s, it was Benny Moré. While born in Cuba, Moré honed his craft in the booming clubs of post-WWII Mexico, before taking his act back to Cuba and on to the United States. An electrifying performer, Moré captured the imagination of listeners throughout the Americas.

A mix of recent immigrants and adventurous natives formed the base for a strong Latin music scene in '50s-era New York. At the same time, bebop musicians like Charlie Parker and Dizzy Gillespie began to view Cuban music as fertile ground for new discoveries. By the late '50s, America had mambo fever and Cuban musicians could easily be seen and heard on American television and radio.

But Latin music in the United States wasn't just confined to East 10 Coast Cubans. With its close proximity to Mexico and large population of Chicanos (Mexican-Americans), Los Angeles reverberated with Latin music. In the '40s, zoot-suit-clad Los Angeles youth had carved out a youth culture so cool it was investigated by the State Un-American Activities Committee. It wasn't just the urban dance styles that Mexican immigrants brought to the American Southwest. Heartrending *corridos,* ballads, and *rancheras* could be heard from Oklahoma to California, inspiring country and western musicians like Marty Robbins and George Strait. More than just entertainment, Mexican folk songs had been used for centuries to record stories and provide social commentary. This spirit lives on in Los Tigres Del Norte's "Los Hijos de Hernandez," which tells the story of a naturalized citizen who has lost his son in service to the United States but is still by many as "an illegal."

Recently, *narcocorrido* (a Mexican genre dedicated to chronicling Mexico's ongoing drug war) made an appearance in the AMC's *Breaking Bad* (season 2 episode 7, *"Negro y Azul"*)—immortalizing the deplorable acts of Walter White in song.

Latin threads were woven into rock 'n' roll as well, most notably the *clave:* a pattern of five accents spread across eight beats, demonstrated here by mambo pioneer Israel "Cachao" Lopez.

In the Spanish-speaking world, *clave* is the heart of salsa or the beat of reggaeton, but in the United States it is the Bo Diddley beat. From the Crickets bopping behind Buddy Holly on "Not Fade Away" to the guitar riff of the White Stripes' "Screwdriver," song's featuring this rhythm are a staple of rock 'n' roll.

Latinos also played an important role in the development of hip-hop. In the '70s, the South Bronx was a war zone. Having been abandoned by city and state authorities, a collection of gangs—usually divided along racial lines—engaged in constant, armed struggle for control of the burned out blocks of the once proud neighborhood. One Puerto Rican gang, the Ghetto Brothers, also doubled as a band, serving up Latin dance music with a fiery rock 'n' roll edge.

In support of a peace treaty that was beginning to take root in 1972, 15 the Ghetto Brothers started playing block parties that were open to everyone, regardless of gang affiliation. These parties gave birth to the idea that music could serve to bind the hopelessly splintered South Bronx—an idea seized upon by party-goer Afrika Bambaataa. The story of early hip-hop is the story of American immigrants trying to craft a new identity, and it's no coincidence that Latin records from artists like Mongo Santamaria and Incredible Bongo Band were staples of early hip-hop DJs. Recently, son of Afro-Cuban percussion legend Willie Bobo. Eric Bobo and critically acclaimed artist Argentine DJ Latin Bitman formed Ritmo Machine, a group that recalls the spirit of the early days of hip-hop.

These are only a few examples of cultural contributions from Latino immigrants. It's true that cities with large Latino populations have developed their own Spanish-speaking subcultures, but this is nothing new, nor does it pose a threat to a city's cultural identity. Like Boston's Southie or Chicago's Polish Downtown, these neighborhoods, and the people who inhabit them, enrich and define their cities.

> "It's true that cities with large Latino populations have developed their own Spanish-speaking subcultures, but this is nothing new, nor does it pose a threat to a city's cultural identity."

Likewise, the trade, immigration, and migration between the United States and the rest of the Americas has given life to American pop culture. So the next time you hear someone crying that the United States is going to hell in a tamale wrapper because a kid in a mariachi suit sang the national anthem on TV, tell them to relax, grab an empanada from their neighborhood food truck, and enjoy this King Chango song. Because nothing is more American than a New York ska band, with Venezuelan roots, covering a song written by an Englishman who was trying to sound Jamaican.

Understanding the Text

1. According to Kjorness, what underlying concern motivates those who fear or oppose immigration?
2. What important role did Latinos play in the development of hip-hop?

Reflection and Response

3. How would you characterize Kjorness's overall view of immigrant assimilation in America? Do you agree or disagree?
4. Kjorness concludes his essay with the sentence, "Because nothing is more American than a New York ska band, with Venezuelan roots, covering a song written by an Englishman who was trying to sound Jamaican" (17). What point is he making? Do you agree? What other similar examples of such hybrid musical artists and styles could you add?

Making Connections

5. To what degree does Kjorness's argument overlap with Deborah Pacini Hernandez's in "To Rock or Not to Rock: Cultural Nationalism and Latino Engagement with Rock 'n' Roll" (p. 217)? Inversely, how are their claims and analyses different?

6. The writer cites a controversial and provocative 2004 article by the late Harvard political science professor Samuel Huntington, "The Hispanic Challenge," which appeared in the journal *Foreign Policy*. Find the article online or through your college library's databases. How do you respond to it? Does Kjorness's article provide a meaningful response to views such as Huntington's? Why or why not?

How the "Kung Fu Fighting" Melody Came to Represent Asia

Kat Chow

Kat Chow's "How the 'Kung Fu Fighting' Melody Came to Represent Asia" suggests a deceptively simple model of inquiry-based writing. Her topic is a familiar, nine-note melody that has long been a musical shorthand "to signal that something vaguely Asian is happening or is about to happen." She asks: Where did it come from? Does it refer to a real Asian tune, or is it merely an "orientalist" invention of the West? These questions lead her to both scholarly and popular sources, as well as a range of related topics, from the popularity of the pentatonic scale to the influx of Chinese immigrants to the United States in the nineteenth century.

Kat Chow is part of National Public Radio's *Code Switch* team, a group of reporters who cover stories about race, ethnicity, and culture for NPR broadcasts such as *Morning Edition* and *All Things Considered*.

There's a tune that you've probably heard throughout your life. It's nine notes long, and it's almost always used to signal that something vaguely Asian is happening or is about to happen.

You know what I'm talking about. The tune's most prominent role is probably in that 1974 song "Kung Fu Fighting." It comes in right as Carl Douglas is singing that anthemic "Oh-hoh-hoh-hoah."

It was in the Vapors' "Turning Japanese." It was in every cat lover's childhood favorite, *The Aristocats*. (Yes, before you even ask, it *was* in the outlandishly racist Siamese cat scene.) It even made an appearance in Super Mario Land.

The tune is ubiquitous. And like many things that are just in the air, few ever ask where it came from. But we did.

The Quest

We're not the first to ask the question. Back in February 2005, on the Straight 5 Dope message board, a person with a username "Doctorduck" asked:

"Where does that stereotypical 'oriental' song come from? You know, the one that goes *dee dee dee dee duh duh dee dee duh*. Featured heavily in braindead Hollywood flicks made by clueless directors who want to give a scene an 'oriental' feel. Also a variation of it can be heard in David Bowie's 'China Girl.'" It was a question that confounded many. Trying to pin down this nameless tune and its place in history turned out to be difficult.

"Where does that stereotypical 'oriental' song come from? It was a question that confounded many. Trying to pin down this nameless tune and its place in history turned out to be difficult."

Across dozens of comments, people agreed 1) that the canonical example of the melody was in "Kung Fu Fighting," 2) the melody also appeared in many other places, and 3) it probably pre-dated Douglas' song. But for weeks, no one could name an incontrovertible pre-1974 example of the tune.

They even called in the experts. One user reached out to Charles Hiroshi Garrett, a professor at the University of Michigan. In 2004, Garrett had written an academic paper referring to the riff, which a user in the Straight Dope forum quoted:

"[The opening phrase from the song 'Chinatown, My Chinatown'] resembles an extremely well known trope of musical orientalism—one of the most efficient that the West has developed to signal "Asia" . . . Such orientalist shorthand remains recognizable to twenty-first-century listeners, since these tropes continue to inhabit today's popular music. Thus, as clearly as the song's title captures its subject, the opening moments of 'Chinatown, My Chinatown' inform listeners that the song aims to fashion Asian difference."

I sent the following email to Charles Garrett, the author of "China-town, Whose Chinatown? Defining America's Borders with Musical Orientalism":   10

Dr. Garrett,

I'm a member of a general-knowledge Internet message board where we're currently discussing the origin of that stereotypical riff, used in movies and popular songs, that signifies "Asian"—the one heard in "Turning Japanese" by the Vapors or "Kung Fu Fighting" by Carl Douglas. . . .

The problem is, none of us have any background in musical history, or any formal training, so we're pretty much reduced to throwing around anecdotal statements, and, unfortunately, we're not getting very far. However, I *did* find that the opening notes of "Chinatown, My Chinatown" are *similar* to the riff in question, which led me to your paper, "Chinatown, Whose Chinatown? Defining America's Borders with Musical Orientalism." In that paper, you mention the "extremely well known trope of musical orientalism—one of the most efficient that the West has developed to signal "Asia"—which employs the same rhythmic pattern" as found in "Chinatown, My Chinatown."

So, by chance, can you shed some light on the origins of this particular riff? *Is* there a particular known origin, or did the riff grow organically from the *total body of Orientalist music? Did it grow out of the music found in "China-town, My Chinatown"? When did this riff first show up?*

Thanks for any information you might have.

Dr. Garrett was kind enough to take my out-of-the-blue question seriously, and his response was:

I'm intrigued by your question, but unfortunately I can't provide you a conclusive answer. In part, that is why the sentence you noted in my article does not spell out things further. I can say that the trope became popular over the years, but I am not sure exactly where or when it got started. I do know that that lick, and similar ones, show up in orientalist novelty songs of the 1940s, as well as in film scores and commercials. And I wouldn't be surprised to discover it in much earlier recordings of songs from the 1900s and 1910s and in ethnic songs written for the vaudeville stage. I've never looked, but there are hundreds of examples. It may even go back further than that to orientalist operas and so forth. I haven't looked for that musical passage in Madame Butterfly or The Mikado, but those sorts of works do use similar pentatonic techniques, too.

After receiving your e-mail, I exchanged some e-mail of my own with one of the experts in the field of musical orientalism. His feeling was that this is a very simplistic lick that anyone can play on the black keys of the piano (if one adds the parallel fourths above and below). In other words, it's a very simple, childlike maneuver that instantly can mimic pentatonic (aka "Asian") music. So, it may just have developed that way—as composers looked for the first recognizable and arguably comic way to imitate pentatonicism.

I hope that helps. If you turn up any other theories, I'd be happy to hear about them. Will do the same for you if I come across anything.

The second paragraph seems like a plausible explanation *how* the riff was established, although not exactly *where* or *when*. And, although he doesn't give a specific example of the "orientalist novelty songs of the 1940s," I'm inclined to believe that he'd be a reasonably reliable source for their existence.

But then, the trail turned cold. Radio silence for a year. Then, suddenly, in June 2006, a user named "mani" announced that he'd built a whole website devoted to the question:

"I got fascinated with this question, and for the past month I've done some research, mostly utilising various online archives of old sheet music and recordings whose copyright claims have expired. My findings soon became far too voluminous to fit in a single post, so I created a website dedicated to the 'Asian riff': chinoiserie.atspace.com."

The user was Martin Nilsson, a Web designer in Sweden. He'd been 15
studying piano at a conservatory and had a lot of free time to devote
to this "hobby research," as he told me over the phone. (It's "hobby
research" that lots of different folks have cited, including music
professors I chatted with, and bloggers at You Offend Me You Offend My
Family.)

Nilsson found that the melody's roots went back way further than
"Kung Fu Fighting"—at least as far as the 19th century.

Defining the Cliché

One of the things Nilsson was trying to discover was whether the melody
was ever a reference to a real Asian tune—or if it was purely a Western
invention.

"It doesn't come from Chinese folk music, really," Nilsson says. "It's
just a caricature of how [Westerners] think Chinese music would sound."

While digging through American sheet music archives, Nilsson
reached a point where the line between references to the riff and very
similar ones got blurry. So he dubbed the similar riffs the "Far East Proto
Cliche," based on specific musical characteristics. The definition: "Any
melody with this particular rhythmical pattern and whose first four
tones are identical" that usually uses a pentatonic scale, Nilsson wrote
on his website. (Some melodies that fit this pattern make no reference to
Asia whatsoever—you might recognize it in Peter, Bjorn and John's song
"Young Folks.")

This nine-note tune and its cousins rely heavily on the pentatonic 20
scale, which music from many East Asian and West African countries
used.

"We get the sense of another culture when we hear the scale," says
Nilanjana Bhattacharjya, an ethnomusicologist at Arizona State University. "It's worth thinking about the fact that the scale isn't necessarily
something we would've been listening to in the United States in a significant way before the end of the 19th century, early 20th."

The pentatonic scale gained global popularity in 1889, during the
Paris World's Fair. The French exhibition—along with other world exhi-
bitions that were popular in that time—was where folks exchanged ideas
and learned about other cultures. It was home to a range of exhibits,
like the human zoo (also known as the Negro Village) and a Javanese
gamelan showcase. The latter inspired composers like Claude Debussy,
whose work often used the pentatonic scale.

But the "Far East Proto Cliche," Nilsson found, went back even further than that World's Fair.

The Backdrop of the Riff

One of the first instances of the cliche Nilsson found was in a show in 1847 called *The Grand Chinese Spectacle of Aladdin,* or *The Wonderful Lamp.*

And to understand the evolution of this riff, we need to look at the 25 backdrop against which this tune emerged.

In the 1800s, men from China were coming to the U.S. to work in gold mines and on railroads. By 1880, there were 300,000 Chinese in the States—and there was a lot of anti-Chinese sentiment. In 1882, the U.S. banned Chinese immigration with the Chinese Exclusion Act. It took until 1968 for such restrictions to be lifted.

Think about it: Most people back then had limited interactions with people from China and other Asian countries. So playwrights and writers had to come up with a shorthand way of saying, "This is Chinese; this is Asian."

This building of a viewpoint—a viewpoint that in many ways is still with us, that people of Asian descent are intrinsically foreign—is echoed time and time again in various cartoons from the early 1900s that feature the riff.

Someone, somewhere decided that this short musical phrase—and others like it—could represent an entire region or identity. And it stuck.

Understanding the Text

1. According to Chow, when did the pentatonic scale first gain global popularity? Why is this fact important to the history of the "Asian riff"?

2. Chow writes, "And to understand the evolution of this riff, we need to look at the backdrop against which this tune emerged" (25). What American historical "backdrop" is she referring to?

Reflection and Response

3. According to the writer, the development of the Asian riff was part of the "building of a viewpoint — a viewpoint that in many ways is still with us that people of Asian descent are intrinsically foreign . . ." (28). How does knowing this history affect the way you hear the Asian riff? For example, do you think the melody is offensive? Why or why not?

4. As Chow establishes in her article, the riff has no connection to authentic Chinese music. What do you think accounts for its persistence and power as a "shorthand" for "Asian"? If you are unfamiliar with the melody, access it online — for example, by listening to Carl Douglas's "Kung Fu Fighting."

Making Connections

5. As musicologist Charles Garrett notes, the Asian riff is a "trope of musical orientalism" and "orientalist shorthand." What other musical melodies, tropes, or musical motifs serve similar purposes for other ethnicities or nationalities? Are they authentic and rooted in those cultures, or are they artificial, like the Asian riff? Does this distinction matter? Why or why not?

6. In "The Most Beautiful Melody in the World" (p. 54), Jan Swafford writes about melody, as well as the ways in which our ideas about melody are shaped by culture: "You know [a tune] when you hear it — according to how you've been conditioned by your culture and experience to hear it. . . . Each culture has its own sense of melody, one that often seems peculiar to the next culture." What insight might this give us into the development and persistence of the "Asian riff"? The American poet Henry Wadsworth Longfellow referred to music as a "universal language," but how might that claim be misleading when applied to melodies from different parts of the world?

It's a Hip-Hop World

Jeff Chang

While hip-hop is considered a distinctly American musical form, originating in New York in the 1970s, it has grown into a sprawling global phenomenon. In this article from *Foreign Policy*, Jeff Chang follows hip-hop in its many musical, cultural, and political manifestations from France and Shanghai to Kenya and Germany. It is often the voice of the oppressed, but it also serves "as the soundtrack for aggressive, youth-oriented consumer goods marketing." Indeed, this tension between commercialism and an "outsider ethos" seems to follow hip-hop wherever it goes. Ultimately, however, Chang sees this music and culture as a positive force for connection in the context of globalism.

Jeff Chang is a journalist and music critic whose work has appeared in *Spin*, the *Nation*, *Vibe*, the *Guardian*, and many other publications. He is the author of *Can't Stop, Won't Stop: A History of the Hip-Hop Generation* (2005) and *Total Chaos: The Art and Aesthetics of Hip-Hop* (2007).

Inside the steaming walls of a nightclub in the heart of one of the world's most dynamic cities, you can hear the sounds of the future. Hundreds of people gyrate rhythmically as a DJ spins hot beats. On stage, a pair of rappers face off, microphones in hand, trading verses of improvised rhyme. They look like typical hip-hop artists, dressed in baggy pants and baseball caps. But listen closely and you notice something unusual: They're performing in Chinese. One rapper spits out words in a distinctive Beijing accent, scolding the other for not speaking proper Mandarin. His opponent from Hong Kong snaps back to the beat in a trilingual torrent of Cantonese, English, and Mandarin, dissing the Beijing rapper for not representing the people. The crowd goes wild, raucously voicing delight and dismay.

This annual rap battle, called the Iron Mic, isn't taking place in New York or Los Angeles, but in Shanghai, where its founder, 32-year-old Dana Burton, has unexpectedly found fame and fortune. The Detroit native arrived in China in 1999 to take a job teaching English. During his first week in town, he went to a nightclub that advertised hip-hop music. But the closest thing to hip-hop was a Michael Jackson impersonator. So, Burton embarked on a mission to bring the real thing to the Middle Kingdom. "I thought about what I could offer China," he says. "It was hip-hop." Burton began to moonlight as a rapper and developed a following. He not only performed himself but also helped others—foreigners and Chinese—get their own acts off the ground by hosting parties and hip-hop nights such as Iron Mic. Admirers called him "the godfather of Chinese hip-hop."

Burton soon began to promote tours for famous hip-hop artists visiting from the United States. Today, multinational corporations including Intel, Coca-Cola, and Adidas turn to him when they want help in marketing their consumer goods to China's booming youth market. Burton then taps into his pool of more than 300 Chinese rappers, DJs, dancers, and graffiti artists.

In a recent campaign for Wyborowa vodka, Burton took his crew on the road, presenting 150 shows in 40 Chinese cities. His artists performed a mini history of hip-hop, from its urban American beginnings to its Chinese apotheosis. It was the perfect brew—an African-American entrepreneur promoting a Polish vodka owned by a French corporation using Chinese performers practicing an Afro-Latin-influenced art form that originated in the inner cities of the United States. Welcome to hip-hop's new world.

A Serious Business

To the uninitiated, hip-hop hardly looks or sounds like a brave, new 5 art form. It's more like a sonic jackhammer, a visual eyesore, and a conceptual nuisance. Critics often call hip-hop materialistic, misogynistic, homophobic, racist, vulgar, and violent. It's a hot mess, the roar of total chaos.

Some of that is true. But rap music is only a part of the movement, and if you look beyond stereotypes, it's clear that hip-hop culture has become one of the most far-reaching arts movements of the past three decades. The best artists share a desire to break down boundaries between "high" and "low" art—to make urgent, truth-telling work that reflects the lives, loves, histories, hopes, and fears of their generation. Hip-hop is about rebellion, yes, but it's also about transformation.

At the core of hip-hop is the notion of something called the "cipher." Partly for competition and partly for community, the cipher is the circle of participants and onlookers that closes around battling rappers or dancers as they improvise for each other. If you have the guts to step into the cipher and tell your story and, above all, demonstrate your uniqueness, you might be accepted into the community. Here is where reputations are made and risked and stylistic change is fostered. That this communitarian honoring of merit—whether it's called "style," "hotness," or whatever the latest slang for it is—can transcend geography, culture, and even skin color remains hip-hop's central promise.

Today, the message of hip-hop is even transcending borders. From *xi ha* in China to "hip-life" in Ghana, hip-hop is a lingua franca that binds young people all around the world, all while giving them the chance to alter it with their own national flavor. It is the foundation for global dance competitions, the meeting ground for local progressive activism, even the subject of study at Harvard and the London School of Economics.

But one thing about hip-hop has remained consistent across cultures: a vital progressive agenda that challenges the status quo. Thousands of organizers from Cape Town to Paris use hip-hop in their communities to address environmental justice, policing and prisons, media justice, and education. In Gothenburg, Sweden, non-governmental organizations (NGOs) incorporate graffiti and dance to engage disaffected immigrant and working-class youths. And indigenous young people in places as disparate as Chile, Indonesia, New Zealand, and Norway use hip-hop to push their generation's views into the local conversation.

> "From *xi ha* in China to "hip-life" in Ghana, hip-hop is a lingua franca that binds young people all around the world, all while giving them the chance to alter it with their own national flavor."

Hip-hop is also a serious business. More than 59 million rap albums were sold in the United States alone last year. But that number represents only a small part of hip-hop's influence. It sells an estimated $10 billion worth of trendsetting luxury and consumer goods every year—not just in movies, shoes, and clothing but in everything from snack crackers and soda drinks to cars and computers. This "urban aspirational lifestyle" market is expected to continue to grow exponentially. According to a 2006 report by business research company Packaged Facts, the potential purchasing power available to this market in the United States alone is worth $780 billion. American rapper 50 Cent is one of the many savvy businessmen in hip-hop who's fully grasped this potential. In 2004, he agreed to endorse flavored beverage VitaminWater for a small stake in Glacéau, the company that produced it. In June, Coca-Cola purchased Glacéau for $4.1 billion. When the deal closed, 50 Cent walked away with a rumored $100 million overnight, just for lending his name to a drink. 10

Of all the rappers out there, mogul and renaissance man Shawn Carter, better known as Jay-Z, is the most successful example of the growing power of hip-hop. When he took over Universal Records' Def Jam unit in 2004, Jay-Z was put in charge of a billion-dollar business. Some industry insiders believe that today, Def Jam's overseas business outpaces its domestic business. Jay-Z's own albums have sold 33 million copies worldwide, and his latest album, released last November, sold 680,000 copies in the United States alone during the first week. He runs popular nightclubs in New York and Atlantic City—with plans to open more next year in Las Vegas, Tokyo, and Macao. The former drug dealer who grew up in poverty in the housing projects of Brooklyn is now worth an estimated $500 million.

Rising Up

With its humble origins, no one could have foreseen the global phenomenon that hip-hop would become. Thirty years ago, New York City bore little resemblance to the glittering metropolis of today, particularly the embattled streets of the Bronx. Race riots, urban renewal, arson, and government neglect wiped out educational and social service programs, eviscerated housing stock, accelerated white flight and job loss, and created an international symbol of urban despair.

Figure 4.3   "It's clear that hip-hop culture has become one of the most far-reaching arts movements of the past three decades": A South Korean breakdancer. AP Images/ Lee Jin-man

Meanwhile, the poor youth of the Bronx found ways to pass the time: rapping in a style adapted from Jamaican reggae with Bronx slang over funky Afro-Latin-influenced grooves, dancing wildly to the percussive breaks, spraypainting their nicknames on walls, buses, and subway trains. These were hip-hop's original "four elements"—MCing, DJing, b-boying (or "breakdancing"), and graffiti. The street culture was alive to the eccentricities of the politically abandoned neighborhood and the children who still populated it. And the innocent leisure choices of teens, taken together, represented the early makings of an artistic vanguard.

In 1973, two Jamaican-American immigrant teenagers decided to throw a back-to-school party. Cindy Campbell and her brother Clive, better known in the neighborhood as DJ Kool Herc, organized the dance in the recreation room of their government-subsidized apartment building at the now famous address of 1520 Sedgwick Avenue. They had exquisite timing. After years of gang violence, teens in the area were growing weary and looking for a new way to express themselves. "When I went to [the] party, it was like stepping into another universe. The vibe was so strong," says Tony Tone, a gang member who later became part of the pioneering rap group the Cold Crush Brothers. The Campbells' Bronx parties became so popular they soon had to move them outdoors to a nearby park. Crowds flocked to them. Instead of getting into trouble on the streets, teens now had a place to expend their pent-up energy. "Hip-hop saved a lot of lives," recalls Tone.

One such lifesaver was a gang leader named Afrika Bambaataa. 15 Inspired by DJ Kool Herc, he too began hosting hip-hop parties. After a soul-altering visit to Africa, he vowed to use hip-hop to draw poor, angry kids out of gangs, and formed a street organization called Universal Zulu Nation to help spread his message. Soon, New York underground journalists were writing that Bambaataa was "stopping bullets with two turntables." With this message of empowerment, rap updated African-American poetic traditions, and bore witness to the joyful, soulful, and sometimes angry stories of life in their forgotten America.

Planet Hip-Hop

Less than a decade after the Campbells' famous party, hip-hop began to seep outside the United States. In 1982, Afrika Bambaataa and his group Soulsonic Force released a single called "Planet Rock," which borrowed musical motifs from German electropop, British rock, and African-American disco rap. They blended the elements together, offering hip-hop as a new vision for global harmony. The record stormed the charts worldwide. That same year, Bambaataa led New York's leading rappers, dancers, artists, and DJs on the first hip-hop tour outside the United States. Bambaataa saw such visits as a key way to expand Universal Zulu Nation and to espouse what he considered the core values of hip-hop: peace, unity, love, and having fun. Everywhere he went, he planted the seeds for the hip-hop movement in Europe, Africa, and Asia.

France, in particular, caught the hip-hop virus. In the 1990s, MC Solaar became the first non-American rap superstar. Solaar was born in Senegal to parents from Chad, and discovered Zulu Nation and the music of Afrika Bambaataa as a young teenager in Paris. His multicultural background appealed to youths throughout the Francophone world, which quickly developed into the largest non-English-speaking rap market. The emerging popularity of cable and satellite television throughout the world in the late 1980s further spread the seeds of hip-hop. In 1988, MTV debuted an experimental pilot program in the United States called *Yo! MTV Raps*, which aired hip-hop videos once a week in an after-hours slot. Soon, the show grew so popular it was broadcast six days a week. African-American and Latino urban style was instantly accessible to millions of youths, and not just in the United States. *Yo! MTV Raps* became one of the network's first globally televised shows — airing in dozens of countries, first on MTV Europe, and then on MTV Asia and MTV Latino a few years later.

One of the groups to get the most airtime was Public Enemy, a collective of mostly college-educated, activist-minded young men with audacious ambitions and the outsized talent to match. Emerging from the largely black inner suburbs of Long Island, New York, the group's lyrics decried police brutality, racial profiling, gang violence, and political apathy. Their rise convinced many skeptics that hip-hop could be a lasting, potentially lucrative, even socially important art form. Taking a page from Bambaataa's book, Public Enemy embarked on extended world tours. Its influence was far-reaching. When Public Enemy reached Brazil's shores in the late 1980s, hip-hop exploded in Latin America. "[Their] song 'Don't Believe the Hype' was so important," says legendary Brazilian rapper Eliefi of the hit single that championed black power. "We had never seen black folks in a militant stance before."

Although hip-hop has become mainstream in many parts of the world today, it is still considered a voice for the oppressed, and a provocation to those in power. In fact, the culture wars that hip-hop spawned in the mid-1990s in the United States, with congressional hearings and CD-crushing campaigns, have appeared in Britain, where national debates over hip-hop have stood in for deeper discussions over the thorny issues of race and immigration. In 2003, British Culture Minister Kim Howells turned his bully pulpit on "hateful lyrics that these boasting macho idiot rappers come up with." Hip-hop has come up against the same resistance in France. Two years ago, angry rap made by the sons of disenfranchised African and Arab immigrants served as the soundtrack to riots in the French *banlieues*, and again in post-election riots this past spring. Two hundred French members of Parliament signed a petition to curb hip-hop. The petition failed, but the episode was another reminder of how hip-hop can clash with the powers that be.

All Hip-Hop Is Local

As hip-hop grows ever more popular, it becomes squeezed in the uneasy space between commercial and economic globalization from above and borderless, cultural grassroots globalization from below. Commercial rap made in the United States — with its ethic of "get rich or die tryin'" — is displacing local rappers and musicians on the radio and television airwaves in Africa, Asia, the Caribbean, and South America, while serving as the soundtrack for aggressive, youth-oriented consumer goods marketing.

This rampant commercialism is often at odds with hip-hop's outsider ethos. In Kenya, for instance, two differing visions — one as a resistance culture oriented toward social justice, the other as a popular culture focused on commodity capitalism — may be increasingly headed toward a reckoning. For some Kenyans, hip-hop has allowed a new generation of postcolonial Africans to speak out. Young Kenyan rappers' lyrics — in *sheng*, a creolized language that includes English, Swahili, and Kikuyu words — tackle the themes of joblessness, poverty, and the older generation's failures. Indeed, young artists are building communities that actively support the development of cultural politics unique to the continent. One Kenyan NGO, Words and Pictures, has been traveling to Ghana, Senegal, South Africa, and Tanzania to promote networking among local hip-hop pioneers. The recent arrival of MTV Base Africa may accelerate these trends. The network was launched in South Africa at the beginning of 2005 with a playlist that was roughly one third African. Since then, the proportion of artists from the continent has risen, and the network says it hopes to reach 50 percent African programming in the next year. But on the radio, hip-hop from overseas is increasingly becoming the norm. Stations such as Britain's Capital FM and locally owned KISS FM sell advertising to multinational corporations like Motorola and Nokia. They prefer to program American artists such as 50 Cent because such rap helps corporations sell consumer goods. But local rappers, whose music critiques government and poverty, dub American rap, ironically, "white-boy oppressor music," even though the artists are predominantly African American.

Nairobi native Michael Wanguhu, who created the documentary film *Hip-Hop Colony*, says this kind of cultural homogenization and commercial sponsorship are becoming major worries. "It's creating opportunities where there were none before," he says, "but there's no room for music that is enlightened and empowers people." Still, he is bullish on hip-hop's expansion.

"Hip-hop in Africa is like the new Pan-Africanism," he says. "It's diffusing all the borders we have and creating new organizations and expanding that whole market."

The Global Cipher

Every October in Braunschweig, Germany, 8,500 hip-hop fans from around the world gather to witness the biggest global hip-hop dance competition, the Battle of the Year. First organized by German b-boy Thomas Hergenröther 16 years ago as a tiny showcase for a handful of dance crews from Germany and Hungary, the event has expanded into nothing less than the World Cup of hip-hop dance. Elimination competitions are held in 20 countries, including Albania, China, Estonia, Malaysia, New Zealand, Serbia, and South Africa. At the finals, 20 teams featuring about 200 dancers represent their respective countries on the main stage of Braunschweig's Volkswagen Halle.

Film director Benson Lee captured the 2005 competition for his doc- 25 umentary, *Planet B-Boy*. In telling the story of one year in the contest, Lee reveals the diversity of hip-hop's global participants—working-class immigrants rejecting the hopelessness of the Parisian suburbs, youths trying to spring themselves from the homogeneity of Tokyo's urban retailscapes, even conscripts from the South Korean army. "These kids aren't thugs. They are artists," says Lee. "The main essence of hip-hop is community."

Hip-hop events such as the Battle of the Year create spaces for a globalization from the bottom, bringing people together across the barriers of geography, language, and race. Lee's movie reveals tensions between the American and French teams, which both perform with aggressive, bold attitudes. Everyone fears the upstart South Koreans, a team of superbly synchronized underdogs sporting patriotic white, red, and aqua-colored hooded track suits. "What Germany or France did in 15 years," Hergenröther says with awe, "they managed in five."

In one scene, the German team—whose crew prominently features African and Arab immigrants—choreographs a humorous Aladdin's magic carpet sequence, taking a pointed jab at the country's continuing immigration wars. "So many different people came together under the name of hip-hop, that hip-hop changed music, arts completely," says a German b-boy who goes by the name "Storm."

But the essence of hip-hop is the cipher, born in the Bronx, where competition and community feed each other. It is here that hip-hop always returns. In the final round of Battle of the Year, the crews line up and verbally attack each other, either one-on-one or "commando style," all at once. It is always a night of riotous explosion of bodies, as dancers burst to the breakbeats. The climax of the battle, the most thrilling part, is itself the deepest kind of communication. "It happens in an exchange," says Storm. "He's giving me something that I can relate to and I have to answer with something that he can relate to so that we can continue this battle." It's the kind of exchange that happens daily, among millions, in almost every corner of the world.

Understanding the Text

1. According to Chang, what is the "one thing about hip-hop" that "has remained consistent across cultures" (9)?

2. Chang writes, "At the core of hip-hop is the notion of something called the 'cipher'" (7). What is the "cipher"? What tensions does it resolve in hip-hop?

Reflection and Response

3. The writer acknowledges: "Critics often call hip-hop materialistic, misogynistic, homophobic, racist, vulgar, and violent" (5). How does he respond to these characterizations? Do you find his alternative view of hip-hop persuasive?

4. Chang traces hip-hop's growth from the Bronx in the 1970s to a global phenomenon now. What do you think accounts for its powerful international appeal? Is that appeal related to the perception that the form is a "voice for the oppressed" (19)?

Making Connections

5. In "Black Rhythm, White Power" (p. 193), Samantha Ainsley writes about the white misappropriation of black musical forms, including hip-hop, as well as the ways in which hip-hop's popularity only perpetuates white supremacy and the marginalization of black people: "White America's

embrace of hip-hop culture is hardly a move toward racial acceptance and cultural understanding. . . . In the eyes of the mainstream, hip-hop reinforces conventions and stereotypes of blackness that foster white power." How does Chang's reframing of hip-hop as a global "arts movement" complicate and problematize Ainsley's argument? For example, does the global diffusion and influence of hip-hop foster "white power" internationally? Why or why not?

6. Chang writes: "Hip-hop is about rebellion, yes, but it's also about transformation" (6). What do you think he means by this? How do styles, musical expression, and consumption enable "transformation"? Have you had any transformative experiences — whether personal or collective — with particular forms of music? Explain.

5

What Does Music Reveal about Sexuality and Gender?

More than any other modern, mass-culture art form, popular music has placed sex, sexual orientation, sexual politics, and gender roles near the center of its existence. In fact, gender-as-performance may be one of the most prominent and perennial of musical themes, enacted in songs from Bo Diddley's "I'm a Man" and Lou Reed's "Walk on the Wild Side" to Lady Gaga's "Born This Way" and Beyoncé's "If I Were a Boy," to name just a few. Likewise, sex and popular music have long been twinned: lust and romantic longing remain, perhaps, the most common preoccupations of popular songs across nearly all genres. That should not be surprising: the very terms *jazz* and *rock and roll*, for example, originally had strong sexual connotations, while the disco genre originated mainly in the subculture of gay dance clubs before achieving mainstream acceptance. Of course, gender roles and sexuality do more than merely shape genres or provide thematic content for songwriters and performers: they also provide the cultural context for the creation, performance, distribution, and consumption of popular music.

The writers in this chapter focus on music from the perspective of sexual identity and gender roles. In "All Hail the Queen?," Tamara Winfrey Harris writes about the complex and misunderstood feminism of superstar Beyoncé — particularly in the context of her status as a black female superstar. Susan Hiwatt's "Macho Rock: Men Always Seem to End Up on Top" offers a raw and provocative exposé of chauvinism and misogyny in the world of late 1960s and early 1970s rock music. In "They've Got the Beat," Hannah Steinkopf-Frank provides a perceptive and necessary reevaluation of the "girl-group" genre, from the late 1950s to the present. Amy Clements-Cortes looks at the way the music and images of popular female musical stars shape the identities of young women who aspire to be performers themselves. Last, Madison Moore's "Tina Theory: Notes on Fierceness" gives an illuminating scholarly interpretation of Tina Turner's career as a performer, as well as a deeply personal account of her influence on the author as a young, gay man.

photo: Flashpop/Getty Images

All Hail the Queen?

Tamara Winfrey Harris

Beyoncé Knowles has been a public figure since her teenage years as part of the group Destiny's Child in the 1990s. Over the past decade, however, she has emerged as an iconic figure in popular culture, both as an enormously successful solo artist, record producer, and actress, as well as the partner (both musically and personally) of rapper and business mogul Jay Z. As Tamara Winfrey Harris writes, feminists should be celebrating her example. Instead, writes Winfrey Harris, Beyoncé is trapped in a double-bind of conflicting expectations and stereotypes, as feminist responses to her reveal the "conflicting pressures on black women and the complicated way our bodies and relationships are policed."

Tamara Winfrey Harris regularly writes about the intersection of race, gender, and popular culture. Her work has appeared in the *New York Times*, *Salon*, *Ms.*, and other publications. She is the author of *The Sisters Are Alright: Changing the Broken Narrative for Black Women in America* (2015).

*W*ho *run the world?* If entertainment domination is the litmus test, then all hail Queen Bey. Beyoncé. She who, in the last few months alone, whipped her golden lace-front and shook her booty fiercely enough to zap the power in the Superdome (electrical relay device, bah!); produced, directed, and starred in *Life Is But a Dream*, HBO's most-watched documentary in nearly a decade; and launched the Mrs. Carter Show—the must-see concert of the summer.

Beyoncé's success would seem to offer many reasons for feminists to cheer. The performer has enjoyed record-breaking career success and has taken control of a multimillion-dollar empire in a male-run industry, while being frank about gender inequities and the sacrifices required of women. She employs an all-woman band of ace musicians—the Sugar Mamas—that she formed to give girls more musical role models. And she speaks passionately about the power of female relationships.

But some pundits are hesitant to award the singer feminist laurels. For instance, Anne Helen Petersen, writer for the blog *Celebrity Gossip, Academic Style*, says, "What bothers me—what causes such profound ambivalence—is the way in which [Beyoncé has] been held up as an exemplar of female power and, by extension, become a de facto feminist icon. . . . Beyoncé is powerful. F*cking powerful. And that, in truth, is what concerns me."

Petersen says the singer's lyrical feminism swings between fantasy ("Run the World [Girls]") and "bemoaning and satirizing men's inability to commit to monogamous relationships" ("Single Ladies"). The writer also accuses Beyoncé of performing for the male gaze and admits, in comments to the post, to feeling "grossed out" by the "Mrs. Carter" tour name. And Petersen is surely not alone in her displeasure.

Turns out, booty shaking and stamping your husband's last name   5 on a product of your own creativity makes a lot of folks question your feminist values. (Beyoncé recently told *Vogue UK* that though the word "can be extreme . . . I guess I am a modern-day feminist. I believe in equality.") Some of the equivocation is no doubt caused by Beyoncé's slick, pop-princess brand. It is difficult to square the singer's mainstream packaging with subversion of conventional and sexist views of gender. But ultimately, the policing of feminist cred is the real moral contradiction. And the judgment of how Beyoncé expresses her womanhood is emblematic of the way women in the public eye are routinely picked apart — in particular, it's a demonstration of the conflicting pressures on black women and the complicated way our bodies and relationships are policed.

In a January 2013 *Guardian* article titled "Beyoncé: Being Photographed in Your Underwear Doesn't Help Feminism," writer Hadley Freeman blasts the singer for posing in the February issue of *GQ* "nearly naked in seven photos, including one on the cover in which she is wearing a pair of tiny knickers and a man's shirt so cropped that her breasts are visible."

Of course, in that very same issue of *GQ*, Beyoncé makes several statements about gender inequity — the sort not often showcased in men's magazines. Among them: "Let's face it, money gives men the power to run the show. It gives men the power to define value. They define what's sexy. And men define what's feminine. It's ridiculous."

That Beyoncé speaks the language of feminism so publicly is even more notable in a climate where high-profile mainstream female entertainers often explicitly reject the very word. Katy Perry, while accepting a Woman of the Year Award from *Billboard*, announced that she is not a feminist (but she believes in the "power of women"). And when asked by *The Daily Beast* if she is a feminist, Taylor Swift offered, "I don't really think about things as guys versus girls. I never have. I was raised by parents who brought me up to think if you work as hard as guys, you can go far in life."

A popular star willing to talk about gender inequity, as Beyoncé has, is depressingly rare. But Freeman insists flashes of underboob and feminist critique don't mix. Petersen concurs, calling the thigh-baring, lace-meets-leather outfit Beyoncé wore during her Super Bowl XLVII halftime show an "outfit that basically taught my lesson on the way that the male gaze objectifies and fetishizes the otherwise powerful female body."

Figure 5.1 "That Beyoncé speaks the language of feminism so publicly is even more notable in a climate where high-profile mainstream female entertainers often explicitly reject the very word." Kevin Mazur/Getty Images

A commenter on Jezebel summed up the charge: "That's pretty much the Beyoncé contradiction right there. Lip service for female fans, fan service for the guys."

These appraisals are perplexing amid a wave of feminist ideology 10 rooted in the idea that women own their bodies. It is the feminism of SlutWalk, the anti-rape movement that proclaims a skimpy skirt does not equal a desire for male attention or sexual availability. Why, then, are cultural critics like Freeman and Petersen convinced that when Beyoncé pops a leather-clad pelvis on stage, it is solely for the benefit of men? Why do others think her acknowledgment of how patriarchy influences our understanding of what's sexy is mere "lip service"?

Dr. Sarah Jackson, a race and media scholar at Boston's Northeastern University, says, "The idea that Beyoncé being sexy is only her performing for male viewers assumes that embracing sexuality isn't also for women." Jackson adds that the criticism also ignores "the limited choices available to women in the entertainment industry and the limited ways Beyoncé is allowed to express her sexuality, because of her gender and her race."

Her confounding mainstream persona, Jackson points out, is one key to the entertainer's success as a black artist. "You don't see black versions of Lady Gaga crossing over to the extent that Beyoncé has or reaching her levels of success. Black artists rarely have the same privilege of not conforming to dominant image expectations."

Solange, Beyoncé's sister, who has gone for a natural-haired, boho, less sexified approach to her music, remains a niche artist, as do Erykah Badu, Janelle Monáe, and Shingai Shoniwa of the Noisettes, like so many black female artists before them. Grace Jones, Joan Armatrading, Tracy Chapman, Meshell Ndegeocello—talented all, but quirky black girls, especially androgynous ones, don't sell pop music, perform at the Super Bowl, or get starring roles in Hollywood films.

Black women (and girls) have also historically battled the stereotype of innate and uncontrolled lasciviousness, which may explain why Beyoncé's sexuality is viewed differently from that of white artists like Madonna, who is lauded for performing in very similar ways.

A *Seattle Times* review of a recent Madonna tour stop praises the artist 15 for "rocking us as a feminist icon" and applauds the singer for her brazen sexuality: "stripping down to a bra, then pulling her pants down below a thong and baring her cheeks to the Key [Arena]." Even the *Guardian*'s Freeman, in an ode to *Like a Prayer*, the writer's favorite album, speaks longingly about Madonna's midriff-baring '80s fashion and the video to the title track.

Through a career that has included crotch-grabbing, nudity, BDSM, Marilyn Monroe fetishizing, and a 1992 book devoted to sex, Madonna has been viewed as a feminist provocateur, pushing the boundaries of acceptable femininity. But Beyoncé's use of her body is criticized as thoughtless and without value beyond male titillation, providing a modern example of the age-old racist juxtaposition of animalistic black sexuality vs. controlled, intentional, and civilized white sexuality.

And then there's the fact that some cultural critics are adding to this dissection of Beyoncé's feminism through commentary on her relationship with husband Shawn Knowles-Carter, a.k.a. hip hop mogul Jay-Z. During an interview with Oprah Winfrey before the *Life Is But a Dream* premiere, Beyoncé spoke passionately about her partner of more than a decade, saying, "I would not be the woman I am if I did not go home to that man." This comment prompted Dodai Stewart at Jezebel to write, "Wouldn't you like to believe she'd be amazing whether or not she went home to a man? (She would be.) It's a much better message when she talks about how powerful she is as a woman and what a woman can do—without mentioning Mr. Carter."

Surely a woman can be powerful and simultaneously admit that her marriage is profound and life altering. Beyoncé did not pronounce herself useless without marriage. On the contrary, she has said she was in no rush to marry the man she met at 18. "I feel like you have to get to know yourself, know what you want, spend some time by yourself and be proud of who you are before you can share that with someone else."

Being a feminist in the public eye should not require remaining aloof about relationships, including those with men who have helped shape who you are. We don't require this of men. None other than Bey and Jay's bestie, President Barack Obama, made a very similar claim about his spouse post-2008 election: "I would not be standing here tonight without the unyielding support of my best friend for the last 16 years . . . Michelle Obama."

Feminist media activist Jamia Wilson says, "I think that it's just hard   20 for people to really grasp what it's like to be extremely powerful but also vulnerable. Black women, in particular, are characterized as singularly strong figures. How can you be the mule of the world for everybody, but also have somebody carry you when you need them to?"

More problematic to some is the name of Beyoncé's world tour—the Mrs. Carter Show. Jane Martinson of the *Guardian* wrote in a February 2013 op-ed, "There is almost something subversive about waiting until the strongest moment of your career, which is where Beyoncé finds herself now, to do away with the infamous glossy mononym in favour of a second name your own husband doesn't even use."

In a recent *Slate* article titled "Who Run the World? Husbands?" Aisha Harris wonders, "as a woman who has earned enough clout to inspire dance crazes, earn lucrative (if controversial) advertising deals, and perform for the U.S. president on multiple occasions, one can't help but wonder why she felt the need to evoke the name of her beau in her solo world tour."

If a woman loses feminist bona fides by becoming Mrs. So-and-So, someone best tell the 86 percent of American women who take their husbands' names at marriage. If there is any woman not in danger of being subsumed by a man's identity—no matter her last name—it is Beyoncé. In fact, the singer's married name is not "Mrs. Carter." She and her husband combined their names to create the hyphenate "Knowles-Carter."

"This man, who has made a living—an extremely good one—perpetuating hyper-masculinity, patriarchal masculinity, took the last name of the woman he married," Jackson says. "That in itself, to me, says something about gender in their relationship and the respect that exists there."

Beyoncé's race, once again, complicates the discussion. She is criti-   25 cized for toying with the traditional "Mrs." moniker at a time of relentless public hand-wringing about black women being half as likely to marry as white women. ABC News actually convened a panel to weigh in on "Why Can't a Successful Black Woman Find a Man?" CNN has aired segments exploring whether the black church or single motherhood is to blame for rampant black female singleness. And men like comedian–turned–relationship guru Steve Harvey are making bank explaining to single black women what they surely must be doing wrong. And what they are doing wrong is understood to be not conforming to traditional ideas of femininity and not mothering in the "right" way (i.e., too often being unmarried "baby mamas" rather than married mommies).

Black women are, it seems, damned if we do and damned if we don't. Our collective singleness, independence, and unsanctioned mothering are an affront to mainstream womanhood. But a high-profile married black woman who uses her husband's name (if only for purposes of showbiz) or admits the influence her male partner has had on her life is an affront to feminism.

Wilson says that in the context of pathologized black womanhood and black relationships, Beyoncé and the Knowles-Carter clan "counter a narrative about our families that has been defined by the media for too long about what our families must look like and how they're comprised." Black women's sexuality and our roles as mothers and partners have been treated as public issues as far back as slavery, even as family life for most citizens has been viewed as a private matter. Our nation's "peculiar institution" treated human beings—black human beings—as property. And so, black women's partnering—when and whom we partnered with and the offspring of those unions—were at the very foundation of the American economy. According to Jackson, "People would talk about black women's sexuality in polite company like they would talk about race horses foaling calves."

Like critiques of her sexed-up performances, response to Beyoncé's recent pregnancy illustrates that black female bodies remain fodder for public gossip. Even with the devotion of mainstream media (especially the entertainment and gossip genres) to monitoring female celebrities' sexuality, "baby bumps," and engagement rocks, the speculation about Beyoncé's womb stands apart as truly bizarre. Almost as soon as the singer revealed her pregnancy at the 2011 MTV Video Music Awards, there was conjecture—amplified by a televised interview in which the singer's dress folded "suspiciously" around her middle—that it was all a ruse to cover for the use of a surrogate.

The HBO documentary, which chronicled her pregnancy, failed to quiet the deliberation. Gawker writer Rich Juzwiak proclaimed, "Beyoncé has never been less convincing about the veracity of her pregnancy than she was in her own movie. . . . We never see a full, clear shot of Beyoncé's pregnant, swanlike body. Instead it's presented in pieces, owing to the limitations of her Mac webcam. When her body is shown in full, it's in grainy, black-and-white footage in which her face is shadowed." There is, in this assessment, a disturbing assumption of ownership over Beyoncé's body. Why won't this woman display her naked body on television to prove to the world that she carried a baby in her uterus?

The conversation surrounding Beyoncé feels like assessing a prize thoroughbred rather than observing a human woman, and it is dismaying when so-called feminist discourse contributes to that. Feminism is about challenging structural inequalities in society, but the criticism of Beyoncé as a feminist figure smacks of hating the player and ignoring the game, to twist an old phrase.

"The conversation surrounding Beyoncé feels like assessing a prize thoroughbred rather than observing a human woman, and it is dismaying when so-called feminist discourse contributes to that."

"Beyoncé has no role in reinforcing or creating sexist structures," says Jackson. "Despite the privilege of celebrity, she is subject to the same limitations other women are. In some ways, she is constrained even more, because she has to always be conscious about her image. It seems odd to critique her instead of the larger structure that creates the boundaries and limitations under which she exists."

Beyoncé exacts considerable control over her public image. (And she wrested that control from her own father.) *GQ* revealed that she has an on-staff videographer and photographer documenting most every move. The singer, or rather, her "people," famously requested that Buzzfeed remove some images from a slide show of the performer's "fiercest" Super Bowl moments. (It seems that the Queen was looking less than serene in a few shots.) Beyoncé's public life, from the reveal of her pregnancy to the first photos of daughter Blue Ivy's face, appears choreographed. And while many critics view that control as merely mercenary, it is well worth noting that this level of power is an achievement in an industry where "suits" retain significant control over "creatives."

Beyoncé's attention to her image may well be her way of moving within the boundaries and limitations of gender and race that Jackson mentions. In *GQ*, Beyoncé noted, "I try to perfect myself." A quest for perfection may not result in raw realness, but it just might keep a sister on top in a society still plagued with biases.

The dogged criticism of the way Beyoncé chooses to live out her feminism must add to the pressure of being a famous woman of color. But celebrity brings with it scrutiny. More problematic is that many challenges to Beyoncé's status as a feminist role model make perfection the enemy of the good for all women concerned with equality, positioning feminism as nigh impossible to everyday women who can imagine being scrutinized for making the same choices Beyoncé has made.

Samhita Mukhopadhyay, executive editor of the popular blog 35 Feministing, says, "[Beyoncé] is not allowed to be groundbreaking and traditional. She has to be Supermom or super hot stuff or super feminist. There isn't enough flexibility for her to just be who she is and for us to be able to say 'I'm not crazy about that decision, but this decision was amazing.'"

Juggling the personal with the political isn't easy in a biased society. We are, even the most diligent of us, influenced by gender, race, and other identities. And we make personal and professional decisions based on a variety of needs and pressures. Judging each other without acknowledging these influences is uncharitable at best and dishonest at worst. A tiny top and a traditional marriage should not be enough to strip a woman otherwise committed to gender equality of the feminist mantle. If we all had pundits assessing our actions against a feminist litmus test, I reckon not even Gloria Steinem° and bell hooks° would pass muster. Women must be allowed their humanity and complexity. Even self-proclaimed feminists. Even Queen Beys.

Understanding the Text

1. What is a "real moral contradiction" (5), according to Winfrey Harris?

2. What contrast does the writer draw between Beyoncé and singer Katy Perry? Why is it important to her argument?

Reflection and Response

3. Winfrey Harris uses the lens of race to interpret public reactions to Beyoncé and Madonna, respectively, as Madonna is "lauded" for her performance persona. According to the writer, how does race explain the different responses? Do you agree? Why or why not?

4. According to the writer, "Feminism is about challenging structural inequalities in society . . ." (30). What are "structural inequalities in society"? How does Winfrey Harris's definition encompass or complicate other definitions or understandings of feminism, including your own?

Gloria Steinem (1934–): prominent American feminist and founder of *Ms.* Magazine.
bell hooks (1952–): activist, author, and theorist who often focuses on the intersections of race and gender.

5. In this essay, the writer discusses Beyoncé — and the public conversation around Beyoncé — in the context of feminism and race. "Juggling the personal with the political isn't easy in a biased society," she writes. "We are, even the most diligent of us, influenced by gender, race, and other identities" (36). How useful or relevant do you think it is to analyze pop stars in the context of wider social issues? For example, do you consider these issues when you listen to music or read about musical artists? Explain your answer.

Making Connections

6. In "The Role of Pop Music and Pop Singers in the Construction of a Singer's Identity in Three Early Adolescent Females" (p. 286), Amy Clements-Cortes writes about the "essential role" music plays in the "identity construction" of younger people: "Music and its texts represent a scheme of significance that consumers may use to delineate their self-concepts as well as personal and social identities." How might you interpret Beyoncé in light of Clements-Cortes's article? For example, does Beyoncé seem similar to the role models in Clements-Cortes's research? Different? Explain your answer.

7. Winfrey Harris writes about Beyoncé and her music, but also the broader cultural conversation *about* the singer, including both popular and more scholarly sources. Choose another female recording artist and perform a similar interpretation, including outside sources. How does the topic of your analysis compare with Beyoncé in the context of race and gender questions? In what ways does she support, refute, or otherwise problematize Winfrey Harris's argument? One suggestion: The writer mentions several other singers, including Erykah Badu, Katy Perry, Madonna, and Taylor Swift. You may wish to use one of them for your topic.

Macho Rock: Men Always Seem to End Up on Top

Susan Hiwatt

This article, which originally appeared in *Rat* magazine in 1970, was written under the pseudonym "Susan Hiwatt" and reflects the communal feminine ethos of the magazine. The author excoriates rock music's misogyny and exclusion of women. For her, the "whole rock scene" requires "groovy" women who never "cut back on a man's freedom," even as they remain "the last legitimate form of property that the brothers can share in a communal world." Hiwatt's voice and slang terms are of their time, as are her musical reference points, but the seriousness of her grievance — and her purpose — still burns brightly underneath the style. Moreover, the prose suggests a sincere "thinking-through": a process whereby the writing serves as not only a catharsis, but as a way of organizing and understanding the writer's "heavy bad feelings." The article should get readers to reflect on rock and popular music in the decades since this essay appeared — and the spaces these forms now make (or refuse) for women, as both creators and consumers.

I. This Was the World that Rock Built

I grew up on Peter Trip, the curly-headed kid in the third row (an AM D.J. in New York City in the late '50s). I spent a lot of time after school following the social life of the kids on *American Bandstand*.° Then in high school I spent most of my time in my room with the radio, avoiding family fights. Rock became the thing that helped fill the loneliness and empty spaces in my life. The sound became sort of an alter-world where I daydreamed—a whole vicarious living out of other people's romances and lives. "Sally Go 'round the Roses." "Donna."

In college, rock was one of the things that got me together with other people: hours spent in front of a mirror learning how to dance, going to twist parties—getting freakier—tripping off the whole outlaw thing of "My Generation" and "Satisfaction." I was able to dance rock and talk rock comfortably in a college atmosphere when other things were mystified and intellectualized out of my comprehension and control. You didn't have to have heavy or profound thoughts about rock—you just knew that you dug it.

American Bandstand: an American television show that ran from 1952 to 1989 and featured Top-40 music stars along with an audience of dancing teenagers.

A whole sense of people together, behind their own music. It was the only thing we had of our own, where the values weren't set up by the famous wise professors. It was the way not to have to get old and deadened in White America. We wore hip clothes and smoked dope and dropped acid. Going to San Francisco with flowers in our hair.

For a couple of years, when I was with a man, I remember feeling pretty good — lots of people around, a scene I felt I had some control over, getting a lot of mileage off being a groovy couple. For as long as I was his woman, I was protected and being a freak was an up because it made me feel like I had an identity.

When I split from him a whole other trip started. It got harder and harder 5 to be a groovy chick when I had to deal with an endless series of one-night stands and people crashing and always doing the shitwork — thinking and being told that the only reason I wasn't being a freak was because I was too uptight. Going to Woodstock all but bare-breasted somewhere in the middle of all that and thinking I was messed up for not being able to have more fun than I was having. In a world where the ups were getting fewer and fewer, rock still continued to turn me on.

Then I connected to the women's movement and took a second look at rock.

II. Crashing: Women is Losers

The Sound of Silence

It took me a whole lot of going to the Fillmore and listening to records and reading *Rolling Stone* before it even registered that what I was seeing and hearing was not all these different groups, but all these different groups of men. And once I noticed that, it was hard not to be constantly noticing: all the names on the albums, all the people doing sound and lights, all the voices on the radio, even the D.J.'s between the songs — they are *all* men. In fact, the only place I could look to see anyone who looked anything like me was in the audience, and even there, there were usually more men than women.

It occurred to me that maybe there were some good reasons, besides inadequacy, that I had never taken all my fantasies about being a rock musician very seriously. I don't think I ever told anyone about them. Because in the female 51 percent of Woodstock Nation that I belong to, there isn't any place to be creative in any way. It's a pretty exclusive world.

There are, of course, exceptions. I remember hearing about some "all-chick" bands on the West Coast, like the Ace of Cups, and I also remember reading about how they were laughed and hooted at. And how they were given the spot between the up-and-coming group and the big-name group—sort of for comic relief. Or the two women I saw once who played with the Incredible String Band. They both played instruments and looked terrified throughout the entire concert (I kept thinking how brave they were to be there at all). The two men treated them like backdrops. They played back-up and sang harmony, and in fact, they were introduced as Rose and Licorice—no last names. The men thought it was cute that they were there and they had such cute names. No one, either on stage or in the audience, related to them as musicians. But they sure were sweet and pretty.

It blew my mind the first time I heard about a woman playing an elec- 10 tric guitar. Partly because of the whole idea we have that women can't understand anything about electronics (and we're not even supposed to want to), and also because women are supposed to be composed, gentle, play soft songs. A guy once told my sister when she picked up his electric guitar that women were meant to play only folk guitar, like Joan Baez or Judy Collins, that electric guitars were unfeminine. There are other parallel myths that have kept us out of rock: women aren't strong enough to play the drums; women aren't aggressive enough to play good, driving rock.

And then there is the whole other category of exception—the "chick" singer. The one place, besides being a groupie, where the stag club allows women to exist. And women who make it there pretty much have to be incredible to break in, and they are—take, for example, Janis Joplin and Aretha Franklin. It's a lot like the rest of the world where women have to be twice as good just to be acceptable.

Words of Love

Getting all this together in my head about the massive exclusion of women from rock left me with some heavy bad feelings. But still there was all that charged rock energy to dig. But what was that all about, anyway? Stokely Carmichael once said that all through his childhood he went to movies to see westerns and cheered wildly for the cowboys, until one day he realized that being black, he was really an Indian, and all those years he had been rooting for his own destruction. Listening to rock songs became an experience a lot like that for me. Getting turned on to "Under My Thumb," a revenge song filled with hatred for women, made me feel crazy.

> "Getting all this together in my head about the massive exclusion of women from rock left me with some heavy bad feelings."

And it wasn't an isolated musical moment that I could frown about and forget. Because when you get to listening to male rock lyrics, the message to women is devastating. And all that sexual energy that seems to be in the essence of rock is really energy that climaxes in screwing over women—endless lyrics and a sound filled with feeling I thought I was relating to but couldn't relate to, attitudes about women like put-downs, domination, threats, pride, mockery, and a million different levels of women-hating. For some reason, the Beatles' "rather see you dead, little girl, than see you with another man" pops into my head. But it's a random choice. Admittedly, there are some other kinds of songs—a few with nice feelings, a lot with a cool *macho* stance toward life and a lot with no feelings at all, a realm where, say, the Procol Harum shines pretty well at being insipid or obscure ("A Whiter Shade of Pale"). But to catalog the anti-women songs alone would make up almost a complete history of rock.

This all hit home to me with knock-out force at a recent Stones concert when Mick, prancing about enticingly with whip in hand, suddenly switched gears and went into "Under My Thumb," with an incredible vengeance that upped the energy level and brought the entire audience to its feet, dancing on the chairs. Mass wipeout for women—myself included.

Contrast this with the songs that really do speak to women where our feelings are at, songs that Janis and Aretha sing of their own experience of being women, of pain and humiliation and the love. And it's not all in the lyrics. When Aretha sings the Beatles' "Let It Be," she changes it from a sort of decadent-sounding song to a hymn of hope. A different tone coming from a different place.

The Great Pretenders

The whole star trip in rock is another realm where *macho* reigns supreme. At the center of the rock universe is the star—flooded in light, offset by the light show and the source of incredible volumes of sound. The audience remains totally in darkness: the Stones kept thousands waiting several hours, till nightfall, before they would come on stage at Altamont. The stage is set for the men to parade around acting out violence/sex fantasies, smashing their guitars and writhing bare-chested with leather fringe flying, while the whole spectacle is enlarged a hundred times on a movie screen behind them. And watching a group like the Mothers of Invention perform is a lesson in totalitarianism—seeing Frank Zappa define sound and silence with a mere gesture of his hand. There is no psychic or visual or auditory space for anyone but the performer. Remember Jesse Colin Young of the Youngbloods turning to his audience with disdain and saying, "the least you could do is clap along"? First you force the audience into passivity and then you imply that they are messed up for not moving.

Smile on Your Brother

Something else about the audience. Even after I realized women were barred from any active participation in rock music, it took me a while to see that we weren't even considered a real part of the listening audience. At first I thought I was being paranoid, but then I heard so many musicians address the audience as if it were all male: "I know you all want to find a good woman," "When you take your ol' lady home tonight . . ." "This is what you do with a no-good woman," etc., etc. It was clear that the concerts were directed only to men and the women were not considered people, but more on the level of exotic domestic animals that come with their masters or come to find masters. Only men are assumed smart enough to understand the intricacies of the music. Frank Zappa laid it out when he said that men come to hear the music and chicks come for sex thrills. Dig it!

It was a real shock to put this all together and realize rock music itself—all the way from performing artist to listener—refuses to allow any valid place for women. And yet I know there would never be rock festivals and concerts if women weren't there—even though we have nothing to do with the music. Somehow we're very necessary to rock culture.

Women are required at rock events to pay homage to the rock world—a world made up of thousands of men, usually found in groups of fours and fives. Homage paid by offering sexual accessibility, orgiastic applause, group worship, gang bangs at Altamont. The whole rock scene (as opposed to rock music) depends on our being there. Women are necessary at these places of worship so that, in between the sets, the real audience (men) can be assured of getting that woman they're supposed to like. Well, it's not enough just to be a plain old woman. We have to be beautiful and even that's not enough: we've got to be groovy, you know, not uptight, not demanding, not jealous or clinging or strong or smart or anything but loving in a way that never cuts back on a man's freedom. And so women remain the last legitimate form of property that the brothers can share in a communal world. Can't have a tribal gathering without music and dope and beautiful groovy chicks.

For the musicians themselves there is their own special property—groupies. As one groupie put it: "Being a groupie is a fulltime gig. Sort of like being a musician. You have two or three girl friends you hang out with, and you stay as high and as intellectually enlightened as a group of musicians. You've got to if you're going to have anything to offer. You are a non-profit call girl, geisha, friend, housekeeper—whatever the musician needs."

This total disregard and disrespect for women is constant in the rock 20
world and has no exceptions. Not even Janis Joplin, the all-time queen of
rock. She made her pain evident in all her blues—that's what made them
real. And the male rock world made her pay for that vulnerability in
countless ways. Since women don't get to play the instruments, it means
they're always on stage with nothing to relate to but the microphone,
and nothing between them and the audience but their own bodies. So
it is not surprising that Janis became an incredible sex object and was
related to as a woman with an outasight voice. Almost everyone even
vaguely connected to rock heard malicious stories about her. This became
part of her legend, and no level of stardom could protect her because
when you get down to it, she was just a woman.

And Who Could Be Fooling Me?

And who ever thought this was all the brothers were offering us when
they rapped about the revolution? Why do we stick with it? Women identified with youth culture as the only alternative to our parents' uptight
and unhappy way of life. We linked up with rock and never said how it
screwed us over. Partly this was because we had no sense of being women
together with other women. Partly because it was impossible to think of
ourselves as performing as exhibitionists in *macho* sex roles, so we didn't
wonder why there weren't more of us on stage. Partly because we identified with the men and not other women when we heard lyrics that put
women down. And a lot because we have been completely cut off from
perceiving what and who really are on our side and what and who don't
want to see us as whole people.

In a world of men, Janis sang our stories. When she died, one of the
few ties that I still had left with rock snapped. It can't be that women are
a people without a culture.

Understanding the Text

1. What event made Hiwatt take a second look at — and reevaluate — rock
   music, from her perspective as a woman?

2. According to the writer, what was the one role "besides being a groupie"
   that rock's all-male "stag club" allowed women? How did this role reflect a
   problem faced by women more generally?

3. If you had to summarize the writer's main point or thesis in a sentence, what
   would it be?

Reflection and Response

4. How would you characterize Hiwatt's style and voice as a writer? How do you react to it? For example, do you find it distracting? Do you find it conversational and appealing? How does her style reflect her subject matter?

5. Hiwatt takes a provocative stance on the misogyny of rock music, particularly its lyrics: "Because when you get to listen to male rock lyrics, the message to women is devastating ... To catalog the anti-women songs alone would make up almost a complete history of rock" (12). This essay was first published in 1970. Do you think the lyrics of popular music (including rock and hip hop) have changed significantly? Would Hiwatt's criticism still apply? Explain your answers.

Making Connections

6. The writer is highly critical of live music's focus on the male star, as "the stage is set for men to parade around acting out violence/sex fantasies ... [while there] is no psychic or visual or auditory space for anyone but the performer" (15). How would you compare and contrast this critique with Judy Berman's description of indie-rock shows in "Concerning the Spiritual in Indie Rock" (p. 98)? Do you think Hiwatt would still find contemporary live shows — small or large — oppressive and "totalitarian"? Why or why not?

7. Hiwatt describes the limited roles allowed for women in rock, whether as consumers or producers of music: ignored, dismissed, turned into sex objects, restricted to performing with "nothing between them and the audience but their own bodies." How have women's roles in rock and popular music changed in the decades since this essay was written? How have they stayed the same?

They've Got the Beat

Hannah Steinkopf-Frank

Hannah Steinkopf-Frank is a student at the University of Oregon Robert D. Clark Honors College. She is also an editorial intern and freelance writer at Bitch Media, where this article originally appeared in 2014. Here, she aims to recover a pop music tradition and genre that, according to Steinkopf-Frank, has often been dismissed by pop-culture critics: the girl group. The classic era of girl groups in the United States occurred during the late 1950s and 1960s, when acts such as the Chordettes, the Chantels, the Shirelles, the Shangri-Las, the Supremes, and many others became popular. But for Steinkopf-Frank, these all-female groups did more than produce catchy hit songs. Rather, they provided "a space not just for young female musicians but for female baby boomers to explore the social issues of the time." She also traces their legacy up through more recent and disparate girl groups, such as Destiny's Child, Dum Dum Girls, and Haim.

They've been called gimmicky, not *real* musicians, and, according to *Rock of Ages: The Rolling Stone History of Rock & Roll*, "the low point in the history of rock 'n' roll."

Girl groups, despite their ongoing legacy and steady influence on popular culture, remain maligned by pop culture gatekeepers. In fact, girl groups are feminist icons, influential musicians, and cultural figures in their own right. Despite the conflicting connotations, since the 1960s, the girl group has created not only a space for female musicians and fans—especially young women—but has been a persistent cultural force within pop music.

All-female groups have long been and continue to be considered a novelty. Most of this criticism is based on the fact that girl groups traditionally didn't write their own music or play their own instruments, and were heavily influenced by producers—all factors shaped by the culture at large. As such, critics have been dismissing girl groups as inauthentic and their fans as equally insignificant for decades.

Girl groups emerged in a specific climate within the music industry and American politics. During the first part of the 20th century, girls were not provided the same opportunities for a music education as young men, especially not when it came to the electric guitar, bass, or drums. Young women also had few female musical role models. During the 1950s, no female artist, specifically one who played an instrument, had had the commercial and also critical success of Elvis, Buddy Holly, or even Chuck Berry. Instead, many first-generation girl groups were formed by friends who learned to sing and harmonize in church and school settings and used these choral techniques as well as the influence of schoolyard rhymes in their music. The success of early girl group the Chantels' 1958 hit "Maybe" inspired other young women to form their own groups.

After some of these early groups garnered commercial success with their own music, record labels quickly took interest. Members of these groups—many under the age of 18—were often carefully coached by producers and record-label executives who influenced not only their music but also their public image. One infamous example of this was Motown's artist development program, which focused specially on molding black artists, such as Martha and the Vandellas and the Supremes, as a way for young black women to achieve upward mobility in a white-run music industry. This program was especially strict for female performers—they were expected to attend a "finishing school," where they were taught posture, table manners, elocution, and choreography.

Before the British Invasion of the mid-'60s, girl groups such as the Shangri-Las, the Supremes, and the Ronettes were the cultural zeitgeist. They were not the first all-female singing groups, but they were younger, lived in urban areas, and were more racially diverse than the all-female, mostly white barbershop groups of the 1950s like the Chordettes. Most significant, this new wave of girl groups was one of the first examples of popular music made by and geared toward teenage girls.

White girl groups were able to take more liberties than those nurtured by Motown, especially with their public image and song topics. In contrast to the Chantels' tea-length dresses, kitten heels, and careful coifs, the Shangri-Las adopted a tough persona with tight pants and menswear-inspired blazers and vests. Having grown up in Queens, New York, the Shangri-Las' "bad girl" reputation was marketed to distance them from other girl groups. By adopting a more masculine-inspired image and performing songs about falling in love with someone "from the wrong side of town" ("Leader of the Pack") and boys who are "good-bad," but "not evil" ("Give Him a Great Big Kiss"), the Shangri-Las are remembered as being more radical and in line with the rock 'n' roll music of that era than most black girl groups, even if the persona was engineered by a record label.

"Even as African Americans were fighting for equal rights, black girl groups achieved as much, if not more, commercial success than their white counterparts."

Still, these groups were able to provide a space not just for young female musicians but for female baby boomers to explore the social issues of the time. Even as African Americans were fighting for equal rights, black girl groups achieved as much, if not more, commercial success than their white counterparts. These teen black musicians were topping the charts while the Little Rock Nine were fighting for the opportunity to attend a desegregated school. Girl groups may have still been segregated by race but they were connected through a common audience. In addition, many girl groups also used their music to question the sexual and gender norms of the 1950s, particularly concerning the sexual double standard and power dynamics in relations.

The Shirelles, an early girl group consisting of school friends from New Jersey, took control of the boy-girl relationship in their 1958 hit "I Met Him on a Sunday," which they wrote themselves. By singing in the first person and breaking up with their nameless lover after he misses a date, the Shirelles crafted an assertive standout in a sea of sappy love songs, the simple lyrics belying a powerful message. (It's probably not a coincidence this song was released by Tiara Records, one of the few labels at the time run by a woman, Florence Greenberg.)

In their 1960 classic "Will You Still Love Me Tomorrow?"—the first   10
song by a girl group to reach number one—lead singer Shirley Owens isn't just swooning over some guy, she's questioning how both he and society will treat her after they have sex. The birth-control pill had come out that same year, and sex, along with its double standard and taboos, was getting more complicated for young women. The song was cowritten by Carole King and Gerry Goffin. King, who was 18 at the time she cowrote the song, had had a child the previous year and quickly married Goffin. Knowing this, it's hard to not feel the weight of the decision concerning premarital sex in the song.

In "Why the Shirelles Mattered," Susan J. Douglas's love letter to '60s girl groups in *Where the Girls Are: Growing Up Female with the Mass Media* (1994), what mattered was the ability of girl groups to speak to complex and often contradictory messages young women received at the time. "Girl group music acknowledged—even celebrated—our confusion and ambivalence. [It] let us try on and act out a host of identities, from traditional, obedient girlfriend to brassy, independent rebel, and lots in between."

After 1965, the girl-group genre saw a decline in popularity. British imports and the rise of psychedelic, folk, and protest music pushed the polished pop groups out of the mainstream. The late-'70s and early-'80s New Wave, and the coinciding advent of MTV, gave girl groups a bit of a boost, uniting the disparate styles of the Go-Go's, the Belle Stars, and Bananarama under the banner of video-friendly pop.

But a more unified girl-group revival didn't happen until the mid-'90s, pioneered by the R&B and hip hop world. Female collaborations, such as Salt-N-Pepa and En Vogue's "Whatta Man," encouraged women to never settle for less and to own and value their sexuality. Subsequent groups like TLC, Xscape, and later, Destiny's Child carried on the message of female friendship and solidarity. These groups revitalized and reinvented the genre, experimenting with R&B, rap, and reggae while still employing girl-group standards of harmonizing and trading verses.

TLC, arguably the most political of these groups, promoted sexual health and questioned social inequality in both their music and public image (TLC member Lisa "Left Eye" Lopes, who wrote much of the group's music with professional songwriters, rocked condom-eyeglasses for safe-sex awareness.)

Destiny's Child also used their music to explore feminist issues. While   15
the Houston, Texas, group had early success with hits like "Bills, Bills, Bills," it was in their later work with songs like "Survivor" and "Bootylicious" that the group exuded a confidence not only in their sexuality but also as women. It may arguably have been the group's 2002 hiatus and Beyoncé's subsequent solo career that marked the end of the '90s girl group.

In the pop realm, the Spice Girls became a global phenomenon, becoming the best-selling female group of all time. Like their '60s predecessors, the six women were handpicked by record executives to fit squarely within the pop music machine. And while feminists — including *Bitch* — have called out the group for their more-fluff-than-fury "girl power," the Spice Girls were a top-selling ensemble of women who put friendship first. As Sady Doyle penned in her *Rookie* article, "In Defense of the Spice Girls," their feminism may have been fingernail-thin, but in the long run "girlhood wouldn't get such good publicity for at least another decade." This same sense of cohesion is what Douglas saw as so important to the groups of the '60s: "Girl group music — precisely because these were groups, not just individual singers — insisted that it was critically important for girls to band together."

Since the early aughts, few girl groups have found real mainstream success — the decade was dominated by indie-rock boy bands and solo pop stars like Alicia Keys and Avril Lavigne. But in recent years, girl groups have been breaking through again and branching out from the Top 40.

Some groups like Little Mix, a four-piece British pop group that was formed for the U.K. talent-competition show *The X Factor*, resemble groups of the '90s with calculated branding and imaging. Little Mix is presented as a group of close mates, though without the distinct personalities of the Spice Girls or the politics of TLC. Their songs use the girl-group trope of switching vocals, to make each song a conversation between friends. In the video for "How Ya Doin?" (which features Missy

Elliott), each member sings about going through a breakup but brushing it off in favor of putting on makeup and going out with friends.

A new wave of girl groups is also blooming in South Korea with the rise of K-Pop (Korean pop) and groups like the Wonder Girls and 2NE1. K-Pop is a powerful musical and commercial force in South Korea, grossing nearly $3.4 billion in the first half of 2012, but has had little relative success outside of Asian markets with the rare crossover (like Psy). So it's especially exciting for 2NE1 to finally get their due overseas with American audiences. Their new album *Crush* set the record for the highest-charting and best-selling K-Pop album in the United States. Like Little Mix, 2NE1's sing-along melodies are simple yet cathartic, but they play off other popular music by infusing a variety of genres into their songs, be it Nicki Minaj–inspired rapping or a reggae beat straight out of a Rihanna single.

Outside of the realm of mainstream pop music, bands like the Dum Dum Girls, Haim, and La Luz have made waves in the past decade, each one hailed by the music press as the younger siblings of '60s girl groups. And many do play off the bad-girl reputation that those bands defined. Dum Dum Girls tracks like "Jail La La" (about waking up in a holding cell) and "Bhang Bhang, I'm a Burnout" (about, well, being a burnout) are throwbacks to the Shangri-Las, knowingly and cheekily nodding to a girl-group legacy.

And still, bands like Deap Vally, La Luz, and Chastity Belt, whose members all play instruments as well as sing, express a complicated relationship with the idea of being a "girl group." Their respective sounds fit into a variety of genres — from indie rock to punk to surf rock — yet perhaps only because of gender, they are still put into the girl-group box.

"It's funny because now a lot of times that is the description of our band: 'All-female' and then something else," said Marian Li Pino, the drummer of Seattle-based La Luz. At the same time, many of these bands agree that there is something special that comes with playing music with other women. "It's different in terms of energy, and we are all very conscientious of leaving space for each other. That is something that when I play with men I haven't experienced," said Chastity Belt lead singer, Julia Shapiro.

While these new groups may not be singing about pining for boys or doing synchronized dance moves like the groups that came before them, they have created a safer space not just for themselves but also their fans. Even if these 21st-century groups might not be "girl groups" in the traditional sense, they are role models in an industry still dominated by white men. It was arguably the first generation of '60s girl groups who paved the way for the girl groups of the '90s and today. Even though these early

Figure 5.2 "Even if these 21st-century groups might not be 'girl groups' in the traditional sense, they are role models in an industry still dominated by white men": Los Angeles–based pop rock band Haim. Daniel Zuchnik/Getty Images

groups were often manufactured and run by labels, they have allowed modern groups to form organically and not necessarily be warped to appeal to a specific audience of teenage girls. These modern girl groups no longer have to be "girls," just musicians making their own music.

Being stuck in a phase of perpetual girlhood is not necessarily a bad thing. The girl groups of the '60s and '90s are some of the few musical examples of when artists of color, specifically young female ones, were just as successful—if not more—than their older, white male counterparts. Whether in matching sequined dresses or '90s crop tops, the girl group persists as a cultural monument to the changing image of popular girlhood. The voice of young womanhood will always need an outlet in popular music, and the girl group, whatever form it takes, is there to fill the role.

Understanding the Text

1. How would you express Steinkopf-Frank's thesis in your own words?
2. Why have all-female groups traditionally been dismissed or devalued as a "novelty" by critics and others?
3. What musical trends caused the girl-group genre to decline in the 1960s?

Reflection and Response

4. Steinkopf-Frank writes that before the mid-1960s, "girl groups such as the Shangri-Las, the Supremes, and the Ronettes were the cultural zeitgeist" (6). What does the term "cultural zeitgeist" mean? How would musical groups reflect or express a cultural zeitgeist? Can you think of other examples?

5. The writer argues that there are continuities between girl groups of the 1960s, on one hand, and girl groups of the 1990s and beyond, on the other. How does she support these claims? Do you agree that these latter groups play a similar role for girls and women that their predecessors did? Why or why not? What social, political, and cultural changes complicate Steinkopf-Frank's assertions?

Making Connections

6. Not surprisingly given her topic, Steinkopf-Frank writes about music in explicitly gendered terms. For instance, she claims that girl groups, whether in the past or in the present, create important "spaces" for both female fans and female artists. Generally, do you think about the music you listen to (or play), or the bands and artists you like, in gendered terms — as "girl bands" or as "music for guys," for example? What are the advantages and drawbacks of using gender to frame musical tastes, styles, and artists?

7. How does Amy Clements-Cortes's "The Role of Pop Music and Pop Singers in the Construction of a Singer's Identity in Three Early Adolescent Females" (p. 286) provide hard data to support Steinkopf-Frank's argument about the importance of girl groups? In what ways do these two articles overlap in their assertions and analysis? How do they diverge?

8. According to Steinkopf-Frank, girl groups are generally "maligned by pop culture gatekeepers" (2). She quotes the authors of *Rock of Ages: The Rolling Stone History of Rock*, who describe girl groups as "the low point in the history of rock 'n' roll." Do you agree that this subgenre — whether in the form of the Supremes or Destiny's Child — has been rightfully or unfairly denigrated? Why or why not? What biases might account for such judgments?

The Role of Pop Music and Pop Singers in the Construction of a Singer's Identity in Three Early Adolescent Females

Amy Clements-Cortes

No doubt, music plays a key role in adolescent identity formation for most young people engaged in popular culture. Our musical preferences express and reflect our tastes, interests, sensibilities, temperaments, and group memberships, among other elements that comprise who we are, both publicly and privately. That is especially true for young, aspiring performers. In this scholarly article from the *Canadian Music Educators Journal*, Amy Clements-Cortes profiles and presents three aspiring early adolescents and examines the role of female pop artists in their own development as performers. As she writes, "What emerged from the three girls was that performing as singers on stage gave them an opportunity to 'try on' new identities, or to experiment with different parts of their personalities."

Amy Clements-Cortes is Assistant Professor, University of Toronto; Instructor/Supervisor, Wilfrid Laurier University; Academic Coordinator/Instructor, Ryerson Chang School; Registered Psychotherapist; Certified Music Therapist; President of the World Federation of Music Therapy; and Managing Editor, *Music and Medicine*.

The prevalence of music in today's society is enormous. Not only do we actively choose to listen to music by turning on the radio, or listening to a favorite CD, but we are exposed to music in many public places including shopping malls, waiting rooms, restaurants, etcetera. Willis (1990) acknowledges that popular music is always listened to within specific social settings and locations, and operates as a background to a variety of activities ranging from dancing in clubs, to surviving the workday, to defeating boredom in the home.

According to Roberts and Christenson (2001) pre-adolescents (11–14) and adolescents (15–18) listen to music between three and four hours a day; and by grade 11, girls typically listen to 30 minutes more music a day than boys. The music industry is keenly aware of this fact, and produces and markets music specifically to this audience. "Teen pop" is a thriving form of music that is defined by Vannini and Myers (2002) as the genre of music that is the most popular with teenage audiences, and is produced, targeted, and consumed by both pre-adolescents and adolescents. It is not a stretch then to see that extended exposure to, and consumption of, music will have an impact and influence on adolescents.

Regardless of the role of popular culture in shaping our identities, consumer culture and cultural activities such as buying clothes, and selecting the food we eat are identity resources pointing to particular lifestyle choices a person makes. Essentially, identity and consumption have become linked together. Fisher (2002) acknowledges that music, movies, and fashion serve as key informants of identity in today's society, and "Even at the origin of modern western capitalism, identity and status were contested and re-made through consumption choices" (p. 18). He goes on to explain that traditionally what we consumed was determined by our identity; however in today's culture of consumerism, the pattern has become reversed, and consumption determines and defines our identity. Stryker and Burke (2000) (identity theorists), argue that an individual consists of a group of identities, each of which is based on occupying a particular role.

According to Roe (1999), since the 1950's music has played an essential role in the process of identity construction in youth. Music and its texts represent a scheme of significance that consumers may use to delineate their self-concepts as well as personal and social identities. Adolescents are a consumer group that may be particularly influenced by pop music and are apt to appropriate the texts of this music, and the meanings they derive from it, to define themselves. Musicians and aspiring musicians, specifically singers, are likely to be even more influenced or affected in different ways than non-musicians by the music they choose to sing, perform, and study, as well as by their favorite singers, and the images and lifestyles projected by those singers.

This paper seeks to explore how early adolescent female singers use 5 popular music, both the songs and images of their favorite singers, to construct their identities as "musical performers or singers." This theme will be explored by drawing on the literature in the area and personal conversations with three twelve-year-old female vocal students. For the purposes of this paper, Levy-Warren's (1996) classification of early adolescence as those persons aged 10–14 will be employed. (The real names of the students quoted in this paper have been changed. Verbal permission to discuss issues of popular music and identity was granted by the students themselves, and written consent was obtained from a parental guardian for each of the girls.)

Early Adolescence

Early adolescence is marked by: the onset of puberty, development of new cognitive skills such as abstract thinking and seeing things as relative rather than absolute, continued egocentrism, and the desire to gain social approval. Adolescence is a time of establishing an identity, autonomy, and intimacy, as well as becoming comfortable with one's sexuality and achievement (Huebner, 2000). The early adolescent's self-concept may be challenged by the changes his/her body is making, and females are especially susceptible to pressure to conform to gender stereotypes.

Hamilton and Masecar (1997) discuss the tasks of early adolescence as a time for: withdrawing from parents; achieving emotional independence; being accepted by peers; biological maturity; identity formation; and, development of self-esteem and independence.

Psychologically, the self-focus that adolescents have at this time causes them to worry what others think about them. Greater importance is given to peer relationships as adolescents begin the process of establishing their own identities as separate from their parents and families. There can be increased conflict between parents, and peer relationships may involve the development of cliques and become based on sharing of values and confidences. Some adolescents begin dating, and romantic crushes are common (Ozretich & Bowman, 2001).

Adolescents have complex relationships with popular culture and there are many messages that they receive and interpret from such engagements during their process of negotiating the developmental tasks. Many of these messages address issues that are at the forefront for them during early adolescence such as romance, sexuality, and independence. How teens go about interpreting these discourses plays a role in how they construct their identities as they learn about their sense of place in the world, and in the many roles that they hold.

"Adolescents have complex relationships with popular culture and there are many messages that they receive and interpret from such engagements during their process of negotiating the developmental tasks."

Identity

There are numerous definitions of identity and many psychologists have studied identity formation at great length. One of the most well-known theories of personal identity was developed by Erikson (1974) (as cited in Head, 1997), who described identity as simultaneous sameness and differences. Identity has also been described as "The distinct personality of an individual regarded as a persisting entity" (American Heritage, 2000). Huntemann and Morgan (2001) acknowledge that "Identity is fluid, partly situational, and thus constantly under construction, negotiation, and modification" (p. 311). The process of constructing one's identity is central in adolescence, and therefore this time period poses an interesting point not only to look at how identity unfolds, but also how the identity of specific roles that a person holds are formed. Erikson (1968) elucidates adolescence is a phase of exploratory self-analysis and self-evaluation, which brings about the development of an integrative self or identity. According to Allison and Schultz (2001) there has been a lack of attention to identity development in early adolescence as the substantial body of knowledge established has focused on older adolescents and college-age persons.

Literature

There is a growing body of literature that began in the 1950's that looks at how youth engage with and consume music, and how this impacts their identities. The following four studies focused on adolescent females and their engagements with popular music and provide a framework for my group discussion with the three adolescents. Frith (1978) maintains that boys and girls build their identities differently from their engagements with music icons, therefore supporting a need to study males and females separately.

Tracy (2001) explored how pre-teen urban elementary school girls' engagement with popular music impacted their identity construction and how their interactions and interpretations of music were entrenched in their daily lives. She found that when the girls talked about popular music, and sang and danced in the lunchroom and playground, they expressed pleasure but also showed their racial, gender, and age-related identities. Essentially Tracy found that these girls constructed a sense of self through their performances which was dependent on contextual conditions, the girls' understandings of socio-cultural relationships, and their interpretation of "what it means to be me."

Jennings (1999) interviewed six teenage girls in an attempt to show how they use their music, in this case by playing musical instruments typically defined as masculine (drums, and electric guitar) to create and communicate their identities. Making music provided these girls with pleasure, self-confidence, and a voice. These girls showed that popular culture continues to present stereotyped messages about femaleness to girls; yet through their music they were trying to resist these stereotypes.

Lowe (2003) conducted two focus groups with groups of five and six early-adolescent middle-class girls, which focused on current "teen pop," and in the end revolved around Britney Spears. The girls had a certain amount of admiration for Britney even though they identified and described her in very negative terms and they were envious of her fame and lifestyle. They recognized that Britney used her body image to sell her CDs, and they applauded her ability to manipulate men and get what she wanted. These girls were articulate about condemning patriarchal views and seemed aware of the media texts and the messages that they received from them. They had strong feminine convictions, but were still able to consume pop music that did not go along with the beliefs they articulated.

O'Neill (2002) interviewed four female musicians aged 17 and 18 on how they construct an identity around music. One student saw music as a private experience; another saw being a musician as both personal and social; the third expressed confusion over being rejected and then validated by adjudicators of a musical performance; and the fourth said that musical identity was core to her being. 15

These smaller studies have produced rich descriptive results; however, there is very little that can be extrapolated to the population of "preteen girls" with such small sample sizes. Similarly, there are problems generalizing results from a group of middle-class or urban subjects to the whole population, and different ethnic groups will experience music, pop culture, and identity-formation differently. Some studies have focused on various ethnic groups and genres of music (St. Lawrence & Joyner, 1991; Hansen & Hansen, 1991; Arnett, 1991; Frith, 1996; Brown & Schulze, 1990; Zillmann et al., 1995). For example, there may be a tendency towards "subversive" listening to or purchasing of certain kinds of music if it is not permitted in the home. That being said, these studies do form a basis for future research and provide useful information for pedagogical consideration especially in designing musical programs in the school system for this age group.

Interviews

The information from the three girls was obtained in a group interview. "Jessica," "Sarah," and "Sydney" are each twelve years of age, and are private voice students of the author. The girls know each other from their participation in recitals at the music studio over the past few years. Jessica has been studying voice and performing on stage since she was seven; Sarah has been taking vocal lessons and performing since she was eight; and Sydney has been taking voice lessons and performing for two years.

The group conversation focused on how each of the girls sees and portrays themselves as singers and performers and their engagements with music, pop music, and pop icons. The conversation was open and built from comments received from each of the girls. Some of the questions that guided the interview were: How do the girls experience and use popular music? and What influence does the text of music have on them, and their choice to sing or not to sing it? (Please note this was not a formal research study. The group conversation was tape-recorded and transcribed by the author. Sentences were coded, broken down into points where necessary and analyzed. Several quotes from the girls have been included below and a few of the comments were clarified individually with the girls.)

In the discussion with these three early adolescents, it should be noted that it is not feasible to focus solely on how popular music and the images of pop stars contribute to their identity formation as singers. Peers, parents, and the community also contribute to their identity formations and are not easily separated out of the discussion.

The following are the themes that arose out of the group conversation and individual follow up with each of the girls: the need to continually evolve; authenticity; multi-threat (i.e. multiple talents such as singing, song-writing, and dancing); independence; seeking admiration and being glamorous; career women; beauty: the body is the voice; popularity and power. Details of the discussions are provided below.

Space to Try On a New Identity, and the Need to Continually Evolve

What emerged from the three girls was that performing as singers on stage gave them an opportunity to "try on" new identities, or to experiment with different parts of their personalities. They felt they could portray themselves as different people on stage, and essentially change their identity as performers depending on what they were singing and for whom. Their comments appeared to indicate that they saw their "singer" identities as separate from their identities as regular twelve-year-old girls. As singers they described feeling powerful on stage, but that power did not necessarily translate to their everyday lives. Sarah said, *"On stage I feel so important and like everyone is watching me, but normally I just blend in with everyone else, no one really notices me, or listens to me all that much."*

In the group conversation the girls arrived at the conclusion themselves that some of the singers they talked about (Kelly Clarkson, Taylor Swift, and Avril Lavigne) were probably very different people on stage than off, and they too wanted to be able to have this ability to create, re-create, and have a stage persona. Sarah said, *"It's fun to pretend to be someone else."* Sydney's comments made it evident that she recognized that it was important for singers to change who they are from time to time or the audience gets bored.

Through these realizations which can be extrapolated to their engagements with "pop stars," the adolescents learned that identity is not purely a process of discovering oneself, but also a process of creating oneself, and as singers they wanted to change their images and identities frequently to maintain the audience's interest. Further to their realization that one could re-define oneself, the girls appeared to like that this re-defining was playful and spontaneous, and these were characteristics that they wanted to be part of their own personas as singers. Jessica said, *"I really like how I can change how I look on stage depending on what I'm singing, and it's like important to do that so that your look goes along with the song."*

Authenticity

The three girls felt they could relate to their favorite singers and the songs that these artists performed, and they imagined personal relationships with their icons. The fact that they felt like the texts of the songs spoke to them was important, and they wanted others to feel that way about the songs they sang. Longhurst (1995) found that the identity of a fan may be designed by their affect for a particular musical personality or type of music. These girls know all the words to their favorite songs and can tell you a multitude of facts about their favorite singers.

Jessica said, *"They sing about things that I've been through, and when I* 25 *am on stage I want others to um . . . well kinda think that I sing about things that matter to them too?"* As singers these girls wanted to be seen as having something important to contribute to their audience, which they realized through their own consumption of popular music. Perhaps this desire for their audiences to feel a connection with them spoke to their need to fit in and be accepted by their peers, which of course is one of the developmental tasks of adolescence that Hamilton and Masecar (1997) outline.

Essentially, they spoke about what could be described as an "authenticity" of their favorite singers' performances, and they too expressed a desire to display this authenticity to their audiences, and be seen as genuine. Sarah said, *"Well remember when Ashlee Simpson got caught for lip-singing, like I lost all respect for her. I would just die if that happened to me."* Jessica said, *"I like Gwen Stefani because she seems to really care about her fans and she is really nice in interviews. That's how I want others to think of me."*

It seems that that the girls learned that in order to be considered a favorite performer, or even a legitimate performer, an artist must be perceived as authentic, both in the lyrics of their music and in their public appearances, and in constructing their own identities as singers they too wanted to display authenticity and genuineness in order that they along with their music would be viewed favorably, and as making a valuable contribution to the music scene.

Multi-Threat

The girls spoke at length about how they admired singers who wrote and sang their own songs, choreographed, danced, played instruments, acted, and produced. They saw value in being more than just a singer and these additional abilities made the singer more legitimate as a performer, and someone who would be taken seriously as a true musician or entertainer. They learned this through their own engagements with popular music and also by their peers' and others' engagements. Jessica said, "*That's totally why I started guitar lessons, like its kinda cool to play, and I want people to think that I am a serious musician. My Mom wanted me to take piano lessons, but guitar is way cooler.*"

Through this recognition they came to understand that substance and legitimacy can be constructed to some degree, and that by the singers' representations of themselves as more than just singers they potentially appealed further to their audiences and built up their potential for consumption. As part of their identity construction as singers, these girls wanted to have several areas in which they were talented or had skills, such as being able to write music or act in addition to singing. In essence, they wanted to be known as "multi-threats" and saw this as an integral part of their identities as singers. They recognized that being seen in this light created more respect for them as entertainers and would potentially contribute to them becoming or remaining successful for longer.

Independence

The majority of the musical texts that the girls spoke about, and the 30 songs they wanted to sing themselves, dealt with intimate relationships, and portrayed the image of girls being independent. The texts appear to have meaning for them because what they articulate speaks to their lived experiences and understandings of social expectations (e.g.: *Beautiful* by Christina Aguilera; and *Because of You* by Kelly Clarkson).

Sydney, Sarah, and Jessica wanted their audiences to see them as independent and strong females and incorporated these aspects into their singer identities. Their desire to portray themselves as independent coincides with Schave and Schave (1989) who claim early adolescents struggle ". . . for increased independence and sense of psychological separateness from their parents" (p. 3).

In particular the song *Don't Tell Me* written by Avril Lavigne and Evan Taubenfeld (2004), and sung by Avril Lavigne was one that appeared to resonate with each of the girls, and one that was discussed in detail during the group conversation.

The text of this song along with others that were discussed demonstrate that women have power by: resisting male dominance; negotiating the terms of an intimate relationship; leaving relationships that were not satisfying to them; being assertive; and, raising their levels of self-esteem.

Sydney said, *"I really like Avril Lavigne because she isn't a sell-out. She sings about what's important to her and that's how I wanna be too."* Jessica felt *"Avril looks in control, she doesn't let anyone tell her what to do."*

In addition to the overriding theme of independence and strength, 35 within the category of independence two sub-themes emerged as being incorporated in the girls' identities as singers: being admired and glamorized; and, career-focused.

Seeking admiration and being glamorous

In creating their identities as performers, the girls wanted their audiences to see that they had the same potential and independent lifestyles as singers like Kelly Clarkson. The allure of these singer's lifestyles, for example, the fact that singers like Kelly travel on the road and are not living at home with their parents, was attractive to them and speaks to their desire to withdraw from their parents and be admired by their peers, much in the way they admired the singers. Another example is Avril Lavigne who began writing her own songs at the age of 12. These girls admired her abilities and wanted to portray similar images to their audiences. Hall and Whannel (1994) maintain that pop stars that girls admire "are not remote stars, but tangible idealizations of the life of the average teenager" (p. 35).

The girls also glamorized the world of famous singers, such as Gwen Stephani from watching her videos, and from watching how she is portrayed in the media. Sarah said, *"Gwen has everything. She's pretty, she's loaded, she has a hot husband and she like gets to go to all the best parties and she doesn't even have to work that hard."* Jessica replied, *"It would be so awesome to be that famous, you get pretty much whatever you want."*

In shaping their own identities as singers, they wanted to create an allure and lifestyle that was seen by others as glamorous and admired.

Career women

In constructing their identities as singers the adolescents wanted vocal music to be their career, and to be seen as serious musicians who could successfully navigate careers as singers and performers, independent of men. Sydney stated, *"I want to be a singer. I know not everyone can make it, but maybe I'll try out for like Canadian Idol when I am a little older and see if I make it to the finals."* Sarah said, *"My dream is to be a famous singer, like Kelly Clarkson, who girls will look up to."* Jessica said, *"The only thing I want to do is be a singer. Well, I guess I could also act and perform in musicals and stuff like that but I probably wouldn't be famous doing that."* What was surprising was that even though the girls wanted to be famous singers, and to be known as serious musicians as part of their overall identities, they did see that they could have performing identities separate from their identities as 12-year-old girls as was discussed earlier.

Interestingly, none of the early adolescents were at a stage yet where 40 they identified that studying music might help them to attain success as musicians, and appeared to have developed that thinking pattern from viewing young singers who had already garnered success without fully understanding the study or amount of work it would take to maintain a successful career. They idealized the worlds of their favorite pop singers.

Beauty: The Body Is the Voice

It materialized for these three girls that their personal identity constructions as singers were closely linked to their physical appearance and body image. This aligns with Brumberg (1997) who acknowledges that girls make their bodies a passionate focus and engage in "body projects" in order to fit into a culturally imposed beauty ideal. Mazzarella and Odom-Pecora (1999) convincingly argue that culture submerges girls with messages that their bodies are their voices, and their identities. Certainly these three girls learned and subsequently held this belief from their engagements with popular culture.

By watching their favorite singers perform in videos and seeing how they are portrayed in the media in magazines and television the girls learned that women who are defined by our culture as "attractive" have prestige and command male attention. They appeared to understand that these performers' success as singers was closely tied to their physical attractiveness (e.g. slim build, long hair, smooth acne-free skin, et cetera) and that this attractiveness was what was of value, not necessarily the fact that the performer was talented or could sing. They too, wanted to portray this attractiveness on stage in order to feel that prestige and power, and spoke about that in the group conversation.

Sarah said, *"At the last recital, do you remember I totally wore that cute hat and you* [referring to Jessica] *wore that t-shirt with the glitter. It's really important to like look the right way."* Jessica responded by saying, *"You're right 'cause look how we dissed Lady Gaga."* Jessica said, *"And what about*

Kelly Clarkson, her weight goes up and down." They also talked about how many of the songs and CD titles had to do with physical attractiveness.

The girls learned to understand that society tied their worth as singers up in their physical appearance, and therefore they had to make themselves physically attractive and portray a certain image in order to be good and valuable singers. This need to become a singer whom others view as attractive became a central part in their identity construction as performers.

Popularity and Power

By choosing to perform "pop songs" at their semi-annual recitals as   45 opposed to the other genres of music that they also studied (and admitted liking), the girls showed that they liked the empowerment, interest, and acceptance they felt they received from the audience as described in their comments, and they recognized that it was important for a singer to please their audience even if it meant not singing something that they liked more because others might not like it. For example, Sarah said "*It seems like I get a lot more attention when I sing pop songs instead of those classical songs we have to learn. Well I guess I actually like some of those songs too, but nobody cares if you sing them on stage, that's why I like to sing the stuff that everyone knows. Like I'll never be famous singing The Water Is Wide, even though I love that song. I don't mind singing those songs at the competitions but everyone's singing stuff like that, and well only older people like my parents and other people's parents are there.*" These comments point to Sarah's desire to construct her identity as a singer as one that conforms to society's expectations of what a pop singer is; and her need to fit in with her peer group and audience by performing the type of music that will resonate with them.

These girls wanted to be identified by others as pop singers because that is by definition what is popular amongst their peers. They were not interested in performing other genres of music at the recitals because they felt that no one else would like it, and in turn perhaps would not value their performance as much. Jessica said, "*We had like Grand River Idol at our school and half the people that got to the finals couldn't even sing, but they are popular at school and so their friends voted for them and they sang like, what's most popular now. Can you imagine if I sang one of those Italian pieces? I would have been talked about for days!*"

The girls wanted to be popular so that they would be appreciated and realized that popularity was an important part of being a successful performer, and therefore they tried to create themselves in a way that would be most appealing to the majority of potential audience members.

Conclusion

Frith (1981) acknowledged that there is a special relationship between pop music and youth. According to Bennett (2000) music is to be considered "a primary, if not the primary, leisure resource for young people" (p. 34). For those persons studying and pursing music as a career choice, music may have an even greater influence on their identity constructions. Music is very prevalent in the lives of adolescents, and it plays an influential role in identity formation. In particular, for these three girls it played a central role in shaping their identities as singers.

Through the group conversation with these early adolescents it became evident that they recognized the need for performers to continually change their identities. They wanted to been seen as authentic singers with important and valuable messages that spoke to their audiences. They wanted to possess many talents (multi-threat), and be known as independent career women who were: playful; spontaneous; admired; glamorous women who were beautiful and popular; and, powerful and serious musicians.

They learned that on stage they could construct, re-construct, and experiment with their identities, and this experimentation was enhanced by their negotiation of the developmental tasks of early adolescents such as withdrawing from their parents, becoming more independent, and trying to gain the acceptance of their peers.

Surprisingly to this author, the issue of national identity did not come up as a factor in creating an identity as a singer for these three females. Even though several of the singers they had a connection with, and subsequently were influenced by, were Canadian there did not appear to be any identification with or pride in these singers as fellow Canadians. Perhaps this is not a central issue for adolescents of this age group. Additionally, there was no mention of interest in music from their own ethnic cultures.

One area that would have been interesting to spend more time on, or perhaps to focus on in future investigations is that of expression. What specific messages did the girls want to communicate to their audiences? They spoke about sending messages that were seen by others as important, but what would those messages contain? The discussion touched on those issues specifically with reference to independence, but there are additional messages there that were not fully explored due to the time frame of only conducting one group session.

Investigations to consider for the future would be to conduct in-depth individual interviews with early adolescent singers and assess whether or not there are similar themes amongst a larger group. Other studies could follow previous interviewees to see how their identities and interests change later into their teen years. Another investigation might compare singers with other instrumentalists to examine how they form their performing identities, and to see if any similarities exist.

Relevance to Music Educators

This topic raises issues and question for music educators to reflect upon. These include such things as: repertoire selection, and adolescent participation in choirs, bands, ensembles, and other music programs. How can we get more musicians to join our ensembles if they are lacking in numbers? Why are some schools more successful at recruiting for ensembles? Does difficult ensemble recruitment stem from how the ensemble will be perceived by the students' peers, or from the repertoire that has been selected?

The role of music in identity construction also raises questions about performance venues, performance opportunities, instrument choice, and audience members. In designing course syllabi for the music classroom and for those teachers selecting teaching material for private lessons it is important to reflect and think on how we can encourage the development of the complete musician, via experiences in music history, theory, playing, and performance. It is also fundamental to determine how we may implement programming for students to maximize their independence and allow them opportunities to feel strong and comfortable as "musicians." 55

References

Allison, Barbara N., and Schultz, Jerelyn. B. Interpersonal Identity Formation During Early Adolescence. *Adolescence,* vol. 36, no. 142, 2001, pp. 509–23.

American Heritage Dictionary of the English Language. 4th ed., Houghton Mifflin, 2000, http://www.thefreedictionary.com/identity.

Arnett, Jeffrey. "Heavy metal music and reckless behaviour among adolescents." *Journal of Youth and Adolescence,* vol. 20, 1991, pp. 573–92.

Bennett, Andy. *Popular Music and Youth Culture: Music, Identity and Place.* Macmillan.

Brown, Jane D, and Schulze, Laurie "The Effects of Race, Gender and Fandom on Audience Interpretations of Madonna's Music Videos." *Journal of Communication,* vol. 40, 1990, pp. 88–102.

Brumberg, Joan J. *The Body Project: An Intimate History of American Girls.* Random House, 1997.

Erikson, Erik H. *Identity: Youth and Crisis.* Norton, 1986.

Fisher, Dan. *Music and Identity: Escape, Engagement, and the Quest for Authenticity in a Commodity Culture.* Doctoral dissertation, University of Arkansas, AAT 3067038, 2002.

Frith, Simon. "Music and Identity." *Questions of Cultural Identity*, edited by S. Hall and P. Du Gay, Sage, 1996.

Frith, Simon. *Sound Effects: Youth, Leisure, and the Politics of Rock n Roll*. Pantheon, 1981.

Frith, Simon. *The Sociology of Rock*. Constable, 1978.

Jennings, Carol. "Girls Make Music: Polyphony and Identity in Teenage Rock Bands." *Growing Up Girls: Popular Culture and the Construction of Identity*, edited by S.R. Mazzarella and N. Odom-Pecora, Peter Lang Publishing, 1999, pp. 175–92.

Grossberg, Laurence. "Is There a Fan in the House? The Affective Sensibility of Fandom." *The Adoring Audience: Fan Culture and Popular Media*, edited by L. Lewis, Penguin, 1992.

Hall, Stuart, and Whannel, Paddy. "The Young Audience." *Popular Culture and Cultural Theory: A Reader*, edited by J. Storey, Harvester Wheatsheaf, 1994, pp. 69–75.

Hansen, Christine, and Hansen, Ranald. "Constructing Personality and Social Reality Through Music: Individual Differences Among Fans of Punk and Heavy Metal Music." *Journal of Broadcasting and Electronic Media*, vol. 35, pp. 335–50.

Hamilton, Laurell, and Masecar, David. *Counselling the Bereaved: Caregiver Handbook Revised*. Canadian Mental Health Association, Alberta Division, 1997.

Head, John. *Working with Adolescents: Constructing Identity*. Falmer Press, 1997.

Huebner, Angela. *Adolescent Growth and Development: Family and Child Development Publication 350–850*. Virginia Polytechnic Institute and State University Website, 2000, http://www.ext.vt.edu/pubs/family/350–850/350–850.html.

Huntermann, Nina, and Morgan, Michael. "Mass Media and Identity Development." *Handbook of Children and the Media*, edited by D.G. Singer and J.L. Singer, Sage Publications, 2001, pp. 309–22.

Lavigne, Avril, and Taubenfeld, Evan. *Don't Tell Me*. AZ Lyrics.com Website, 2004, http://www.azlyrics.com/lyrics/avrillavigne/donttellme.html.

Levy-Warren, Marsha H. *The Adolescent Journey: Development, Identity Formation, and Psychotherapy*. Jason Aronson Inc, 1996.

Longhurst, Brian. *Popular Music and Society*. Blackwell Publishing, 1995.

Lowe, Melanie. "Colliding Feminisms: Britney Spears, "Tweens," and the Politics of Reception." [Electronic version]. *Popular Music and Society*, vol. 26, no. 2, pp. 123–40.

Mazzarella, Sharon R., and Odom-Pecora, Norma. *Growing Up Girls: Popular Culture and the Construction of Identity*. Peter Lang, 1999.

O'Neill, Susan. "The Self-identity of Young Musicians." *Musical Identities*, edited by R. MacDonald, D. Hargreaves, and D. Miell, Oxford University Press, 2002, pp. 79–96.

Ozretich, Rachel A., and Bowman, Sally R. *"Middle Childhood and Adolescent Development."* Oregon State University Extension Service, 2001, http://eesc.orst.edu/agcomwebfile/edmat/html/ec/ec1527/ec1527.html.

Roberts, Donald F., and Christenson, Peter G. "Popular Music in Childhood and Adolescence." *Handbook of Children and the Media*, edited by D.G. Singer and J.L. Singer, Sage Publications, 2001, pp. 95–414.

Roe, Keith. "Music and Identity Among European Youth." *Soundscapes-Journal on Media Culture*, vol. 2, 1999, ISSN 1567–7745, http://www.icce.rug.nl/~soundscapes/DATABASES/MIE/Part2_chapter03.html.

Schave, Douglas, and Schave, Barbara. *Early Adolescence and the Search for Self: A Developmental Perspective*. Praeger Publishing, 1989.

St. Lawrence, Janet S., and Joyner, Doris J. "The Effects of Sexually Violent Rock Music on Males' Acceptance of Violence Against Women." *Psychology of Women Quarterly*, vol. 15, 1991, pp. 49–63.

Stryker, Sheldon, and Burke, Peter J. "The Past, Present and Future of Identity Theory." *Social Psychology Quarterly*, vol. 63, 2000, pp. 284–97.

Tracy, Pamela J. *Pre-teen Girls' Popular Music Experiences: Performing Identities and Building Literacies*. Doctoral dissertation, Ohio State University, AAT 3022590, 2001.

Vannini, Phillip, and Myers, Scott M. "Crazy About You: Reflections on the Meanings of Contemporary Teen Pop Music." *Electronic Journal of Sociology*, ISSN 1198 3655, http://www.sociology.org/content/vol006.002/vannini_myers.html.

Willis, Paul. *Common Culture*. Open University Press, 1990.

Zillmann, Dolf, Aust, Charles F., Hoffman, Kathleen D., Love, Curtis C., Ordman, Virginia L., Pope, Janice T., Siegler, Patrick D., and Gibson, Rhonda J. "Radical Rap: Does It Further Ethnic Division?" *Basic and Applied Social Psychology*, vol. 16, 1995, pp. 1–25.

Understanding the Text

1. What is the purpose of this paper, according to the author?

2. While Clements-Cortes focuses on the role of music as it contributes to identity formation, she acknowledges other important factors that cannot be "easily separated" from this process. What are they?

Reflection and Response

3. The author writes that through their engagements with "pop stars," her adolescent subjects "learned that identity is not purely a process of discovering oneself, but also a process of creating oneself" (23). How would you explain this distinction in the formation of personal identity? To what degree do you think identity is a matter of "discovery" or "creation"?

4. According to the article, the adolescent performers in the study learned (among other things) that "society tied their worth as singers up in their physical appearance" and that they had to make themselves attractive "to be good and valuable singers" (44). Likewise, they realized that being

"popular" is important; therefore, "they tried to create themselves in a way that would be most appealing to the majority of potential audience members" (47). How do you react to this? Does this seem like a healthy response to pop culture role models, and popular culture, generally? Are these young performers succumbing to unhealthy expectations, or are they merely accepting the reality of being a performer? Explain.

Making Connections

5. Clements-Cortes paraphrases one of her scholarly sources, who asserts that "traditionally what we consumed was determined by our identity; however in today's culture of consumerism, the pattern has become reversed, and consumption determines and defines our identity" (3). How would you apply the principle of consumerism and identity to the consumption of music? That is: Does who we are determine what music we listen to? Or, does what we listen to determine our identity? Using your own experience and observations, as well as other examples in this book, how would you address these questions?

6. This article focuses on young female performers and female performing artists in the context of adolescent identity formation. Widening the context beyond aspiring performers to include all adolescents and young people, do you think male and female children, teenagers, and adults use music in similar ways to discover, create, and signal their identities? Or is there a gendered difference in the processes, depending on whether a person is male or female? You might consider several selections in this book to compare and contrast, including "Left of the Dial" by Rob Sheffield (p. 70); "Hardcore Persona" by Laina Dawes (p. 90); "Country Music, Openness to Experience, and the Psychology of Culture War" by Will Wilkinson (p. 105); "Music Is My Bag" by Meghan Daum (p. 136); and "Tina Theory: Notes on Fierceness" by Madison Moore (p. 302), among other options.

Tina Theory: Notes on Fierceness

Madison Moore

In the pantheon of musical divas, Tina Turner (b. 1939) has had one of the longest and most legendary careers. She has also been an inspiration for many, including writer and scholar Madison Moore. Indeed, he begins this scholarly essay by recalling his fascination with her when he was a child, lip-syncing and dancing to her music at family parties: "But what was it that drew me — a black gay boy ... into her style of performance?" From this basic question, he moves through a demanding and illuminating argument about race, gender, culture, and "fierceness" that manages to be both deeply personal and theoretically rigorous.

Madison Moore, who earned his PhD at Yale University, is currently a postdoctoral research associate at King's College in London. His work has appeared in both popular and scholarly publications, including *Vice*, *Interview*, and *Journal of Popular Music Studies*, where this article was first published.

Touching Queerness

Everything I know about being queer I learned from Tina Turner. More specifically, you might say that Ike and Tina's cover of "Proud Mary" — the soundtrack of my childhood — taught me, through camp performance, how to be a "Mary." During the holiday parties at my great-grandmother Lucille "Big Momma" Jones' house, for as long as I can remember, we kids ended up in the "Children's Room" so the grown folks could curse, drink whiskey, smoke, laugh, and be as loose as they felt. The "Children's Room" was not that special. It was usually a bedroom with a computer or television and a few board games, located next to the food which was always laid out buffet style. My favorite moments were when we would lip sync for our lives by doing drag karaoke, where my cousins and I would lock ourselves away and perform great popular music hits for an invisible audience. We pulled songs from Christina Aguilera or Britney Spears' latest album to older joints that circulated long before our time, songs like "Stop! (In the Name of Love)" by Diana Ross and the Supremes and Patti LaBelle's "Lady Marmalade." But one song we kept in our catalog and that we seemed to have the most fun with was the Ike and Tina Turner cover of "Proud Mary."

Whenever we did "Mary" I insisted in being Tina. But what was it that drew me — a black gay boy rooted, like Tina, in Saint Louis, which is either the South or the Midwest depending on who you ask — into her style of performance? And why "Proud Mary" in particular? Was it Tina's way with sequins and fringe that turned me on? Or did it have to do with the way she instinctively knew how to work a stage? Gay men idolize many kinds of divas, as the cultural critic Wayne Koestenbaum has revealed.[1] But perhaps the one commonality they share among them is the virtuosic styling of the body: the use of sequins, fringe, sunglasses, big shoulder pads, and bedazzled hats—accessories that help transform the diva from a mere mortal into a fantastical image, or what Guy Debord might describe as "capital accumulated to the point where it becomes image" even if the pearls are fake (24).

I did not have a bedazzler when we did "Proud Mary," but I did put a T-shirt on my head since I did not have hair or wigs. There we were, performing Tina's exact choreography, quoting her dance moves and facial expressions. Eyebrows furrowed, I would strut around the room back and forth on the tips of my toes, mouthing the lyrics to the song. I felt like I was wearing a pair of stilettos, swinging my makeshift T-shirt hair extensions in the service of working an invisible crowd. As I now arrive at my own theorizations of black glamour and the political thrust of spectacular sartorial style, I've come to realize that it was through my performances as Tina Turner that I learned what queerness meant for me—it meant a spectacular presence—and this is how, as a Midwestern boy trapped in a basement and quoting a diva five times my age, that I was able to touch queerness.

I idolized many divas and pop singers during my youth but there was always something extra that drew me to Tina Turner. Now, as I join scholars such as Deborah Willis, Monica Miller, and Nicole Fleetwood in thinking about how black and queer bodies are made visible through fashion and performance, and as I hone my thinking around black sartorial culture and the political potential of black glamour, I've realized that my interest in Tina Turner has to do with her embodiment of "fierceness" as a disruptive strategy of performance. By fierceness, I mean a spectacular way of being in the world—a transgressive over-performance of the self through aesthetics. This over-performance works simultaneously to change the dynamics of a room by introducing one's sartorial, creative presence into the space as well as it is to crystallize, highlight, and push back against limiting identity categories. Like divas, to quote Alexander Doty in a special double issue of *Camera Obscura*° devoted to divas, fierceness "offers the world a compelling brass standard that has plenty to say to women, queer men, blacks, Latinos, and other marginalized groups about the costs and the rewards that can come when you decide both to live a conspicuous public life within white patriarchy and

Camera Obscura: a feminist film journal.

try and live that life on your own terms . . . the diva will make certain that it is tradition and convention that yields to her" (2). In other words, to be fierce is to transcend and to unravel, to self-actualize and to return the gaze. Because of its transgressive potential and deep connection to showmanship, fierceness allows its users to fabricate a new sense of self that radiates a defiant sense of ownership through aesthetics, and in this way fierceness becomes a social, political, and aesthetic intervention.

In many ways fierceness is It: "a quality that makes certain people 5 interesting all the time" (Roach 9). But even as I front load my remarks on fierceness with a definition of the term, I need to point out that, like It, fierceness embodies several contradictions all at once. As I will show, fierceness is both ownership and the loss of control, simultaneously deliberateness and spontaneity. If fierceness presents this set of contradictions, it is because, as Joseph Roach describes, "It is the power of effortless embodiment of contradictory qualities simultaneously: strength and vulnerability, innocence and experience, and singularity and typicality" (5). This set of contradictions allows the term to be noticeable yet unpredictable which, the way I see it, helps to keep it interesting.

To illustrate my theory of fierceness, I'd like to focus on how Tina Turner employs the term by doing a close reading of a range of Tina's performances and images across media. I look at Tina Turner as she appeared on the first cover of *Rolling Stone* in 1967; I play the athletic twelve-minute rendition of "Proud Mary" on Ike and Tina's 1971 live album *What You Hear Is What You Get*; and I conclude by moving away from "Proud Mary" to consider her live video performance of "I Want to Take You Higher" as performed in Holland in 1971. What links this select archive is the way in which Tina's voice—her literal voice as well as the vocality of her fashion image—shows the process of fierceness. Whether Tina appears in print, sound, or through a video-documented live performance, the fact is that fierceness remains.

Fashion and Fierceness

On November 23, 1967, a roaring Tina Turner, born as Anna Mae Bullock in Nutbush, Tennessee, appeared on the cover of *Rolling Stone* magazine—only the second issue of the newly formed San Francisco–based rock journal. The black and white image, a still from a live performance, captures the magic of Tina Turner's fierceness. Her mouth agape and muscular arms outstretched, Tina wears a short, form-fitting dress made entirely of sequins. The image of her open mouth, coupled with the creases in her be-sequined dress proffers the sense of movement. When we look at the image, we know that something *happened* at the

Figure 5.3   "But what was so exciting to audiences about 'Proud Mary,' and how did the song capture Tina's fierceness?" Tina and Ike Turner onstage. Gijsbert Hanekroot/ Getty Images

moment during which the picture was taken. Tina's "Tinaness" is what this image is about; she is frozen, caught in *medias res*, and this image summarizes how she will look from 1967 onwards. More than simply a performance shot placed on the cover of a magazine, Tina's pose raises important questions about the specific role that fashion played in framing her specific brand of performance. But what is the visual power of her look as a black female on the cover of a mainstream rock journal? Is this simply style for the sake of glamour?

To address these questions, it is important to note that a few studies of glamour have sufficiently addressed the crucial role of people of color in the making and consuming of glamour. This omission may have to do with the historical lack of people of color across all mainstream media. In fact, Tina Turner appeared on the cover of *Rolling Stone* at a moment when black women were emphatically not on the covers of any magazines, and it would take still another seven years—in 1974—for a black face to be splashed across the cover of American *Vogue*, the most coveted fashion magazine in the United States. The silence around black bodies in the marketplace of glamour led literary critic Francesca Royster, in an article on Cleopatra, to beg the polemical question, one I share: "What color is glamour" ("Becoming Cleopatra" 97)? As Royster describes, notions of glamour are tied to Hollywood, which has always been about framing a specific vision of idealized white femininity. For Royster, "Hollywood glamour is framed by a white, western eye . . . thus we might think more about what glamour and whiteness have in common" (98). Other scholars, most notably Richard Dyer, have written about the relationship between Hollywood and the construction and maintenance of whiteness in visual culture, as well as through the technologies of lighting in particular.[2]

But the fact is that the silence around black bodies and glamour does not only surface in visual culture. Even in scholarly conversations about glamour—a subject that over the past several years has come into vogue as a serious academic and curatorial line of inquiry—there is a peculiar lack of focus on black bodies. Film historian Stephen Gundle's own book *Glamour: A History*, one of the first academic tomes devoted to the historical study of modern glamour, makes virtually no mention of the African American consumption or production of glamour, though it is rigorous otherwise.[3] But scholars of late have attended to this lack of discussion by ushering in new ways of thinking through the color of glamour. Anne Cheng, in her work on Anna May Wong, sees celebrity as "a politics of recognition and glamour as a politics of personhood," which places an emphasis on personhood and humanity, rather than whiteness and not-whiteness. To think through race and glamour "presses us to think in more nuanced terms about what celebrity and glamour mean for the woman of color," which points towards the study of the use-value of glamour and celebrity for people of color (1023). The way I see it, fierceness and its use-value have much to do with the way fierceness gets used as a strategy of transgression, and in particular for the disenfranchised and groups of color.

My thinking around "fierceness" follows a sentiment that a num- 10
ber of scholars, such as Monica Miller and Richard Powell, have theorized as a way to talk about the relationship between excess, style, and performance in black popular culture. Miller calls black sartorial practice "stylin' out"—a colloquialism describing the act of "dressing to the nines, showing sartorial stuff, especially when the occasion calls for it and, more tellingly, often when it does not" (1). In her history of the black dandy,° Miller suggests that dandies "are creatures of invention who continually and characteristically break down limiting

---

dandy: a male excessively preoccupied with style, fashion, dress, and appearance.

identity markers and propose new, more fluid categories within which to constitute themselves" (11). Powell, in his recent work on black portraiture, prefers the term "sharp"—another colloquialism used to describe someone who is ostentatiously stylish. Commenting on a nuanced sense of sharpness within the black sartorial community, Powell argues that "many fashionable people have a precise and exacting edge, a sense of how to look, of how, figuratively speaking, to 'stand out' and be 'a cut above' the dull and commonplace" (4). This notion of knowing how to stand out, of being above the dull and the commonplace, is key for understanding how fierceness functions as a category of self-making that challenges readymade categories of normative identity.

But as I started examining Tina Turner's fashion and performances to develop a language for speaking about fierceness, and as I created an archive of spectacular performances by other recent black entertainers—Grace Jones, Sylvester, Freddie Mercury, Prince, and Michael Jackson to cite these few—I began to wonder whether "black glamour" was something different altogether, a not quite glamour, a not quite *not* glamour; a "something else." I noticed in each black performer I studied a deliberate element of transgression in their performance persona, and the single trait that links the majority of artists I've examined is fierceness. Through fashion, style, and self-presentation, black performers used fierceness to transgress and transcend restrictive boundaries of race and gender. But what difference does performance make? As the cultural critic Daphne Brooks reveals in her in-depth study of the ways in which black artists and performers utilized performance as a way to forge revised notions of blackness, we see that black female celebrity performers turned to performance "as a place from which to explore and express the social, political, and sexual politics of black womanhood in America" (286). This suggests that performance has been the long space where black bodies have thrown quotation marks around particular identity categories as a way to test, revise, and debunk them. This thinking fits in with recent scholarship that specifically addresses the relationship between the body of color and glamour, work that focuses on black glamour and performance with a particular interest in fashion, a major intervention for the field of fashion studies which still fetishizes white women's bodies and white femininity. But what does black glamour as a test or as a debunking look like?

> "I noticed in each black performer I studied a deliberate element of transgression in their performance persona, and the single trait that links the majority of artists I've examined is fierceness."

Listen to this *Rolling Stone* reporter try to capture Tina Turner's unique style: "Tina Turner is an incredible chick. She comes in this very short miniskirt, way above her knees, with zillions of silver sequins and sparklers pasted on it" ("Ike and Tina Turner"), the reviewer said in 1967. One way to interpret this phrase is as a way to sexualize Tina by placing an emphasis on the visibility of the legs, but no matter how seductive or sparkly Tina's clothes became, her flashy style of dress had more to do with the politics of race and beauty at the time than with mere style or seduction. I said that Tina took the cover of *Rolling Stone* at a time when black women were emphatically not on the covers of any mainstream magazines, and it is impossible to understand Tina Turner's impact on the popular culture of the late 1960s without paying due attention to the fashion and styling of her musical peers. Seen this way, the real news of the 1967 *Rolling Stone* article is not that she wears sequins or short skirts, but that she does it as a contrast against the equally successful but more visually sedate acts of the time. "Unlike the polite handclapping Motown groups, [Tina] and the Ikettes scream, wail, and do some fantastic boogaloo," the article said. Look at this 1965 photo of the Supremes captured by Bruce Davidson, an iconic photographer of the Civil Rights Movement, and you will see a rather proper looking Supremes at the Motown recording studio in Detroit. In the image, Diana Ross appears feminine and tasteful in a bouffant wig, her head wrapped in a silk scarf. A pearl necklace and white suit accentuate her value not only as the star of the group, but as a respectable black woman dressed in her Sunday best. Indeed, if Diana Ross appears diva-like, as the lead singer and visual focal point of this image, it may have to do less with projecting star quality than it does with the diva as a model of uplift. Brooks suggests the way in which divas "were often expected to shoulder the demands that the race puts its best face forward. 'Divine' as they may seem, these women were often forced to place the material and representational desires of their community before themselves, to perform the hopeful ideals of people above all else" (Brooks 320).

Tina and the Supremes, as well as other contemporary acts such as Martha and the Vandellas who penned the song "Dancing in the Streets," were making music at a time when black women in America were fighting for inclusion and representation in all areas of American culture, from real estate to the workplace, and from consumerism to media. Positive representations of black women in particular became a highly political issue. As Maxine Leeds Craig shows in her study of the rise of black beauty and first black beauty pageants in America, African Americans had been subject to negativist and degrading images of themselves in the media, thus "donning fabulous hats on Sunday at church; wearing clean, pretty dresses; and having their hair straightened and styled to motionless perfection were ways of displaying dignity. A woman who put time and money into her appearance was dignified, and her dignity spoke well of the race. Grooming was a weapon in the battle to defeat racist depictions of blacks" (Craig 34). Indeed, as a number of popular music scholars have shown, Motown worked as a vehicle to promote positive images of middle-class black America. Motown "saw black progress in terms of the integration of mainstream and elite American institutions by blacks with highly textured middle-class sensibilities" (Neal 88–89). The narratives of sophistication, respectability, and upward mobility were crucial enough that Motown hired Maxine Powell—a well-known professional stage actress—as a finishing school consultant to groom a number of Motown acts, including Diana Ross. Powell taught each performer that they were being trained for concerts at "The White House" and "Buckingham Palace," placing an emphasis on poise, glamour, and sophistication (Murphy). Contrast this image of finishing school primness with the fire-spitting Tina Turner—whose dresses rarely fell much below her knees—and the impact of Tina's presence in 1967 becomes clear: glamour contra fierceness.[4]

But when we position the Supremes' performance of glamour, of whiteness, next to Tina Turner's performance of fierceness, of blackness, what we are actually witnessing is the performance of class. As scholars of conspicuous consumption such as Thorstein Veblen have shown, one marker of the leisure class is a certain style of dress that implies the wearer does no work. Fancy clothes do not necessarily lend themselves to sweat and physical labor. Reading the fashions of the Supremes, dressed as they were in evening gowns and arm length satin gloves, next to Tina Turner's sparkly, cabaret-influenced ensembles, we notice that the Supremes are dressed for *class*. Tina Turner, on the other hand, whose skirts are shorter and who drips sweat, is dressed for labor. Read this way, Tina's *Rolling Stone* cover frames her fierceness simultaneously as a particular styling of the body and as a type of *excess*.

Fierceness as Sound

At her highest point, Tina Turner was an unshakable vocal powerhouse. 15
She changed the popular music scene. Speaking to a reporter in 1968, Janis Joplin described the impact Tina Turner had on her own performance: "currently, Tina Turner is my biggest influence. I saw her a short while ago and I realized that this was what I'm trying to do. I mean, she just comes on stage and *aaagh!* She hits you right there" (Jackson 182). What I'm interested in theorizing here is the astonishment of *"aaagh!"*

that Joplin quotes. Specifically, I take Joplin's term and call it fierceness, and I aim to show what this term means and how it relates to what Patricia Hill Collins has called "the power of self-definition." In what ways does the astonishment of Tina's live performance describe how fierceness can be used to assert social and cultural presence?

Throughout her career, Tina has perfected the notion of the volcanic stage persona, leading critics to pen a range of sensational headlines about Tina's performances over the years that evoke the blaze of fire: "A volcano that just can't stop erupting"; "Tina Turner: Sizzling at 45"; "Proud Tina Keep On Burnin'"; "Tina Turner Still Setting the Stage Afire"; and "Tina Treats Ravinia to Early Fireworks." What are the racial implications of using descriptors such as "sizzling" and "fireworks" to describe Tina's performance practice? How can looking at Tina as a persona of fierceness complicate the colloquialism's use and meaning in gay culture, and in popular culture more broadly?

All told, Ike and Tina's version of "Proud Mary," which appeared on their 1971 album *Working Together*, stands among the most prolific demonstrations of "fierceness" in black popular culture. The American rock group Creedence Clearwater Revival recorded the original song in 1969, but the original Creedence version was rather more Cajun flavored. As Tina remembered, "In the beginning Ike hated the Creedence Clearwater Revival song, but then he heard the version by the Checkmates and took notice" (Turner 139).

Recorded in 1970 at a studio in Florida, Tina recalls: "We made that song our own. I loved the Creedence version, but I liked ours better after we got it down, with the talking and all. I thought it was more rock 'n' roll. That was the beginning of me liking rock music" (146). Almost overnight, "Proud Mary" became the biggest song in Ike and Tina's catalog. It reached Number 4 on the *Billboard* charts. It was their first million-selling record, and the song pulled their album *Workin' Together* to number 25 on the *Billboard* charts. Tina even earned a Grammy for Best Vocal Performance (Bego 108). Speaking to *The Independent*, John Fogerty remarked that he was surprised when Tina Turner decided "to cover 'Proud Mary' two years after we had a hit with it. They had a whole different take on it, with the slow start and then, *boom*, they went into the Las Vegas revue! Tina was shaking her moneymaker, just rocking out. Tina Turner shot my song 'Proud Mary' into the stratosphere" (Perrone).

The magic and fierceness of "Proud Mary" can be heard best during an iconic live recording of the Ike and Tina Turner Review at Carnegie Hall in 1971, which resulted in an album called *What You Hear Is What You Get*. As the concert begins, a series of musical interludes and announcements occur that serve to build anticipation for Tina's imminent, dramatic entrance. Though we do not see her, the listener can tell when she emerges onto the stage as the audience applauds and cheers in excitement, and the band — which sways sonically in the backdrop — introduces her not just by name, but with a sudden, acrobatic-sounding, quick-paced tune called "Doin the Tina Turner." At this point in the performance, Tina has been on stage for nearly two minutes yet she has not sung a word before, at last, she spins around once the music drops, hair flying in her face, this is what I imagine, and she grabs hold of the microphone to sting the audience at the top of her lungs with the question, "*Do you like good music?*" the opening verse of "Sweet Soul Music," a 1967 classic originally performed by Arthur Conley and written with Otis Redding. The fierceness of this particular entrance hinges on the piercing quality of Tina's voice — the peculiarly pleasant-sounding strain of the voice, which is evoked each time Tina sings "yeah." I said that she had been on stage for two minutes before singing or otherwise addressing the audience, and in this way when she finally did sing, she cut through the vocal silence in the concert hall, literally piercing the audience with her raw sound.

But the crown jewel of this recording, aside from being one of the best 20 live Ike and Tina albums ever made, is the rendition of "Proud Mary." If anyone around in 1971 ever doubted the scale of "Proud Mary" as a major Ike and Tina hit, proof of its success lies in the fact that on this recording, Tina performed the song a staggering three times in a row. As the song begins — the tenth number out of sixteen — Tina teases the audience with the by then already familiar line, "And right about now . . . I think you . . . I think you might like to hear something from us . . . nice . . . *easy*" before the crowd erupts in anticipation. The Ikettes, at the background, cheer Tina on by singing "Go 'Head!," urging her and helping to build momentum for the crowd-pleasing, orgasmic release of the faster second half of the song. But by the time Tina delivers the final "rollin' on the river," we can already hear the audience's anxiousness for the good part. Ike shouts, "2, 3, 4!" and instantly we imagine Tina and the Ikettes spinning, running around on stage, all of which mirrors the music which sounds like a strobe light thrusting attention on the moment of action. Tina electrifies the audience by performing "Proud Mary" three times in a row, each time more energetic than the last. In other words, "Proud Mary" becomes a performance of endurance. At the precise moment we think Tina cannot keep screaming and spinning to "Proud Mary," she does it one more time just to prove us wrong. One album review of *What You Hear Is What You Get* from *The Hartford Courant* warned: "Anyone who buys this record better like 'Proud Mary,' because there's 12 minutes and 35 seconds worth" (McNulty).

"Proud Mary" stands as the fiercest song in Ike and Tina Turner's catalog. But what was so exciting to audiences about "Proud Mary," and how did the song capture Tina's fierceness? What has always struck me about the song in particular is the drastic separation between the spoken word first half and the speedy second. This might seem obvious, but I'm not thinking in terms of fastness and slowness. Rather, I see it as it relates to what I would call the "diva moment." By "diva moment," I mean the special, unique quality that a performer brings to their version of a cover song that stamps their identity and makes the song their own. What made "Proud Mary" Ike and Tina's was not simply the change in musical form, but the addition of the call-and-response. I have always thought that the one quality that separates divas from the conveyor belt of traditional pop singers is the ability to work a crowd through spoken word. We need the rawness and immediacy of the spoken. Sometimes the most interesting moments during a concert occur not when the singer sings, but when she or he narrates the space between the songs with camp stories and witty dialogue. The diva moment is precisely when fierceness *speaks*.

So far I've used "Proud Mary" to center my remarks on fierceness, but now I'd like to move away from that song to consider a live performance of a different, somewhat lesser known Ike and Tina cover. One archival video I found shows Tina doing a version of Sly and the Family Stone's 1969 single "I Want to Take You Higher," and the video stands as her most intense demonstration of fierceness yet. The performance occurred in 1971 in Holland—a rare full-length concert video of the Ike and Tina Turner Revue. The video opens with a funk interlude performed by Ike and his eight-piece band, who are all dressed in '70s psychedelia—bell bottoms, sunglasses and floral prints abound—with Ike playing the guitar in the background, dressed in an all red velvet suit and black wig. After the interlude, the Ikettes—"three very bold soul sisters"—emerge on stage, and they are all styled identically in short pink dresses that reveal their arms and legs, a specific fashion choice that frames blackness as different/other/desirable for a largely white, Dutch audience. The Ikettes, an all black three-piece that suggests a rawer version of the prim and proper Supremes, sing and dance freely around stage to build the anticipation and set the tone for Tina Turner's eventual entrance.

"She's known as the hardest working woman in show business today. Ladies and gentlemen, Miss Tina Turner!" the announcer says before the Ikettes and Tina Turner emerge on stage. Tina, for her turn, wears a short, tight-fitting purple sequined dress that covers the arms but reveals the legs. She and the Ikettes dance back onto the stage to a medley of the songs they will play; their arms flailing about, hair in constant motion.

Everything, in fact, is in constant motion. But what is immediately present the moment Tina takes the stage is the sense of her being possessed by the performance before she has even started to sing—her level of intensity. She and the Ikettes are all performing the same moves, but Tina is offering *more*—fierceness, that is, as a kind of generosity. At first, she and the Ikettes glide onto the stage performing balletic moves. But when the rock and roll medley begins, with classic rock and roll guitar riffs, "Tina Turner" is immediately turned "on," ready to work. Her face stretches out of control, the mouth at turns wide open, the lips pursing themselves outward, her eyebrows are furrowed. All of this is to suggest the connection between music, possession, and the intensity of performing against it.

After the opening dance routine, Tina takes to the microphone and sings her first song of the concert, a cover of "I Want to Take You Higher." As the Ikettes sing "Higher" behind her, Tina is constantly moving: her leg tapping the stage, shaking the hips to make the purple sequins sparkle. Hair creates drama, and its length in this performance allows her to work it from right to left in a way that sustains the sense of intensity and action on the stage. At the end of the song, Tina pulls away from the microphone and performs a dance which involves the rhythmic stomping on the ground and the simultaneous punching of the air with the head going from down to up on the downbeat, which turns the stage into a symphony of hair flying all around.

If this performance shows that half the power of the Ike and Tina 25 Turner Revue is visual and kinesthetic, then fierceness emerges as a constant flux that pushes boundaries because of its sheer force. When something is moving, say a falling object out of the sky, one is inclined to move out of the way because the object falls with such force that one could be injured if hit. Fierceness—in this case Tina Turner—is that falling object. Fierceness is cognizant of its own force, of its own disruptive strategy. We see this especially at the end of Tina's songs, which in this concert like many others she closes by saying "Yeah" or "Okay"; she knows the value of what she's just done.

At the end of the concert when Tina and the Ikettes walk off stage, the audience offers up warm in-unison applause and they begin to chant "We want more! We want more!" At this point, the audience can barely stay seated, and throughout the concert we see the theater go from respectful concertgoers to rabid fans. Tina has essentially, over the last forty minutes, succeeded at working the room. With Tina now off stage, a few moments of tantalization go by, and she struts back out and performs "I Want to Take You Higher" as an encore. It was as appropriate a moment for "Higher" as ever, as Tina sings: "The beat is getting stronger / the beat is getting longer too / music sounding good to me / I wanna, I wanna,

I wanna take you higher." When the grain/strain of Tina's smoky voice wraps around those words, the meaning transforms the song into an anthem, a manifesto, about what "Tina Turner" brings to the stage as a performer. Tina has been sweating throughout the concert, but now the sweat is particularly telling. With each passing note, Tina's eyes flutter quickly, and she bumps and shakes rhythmically. Here, Tina's soul and fierceness takes the audience to a "higher" plateau of live performance. As the camera pans away from Tina to show the theater, one can see the audience boiling in their seats, unable to contain themselves through the intensity of Tina's performance. As she presides over the room, the audience claps, shakes, nods their heads, and reacts to the music, sometimes raising their arms in the air as if they have been spiritually possessed.

As Nicole Fleetwood reveals in her work on the way the black body is produced through visual culture and performance, "the black female body functions as the site of excess in dominant visual culture [. . .] in excess of idealized white femininity" (109, 111). She coins the term "excess flesh" to think through the ways in which black women "engage with visual practices as a re-inscription of their corporeality" (105). Tina's gymnastic choreography in "Higher" puts into motion the relationship between "excess flesh" and her ownership of her fierceness and sexuality—this is, in other words, about being in control of how her image is read. She knows the audience desires to see her body and her excessiveness in motion, and she allows them to have a taste. But like any good diva, she only gives them a taste. Here, ownership and the contradictory nature of fierceness emerges with a particular force: you can have her, but you cannot really have her. She is on stage, but of course she is not really on stage. Fierceness is a mask that draws attention to the fact that it simultaneously is and is not a mask.

I said that Tina Turner is a nodal point in terms of fierceness as a whole-body aesthetic, and by whole-body I mean fierceness as the use of fashion, style, and movement. Across Tina's performance practice we witness fierceness as a spastic bodily possession—a seemingly uncontrollable, unrestrained energy. For Tina, every handclap, ad lib, stomp, and bead of sweat is a moment of possession; she is taken over by the performance. At several points throughout the performance, Tina's face appears glazed over, her eyes fluttering quickly. She reaches, both physically and emotionally, for the right character of note to sing, and makes heroic attempts to pull the song out. When she does a cover of "Come Together" by the Beatles and sings "got to be a joker he just do what he please," her eyes remain closed, the head tilted back and the neck pulled tight, as if she is trying to pull the song out of her vocal cords, as if not even she can tame the song. The live performance, like an exorcism, possesses her. This is what the cultural critic Francesca Royster has called a "playfully outrageous bodily knowledge" ("Nice and Rough" 4). But even as fierceness evokes the sense of being out of control, the fact is that it also requires a certain level of mastery, of virtuosity and deliberateness. In her performance work, Tina demonstrates a sense of control and expertise. More than simply singing the song, she means it. Meaning it implies ownership. Fierceness demonstrates a mastery and an ownership of the self that gives minoritarian subjects the power to re-create and assert themselves through aesthetics.

Conclusion

I have always thought that one of the most interesting things about Tina Turner was the way "she" circulates through popular culture even when she is nowhere to be found. How do we come to perform Tina, or to know Tina through performance? I knew her through standing on my tippy toes and putting a shirt on my head. Angela Bassett knows her—not unlike drag queens or cabaret performers across the world—through platinum gold fringe dresses. In the "Proud Mary" scene of the movie *What's Love Got to Do With It?*, where Bassett plays Tina, she *works* her dress, slowly moving the fringe from side to side. But when she pulls away from the microphone for the up tempo second half of the song, Bassett violently spins in circles—seeming on the verge of falling several times—with the gold fringe, hair, and arms flailing about. During the dance sequence, Bassett and the Ikettes pull and stretch their arms and backs in a dizzying gymnastic workout which is keyed to mime "swimming" or rolling down the river, original choreography that helped shoot "Proud Mary" into iconicity, and which basically has not changed since it was first performed.

What draws me into this performance of "Proud Mary" as a way of 30 concluding this article on fierceness is its *representation* of Tina Turner, its presentation of "Tina-ness." Tina Turner the person becomes "Tina Turner" the specific, easily quotable idea. I do not mean to say that Tina is nothing but a fringe dress, but what is interesting about "Tina-ness" is precisely how quotable it is. "Tina-ness," like fierceness, is about presenting a style that is so one's own that that presence eclipses anything that tries to step into it; anybody wearing a fringe dress can automatically be read as Tina Turner, whether they intended it or not. And that is where I locate the value of fierceness—in its ability to crystallize a solid identity for people who might otherwise be overlooked. "The diva makes herself a force to be reckoned with, so that even in defeat there is something gloriously iconoclastic about the 'bitch'" (Doty 3).

In writing about Tina Turner, I hope to restore the power and novelty of her performance practice as something that she owned and which was her own fierce labor. Famously, all Tina asked for in the divorce proceedings from Ike was her name—"Tina Turner"—perhaps because her name had become synonymous, like the wigs and the fringe, with the style of fierceness and ownership that she made her own.

Notes

1. For more on opera divas and homosexuality, see Wayne Koestenbaum, *The Queen's Throat: Opera, Homosexuality, and the Mystery of Desire* (New York: Da Capo p, 2001).

2. For additional context on the framing of whiteness, see Richard Dyer, *White* (New York: Routledge, 1997).

3. For more on Stephen Gundle, see *Glamour: A History* (Oxford: Oxford UP, 2008).

4. It is important to note that Tina's stage image at the beginning of her career was in fact more in line with the visual performance of respectability, right along with the Motown groups. It became the sexualized, "fierce" version around 1967.

Works Cited

Bego, Mark. *Tina Turner: Break Every Rule*. Taylor Trade Publishing, 2003.

Brooks, Daphne. *Bodies in Dissent: Spectacular Performances of Race and Freedom, 1850–1910*. Duke University Press, 2006.

Cheng, Anne A. "Shine: On Race, Glamour, and the Modern." *PMLA*, vol. 126, no. 4, Oct. 2011

Craig, Maxine L. *Ain't I a Beauty Queen: Black Women, Beauty, and the Politics of Race*. Oxford University Press, 2002.

Debord, Guy. *The Society of the Spectacle*. Zone Books, 1995.

Doty, Alexander. "There's Something about Mary." *Camera Obscura*, vol. 22, no. 2, 2007, p. 65

Fleetwood, Nicole. *Troubling Vision: Performance, Visuality, and Blackness*. University of Chicago Press, 2011.

"Ike and Tina Turner." *Rolling Stone*, 1967.

Jackson, Buzzy. *A Bad Woman Feeling Good: Blues and the Women Who Sing Them*. W. W. Norton, 2005.

McNulty, Henry. "Ike, Tina Take You Higher; Paul Gently Cools You Down." *Hartford Courant*, 14 Aug. 1971.

Miller, Monica. *Slaves to Fashion: Black Dandyism and the Styling of Black Diasporic Identity*. Duke University Press, 2009.

Murphy, Michael. "Maxine Powell Buffed Motown's Rough Edges." *Detroit Metro Times*, 1 Oct. 2003.

Neal, Mark A. *What the Music Said: Black Popular Music and Black Public Culture.* Routledge, 1998.

Perrone, Pierre. "'Tina Turner Shot My Song into the Stratosphere': The 5-Minute Interview." *The Independent* (London), 29 June 2006.

Powell, Richard. *Cutting a Figure: Fashioning Black Portraiture.* University of Chicago Press, 2009.

Roach, Joseph. *It.* University of Michigan Press, 2007.

Royster, Francesca. *Becoming Cleopatra: The Shifting Image of an Icon.* Palgrave Macmillan, 2003.

Royster, Francesca. "Nice and Rough: The Promise of Privacy in Tina Turner's 'What's Love Got to Do with It' and *I, Tina.*" *Performance Research: A Journal of the Performing Arts*, vol. 12, no. 3, 2007, pp. 103–13.

Turner, Tina. *I, Tina.* Avon, 1987.

Understanding the Text

1. What does Moore mean by "fierceness"? How does he go about defining it throughout the article — and how is it related to being (in his phrase) a "minoritarian subject" (28)? Can you explain its meaning — and discuss its elements — in your own words?

2. Moore contrasts the appearance of the Motown group the Supremes with Tina Turner's visual style. What point does he make by doing this?

3. According to Moore, what was the only thing Tina Turner asked for in her divorce proceedings from Ike Turner? How does the writer link this detail to his argument?

Reflection and Response

4. This article appeared in the peer-reviewed academic *Journal of Popular Music Studies*, which implies a particular writing context: a specialized audience, an academic purpose, a certain scholarly objectivity or detachment. At the same time, Moore writes in the first person, from a profoundly intimate perspective about a topic that is deeply personal to him. How does he reconcile these two seemingly disparate approaches to his topic? In what ways does the personal inform or illuminate the critical, scholarly, or academic? What does his approach suggest about academic writing, generally?

5. Moore focuses on Tina Turner as his exemplar. What other examples can you find that fit, illustrate, or complicate his definition of "fierceness"?

Making Connections

6. According to Moore, Tina Turner's "fiercest" song was "Proud Mary," which was written and performed by the American rock band, Creedence Clearwater Revival. The article discusses several different versions of the

song, including the original. Turner herself said, "We made that song our own. I loved the Creedence version, but I liked ours better after we got it down, with the talking and all. I thought it was more rock 'n' roll ..." Watch or listen to both the original version of the song and Turner's version. How do you compare and contrast them? For example, how do you evaluate the "authenticity" of each version? What do these performances reveal about how artists make the songs of others their "own"?

7. As the article suggests, Tina Turner was a prominent figure in rock music as early as 1967, when she appeared on an early cover of *Rolling Stone* magazine. In her 1970 essay "Macho Rock: Men Always Seem to End Up on Top" (p. 272), Susan Hiwatt argues that the "total disregard and disrespect for women is constant in the rock world and has no exceptions." How might you read Tina Turner's "fierceness" in the context of Hiwatt's assertions about marginalized women in music? Does Turner seem like an exception to it, or was she just another female performer "on stage with nothing to relate to but the microphone, and nothing between them and the audience but their own bodies"? (For added context, you might want to read about Turner's fraught and sometimes violent personal and professional relationship with her then-husband, Ike Turner.)

Sentence Guides for Academic Writers

Being a college student means being a college writer. No matter what field you are studying, your instructors will ask you to make sense of what you are learning through writing. When you work on writing assignments in college, you are, in most cases, being asked to write for an academic audience.

Writing academically means thinking academically — asking a lot of questions, digging into the ideas of others, and entering into scholarly debates and academic conversations. As a college writer, you will be asked to read different kinds of texts; understand and evaluate authors' ideas, arguments, and methods; and contribute your own ideas. In this way, you present yourself as a participant in an academic conversation.

What does it mean to be part of an *academic conversation*? Well, think of it this way: You and your friends may have an ongoing debate about the best film trilogy of all time. During your conversations with one another, you analyze the details of the films, introduce points you want your friends to consider, listen to their ideas, and perhaps cite what the critics have said about a particular trilogy. This kind of conversation is not unlike what happens among scholars in academic writing — except they could be debating the best public policy for a social problem or the most promising new theory in treating disease.

If you are uncertain about what academic writing *sounds like* or if you're not sure you're any good at it, this booklet offers guidance for you at the sentence level. It helps answer questions such as these:

How can I present the ideas of others in a way that demonstrates my understanding of the debate?

How can I agree with someone, but add a new idea?

How can I disagree with a scholar without seeming, well, rude?

How can I make clear in my writing which ideas are mine and which ideas are someone else's?

The following sections offer sentence guides for you to use and adapt to your own writing situations. As in all writing that you do, you will have to think about your purpose (reason for writing) and your audience (readers) before knowing which guides will be most appropriate for a particular piece of writing or for a certain part of your essay.

The guides are organized to help you present background information, the views and claims of others, and your own views and claims — all in the context of your purpose and audience.

Academic Writers Present Information and Others' Views

When you write in academic situations, you may be asked to spend some time giving background information for or setting a context for your main idea or argument. This often requires you to present or summarize what is known or what has already been said in relation to the question you are asking in your writing.

SG1   Presenting What Is Known or Assumed

When you write, you will find that you occasionally need to present something that is known, such as a specific fact or a statistic. The following structures are useful when you are providing background information.

As we know from history, _____.

X has shown that _____.

Research by X and Y suggests that _____.

According to X, _____ percent of _____ are/favor _____.

In other situations, you may have the need to present information that is assumed or that is conventional wisdom.

People often believe that _____.

Conventional wisdom leads us to believe _____.

Many Americans share the idea that _____.

_____ is a widely held belief.

In order to challenge an assumption or a widely held belief, you have to acknowledge it first. Doing so lets your readers believe that you are placing your ideas in an appropriate context.

Although many people are led to believe X, there is significant benefit to considering the merits of Y.

College students tend to believe that _____ when, in fact, the opposite is much more likely the case.

SG2 Presenting Others' Views

As a writer, you build your own *ethos*, or credibility, by being able to fairly and accurately represent the views of others. As an academic writer, you will be expected to demonstrate your understanding of a text by summarizing the views or arguments of its author(s). To do so, you will use language such as the following.

X argues that _____.

X emphasizes the need for _____.

In this important article, X and Y claim _____.

X endorses _____ because _____.

X and Y have recently criticized the idea that _____.

_____, according to X, is the most critical cause of _____.

Although you will create your own variations of these sentences as you draft and revise, the guides can be useful tools for thinking through how best to present another writer's claim or finding clearly and concisely.

SG3   Presenting Direct Quotations

When the exact words of a source are important for accuracy, authority, emphasis, or flavor, you will want to use a direct quotation. Ordinarily, you will present direct quotations with language of your own that suggests how you are using the source.

X characterizes the problem this way: ". . ."

According to X, _____ is defined as ". . ."

". . . ," explains X.

X argues strongly in favor of the policy, pointing out that ". . ."

Note: You will generally cite direct quotations according to the documentation style your readers expect. MLA style, often used in English and in other humanities courses, recommends using the author name paired with a page number, if there is one. APA style, used in most social sciences, requires the year of publication generally after the mention of the source, with page numbers after the quoted material. In *Chicago* style, used in history and in some humanities courses, writers use superscript numbers (like this[6]) to refer readers to footnotes or endnotes. In-text citations, like the ones shown below, refer readers to entries in the works cited or reference list.

MLA	Lazarín argues that our overreliance on testing in K-12 schools "does not put students first" (20).
APA	Lazarín (2014) argues that our overreliance on testing in K-12 schools "does not put students first." (p. 20)
Chicago	Lazarín argues that our overreliance on testing in K-12 schools "does not put students first."[6]

Many writers use direct quotations to advance an argument of their own:

Standardized testing makes it easier for administrators to measure student performance, but it may not be the best way to measure it. Too much testing wears students out and communicates the idea that recall is the most important skill we want them to develop. Even education policy advisor Melissa Lazarín argues that our overreliance on testing in K-12 schools "does not put students first" (20).

Student writer's idea

Source's idea

SG4   Presenting Alternative Views

Most debates, whether they are scholarly or popular, are complex—often with more than two sides to an issue. Sometimes you will have to synthesize the views of multiple participants in the debate before you introduce your own ideas.

> On the one hand, X reports that _____, but on the other hand, Y insists that _____.

> Even though X endorses the policy, Y refers to it as ". . ."

> X, however, isn't convinced and instead argues _____.

> X and Y have supported the theory in the past, but new research by Z suggests that _____.

Academic Writers Present Their Own Views

When you write for an academic audience, you will indeed have to demonstrate that you are familiar with the views of others who are asking the same kinds of questions as you are. Much writing that is done for academic purposes asks you to put your arguments in the context of existing arguments—in a way asking you to connect the known to the new.

When you are asked to write a summary or an informative text, your own views and arguments are generally not called for. However, much of the writing you will be assigned to do in college asks you to take a persuasive stance and present a reasoned argument—at times in response to a single text, and at other times in response to multiple texts.

SG5   Presenting Your Own Views: Agreement and Extension

Sometimes you agree with the author of a source.

> X's argument is convincing because _____.

> Because X's approach is so _____, it is the best way to _____.

> X makes an important point when she says _____.

Other times you find you agree with the author of a source, but you want to extend the point or go a bit deeper in your own investigation. In a way, you acknowledge the source for getting you so far in the conversation, but then you move the conversation along with a related comment or finding.

> X's proposal for _____ is indeed worth considering. Going one step further, _____.

> X makes the claim that _____. By extension, isn't it also true, then, that _____?

> _____ has been adequately explained by X. Now, let's move beyond that idea and ask whether _____.

SG6   Presenting Your Own Views: Queries and Skepticism

You may be intimidated when you're asked to talk back to a source, especially if the source is a well-known scholar or expert or even just a frequent voice in a particular debate. College-level writing asks you to be skeptical, however, and approach academic questions with the mind of an investigator. It is OK to doubt, to question, to challenge—because the end result is often new knowledge or new understanding about a subject.

> Couldn't it also be argued that _____?

> But is everyone willing to agree that this is the case?

> While X insists that _____ is so, he is perhaps asking the wrong question to begin with.

> The claims that X and Y have made, while intelligent and well-meaning, leave many unconvinced because they have failed to consider _____.

A Note about Using First Person "I"

Some disciplines look favorably upon the use of the first person "I" in academic writing. Others do not and instead stick to using third person. If you are given a writing assignment for a class, you are better off asking your instructor what he or she prefers or reading through any samples given than *guessing* what might be expected.

First person (*I, me, my, we, us, our*)

I question Heddinger's methods and small sample size.

Harnessing children's technology obsession in the classroom is, I believe, the key to improving learning.

Lanza's interpretation focuses on circle imagery as symbolic of the family; my analysis leads me in a different direction entirely.

We would, in fact, benefit from looser laws about farming on our personal property.

Third person (names and other nouns)

Heddinger's methods and small sample size are questionable.

Harnessing children's technology obsession in the classroom is the key to improving learning.

Lanza's interpretation focuses on circle imagery as symbolic of the family; other readers' analyses may point in a different direction entirely.

Many Americans would, in fact, benefit from looser laws about farming on personal property.

You may feel as if not being able to use "I" in an essay in which you present your ideas about a topic is unfair or will lead to weaker statements. Know that you can make a strong argument even if you write in the third person. Third person writing allows you to sound more assertive, credible, and academic.

 Presenting Your Own Views: Disagreement or Correction

You may find that at times the only response you have to a text or to an author is complete disagreement.

X's claims about _____ are completely misguided.

X presents a long metaphor comparing _____ to _____;
in the end, the comparison is unconvincing because _____.

It can be tempting to disregard a source completely if you detect a piece
of information that strikes you as false or that you know to be untrue.

Although X reports that _____, recent studies indicate that is
not the case.

While X and Y insist that is _____ so, an examination of their
figures shows that they have made an important miscalculation.

SG8   Presenting and Countering Objections to Your Argument

Effective college writers know that their arguments are stronger when
they can anticipate objections that others might make.

Some will object to this proposal on the grounds that _____.

Not everyone will embrace _____; they may argue instead that
_____.

Countering, or responding to, opposing voices fairly and respectfully
strengthens your writing and your *ethos*, or credibility.

X and Y might contend that this interpretation is faulty; however,
_____.

Most _____ believe that there is too much risk in this
approach. But what they have failed to take into consideration is
_____.

Academic Writers Persuade by Putting It All Together

Readers of academic writing often want to know what's at stake in a particular debate or text. Aside from crafting individual sentences, you must,
of course, keep the bigger picture in mind as you attempt to persuade,
inform, evaluate, or review.

SG9   **Presenting Stakeholders**

When you write, you may be doing so as a member of a group affected by the research conversation you have entered. For example, you may be among the thousands of students in your state whose level of debt may change as a result of new laws about financing a college education. In this case, you are a *stakeholder* in the matter. In other words, you have an interest in the matter as a person who could be impacted by the outcome of a decision. On the other hand, you may be writing as an investigator of a topic that interests you but that you aren't directly connected with. You may be persuading your audience on behalf of a group of interested stakeholders—a group of which you yourself are not a member.

You can give your writing some teeth if you make it clear who is being affected by the discussion of the issue and the decisions that have or will be made about the issue. The groups of stakeholders are highlighted in the following sentences.

Viewers of Kurosawa's films may not agree with X that _____.

The research will come as a surprise to parents of children with Type 1 diabetes.

X's claims have the power to offend potentially every low-wage earner in the state.

Marathoners might want to reconsider their training regimen if stories such as those told by X and Y are validated by the medical community.

SG10   **Presenting the "So What"**

For readers to be motivated to read your writing, they have to feel as if you're either addressing something that matters to them or addressing something that matters very much to you or that should matter to us all. Good academic writing often hooks readers with a sense of urgency—a serious response to a reader's "So what?"

Having a frank discussion about _____ now will put us in a far better position to deal with _____ in the future. If we are unwilling or unable to do so, we risk _____.

Such a breakthrough will affect _____ in three significant ways.

It is easy to believe that the stakes aren't high enough to be alarming; in fact, _____ will be affected by _____.

Widespread disapproval of and censorship of such fiction/films/art will mean _____ for us in the future. Culture should represent _____.

_____ could bring about unprecedented opportunities for _____ to participate in _____, something never seen before.

New experimentation in _____ could allow scientists to investigate _____ in ways they couldn't have imagined _____ years ago.

SG11 Presenting the Players and Positions in a Debate

Some disciplines ask writers to compose a review of the literature as a part of a larger project—or sometimes as a freestanding assignment. In a review of the literature, the writer sets forth a research question, summarizes the key sources that have addressed the question, puts the current research in the context of other voices in the research conversation, and identifies any gaps in the research.

Writing that presents a debate, its players, and their positions can often be lengthy. What follows, however, can give you the sense of the flow of ideas and turns in such a piece of writing.

_____ affects more than 30% of children in America, and signs point to a worsening situation in years to come because of A, B, and C. Solutions to the problem have eluded even the sharpest policy minds and brightest researchers. In an important 2003 study, W found that _____, which pointed to more problems than solutions. [. . .] Research by X and Y made strides in our understanding of _____ but still didn't offer specific strategies for children and families struggling to _____. [. . .] When Z rejected both the methods and the findings of X and Y, arguing that _____, policy makers and health-care experts were optimistic. [. . .] Too much discussion of _____, however, and too little discussion of _____, may lead us to solutions that are ultimately too expensive to sustain.

Student writer states the problem.

Student writer summarizes the views of others on the topic.

Student writer presents her view in the context of current research.

Appendix: Verbs Matter

Using a variety of verbs in your sentences can add strength and clarity as you present others' views and your own views.

When you want to present a view fairly neutrally

acknowledges   observes
adds   points out
admits   reports
comments   suggest
contends   writes
notes

X points out that the plan had unintended outcomes.

When you want to present a stronger view

argues   emphasizes
asserts   insists
declares

Y argues in favor of a ban on _____; but Z insists the plan is misguided.

When you want to show agreement

agrees
confirms
endorses

An endorsement of X's position is smart for a number of reasons.

When you want to show contrast or disagreement

compares   refutes
denies   rejects
disputes

The town must come together and reject X's claims that _____ is in the best interest of the citizens.

When you want to anticipate an objection

admits
acknowledges
concedes

Y admits that closer study of _____, with a much larger sample, is necessary for _____.

Acknowledgments (continued from page iv)

Samantha Ainsley, "Black Rhythm, White Power," Morningside Review (2007/2008). Copyright © 2008. Reprinted by permission of the author.

Lessley Anderson, "Seduced by 'Perfect' Pitch: How Auto-Tune ConqueredPop Music," *The Verge*, February 27, 2013, http://www.theverge.com/2013/2/27/3964406/seduced-by-perfect-pitch-how-auto-tune-conquered-pop-music. Copyright © 2013 by Vox Media, Inc. Reprinted by permission of Vox Media, Inc.

St. Basil, excerpt from "Homily on the First Psalm," translated by William Strunk Jr. and Oliver Strunk, from *Source Readings in Music History: From Classical Antiquity through the Romantic Era*, ed. Oliver Strunk. Copyright © 1950 by W. W. Norton & Company, Inc. Used by permission of W. W. Norton & Company, Inc.

Judy Berman, "Concerning the Spiritual in Indie Rock," *The Believer*, August 2009. Copyright © 2009 by Judy Berman. Reprinted by permission of the author.

Jeff Chang, "It's a Hip-Hop World," *Foreign Policy* 163 (November/December 2007), pp. 58–65. Copyright © 2007. Republished with permission of Foreign Policy/Slate Group LLC; permission conveyed through Copyright Clearance Center, Inc.

Kat Chow, "How the 'Kung Fu Fighting' Melody Came to Represent Asia," *npr.org*, August 28, 2014. Copyright © 2014 National Public Radio, Inc. NPR news report used with the permission of NPR. Any unauthorized duplication is strictly prohibited.

Amy Clements-Cortes, "The Role of Pop Music and Pop Singers in the Construction of a Singer's Identity in Three Early Adolescent Females," *Canadian Music Educator* 51.4 (Summer 2010), pp. 17–23. Copyright © 2010. This article is reprinted here with permission from the Canadian Music Educators' Association.

Meghan Daum, "Music Is My Bag," from *My Misspent Youth: Essays* by Meghan Daum. Copyright © 2001, 2015 by Meghan Daum. Reprinted by permission of Farrar, Straus and Giroux, LLC.

Justin Davidson, "Beethoven's Kapow," *New York Magazine*, March 21, 2010. Copyright © 2010. Reprinted by permission of *New York Magazine*.

Laina Dawes, "Hardcore Persona," *Bitch Magazine* 57 (Winter 2013). Adapted from Chapter 4, "So You Think You're White?," in *What Are You Doing Here? A Black Woman's Life and Liberation in Heavy Metal* by Laina Dawes (Bazillion Points, 2012). Copyright © 2012 by Laina Dawes. Reprinted by permission.

Stephen A. Diamond, "Why We Love Music—and Freud Despised It." This essay is a slightly revised version of the original by Stephen A. Diamond, PhD, from his blog *Evil Deeds* published by *Psychology Today* (November 10, 2012): https://www.psychologytoday.com/blog/evil-deeds/201211/why-we-love-music-and-freud-despised-it. Copyright © 2012 by Stephen A. Diamond. Reprinted by permission of the author. Dr. Diamond is a clinical and forensic psychologist, a musician, and the author of *Anger, Madness, and the Daimonic: The Psychological Genesis of Violence, Evil, and Creativity* (SUNY Press, 1996).

Sasha Frere-Jones, "A Paler Shade of White: How Indie Rock Lost Its Soul," *New Yorker*, October 22, 2007. Copyrighted 2017. Condé Nast. 126716:010317BN.

Jeremy Gordon, "I Listen to Everything, Except Rap and Country Music," *Pacific Standard Magazine*, February 25, 2014. Copyright © 2014. Republished with permission of the Miller-McCune Center for Research, Media and Public Policy. Permission conveyed through Copyright Clearance Center, Inc.

Tamara Winfrey Harris, "All Hail the Queen?," *Bitch Magazine* 59, the "Micro/Macro" issue (Summer 2013). Copyright © 2013. Reprinted by permission of Bitch Media.

Index of Authors and Titles